The Global Etiquette Guide to Africa and the Middle East

The Global Etiquette Guide to Africa and the Middle East

Everything You Need to Know for Business and Travel Success

Dean Foster

John Wiley & Sons, Inc.

This book is dedicated to my parents, Joseph and Sylvia,
who first showed me the world

Library of Congress Cataloging-in-Publication Data:

Foster, Dean Allen.
    Global etiquette guide to Africa and the Middle East / Dean Foster.
      p.   cm.
    Includes bibliographical references and index.
    ISBN 0-471-41952-4 (pbk. : alk. paper)
    1. Etiquette—Africa—Handbooks, manuals, etc. 2. Africa—Social life and customs—Handbooks, manuals, etc. 3. Etiquette—Middle East—Handbooks, manuals, etc. 4. Middle East—Social life and customs—Handbooks, manuals, etc. I. Title.

    BJ1838 .F669   2002
    395'.0956—dc21

                                            2002001918

Printed in the United States of America

10 9 8 7 6 5 4 3 2 1

Contents

Preface   ix

Introduction: Why Getting It Right around the World
             Is So Important   1

Part One   The Middle East
            The Crucible   **9**

Chapter One: The Gulf Arab Cultures: Saudi Arabia,
             Kuwait, Oman, Qatar, Bahrain, United
             Arab Emirates, and Yemen   11
    Saudi Arabia   *11*
    Kuwait   *36*
    Oman   *37*
    Qatar   *37*
    Bahrain   *38*
    United Arab Emirates   *38*
    Yemen   *38*

Chapter Two: The Arab Levantine Cultures: Lebanon,
             Syria, and Jordan   40
    Lebanon   *40*
    Syria   *40*
    Jordan   *41*

Chapter Three: The Judaic Levantine Cultures: Israel   42

Part Two   North Africa
            The Dry Sea   **51**

Chapter Four: The Classical North African Arab World:
             Egypt, Sudan, and Chad   53
    Egypt   *53*
    Sudan   *78*
    Chad   *81*

Chapter Five: The Maghreb and Sahel: Morocco, Algeria,
             Tunisia, Mali, Mauritania, and Niger   86
    Morocco *86*
    Algeria *89*
    Tunisia *91*
    Mali *92*
    Mauritania *94*
    Niger *97*

Chapter Six: The Horn of Africa: Ethiopia, Eritrea,
             Somalia, and Djibouti   99
    Ethiopia *99*
    Eritrea *102*
    Somalia *104*
    Djibouti *106*

Part Three   West Africa
            The Ancient Traders   **107**

Chapter Seven: The Atlantic Cultures: Senegal,
             The Gambia, Guinea-Bissau, Guinea,
             Sierra Leone and Liberia, and
             Côte d'Ivoire   111
    Senegal *111*
    The Gambia *132*
    Guinea-Bissau *134*
    Guinea *136*
    Sierra Leone and Liberia *137*
    Côte d'Ivoire *139*

Chapter Eight: The West African Gulf: Nigeria, Ghana,
             Togo, Benin, and Burkina Faso   *141*
    Nigeria *141*
    Ghana *162*
    Togo *164*
    Benin *165*
    Burkina Faso *167*

Part Four   Central and Eastern Africa
            The Equatorial Heart   **169**

Chapter Nine: The Center: Cameroon, the Central
             African Republic, Gabon, and Congo   171
    Cameroon *171*
    The Central African Republic *174*

Gabon   *176*
Congo   *178*

Chapter Ten: The East: Kenya, Tanzania, Uganda,
            Rwanda, and Burundi   199
Kenya   *199*
Tanzania   *219*
Uganda, Rwanda, and Burundi   *221*

Part Five   Southern Africa
            The Promise   **225**

Chapter Eleven: The North: Zambia and Zimbabwe,
            Malawi, and Mozambique and
            Madagascar   229
Zambia and Zimbabwe   *229*
Malawi   *232*
Mozambique and Madagascar   *232*

Chapter Twelve: The South: South Africa, Lesotho and
            Swaziland, Botswana, and Namibia   238
South Africa   *238*
Lesotho and Swaziland   *258*
Botswana   *260*
Namibia   *261*

Index   263

Preface

The idea for this series emerged out of the work that my staff and I, and literally thousands of people from around the world that we work with, have been doing for almost two decades: assisting businesspeople and travelers to better understand their colleagues in other cultures. This work has primarily focused on international business and has taken many forms: helping to prepare families of employees adjust to an overseas assignment; assisting individual businesspeople in their negotiations with colleagues abroad; and helping global organizations to build more effective global teams. As business has globalized, the need for cross-cultural information has grown.

But globalization hasn't affected only the businessperson. While most of the work in the cross-cultural field has developed in response to international business needs, the need for cross-cultural information for the nonbusiness international traveler (both actual and of the armchair variety!) has also grown. Unfortunately, the amount of useful, objective, and applicable information, adapted to the needs of the more casual international explorer, has been limited. In most cases, what information was available usually took the form of anecdotal war stories, overgeneralized stereotypes (always interesting, but of dubious veracity), or theoretical statements about culture that were too removed from the day-to-day adventures of the international traveler. As the gap between useful cultural information for international business and international travelers grew, so did the need to bridge it. Hence, the idea for the Global Etiquette Guide series.

Correction: I embarked on this project at first with the goal of writing one book. But the world, as it turned out, was simply too big, and so was the book. Given my work, I for one should not have been surprised at this development, but at first was concerned about how to handle the dilemma. Nevertheless, under the kind and careful guidance of my editor, publisher, and agent, we expanded the original concept into a series. And I am glad we did. For one thing, it gave me the breathing room to explore cultures to the degree that was necessary for the reader; for another, it gave me the opportunity to experience just how fine a team I was working with.

My editor, Tom Miller, did double duty, providing patience and insight, through both the serialization of the original book and the actual editorial review of the material. His input, despite my occasional and incorrect misgivings, gave me focus, pause to rethink when it was important to do so, and perhaps most importantly, impetus and space to keep going in the face of demanding schedules and unpredictable events. A good editor provides the professional expertise to fine-tune the work. A great editor also provides faith. Tom never failed to offer both.

Jane Dystel is everything an author can ask for in an agent. On many levels, this series would not have happened without her. She is always available, always on my side, and equally able to manage scrupulously the details of a particular project while helping me to put the pieces in place for the bigger career; I am very grateful to have her support. This is the third time we have worked together on a project, and I look forward to many more.

Bob Stein is the lawyer behind the scenes. Lawyers are, no doubt, overlooked far too often, and easily forgotten once their job is done. Here I have probably been more neglectful than most, for Bob is also a dear and longtime friend who has never failed to support me, even in my most ridiculous moments, and I fear I have taken advantage of that. Forgive me, Bob, and thank you . . . again.

I also want to thank all the professionals in the cross-cultural field with whom I have had the pleasure to work over the years. They have all contributed in important ways to these books. To my colleagues at Berlitz International and at GMAC Intercultural, who, around the world, have given me opportunities to play a leading role in the cross-cultural field, I am eternally grateful. To the many professionals in both competing and supporting organizations whom I have learned from, and worked and played with, many, many thanks. Finally, to the diverse thousands of individuals around the globe, of all cultures and backgrounds, who, in their work with me and my staff, have provided us with the joy and opportunity to learn about their unique part of the world, my very heartfelt thanks. Without your perspectives, experiences, and input, my work, and ultimately these books, would never have been possible.

When exploring cultural differences, one quickly observes that there are some cultures that "work to live," and others that "live to work." Balancing these two perspectives is a constant challenge for both cultures and individuals, and my world would surely be quite unbalanced without the love and support of my wife, Sheryl. She has been my constant, both the wind beneath my wings and my tether to the shore. I know this has not been easy, as she must also balance her own professional demands with our personal life. That she has done both is a testament to her strength and love. These books, as with so much else in my life, could not have occurred without her.

Leah, my daughter, plays a great role in these books. As I've watched her grow into the intelligent and caring young woman she is today, she serves as a constant reminder that the prize we work so hard for should truly be worth something. It needs to be created in love, based on justice, and worth the struggle. As I hope I have given meaning to her life, she continues to give meaning to mine. We have been growing up together all her life, and although she is now "all grown up," I have no intention of stopping.

Finally, after crediting all these worthy folks for their kind and important contributions, I must now credit myself: all the shortcomings of these books are mine. If I overstated a culture too broadly, overlooked an important cultural consideration, or in any way misrepresented or misjudged a particular way of life, the error is mine and no one else's. I only ask that the reader please consider the cause as the "anthropologist's dilemma": that is, the impossibility of describing a culture objectively, due to the fact that the "describer" is always viewing the culture being observed in reference to his or her own (in my case, the United States). For some, this unfortunate natural law of the social sciences may be an added bonus (for other Americans, perhaps). For others, this may cause some serious and legitimate misgivings. I hear you both. Please take solace in the fact that every effort has been made to minimize the negative effects of this phenomenon whenever and wherever possible. No doubt I have not succeeded completely.

Why Getting It Right around the World Is So Important

Apparently, the world is getting smaller and smaller every day. We can't make it through a twenty-four-hour period without the media informing us of something happening in a distant land, without our local bank accounts being affected by a foreign stock market, without our schools having to make decisions about bilingual education, and without the possibility that our friends, coworkers, neighbors, and possibly family, will have come from somewhere else, speak a language we barely understand, and have a perspective on life that may be radically different from our own. As English speakers, isn't it unnecessary that we learn another language . . . or become familiar with another culture? After all, isn't technology spreading the English language and American pop culture so globally that we're all going to understand each other through the medium of Coca-Cola and rock 'n' roll anyway? The answer to all of the above, as anyone who steps off a plane in a foreign land will learn, is a resounding "No."

I like to think that the world is getting bigger, not smaller; that world cultures, perhaps unique among many aspects of life that are indeed being homogenized, will not be, and that cultures more deeply rooted with far longer histories than that of the American pop culture, along with their languages, will still be with us long after Coca-Cola becomes their favorite soft drink and rock their favorite form of music.

There is no doubt that cultures are in contact with one another to a degree never before experienced in human history. The vastness of human experience, which is the world, is suddenly in our respective faces as never before. Each of us is experiencing not the smallness of the world, but the very bigness of it. For most of us, this is not an easy thing to do. For a variety of reasons, such as the economics of globalization, the development of technology, and the evolution (or devolution, depending upon your point of view) of current political forms, the need to recognize and understand differences in cultures has probably never been more critical than it is today.

Businesspeople traveling the world are learning to appreciate the consequences of the misunderstood gesture, the ill-placed word, the uninformed judgment; workers down the hall are required to communicate effectively with coworkers who may or may not speak their language or understand their ways; world travelers, from tourists to diplomats, evaluate the success of their sojourns more and more according to their ability to understand, appreciate, and bridge the differences that exist between themselves and their new foreign hosts. Understanding, managing, appreciating, and maximizing the benefits of cultural differences, in fact, have become the most critical factors for the success of the global businessperson, the international diplomat, the manager of a multicultural office, or simply the continent-hopping tourist seeking a vacation of reward and richness. No, the world is not getting smaller—but we *are* being required to act much bigger in order to make sense of it all.

This book can help us to do that. There is no doubt that those forces of economics, politics, and technology that are bringing us in closer contact with one another foster, in some measure, a sense of unity. However, the degree to which understanding is developed simply as a result of cultural contact is questionable. Unfortunately, history provides us with evidence that when cultures collide, through whatever forces and for whatever reasons, the initial results are often disastrous. There is nothing inherent in cultural contact that automatically leads to understanding, homogeneity, peace, love, justice, and universal brotherhood. In fact, the reverse, at least in the short run, has been true. Over time, and only when specific structures such as democratic political forms, legal systems, and economic opportunities are in place, can cultures that once did not understand one another begin to accept one another. All one needs to do to better appreciate this sobering fact is to read the international headlines of any major newspaper any day of the week.

Nevertheless, if we are bound, as we apparently are, to hurtle headlong into one another's cultures, the least we can do is prepare ourselves to understand the other a little better. The forces of globalization carry information that both informs and misinforms one culture about the other. So we cannot depend for truth on what Hollywood tells us about Morocco, what Joe Smith relates to us over drinks about his recent trip to Tanzania, or what our coworker Patricia from Abidjan tells us about how people from Côte d'Ivoire think. Neither the global businessperson nor the casual tourist can afford to make mistakes when abroad, to misunderstand the intent of his or her foreign hosts, or to risk inadvertently offending someone. If we are all now working, living, loving, growing, and having to not only survive but thrive in a universe far larger and more complex than anything we were prepared to handle, it's time, to say the least, to get prepared. And that's the purpose of this book.

What This Book Is . . . and Is Not

This book is one of several in the series of Global Etiquette Guides, each of which focuses on a major world region. Each book follows the same format and structure, so whether you are beginning the series with this book or have already read one of the others, you will recognize a structure that makes the reading fun and provides you with the information you need about the countries in the region quickly and easily.

However, no one book can provide you with everything you've ever wanted to know about any particular culture, let alone the major cultures of even one particular world region. People make lifelong careers out of studying one particular culture, and there are sections in most libraries with many books focused solely on one aspect of one culture. Nor can one book provide you with everything you need to know to do business successfully every time in those cultures. But this book will look at most major cultures in Africa and the Middle East, those with which most readers will have some contact or be influenced by in their lifetimes. It will provide important information about the basic day-to-day behaviors in those countries that enable the inhabitants to pursue what they believe to be the best way to live their lives, achieve their goals, and solve their problems; in short, the day-to-day customs, etiquette, and protocols of these cultures that make them what they are, and, perhaps, different from our own.

The information provided about business issues, practical "do's and don't's" for all travelers, and the underlying values and belief systems of the various cultures will be useful for global businesspeople, casual international travelers, and cultural researchers. Most important, this information will address the one issue we all have in common in the face of our amazing diversity: our need to create a day-to-day modus operandi for living, for dealing with other people, and for communicating our needs and desires. *The Global Etiquette Guide to Africa and the Middle East* is intended to be a practical and relatively thorough guide to the protocol, etiquette, and customs that are the ways of life in one of the world's most important cultural regions.

What Do We Mean by "Culture"?

Culture is the normative way in which groups of people behave and the belief systems that they develop to justify and explain these behaviors. These behaviors can differ between groups, generally as a result of the different experiences that disparate groups have had. In turn, these experiences are usually a combination of history, geography, economics, and other factors, which vary from group to group. What makes all cultures similar, however, are the essentially universal problems of life that we all must address, as individuals and as societies. The problems and questions are the same everywhere, but the answers we come up with as societies can be different. This is what defines our individual cultures. Geert Hofstede, one of the seminal researchers in the field of culture, says, "If the mind is the hardware, then culture is the software," meaning that we are all hardwired pretty much the same, but the programs that we run on can be quite dissimilar. Culture is human software, and the challenge is to make the programs compatible.

I also want to emphasize the normative and group aspects of culture. I am constantly amazed at how from person to person we all seem so much alike, and yet from society to society we can be so very different. Culture reveals itself mainly in the group dynamics of the major institutions of society, and not necessarily in the interpersonal behaviors of individuals. In any particular culture, therefore, you may run into people who behave very differently from the way we describe the culture; in these cases, these individuals are behaving outside the norm. Culture is not a predictor of individual behavior, so when we discuss any cultural protocol, we are talking about general tendencies, expectations, and normative preferences. As someone foreign to a culture, you may be very far from its norm; for that very reason, it is important to know what that norm is, respect it, and adjust to it.

This issue of norms also reminds us that the statements we make about any given culture are generalizations. There are certainly situations, individuals, and conditions that would reveal contradictory behaviors within the same culture. When we make a cultural statement, at least in this book, we are speaking of *primary* tendencies; in no way is this meant to imply that contradictory behaviors will not exist. In fact, it is this delicious complexity of cultures that makes them so fascinating and challenging to work with. In most cases, we are usually also referring to situations between strangers, for once personal relationships are established, many formalities fall by the wayside.

So how important is it really to "go native"? The answer: not very. The goal of this book, and the goal of all intercultural understanding, is not to prescribe behaviors for you—behaviors that may be uncomfortable or unnatural to your own culture (many no doubt will be). Rather, the goal of this book is to explain unfamiliar behaviors so that you can come to understand them and why they exist, appreciate the benefits they bring to their culture, and adjust to them to the degree that you are comfortable in order to make someone from that culture equally comfortable with you. No one, however, can be someone he or she is not, and the worst thing you can do is to act inauthentically. There is nothing more awkward than a North American, for example, uncomfortably wearing native Gulf Arabian dress simply because he or she is in Gulf Arabia, or an African American assuming "welcoming arms" in West Africa simply because of a moment of shared—albeit significant—history. The greater benefit from such information comes when the North American understands the meanings behind native Gulf Arabian dress, or the degree of cultural similarity and distance that might exist between themselves as African Americans and their West African colleagues. Wherever you are, be yourself and be true to your own culture, but be true as an enlightened, informed, and respectful cultural being.

How the Book Is Organized

When you approach a world region, such as Africa, from a cultural perspective, there are first megacultures, and to varying degrees, variations on these megacultural themes, which are usually grouped geographically within the region. For example, there is the megacultural category of North African cultures, which can be found from Egypt in the east to Morocco in the west, from Algeria in the north to the Sudan in the south. While the people of many countries in this broad geographical swath are ethnographically Arab, many are not, such as the Senegalese, the Nigerians, and many peoples of southern Sudan. Complicating the picture is the fact that while most of these countries are Islamic, we may see Arabs who are not Muslim (such as Coptic Egyptians). Yet all are technically North African. Much of what is said about the protocols and etiquette of any one North African culture will also be true for many other North African cultures; nevertheless, there can also be many differences among them. And since the protocol and etiquette *topics* that are discussed for any one country are generally the same for all countries, the African cultures are organized according to these main African megacultural or regional groups.

Each group begins with a discussion of those cultures that provide the foundations for all the countries within the group, followed by further explorations of the countries within that cultural region and how they differ from one another. This has been done in order to highlight the distinctions that make each country within a cultural region unique and different without having to repeat information that is common to all the countries. Nevertheless, many readers will probably want to dip into the book country by country, rather than read it as a whole. If that's your style, rest assured that important cultural behaviors and facts are repeated country by country when necessary, so you won't miss too much if you want to read about only one country without referring to others in the same region. To make finding specific countries easy, the contents page lists each country, so you can go straight to the page listed for information on that country's protocol and etiquette if you so desire.

The topics explored for every region or country are generally the same. Each chapter begins with "Some Introductory Background" on the culture, and "Some Historical Context," followed by a quick "Area Briefing," which usually talks about politics and government, schools and education, and religion and demographics. This should give you a good appreciation for the forces that have shaped the culture. "Fundamental Cultural Orientations" explores the belief systems that justify the behaviors people reveal to one another on a day-to-day basis, giving you an understanding of why the protocols and etiquette exist as they do. The rest of the chapter takes an in-depth look at the actual customs of the country: greetings and verbal and nonverbal communication styles; protocol in public; dress; dining and drinking; how to be a good guest or host; gift giving; how to celebrate the major holidays; and important aspects of the business culture. For each of these topics there are subtopics that explore aspects of the culture in relation to men and women, younger and older generations, and both business and social circumstances.

This book does not look at all nations and all cultures within Africa. The world is a dynamic and changing place, and one of the difficulties about writing about culture at this point in world history is the fact that countries and cultures do not necessarily line up, and this is no more profoundly evident than in Africa and the Middle East today (in fact, the failure of nation states and their boundaries to represent the complexity of peoples and cultures in Africa and the Middle East is the source of much of the continued conflict throughout the region). For example, while there is no one country representing the distinct Tutsi and Hutu peoples, Tutsi and Hutu culture infuses many different countries in Central Africa, and the arbitrarily and artificially drawn national boundaries by retreating European colonialists in the Middle East are still one of the root causes for the smoldering disagreements that exist between Iraqis and Kuwaitis, Saudis and Yemenis, Jordanians and Syrians, not to mention the profoundly complex problem of Palestinians and Israelis. For these, and other thorny reasons, the book explores only those countries in the region that are, in the judgment of the author, distinguishably different from one another and of greatest interest to the reader. My apologies if I have not included a country or a culture of interest: it is not out of disrespect or malice, but merely because of space, knowledge, and time limitations.

The Meaning of the Information

In order to understand why the protocol, manners, and etiquette of any particular country are as they are, it is critically important to understand the belief systems and fundamental values that are at the heart of the culture. This is why the beginning of each section of the book includes a brief description of "Fundamental Cultural Orientations." These orientations, of course, change region by region, but the categories themselves remain the same. For example, it is common for meetings in Togo to begin simply when everyone has shown up, not necessarily when the clock says a meeting is to begin. This protocol is based on a more fundamental cultural orientation in Togo around the issue of time. In South Africa, however, especially within the professional community of say, Johannesburg, meetings typically begin at the time indicated on the agenda. This different protocol results from a different fundamental cultural orientation in Johannesburg around the same issue, time. Of course, it's important to remember that Togolese can begin their meetings on time, and South Africans can be far more flexible with time; it's just that there is, from a cultural point of view, a general difference in the concept of what constitutes timeliness. Therefore, let's briefly explore those fundamental orientation issues around which all cultures can differ, because we will be referring to them again and again with each region we visit.

As the example stated earlier illustrated, cultural orientations revolve around some very basic concerns shared by all cultures:

1. What's the Best Way for People to Relate to One Another?

Societies are all about people, and how we organize ourselves in relation to one another is an issue that every culture must sort out for itself. Cultures might insist on honoring a societal hierarchy, structure, and organization, and they do so with all sorts of perks: titles, rank, different signs of respect, different roles for men and women, younger and older, and so on. Other cultures deemphasize the importance of such things, preferring to treat everyone as equals. So we have cultures that are *hierarchy* and *organization* oriented, and on the opposite end of the spectrum, cultures that are *egality* oriented. Some cultures might reward individuals for standing out, empowering them to make decisions on their own, while other cultures insist that individuals fit into the group, making sure that no one does anything without the consent and support of others. So we have cultures that are *other-independent,* and on the opposite end of the spectrum, cultures that are *other-dependent.* A culture might place a value on devising systems for organizing life, creating interconnected rules and regulations that must apply universally to all, while another culture might place more emphasis on the personal relationships that exist between people as the determinant of how to do things. So we have cultures that are *rule* oriented, and others that are *relationship* oriented. All of these orientations have to do with what a culture believes to be the best ways by which people can relate to one another.

2. What's the Best Way to View Time?

All societies have to handle moving through time, creating a way of understanding and simultaneously managing the flow of things. Cultures might place a great deal of importance on managing and controlling time. For these *monochronic* cultures, clocks, agendas, calendars, and deadlines determine what and when things are done, and time is a limited commodity that must be carefully managed. For other cultures, time exists, of course, but it is not the determinant of people's actions. For these *polychronic* cultures, time stands in the background, there is usually plenty of it, and relationships and immediate needs usually determine what and when things are done. Some cultures might move quickly with a limited amount of information, while other cultures need a great deal of information in order to make even a small decision. Therefore, cultures may be *risk-taking* or *risk-averse*. Finally, do the people put more of their energy into maintaining what they already have, or do they value change for change's sake? A culture may be *past* oriented (and often more fatalistic), while another may be more *future* oriented (and often more controlling).

3. What's the Best Way for Society to Work with the World at Large?

All societies must make decisions about how they fit into, process, and deal with the larger world. Essentially, this means how a culture communicates, thinks, and plans. Some cultures might create, analyze, and communicate information directly; they depend upon the meaning of the word, and don't embed information in the larger context of the situation. These cultures often place a high value on confrontation and absolute truth: they are *low-context* communicators. However, other cultures value the importance of communicating indirectly—with actions, not words—and have subtle systems in place for exchanging information appropriate to the situation and the environment, through nonverbal behavior. These cultures place a high value on the maintenance of smooth interpersonal relationships; they are *high-context* communicators. One culture might place the greater emphasis on the process by which goals are achieved, while another culture places the greater emphasis on the goal itself, regardless of how it's achieved. Therefore, cultures can be *process* oriented (relying often on deductive logic), or *results* oriented (relying often on inductive logic). In addition, cultures may be more associative in their thought-processing; that is, they do things based on the way they know things always have been done, or how they are already being done in a similar situation. Finally, cultures might value the formal, established, reliable, and in some cases almost ritualized way of doing things, while other cultures might value change, informality, and spontaneity. Therefore, cultures may be *formal* or *informal* in their general orientation toward protocol itself.

It's important to remember that very few cultures are either absolutely one way or the other in their orientation. Most fall somewhere in between, and are simply more or less inclined to one way than the other. It's also important to remember that any one culture is a profile made up of all of these orientations, so be careful not to prejudge what one culture's orientation might be in one area just because of its orientation in another: you might be very surprised at the diversity and complexity of the combinations that exist when we tour the African and Middle Eastern regions! All world regions, Africa and the Middle East included, provide us with the opportunity to explore an enormous diversity of cultural behaviors; the range, especially in what is considered correct and incorrect, is staggering. Remember, the only constancy is change and the only absolute is complexity. What is correct in one culture may be incorrect in another, and what works in one can be a disaster in the other. As the old saying goes, "When in Rome, do as the Romans," and when in Riyadh we must also do as the Saudis, in Dakar as the Senegalese, in Nairobi as the Kenyans . . .

Regarding Terrorism and Travel in the Region

Recent events have conveyed an image of Africa and the Middle East as uniquely dangerous and violent places. Certainly the post–September 11 world and the U.S. war on terrorism focuses much of its concern on countries in this region, such as Iraq, Iran, Somalia, Sudan, and others, that are in fact dangerous and involved in terrorism. And there is no doubt that some of the twenty-first century's greatest challenges are reflected in the relationship between the developed world and this largely developing and economically deprived region. The continuing grinding poverty, lack of education and opportunity for youth and women, political oppression, and the disparity between fundamentalism and modern values that exist more or less throughout the region create an environment that is ripe for violence, instability, and conflict with the West.

That said, it is important to remember that the region's violence and instability are not new post–September 11 phenomena, nor is violence and instability unique to the Middle East and Africa. In fact, many travelers to the United States from this region find U.S. cities to be far more dangerous to them as individuals than the random political violence that may occur in their home country. In all but the most devastated and deprived nations in the region, people have gotten on with their lives, and the traditional cultures, with all their richness and complexity, have continued, and in some cases, thrived. And while the possibility of violence and danger must always be taken seriously (especially for the adventurous Western traveler who as a stranger does not know his or her way around), what makes the news are still random and unique events in people's day-to-day existence. People still work, raise their families, love one another, and maintain the traditions and beliefs that in many cases have made their cultures, if not now, at least in the past, glorious and worth treasuring, valuing, and certainly visiting. There is much we can learn from many of these cultures, but the bridge of understanding between the West and this region still needs to be built. Go humbly, carefully, wisely, and make your contribution to the bridge.

PART ONE

The Middle East

The Crucible

An Introduction to the Region

Nothing is as it seems in the Middle East, and any Middle Easterner will quickly admit to that. It is, in fact, perhaps the one—and only—perspective that all Middle Easterners share. The exceptions to almost anything stated with certainty about the region become apparent even as one simply attempts to find an appropriate phrase to define the region in the first place. For example, although we will use the term Middle East because of its broad recognition factor, what is commonly known as the Middle East is "middle" only in the sense that it stands between the "Far" East and the "West." In reality, of course, it is its own very complex world, and the term "Middle East" reflects the European—or Western—vantage point. Using an ethnologic perspective, one could also refer to this area as the Arab World, as most Arabs live here, but so do many other ethnic groups, and the Arab world extends well beyond the Middle East into western North Africa and parts of southeast Asia. Using a religious perspective, one could refer to this area as Islamic, as the majority of the population is Muslim, but many people are Jewish, Christian, Druze, Zoroastrian, Baha'i, and so on. Using a geographic perspective, one could call the area southwest Asia, but then we would be ignoring the similarities that unite many of the peoples in this region to peoples in North Africa and other regions beyond southwest Asia. Complicating the picture even further is the fact that combinations of many of the above are rampant: there are Christian Arabs, Arab Israelis, Jewish Syrians, and Christian Palestinians. Historically, the region is the crucible of the three great religious traditions of the West; it remains, despite massive wealth from oil and natural gas reserves, an intractably poor and politically unstable region. And it is the region that along with China will provide the century with one of its most compelling concerns: the coexistence of the West and Islam.

Getting Oriented

The region, however one may choose to define it, for our purposes consists of the following macrocultural groups:

- The Gulf Arab cultures: Saudi Arabia, Kuwait, Oman, Qatar, Bahrain, United Arab Emirates, and Yemen
- The Levantine cultures: Lebanon, Syria, Jordan, and Israel

As all of these countries are highly identified with Islam culturally (with the exception of Israel, which will be treated separately), we will begin our exploration with Saudi Arabia, the country where Arab culture and Islam had their formative roots, and make some comments about country-specific variations as required.

(Please note: in the Arab world, the body of water that lies to the east of Saudi Arabia is generally called the "Arabian Gulf," not the "Persian Gulf.")

The Gulf Arab Cultures: Saudi Arabia, Kuwait, Oman, Qatar, Bahrain, United Arab Emirates, and Yemen

CHAPTER ONE

SAUDI ARABIA

Some Introductory Background on Saudi Arabia and the Gulf Arabs

Arabs and Westerners often bring out the worst in each other, for each is sometimes quick to misunderstand the other, and to lay the blame for the misunderstanding on the other, as well. The stereotypes by each group of the other abound, and exist primarily due to the willful refusal on both sides to understand and accept the culture of the other. Arabs, extremely proud of the historical importance of their culture, which once ruled a substantial part of the world, are very defensive about their current position in the world, having been reduced, in part, by several hundred years of western exploitation to the status of a developing people in their own lands. The countries themselves are often artificially imposed political boundaries created by conquering (and then retreating) Europeans, and often do not accurately reflect the cultural groupings of the Arab peoples themselves. Arabs are also extremely proud of Islam, and have defended its growth and development against what they sometimes see as the aggression and incursions of a morally debased West. Today, many Arabs see their struggle as the inevitable result of hundreds of years of Western exploitation, and find it increasingly difficult to adopt Western customs, institutions, and beliefs as a road out from poverty and underdevelopment; instead, they increasingly turn to their own Islam, and rediscover their pride, their power, and what is, for some (genuinely, and others manipulated for personal or political power), a God-given mission, to renew the world on their terms. Saudi Arabia today is the country responsible for the holiest of Islam's holy sites, Makkah (Mecca) and Medina, where Muhammad was respectively born and received his revelations from God, and as such, is the "center" and most fundamentalist of all Islamic nations. If we understand the Saudi culture, and associated Saudi behaviors, we will be able to modify our behaviors when dealing with other Arab and Islamic nations in the region.

Some Historical Context

Saudi Arabia as a nation is a recent development: only in the late 1920s did the tribes in the region consolidate under the Saud family (al-Saud) to create a sovereign nation. Abdul Aziz al-Saud united the tribes through conquest and marriage, and strengthened his hold on the country through the application of strict Islamic law (justified in part as a way of developing Arab strength against the Westernized and impure Islam of the decaying Ottoman Empire, which governed much of the rest of Southwest Asia up to the end of World War I).

An Area Briefing

Politics and Government

Today, the country is an Islamic monarchy: the king is the absolute ruler of the nation, although he is informed by a Council of Ministers (whom he selects). There is no representative government, and the only restriction on the king's powers is Islamic law, which is the law of the land. The oldest male descendant of the king would technically be in line to become the next king, barring any kind of revolt that could overthrow the system.

Schools and Education

All schooling is free and mandatory through high school, and free universities are available for those who qualify. Girls and boys are educated (although separately), and literacy is growing rapidly. Most Saudis, with the exception of nomadic tribespeople, are fairly well-off, and send their university-bound children abroad for their graduate education. There is, therefore, a knowledge and awareness of the West and its ways among the younger Saudis, and many speak English. Educated girls usually enter teaching and medicine, but women play almost a nonexistent role in business.

Religion and Demographics

Saudi Arabia is a fundamentalist Islamic state, ruled ultimately by the laws of Islam, which are rigorously applied. The majority of the people are Sunni Muslim, and there is fear and concern among the Sunni majority regarding the small Shiite minority that exists in the country. In addition, "guest workers" from other parts of the Arab and Islamic Asian world (particularly Pakistan, the Levant, Yemen, and parts of Africa) are sometimes perceived as a threat to the more puritanical nature of Islam in Saudi Arabia. (These guest workers can never become citizens, as no visitor to Saudi Arabia ever can, but they constitute the bulk of the workforce in the country, with Saudis holding the positions of authority in business, government, and the social world.)

One of the ways that the Saud family unified the nation was by appealing to and adopting the very strict Wahhabi sect of Islam: this group represents a return to a very fundamentalist interpretation of Islam and the Koran. Saudi Arabia, which is an ally of the United States in the region, curiously enough, is the most

Islamic fundamentalist Arab nation (a challenge to the misguided popular belief that all radical Muslims are anti-American). There are no non-Muslim Saudi Arabians, and non-Muslim visitors, in fact, are legally prohibited from visiting the holy cities of Mecca and Medina. Mecca is the site of the annual hajj, during which devout Muslims from around the world converge to pray and become purified in the presence of the site of Muhammad's birth. In the center of the Great Mosque is a draped black cube around which Muslims pray and circle; inside of this cube lie the remains of the stone that Abraham was prepared to use for the sacrifice of his son.

Islam is the youngest of the West's three great religious traditions, beginning with Judaism and Christianity. As a Western religion, it is linked to the Judeo-Christian belief system and rejects Hinduism and Buddhism as "pagan," and not "of the book," or codified. Incorporating both Judaism and Christianity into its system of beliefs, Islam claims that it is the final revelation of a monotheistic God, as revealed to the world through the prophet Muhammad, and that previous "messiahs," such as Jesus and Moses, were merely prophets, along with Muhammad, proclaiming the word of God. Muslims do not worship Muhammad (therefore, they are not Muhammadans, a very derogatory term created by Westerners who did not understand Islam); they worship Allah, which is the Arabic name for the same God worshiped by Christians and Jews. Muhammad and his followers wrote down the law of God as revealed to them in the Koran (or Qu'ran), the Islamic Holy book. It does not negate the Old or New Testaments: it merely provides, in the eyes of the Muslim faithful, the final required text. Muhammad received his revelations from God in Medina; prior to Islam, the nomadic tribes of the region believed in a variety of pagan ideas; but with the notion of one God, and the laws under which people were to behave, Muhammad was able to unify the peoples of the Gulf Arab peninsula into the beginnings of a single Arab culture. This is one of the reasons why Gulf Arabs are singularly Muslim (this is not necessarily the case elsewhere in the Arab world). Islam spread rapidly throughout the Middle East, into Europe, and eastward across Asia. While Islam underwent a serious split almost immediately following Muhammad's death (two major camps emerged, the Shia and the Sunni, in an effort to decide how to continue the faith), it nevertheless rapidly gathered huge followings. Sunni Muslims believe that the caliphs, or religious leaders, subsequent to Muhammad are legitimate; Shiite Muslims believe that the caliphs subsequent to Muhammad are usurpers, and therefore do not believe in Sunni authority. All Muslims must abide by five basic tenets, or Pillars of Faith:

- Proclaim the supremacy of the one true God, Allah, above all others
- Pray to Allah five times daily
- Observe Ramadan, the holy month, the ninth month of the Islamic calendar, which is essentially a celebration of the first time when God revealed his word to Muhammad
- Give alms to the poor and needy
- Perform the hajj, or spiritual (and physical) journey to Mecca, at least once in their lifetime if they are capable of doing so

Specific codes of conduct have developed over time, and have been codified into Islamic law, known as the Shari'a. The degree to which one follows these scriptures often determines how devoutly one applies the Islamic ethical code in day-to-day life; in Saudi Arabia, the Shari'a is enforced by the "religious police," or *mataween:* they are fully empowered to arrest, publicly whip, and otherwise ensure the complete compliance of the entire populace with the rigid fundamentalist Islamic laws.

Women and men play completely different roles in this society, with women primarily handling private life, and men handling public life. This means that women do the nurturing and educating, and men do the business and civic ruling. This does not mean that these roles—and subsequently men and women— are unequal, for both roles cannot be performed by or without the other. It will be very difficult for Western businesswomen who do not establish acceptance of their authority ahead of time to be effective in this male-dominated business environment; they can be, but only if their expertise is required, and only if they behave in their role as subject-matter expert according to all the strict requirements of the Islamic code.

Fundamental Cultural Orientations

1. What's the Best Way for People to Relate to One Another?

OTHER-INDEPENDENT OR OTHER-DEPENDENT?   There is a combination of deep concern for family, clan, and other membership groups (such as work and religion) that defines an individual and individual expression. Saudis, like all Arabs, are deeply connected first to their clan and their families: this is an intensely private life (and therefore, one needs to be very careful about inquiring about the family, among other things). However, individual pride, and how one is seen by others, is perhaps the most important aspect of Arab culture that non-Arabs need to be sensitive to. It is not a heightened sense of individualism separate from others; in fact, it is the opposite. Because of one's intricate relationships with others (there is an old saying that an Arab has one thousand close relatives), one is always keenly aware of how one is being perceived and of one's obligations to others. It is very important that you always show great respect for your Arab colleague. Arab pride must be supported and respected.

HIERARCHY-ORIENTED OR EGALITY-ORIENTED?   As Muslims, all people are technically equal in their submission to Allah and his will; however, Arabs structure the secular world with clearly assigned roles, so that Allah's will can be fulfilled effectively. It is critical that everyone show respect for elders and devout Muslims, and men for women, sons for fathers, older brothers for younger brothers, and so on. All individuals have a role to play in this hierarchy, and are responsible to others and the greater Arab community to fulfill their role. Those above absolutely make the decisions for those below, and those ultimately in charge, the Islamic rulers and their *mataween,* have ultimate authority. There is a saying in Arabic, "The eye cannot rise above the eyebrow": it means that people must know their station and position in life, and make the best of it. Women and men are different and perform different roles: in Saudi Arabia a woman typically may not go out in public alone, or in the company of a man who is not a near relative (husband, father, son, or brother); if she does, both she and the man risk punishment, including jail.

Rule-Oriented or Relationship-Oriented?   While many Saudis have had experience with and in the West, Islamic law, not Western rules, are the rules that are followed, and these are applied universally if they are universal (i.e., part of Islamic law), and subject to interpretation and uneven application if nonuniversal. This leads to a high dependence on power, authority, and subjective decision-making based on the situation and the relationships between the individuals involved. Ultimately, face-to-face knowledge of the individuals involved in any interaction is the basis upon which final decisions are often made.

2. What's the Best Way to View Time?

Monochronic or Polychronic?   Saudi Arabia is essentially very polychronic, due to the influence of both agrarian and religious traditions. The clock is definitely not the determinant of action; it plays a role most certainly, particularly in the larger, more modern urban areas, and there is an acceptance of Western organizational ideas (Westerners should not be late, for example). Nevertheless, there is forgiveness for the inevitable delays, and understanding when things don't go as planned or scheduled; people may or may not show up at invited events, things may or may not happen as planned. Things take the time they take, that's all (the concept of *buqrah*). Muslim laws even view planning too far into the future—or planning at all in some cases—as heretical, for it presumes that individuals can control events that are essentially in the hands of Allah. Even today, schedules tend to be loose and flexible; the workday begins around 9 A.M. and ends around 4 P.M. Most workers take an hour break after lunch. Because who (relationships) is more important than what (tasks) or when (time), there can be many interruptions during a meeting, and people's obligations to other people, who come and go, are more important than doing things according to schedules. If you are being kept waiting, or are ignored because of someone else's needs, it is an indication of your importance relative to the other person, and expressing frustration over being kept waiting only diminishes your importance.

Risk-Taking or Risk-Averse?   Saudis, and most Arabs, are prone to taking risks when in positions of authority, but avoiding them when they are not. Within organizations, the decision makers can be bold, even reckless, but subordinates generally are not, and take action only when instructed to do so. Therefore, comfort with uncertainty, in general, is low, and much information may need to be exchanged with different people before decisions can be made. Even when decisions are made at the top, the concern for others in the group requires decision makers to consult with subordinates before making decisions. There will be much discussion with trusted others about what you, as a foreigner, bring to the table, *after* you leave the meeting.

Past-Oriented or Future-Oriented?   There is a distinct and inherent fatalism in regard to the effect of human action, fundamentally because only Allah determines what and when things will happen. Nevertheless, those empowered by virtue of their position are expected to make the decisions that keep the world running, and by so doing, are fulfilling Allah's will. Therefore, future benefits often do not motivate Saudis; doing nothing, or doing things for the here and now, is sometimes more important, and if things do not work out, that is to be expected—no mortal controls the universe, and all is ultimately determined. There is a deep belief that things will take the time they need to take, and that only Allah knows what that is (this has often been summarized as the "IBM" of the Arab world: I for *inshallah*—as and only if Allah wills it; B for *buqrah*—things will take the time they take; and M for *ma'alesh*—loosely translated as, "don't worry," "don't sweat it," "it'll turn out okay, you may not see it now, but it's all for the best").

3. What's the Best Way for Society to Work with the World at Large?

LOW-CONTEXT DIRECT OR HIGH-CONTEXT INDIRECT COMMUNICATORS? Arabs are very context-driven communicators. They will speak in metaphors, and use stories or codified phrases; they will employ analogies, Islamic precedent, and much nonverbal behavior to convey true meaning. They generally avoid confrontation, and are honor-bound to do everything possible to make strangers like and honor them (they are lavish hosts). They will avoid unpleasant discussions as long as possible, and it is precisely because they shun unpleasantness in discussions that anger, often expressed as an insult to pride, can blow fast and hard when disagreements can no longer be avoided.

PROCESS-ORIENTED OR RESULT-ORIENTED? Islamic law, and the complex study of Islam that developed in the Muslim world into its own field of scholastic inquiry, is fundamentally different from Western Greco-Roman philosophies of knowing. In Islam, interpretation and truth are dependent upon "analogous" reasoning, while in the West, such inquiry is based more on "argument" (proving and disproving). Decisions and actions therefore may be the result of reasoning that is not directed at a determination of truth, but rather context-based "correctness," based on similar experiences, often with strict Islamic code as the only context. Combine this with a tendency to rely also on subjective experience, and the Arab mind is processing information, for the most part, in a different way than the Western mind.

FORMAL OR INFORMAL? Arab society is formal and ritualized, and each group has its own way of honoring the hierarchies, establishing respect and deference, and following (or not following) through on their responsibilities. They are even more formal when one is an outsider, which is always the case with non-Muslims.

Greetings and Introductions

Language and Basic Vocabulary

"Arab" describes the people; "Arabian" describes the culture; "Arabic" describes the language. Arabic is the language of the Koran, and therefore, by extension, is the language of God. There are many forms of Arabic throughout the region, some more formal and some informal, but Arabic is the primary language. As a Semitic language, it is very different from other Asian and European languages, and is written from right to left in a flowing script. Written vowel sounds are assigned to consonant letters with diacritical marks, with words changing tense, agreement, and meaning based on the addition of suffixes and prefixes to the root or stem words.

Words and language have a power all their own in the Arab world; in fact, it has been said that the expression of a feeling or action can sometimes replace the feeling or the action itself. Therefore, the expression of anger, which may involve statements of violence, in fact may be a way of precluding the act of violence. Be extremely sensitive to the meaning of words, the emotion behind them, how they are used, and how you use them. Speech can be flowery, over-blown, hyperbolic, and rich in texture; this is meant to honor both the speaker and the person to whom one is speaking. Arabs will always overemphasize, reassure, insist that they can do something, know something, or solve the problem, whether or not they actually can or will; this is not meant to be deceiving, but to indicate their hope for a mutually positive experience. Words more often indicate what they desire than what might actually be. Many religious phrases are added onto everyday statements (i.e., "_____ , *inshallah*"—"if God wills"; or "_____ , *mash'allah*"—"what God wills," usually said after speaking about someone's health; or "_____ , *alhamdu lillah*"—"thanks be to God," spoken as a way of giving thanks for something that has happened, or that you hope will happen). Never use religious references casually or disrespectfully—it is assumed that all people are religious in some way, even if not a Muslim—and be very careful never to use "God" in any way other than in the most respectful sense. There is a Classical Arabic, which Saudis claim to speak, with essentially three other basic dialects of Arabic spoken in the region: Egyptian/Sudanese, Levantine, and Gulf Arabic. All three are mutually intelligible to one another.

It is important to recognize that other non-Arabic languages are spoken throughout the region, including indigenous languages such as Berber in North Africa, Coptic in Egypt, Hebrew and Aramaic in the Levant, and Farsi (Persian) and South Arabian nomadic languages in the Gulf states.

Here are some basic Arabic phrases and their meanings in English:

marhaba, or *marhaba alan*	hello
marhabtayn, or *marhabtayn alan*	hello (response)
ahlan wasahlan	welcome
ahlan beek	thanks (response)
sabah alkayr	good morning
sabah annoor	good morning (response)
assalamu 'alaykum	peace be with you (general greeting)
wa'alaykum assalam	and upon you, peace (response)
min fadleek	please
aesef	sorry, excuse me
ma'a ssalama (go with safety)	good-bye

allah yisallimak	good-bye (response)
(may God make you safe)	
shukran	thank you
'afwan	you're welcome

English is taught in schools, so young people often speak and understand some English; businesspeople from the upper classes (most Saudis) speak English, since they were educated, in many cases, abroad. Most people on the street in most Arabic-speaking countries, however, speak little English.

Honorifics for Men, Women, and Children

Names will be Arabic in content in the region, but structured according to fairly complex and sometimes differing traditions.

Most people have several names, and the order of the names is similar to that of the West, with the given name first, and the family name last. Other names used may refer to one's role in the family (such as son) or an honorary association with an important or meaningful person (often a reference to an important person in Islamic history). It is important to address Arabs by their given (or first) names, because that is really their only true name (the other names being indications of genealogy or relationship). Several common relationship forms found in names are:

- *Bin* or *ould* (North African and Levantine), or *ibn* (Gulf Arab), meaning " . . . son of": for example: Abdel Azziz ibn Saud (Abdel, son of Saud); or Muhammad ould Haidalla (Muhammad, son of Haidalla)
- *Bint* or *binte,* meaning ". . . daughter of": for example, Fatima bint Saud (Fatima, daughter of Saud)
- *Bou* (North African mainly), meaning " . . . father of": for example, Habib bou Guiba (Habib, father of Guiba)

The honorifics Mr., Mrs., and Miss, are placed before the surname; and you should always use titles, if they are known (doctor, professor, etc.) before the surname, as well: for example, Dr. Habib, Professor Muhammad, Princess Asma, Sheikh Abdullah ("sheikh" is an indication of importance; it does not represent a specific title or position, nor does it in and of itself represent the leadership of any one particular clan, tribe, or group).

Ma'ali is an honorific often used for government officials (it means "Your excellency"); high officials are given the honorific *sa'ada* before their names.

- *Al-* + family name: usually indicates "house of" as the family (final) name: for example, Muhammad ibn Abdallah al-Ahmar (Muhammad, son of Abdallah, house of Ahmar). It is not in any way related to the English nickname "Al," short for "Alan."
- Sometimes grandfathers, and male forebears even further back, are acknowledged in the string of names, so that there may be several *ibn* + name groupings within the name: for example, Muhammad ibn Abdallah ibn Muhammad al-Ahmar (Muhammad, son of Abdallah, son of Muhammad, of the house of Ahmar). Usually, after several generations, the most distant names are dropped. Arabs usually do not give their sons the same first name as the father, but commonly use the grandfather's name, so the first and third names are more often the same.

- A woman does not typically take her husband's family name when she marries: she keeps her family name, and is addressed as "Mrs. + her first name."
- Hyphenated names usually represent an attribute plus the name: for example, Abdel-Allah Muhammad ibn Kamal ibn Muhammad al-Tawil (Servant of God Muhammad, son of Kamal, son of Muhammad, of the house of Tawil).
- Muslim males who have made the hajj often use the honorific *hajji* as a title before the surname and any other honorifics: for example, Hajji Dr. Abdel-Allah Muhammad ibn Kamal ibn Muhammad al-Tawil. Muslim females who have made the hajj often use the honorific *hajja* as a title before the surname and any other honorifics.
- Women retain all male references to genealogy in their name after their given female surname: for example, Hajja Dr. Asmah bint Muhammad ibn Kamal ibn Muhammad al-Tawil (a devout, educated sister of the above-mentioned Abdel-Allah Muhammad who has made the hajj).

Remember that vowel sounds in Arabic are often indicated with diacritical marks rather than with specific letters. Therefore, translating words, especially names, into English is not an exact science; the same name may be spelled with different vowels (e.g., Mohammed, Muhammad, and M'hamad).

Finally, sometimes (especially in the Levant and Egypt) the honorifics *um* (mother) and *abu* (father) may be used in front of the given name, or replace a name completely. This is an affectionate way of referring to someone you may know well and personally.

The What, When, and How of Introducing People

Saudis may, upon greeting you, call you by your last or first name, with or without your title. Always wait to be introduced to strangers; never take that responsibility upon yourself, as doing so is considered inappropriate most of the time. Saudis, and Arabs in general, are most comfortable with third-party introductions, and because business is very personal, you will need an individual to introduce you to the required businesspeople. Never presume to seat yourself at a gathering: if possible, wait to be told where to sit. The seating arrangements have usually been carefully worked out in advance, and in most cases reflect the status of the individuals in the group, and the honor that is being accorded the guests. When departing, it is important to say farewell to every individual present: the American group wave is not appreciated. Once you greet someone you will encounter later that day in the same circumstances (e.g., at the office), you do not need to greet them when you see them again. Seniors, or those who are obviously the oldest in a group, are greeted first, seated first, and allowed to enter a room first (usually as the center of a group, however, and in most cases preceded by their younger aides). Single women traveling in the region may want to consider wearing a wedding band; it can help avoid a myriad of difficult questions and problems.

Physical Greeting Styles

Close associates and businessmen (the operative part of the word is *men,* as this is only between men, and never between men and women) who have developed working relationships often greet each other warmly, with hugs and kisses. Wait until your Saudi host initiates this behavior before initiating it yourself.

Typically, the greeting here is the "salaam," which involves a soft handshake with the right hand, after which, for extra sincerity, you may pull your hand back to your heart and touch it. Additionally, Saudis and other Gulf Arabs also reach out and touch the shoulder of the other person with their left hand. Traditionally, the salaam was performed by quickly and lightly touching your forehead first, then your heart, then the front of your abdomen with your right hand as you bowed slightly; this is still done on very formal occasions. Muslim women and men do not touch or shake hands (unless the woman is Westernized, and you will know if she extends her hand). The handshake may be soft, almost limp sometimes. This does not signify insincerity; rather, it is an accommodation to the Western fashion while remaining humble and considerate.

The traditional business introduction also includes the exchange of business cards. Always take a large supply of business cards with you: you should give one to every new person you are introduced to (there is no need to provide another business card when you are meeting someone again unless information about you has changed, such as a new address, contact number, or position). Be sure your business cards are in fine shape: they are an extension of you as a person, and must look as good as possible. Embossed cards are extremely impressive, especially with logos in green (the color of Islam). Never hand out a dirty, soiled, bent, or written-on card, and always handle business cards with your right hand only. You should translate your business card into Arabic on the reverse side.

When presenting a business card, give it to your colleague so that it is readable for him as you hold it (he will, in turn, present his card so that it is readable for you). Do not worry too much about who receives and gives his business card first: the exchange is very quick, and because you would probably not be introduced to that person in the first place if you were not already seen as having an equivalent rank, there is no need to show deference. There is also no need for bowing.

Smiling and other nonverbal forms of communication may accompany the card exchange. Information about each other's status is the most important information to be exchanged, and this is provided directly on the business card, as well as indirectly through a number of high-context indicators, such as gender, age, and the number of people surrounding and assisting the other person. Should you meet more than one individual at a reception, you will have a handful of cards when the greetings are over.

As the business card exchange usually precedes a sit-down meeting, it is important to arrange the cards you have received in a little seating plan in front of you along the top of the desk or table at your seat, reflecting the order in which people are seated. This will help you connect the correct names with the correct individuals throughout the meeting. Do this even if you are just meeting one person; it is expected. During the meeting, it is important never to play with the business cards (do not write on them—ever!); and when the meeting is over, never put them in your back pants pockets: pick them up carefully and respectfully, and place them neatly in your cardholder (a nice-looking brass card case would be perfect), then place the cardholder in the left inside jacket pocket of your suit (nearest your heart).

Do not photograph people without asking their permission, ever, and do not videotape freely. In some of the countries in the Arab world, videotaping is generally illegal, and traditionally in Islam, images of people and the human form are considered sacrilegious.

Communication Styles

Okay Topics / Not Okay Topics

Okay: anything that reflects your personal interests and hobbies, religion, and your sincere appreciation of and curiosity about things native to the Arab world. Most Saudis whom foreigners meet are relatively wealthy and influential. They love horses and sports; camel racing and horse racing are popular (but there is no betting allowed). *Not okay:* Politics, current events, or any subject that might in any way be controversial needs to be avoided at first. Do not inquire about a person's occupation or income in casual conversation, although it may be inquired of you (if so, this is just a way of getting to know more about your country, and not a personal investigation: answer specifically, and fully, with an explanation as to what things cost at home, why you do what you do, etc.). Other personal questions may be asked of you ("Why are you not married?" or "Do you have any sons?"); the best responses are those that fit the Saudi context ("Allah has not blessed me yet; I wait patiently."). Do not inquire about family life, especially spouses, or the role of servants and household help. Do not give your opinions about Israel, Jews, foreign workers, Islamic fundamentalism, or women's rights. Do not talk about sex or tell dirty jokes: it is in very bad taste. Discussions about your company and its work are very much appreciated, as they give Saudis a chance to learn more about you and your firm. The goal of all conversation, at least at the beginning, is to create and maintain a harmonious atmosphere, despite the difficult or confrontational nature of the topic being discussed. At first, speak about things that you believe you have in common, so that you can build a personal connection that will go far toward maintaining a harmonious bridge between you. This is appropriate for both individuals and organizations.

Tone, Volume, and Speed

The people of this region generally speak in soft, quiet, and restrained tones. Saudis, and most Arabs, raise their voices only when it is necessary to display anger—and at that point, it is usually too late in the relationship. They may speak rapidly, but if you, in turn, speak rather slowly, they may get the hint and slow down.

Use of Silence

Passive silence—allowing time to pass simply without words—can be a form of proactive communication, and is used as a nonverbal way of avoiding confrontation, disagreement, or an unpleasant subject. If confronted with unexplainable silence, gently coax the conversation in a different direction, one that is more mutually harmonious.

Physical Gestures and Facial Expressions

Westerners are advised to reduce the amount of body language they use, although Saudis and most Arabs are very comfortable with nonverbal behavior (you just do not want to inadvertently offend). Winking, whistling, and other similar displays are considered very vulgar. Public displays of familiarity and affection with the opposite sex are never expressed. Never touch anyone on his or her head, even a child; this is considered the holiest part of the body. Do not point with or intentionally show the sole of your shoe to anyone: this is considered vulgar, as the bottom of the shoe touches the ground, and is therefore the dirtiest part of the body. Any gesture involving a closed fist or made with the "thumbs-up" sign is considered quite vulgar. Standing with your hands on your hips is considered very aggressive and should always be avoided. Yawning in public is considered impolite; you must cover your mouth when you yawn.

For any action or gesture that would naturally be done only with one hand, do not use your left hand, as this is considered the unclean hand (the hand used for personal hygiene). Pass all documents, business cards, food, and money with your right hand (if you're a southpaw, you will have to practice this). You must remove your shoes before entering a mosque (and some buildings, as well as homes), and you may need to wash your feet and hands if there is an entrance fountain provided before entering a mosque as well. Women may be restricted to specific areas and times when visiting mosques. Women entering mosques need to have their heads covered, their legs covered to below the knee, and their arms covered to below the elbow; Western women do not necessarily need to have their faces covered. Smile whenever possible: it smooths the way with strangers quickly and easily.

Waving and Counting

The thumb represents number 1, the pinkie represents the number 5, with everything in between ordered from the thumb down; however, instead of raising the fingers when counting, the whole hand is exposed, and each finger is depressed as the counting is done. It is very insulting to beckon someone with the forefinger (instead, turn your hand so that the palm is facing down and motion inward with all four fingers at once). If you need to gesture for a waiter, very subtly raise your hand. Waving or beckoning is done with the palm down and the fingers moving forward and backward in a kind of scratching motion. It may seem as if the person making the gesture is saying good-bye to you, when in fact you are being summoned over. If you need to point to something or someone, close your fingers, open your palm and face it upward, and pass your hand in the direction you want to indicate.

Physicality and Physical Space

Saudis and most Arabs stand closer than most North Americans are accustomed to; resist the urge to move back. Many Arabs are comfortable at a distance where one can feel the warmth of the breath of the other person. Never speak with your hands in your pockets: always keep them firmly at your side when standing. If men and women must cross their legs when they sit, it must never be ankle over knee (for women, the preferred style is to cross ankle over ankle; but the bottom of the shoes must not show to the other person). Remember, even in public, formal is always better than informal: no gum-chewing, *ever;* don't slouch; and don't lean against things. Arabs are most comfortable when they are next to other people: in a nearly empty bus, movie theater, or restaurant, in most cases, Arabs will tend to sit next to or near the other person present, instead of far away from them.

Eye Contact

Eye contact can be very direct between strangers and once relationships are established. As a Westerner, you may be the object of other people's stares: this is not meant to be impolite; it is mere curiosity. However, rank changes eye contact patterns; interest in what one's supervisor says is often best shown by averting the eyes, not by making eye contact. The eyes are used extensively to convey true feelings in formal situations where it is difficult to express things verbally. Tune up your nonverbal antennae.

Emotive Orientation

Arabs are emotive and demonstrative. There can be much touching (at least between members of the same sex) during even the most casual conversation. Two men or two women often walk hand in hand or arm in arm down the street. Verbal communication often employs effusiveness, exaggeration, and flowery phrases: this is meant to show sincerity, not duplicity.

Protocol in Public

Walking Styles and Waiting in Lines

On the street, in stores, and in most public facilities, people pay little attention to maintaining orderly lines. Due to the volume of passengers on public transportation, there can be much pushing and jostling. This is not to get into a bus ahead of someone else, though; it is merely to get in! This is not meant to be disrespectful; if it is bothersome, just say so politely, and you will be treated well. If you ask an Arab for directions, he or she will make every effort to show you the way (even if he or she is not that certain!).

Behavior in Public Places: Airports, Terminals, and the Market

Pride will always demand that Arabs provide you with assistance; even if they do not have an answer, they will give you one. If you feel as if you are on the outside, or being treated as a stranger, strike up a polite and respectful conversation: you will be treated honorably.

Establish a personal relationship with a shopkeeper, and you can expect much assistance; once this is done, you are treated royally. Stores in the cities are open in the evenings and on weekends, as well as during the day, but close during the Muslim Sabbath (Friday) and in preparation for it (Thursday nights), and on all Muslim holidays. A personal verbal thank-you to store owners, waiters, chefs, and hotel managers for their services is important, as it will help establish the relationship you need to get continuing good service. In goods stores, if you buy a product and have problems with it, returning the item is usually difficult. Smoking is endemic, and you may have difficulty finding a no-smoking area on public transportation, in restaurants, and in other public places (be sure not to smoke during the day during Ramadan, when Muslims abstain; this is true for eating and drinking during the day during Ramadan when in the presence of observant Muslims, as well). When and if you do smoke, it is critical that you offer a cigarette first to everyone else at the table before you light up, and then offer to light their cigarettes for them. Bathroom facilities can range from Western-style toilets to Asian-style toilets (holes in the floor, with buckets of water or hoses attached to a water line for cleanup instead of paper); be prepared.

Unless they are in the company of other women or close male relatives, women generally do not go out in public, especially at night. Western women traveling alone in Saudi Arabia will place an unusual burden of consideration on the behavior of others toward them: many people won't know what to do, or how to act toward them; some other women will want to assist them, and certain men, no doubt, will try to take advantage of them. Traveling alone is not a good idea in any part of the Arab world for women.

Never bring anything into the countries of the Arab world that can be construed as pornographic or challenging to Islam in even the slightest way: videotapes, books, and magazines will be inspected and confiscated at most borders if so judged, and you can be subject to harsher penalties, in some cases.

When answering a telephone, say "Hello" or just your given name. Cell phones are ubiquitous.

Bus / Metro / Taxi / Car

Driving is on the right, and whether in the country or the city, being in a car can be hazardous to your health. The roads are not necessarily in good repair in the developing Arab world (but they are generally in very good shape in Gulf Arabia), marked, or where maps says they are; obtaining fuel, however, is usually not a problem. Driving on the good roads in Gulf Arabia, however, poses its own set of problems, since people drive like they own the road: at any speed, in any direction, at any time. It can be very dangerous, and even more so at night. Traveling alone is not done in Saudi Arabia, and in other parts of the Arab world it may be dangerous in towns where you are not known. Driving simply puts you at risk of being stopped by police. Non-Muslims will be prohibited from entering Medina and Mecca.

The best way to catch a cab is at designated taxi stands (hotels are good places, but often charge more for the same ride: a hotel surcharge is added to the meter fare, in some cases). When a taxi has been hailed, negotiate the price. Whenever possible, have the address you need to get to written down on a piece of paper (or use the business card of the person you are going to see, if you can) before you hail the cab.

Tipping

Tipping (the ubiquitous *baksheesh*) is universally required throughout the Arab world, and then some. It is traditional to always give a little something to someone who has helped you out (in Saudi Arabia, these will often be guest workers from abroad). The offer may be refused in some cases, but you must insist, and it will be graciously accepted and appreciated. Tips in restaurants run about 10 percent and are typically not included in the bill (but double-check to be sure); a tip is not necessary if you have negotiated the fare for the taxi ahead of time and already figured in the tip. For everything else, a few coins are all that is needed, but you should always have a lot of spare change handy to see you through the day.

Punctuality

Punctuality is valued, but not required. You should be on time, but you may be kept waiting for quite awhile: patience and good humor are required. Never get upset over time. If you are late, making a general comment about the traffic is all you need to do to get off the hook for being late. It will be understood.

Dress

Saudi men traditionally wear the *ghotra* (head covering) and *thobe* (white robe covering); Saudi women usually wear the black robe (*abaya*), plus a veil. It is *not* appropriate for non-Saudis to dress in traditional Saudi clothes; Westerners should dress in conservative business clothes, but may find it more comfortable to wear items that are as loose fitting as possible (the weather is hot, and you may be required to sit cross-legged from time to time on cushions). In all cases, for men and women, most of the body needs to be covered, including arms down to the wrists, torso up to the neck, and legs down to the ankles. (Men should not wear neck jewelry, even if it is not visible underneath clothing.) Clothes must not be tight-fitting or revealing in any way, for men or women. If you're dressing casually, your shirt must be buttoned up to the neck. Women should not wear pantsuits, as they reveal too much of the shape of the legs. Any clothing that is different from the prescribed norm will engender stares, and perhaps *mataween* intervention. Women whose legs are clearly showing above their ankles risk having their legs whipped in the street. For adults, sneakers and T-shirts are only for the gym or around the house; shorts are never okay, on the street or elsewhere.

Seasonal Variations

In Saudi Arabia, it is always dry and hot: the air conditioning, however, can be frigid, so be prepared with a shawl or another type of cover-up.

Colors

Neutral and muted, whenever possible.

Styles

For visitors, wear conservative Western clothes.

Accessories / Jewelry / Makeup

Makeup, hairstyle, and accessories are important for women, but only if done modestly. In any event, they often can't be seen underneath the veil. Western women should avoid risking too much makeup. The Saudis appreciate men and women who smell good. There is a liberal use of cologne among men at work during the day; and if you visit a Saudi's home, a tray of perfume is often at the entrance, for women to use as they come and go (feel free). Arabs have a keenly developed sense of smell and taste. Colognes and perfumes are typically not made with alcohol (alcohol is generally prohibited in Islam).

Personal Hygiene

In Saudi Arabia, cleanliness is associated with purity. Washing both hands and feet more than once a day is very common. Do not blow your nose in public: it is considered very rude. Spitting does occur on the street, but is also regarded as rude. Muslim men may sport facial hair, usually in the form of a mustache. At the end of a meal, if you use a toothpick, you must cover the "working" hand with the other hand, so that others cannot see your mouth. Consider that Muslims consider dogs very unclean; therefore, do not refer to them or bring them (or pictures of them) along with you.

Dining and Drinking

Mealtimes and Typical Foods

The typical Saudi diet is rich in grains, breads, fresh vegetables, and fruits. Meats will include lamb, goat, and chicken. Gulf Arab cuisine includes a dip made of eggplant (*baba ghanoush*) and hummus (a chickpea and sesame paste). Olive products are varied, and there is liberal use of fruits (fresh and dried, especially figs, dates, raisins, and pomegranates) and nuts. Breads can be the pocket-type pitas and leavened or unleavened breads. Foods can be spicy, but are not necessarily hot. Although they are becoming increasingly familiar with Western food, Saudis and Arabs in general love their food, and most enjoy a fine local meal (if you are hosting them in your country, unless they directly express an interest in trying a local cuisine, take them to the best local Middle Eastern restaurant you can find, and tell the restaurant manager that you are hosting Arab guests: the restaurant management will usually go out of their way to make the meal very fine for you).

If you are serving a meal at home, be sure you do not use alcohol or pork in any of the dishes; and if you do, labeling the dish and serving it separately will still make your Arab guest uncomfortable—simply don't do it. You, as a guest in the region, may be rewarded with favored parts of the animal, such as the goat's eye or head: this is an honor that needs to be acknowledged before the food is consumed or rejected (if you cannot bring yourself to partake, acknowledge the honor, and suggest that while you will always hold the honor in your heart, you in turn will bestow it on someone who can also appreciate it in his or her belly: then pass the honored dish on to an Arab colleague). In fact, in the Gulf area, you if you are invited to someone's home and see a sheep's carcass in front of or on the grounds of the house, this is a honor: it means the animal has been slaughtered in your honor, and you can be sure you will have the meat for dinner.

Most meals begin with tasty appetizers of dips and vegetables and breads, and are served buffet or family style, so there is much for everyone. The amount of food at a meal at which you are a guest in the region can be overwhelming; guests must be treated with great respect and honor. It is far better to return for more than to load up your plate at once and not be able to eat any more later.

Breakfast is served from about 7 to 8 A.M., and usually consists of tea and coffee, breads, jams, cheese, and olives. Tea is usually drunk with milk or sugar. Yogurt and fruit drinks are sometimes served for breakfast. The coffee is rich, dark, very sweet, and served in small cups, usually without milk. It is often flavored with sweet spices, such as cardamom or cinnamon.

Lunch is traditionally the main meal of the day, and even today, in busy cities, it can still be an elaborate affair with several courses—or it can be a simple snack prepared and eaten in a matter of minutes. Lunch is served from about noon to 2 P.M. Lunch consists of meat, fish, and/or vegetables, with rice or yogurt, and can be in a stewlike vegetable sauce. The drinks served with lunch and dinner are usually soft drinks, fruit juices, and/or tea, with Arabic coffee after the meal.

Dinner is served from 8 P.M. on, with 9 P.M. the customary late time. Even if the main meal of the day was lunch, dinner is only slighter lighter—this is often the case with families at home. The dinner menu is often similar to that of the more formal lunch, with *felaffel,* lamb shish kebabs, and other more elaborate dishes. Dinner drinks are similar to thowse served at lunch. When you come to a Saudi home, even for just a brief visit, you will be served some sweet delicacy plus a cool drink (usually iced water, lemonade, or fruit juice) and/or tea and coffee. The sweet is not a dessert; you will get that at the end of the meal as well. Desserts can be very sweet, such as honeyed pastries, not unlike baklava, with puddings made of sweetened yogurts, nuts, rosewater, and eggs.

Regional Differences

Chicken cooked with herbs, tomatoes, and spices is a favorite. Another favorite dish is *foul,* or fava beans prepared with olive oil and lemon. Stuffed grape leaves are a popular appetizer, as is *f'teer,* a kind of pizza filled with meat and vegetables. Cheese is popular, either as a feta-like soft cheese, or as a hard cheddar-like white cheese. Remember, Islam prohibits the use of pork, and most meats of any kind for Muslims need to be prepared *halal* (meat slaughtered according to Islamic prescriptions). A staple grain is couscous, cooked in a thousand different ways with many different ingredients. Do not eat in front of your Muslim colleagues, or invite them to join you for a meal, during the day during Ramadan, as Muslims typically fast (and refrain from drinking and smoking) during the day, and feast with family and friends at night. Ramadan lasts for a lunar month: this is simply not a good time to do business or go out entertaining in the Arab Middle East.

Typical Drinks and Toasting

Tea and coffee are served everywhere, all the time. Sometimes tea or coffee is boiling hot: sometimes it is lukewarm; most of the time tea is served with milk or sugar. Coffee is served in small cups, always without milk; it is strong, black, often intensely presweetened (so taste first before adding sugar!), and sometimes spiced. Always accept the cup of tea and/or coffee, even if you only put it to your lips or just take a few sips. Your cup will always be refilled if it is less than half full. The ceremony of tea/coffee/tea can last hours, as you chat and converse, and do business, and it goes something like this: you will be offered tea; when you are finished, you will be offered coffee; when you are finished, you will be offered tea again, and the whole process can repeat itself. This is an important relationship-building event. Typically, beer and other alcoholic drinks are not served: fruit juices and lemonades, along with tea, may accompany most meals. Because you must never pour your own drink (be it juice or tea or coffee), you must always be alert throughout the meal as to whether or not your neighbor's cup or glass needs refilling. If it is less than half full, it needs refilling; alternately, if yours is less than half full, your neighbor or host is obliged to refill it. If he or she does not, do not refill it yourself, for this will cause your neighbor or host to lose face; instead, diplomatically indicate your need by pouring a little more drink into their glass, even if it doesn't really need it.

If you are the honored guest, you are not expected to make a statement or toast, but it is appropriate to offer a small compliment. It will typically be appreciated and dismissed as unnecessary; you can do this at the end of the meal, just before everyone departs. An appropriate comment would be to wish for the health of the host and all those present, and to the prosperity of the business under discussion. Make it as eloquent and flowery as you like, but always be very sincere.

Avoid drinking tap water anywhere in the region (this means you should brush your teeth with bottled water and not take ice in any of your drinks; drink only bottled water, or brewed tea or coffee or soft drinks, and avoid getting water from the morning shower into your mouth; never eat fresh fruits or vegetables that cannot be peeled first, and ideally cooked later before eating). This is a serious matter: there are some very nasty bugs going around in developing countries. In addition, avoid all dairy products except in the finest hotels, as the required refrigeration may be questionable.

A word about water and its use in the region: consider that most of the region is desert, so despite the graciousness of your hosts, water use is a serious concern in this part of the world. Even if you won't drink tap water, use it judiciously when you do use it.

Table Manners and the Use of Utensils

Before meals, as the food is served, guests say, "*Sahtain*" (the equivalent of "bon appetit"), or "*Bismillah*" (In the name of God); when the meal is over, guests should also say, "*Daimah*" ("may there always be plenty at your table"), or "*Hamdullah*" (thanking God for the meal).

You may or may not be given Western utensils. Throughout the region, people use spoons, forks, and knives, if necessary, or no utensils at all. Since the spoon is more important than the fork, if you are right-handed, keep the spoon in the right hand, and put it down to switch to the fork if and when you need it. Never use your left hand for eating, especially if you are eating directly with your hands.

What do you do when no utensils are available? Why, eat with your fingers, of course! Many think it makes the experience more fun, maybe because you're adding an extra sense to an already very sensory experience: the sense of touch. A great variety of foods can be eaten with the hands, including wonderful vegetarian or meat curries, shish kebobs, and the like, served with rice and sauce. You reach into the rice, take some with your fingers, gently roll it between your index and middle fingers and thumb (not your palms) into a kind of self-sticking ball, dip it into the sauce, mix it with a vegetable or a piece of chicken, then pop the whole thing in your mouth.

Here are some other things to note about eating in Saudi Arabia:

- If you are dining without utensils, wash your hands before you sit down to eat. Many restaurants have washrooms and sinks out in the open specifically for this purpose. (However, you may want to wash your hands with bottled water at the hotel first, since the washing water at the restaurant may be more hazardous to your health than the germs already on your hands!). You will also need to wash your hands again at the end of the meal, especially after eating the saucy dishes, since you've probably got some messy fingers by the end of the meal. Don't worry, it's to be expected.
- Use your right hand when picking up and eating food: never your left hand. Keep your left hand at your side. Do not place your left hand on the table, and do not pass food with your left hand.
- Pork will typically not be on the menu.
- Alcohol will usually not be served with the meal.
- Men and women, in some establishments, may be asked to dine separately.
- If you absolutely cannot eat without some kind of utensil, it's perfectly all right to ask for one. The proprietors, or your hosts, are usually more than pleased to accommodate Westerners.

It is especially important that if men and women are dining together (rare in Saudi Arabia, but more common elsewhere), that women not directly touch food that is being served to a Muslim male, other than those who are her immediate relatives: to do so makes it impure in the eyes of some observant Muslims.

A word about smoking: it is ubiquitous throughout the region. Usually, you do not smoke until the meal is over. In addition, at the end of some meals, particularly in Saudi Arabia and the Gulf region, incense or cologne might be passed around as a final refreshment: you lean over and gently inhale the sweet fragrance. Fresh mints or caraway seeds may be offered as a special treat just before you go.

Most discussion occurs before the meal, not after, although dining at someone's home will last well into the night. Expect to be told that it is too early to leave the first time you try; stay a while longer, but if the hosts serve some ice water or another cool drink, you should leave soon thereafter.

Seating Plans

The most honored position is in the middle of the table, with the second most important person, or the honored guest, seated next to the head of the table. (Spouses are usually not invited to business meals in restaurants. Do not ask if your spouse can join you; it will embarrass your Arab colleague. However, your spouse might be invited to a meal at home, especially if the spouse of the host will be there, which will probably be the case. The invitation will then be phrased, "My spouse invites your spouse." By the way, invitations, business or social, will almost always be verbal, not written.) Be prepared that in some more traditional homes, you might sit on carpets on the floor at very low tables. In addition, the honored guest sits on the side of the table farthest from the door. (This is the same at business meetings, with the key people sitting in the middle, flanked on either side in descending order by their aides, with the least important person sitting at the ends of the table farthest from the middle and closest to the door; the arrangement is mirrored on the other side.) Men and women eating at someone's home may dine in separate areas (and spend the entire evening separated) or at separate times, with the men dining first; this is especially the case in Saudi Arabia and the Gulf region.

Refills and Seconds

You will always be offered more food. Leave a bit on your plate if you do not want more food. You will be implored to take more two or three times, in the form of a little ritual. The game is as follows: first you refuse, then the host insists, then you refuse again, then the host insists again, and then you finally give in and take a little more. This is known as the *uzooma* (the seesaw dialogue of imploring, rejecting, and finally submitting). If you really don't want more, take very little and leave it on your plate. Your host will constantly ask you if you are enjoying yourself and will implore you to have more. You may always have additional beverages; drink enough to cause your cup or glass to be less than half full, and it will generally be refilled. A reminder: never refill your own glass; always refill your neighbor's glass, and he or she will refill yours.

At Home, in a Restaurant, or at Work

The honored guest is served first, then the oldest male, then the rest of the men, then children, and finally women. Do not begin to eat or drink until the oldest male at the table has been served and has begun. At the end of the meal, it is appropriate to thank the host or hostess for a wonderful meal.

In informal restaurants, you may be required to share a table. If so, do not force conversation: act as if you are seated at a private table. Women should be sensitive to the fact that they may be seated only with other women. Waitstaff may be summoned by making eye contact; waving or calling their names is very impolite. The business breakfast is practically unknown in the region, and most business meals are lunches. Business meals are generally not good times to discuss business or make business decisions. Take your cue from your Arab associates: if they bring up business, then it's okay to discuss it, but wait to take your lead from their conversation. It is safer to never host Arabs in a nightclub or any establishment where liquor is served (even if they ask about going to a nightclub, they may be doing so for your sake, and it will make them uncomfortable if you actually go). Music may accompany the meal in restaurants, with performance dancing (usually traditional belly dancing) as well.

When invited to a colleague's home for a formal meal, you will be invited to sit anywhere you like at the table; resist the impulse to sit down, and wait until your host gives you further instructions. These will generally come after the host or eldest man is seated, and often you will be placed at his side. It is an honor to be invited into an Arab home, but a great obligation as well. (You may, in fact, be invited into a private home sooner than you are taken to a restaurant, as Arabs want to get to know you). The "salon," where you will be entertained, is a symbol in Arab culture of the honor and responsibility the host has to the guest. Once invited inside, you may need to remove your shoes; this is still a custom in many homes (this is not a custom in restaurants, however). You will know when you approach the home and see a row of shoes at the door (keep your socks in good shape, and wear comfortable but well-made slip-ons for such occasions). Once inside the home, do not wander around: much of the house is really off-limits to guests. If you move from room to room in a Saudi home or restaurant, be sure to always allow the more senior members of your party to enter the room ahead of you. Servants and household help are very common in middle- and upper-class homes; do not comment on them and do not offer to help: they are there to serve.

Being a Good Guest or Host

Paying the Bill

Usually the one who does the inviting pays the bill, although the guest is expected to make an effort to pay. Sometimes other circumstances determine who pays (such as rank). Making payment arrangements ahead of time so that no exchange occurs at the table is a very classy way to host, and is very common. Western businesswomen, if out with men, will have a problem paying the bill at a restaurant; if you want to, make payment arrangements ahead of time, and don't wait for the check to arrive at the table. It may be easiest to do this at one of the international hotel dining rooms (they are rarely as much fun, but they are very convenient, and they do avoid a lot of problems!).

Transportation

It's a very nice idea, when acting as the host, to inquire ahead of time as to whether your guests will require transportation. If necessary, you should arrange for taxi service at the end of the meal. When seeing your guests off, you must remain at the entrance of the house or restaurant, or at the site where you deposited your guests into the car, until the car is out of sight: it is very important not to leave until your guests can no longer see you, should they look back. Guests are seated in cars (and taxis) by rank, with the honored guest being placed in the back directly behind the front passenger seat; the next honored position is in the back behind the driver, and the least honored position is up front with the driver.

When to Arrive / Chores to Do

If invited to dinner at a private home, do not offer to help with the chores: you are a guest, and the servant or household staff performs such tasks. You should not expect or ask to visit the kitchen. Do not leave the table unless invited to do so. When in the home, be careful not to admire something too effusively: Arabs may feel obligated to give it to you, and you, in turn, will be required to present them with a gift of equal value. Instead of saying things like "I love that vase," say something like "Vases that beautiful in my country are only found in museums." Your compliments will most likely be dismissed, but will be very much appreciated. Remember also that Arabs consider it very bad luck to have their children praised: it can bring ill-fortune to them (comment on the children indirectly, but comment on them positively).

Gift Giving

In general, gift giving is not that common for social occasions, but is common in business situations between trusted colleagues. It is not only done as a gesture of thanks, but as a way of helping to ensure good business relations in the future (be careful not to go overboard here, as a gift that looks like an obvious bribe is not appreciated, and may land you in quite a bit of trouble . . . with the authorities in your home country, more than likely). In business settings, this usually takes the form of a personal gift that symbolically says the correct thing about the nature of the relationship. When going to the region on business, bringing a gift for the key decision maker is usually enough. Your gift does not have to be elaborate or expensive, but it should, whenever possible, be personalized (engraved, or representative of the personalities of the receiver or giver or of an aspect of the relationship). You present your gift when you arrive in the country; before you leave to return home, you will receive a farewell gift, usually at the last meeting. When Arabs visit your country, they will also bring you a gift, and before they leave, you should give them farewell gifts.

The most appropriate gift for a personal visit to a home, or as a thank-you for dinner, would be a box of fruits, pastries, cakes, cookies, or other sweets. Flowers are okay to give as gifts, but avoid roses, as they are too personal. A man typically only gives a gift to a man, a woman to a woman; remember, any gift given by a man to a woman must come with the caveat that it is from his wife/sister/mother, or else it is far too personal. Sending a handwritten thank-you note the day after the dinner is a very good idea. If you are staying with a family, an appropriate thank-you gift would be a high-quality item that represents your country and is difficult or expensive to get in Saudi Arabia; this is also a good idea for a key business associate. Avoid gifts from or about the United States with political implications (although relations between the United States and some Arab states, including Saudi Arabia, are good, the politics of the United States in the region are questioned by many Arabs). In Saudi Arabia and the Gulf, gifts need to be a bit luxurious (these are essentially wealthy countries). Do not give alcohol (and this includes perfumes or colognes made with alcohol), pork, art or photographs that depict natural scenes or people (this runs counter to Islamic beliefs that man must not attempt to reproduce what God has made), or cutlery (which symbolizes the severing of a relationship). A fine gift for a Muslim would be a silver compass, so that he will always know which direction to face when he says his daily prayers (Muslims must face Mecca no matter where they are when they say their prayers).

For both giving and receiving gifts, two hands are used always. Gifts are typically not opened by the receiver in front of the giver; they are usually received after much imploring by you, graciously acknowledged, and placed aside to be opened once the giver is no longer present.

Gifts should be wrapped well. Typically, gifts are wrapped in ordinary paper first then wrapped again in green or other bright colors; white wrapping is perfectly fine.

By the way, if you have a copy of the Koran (received as a gift or not), never place it on the floor or below any object: it must be the highest book on the shelf. Do not give a copy of the Koran as a gift: it is far too significant for a business or social acknowledgment.

Special Holidays and Celebrations

Major Holidays

Avoid doing business the entire month of Ramadan. Many cities have different local holidays as well, so double-check with your Arab associates before making final travel plans.

Islamic holidays are the most important holidays throughout the region (additionally, in Saudi Arabia, September 23 is celebrated as National Day). Islamic holidays are on the lunar calendar, so the dates change each year, and all holidays begin at sundown the day before.

The most important Islamic holidays are (in order of their usual occurrence):

Ramadan
Eid al Fitr: A multiday (usually two or three) celebration of the end of
    the fast at the end of Ramadan
Eid al Adha: The Feast of the Sacrifice, celebrating Abraham's willingness
    to sacrifice his son
Hajj: The first day of the annual pilgrimage to Mecca
Birth of the Prophet Muhammad
Islamic New Year

Business Culture

Daily Office Protocols

The traditional Saudi office can be closed or open, but no matter how the architecture is designed, you can be sure many people will be coming and going. This is not so much a statement on your unimportance as much as it is a statement about the importance of your host: that he is needed by many, and that in the polychronic Arab culture, things are handled in order of their importance and not according to the clock. Be patient. In the Arab organization, hierarchy is strictly observed. Executives are usually placed on different floors than the rank and file. You probably will not be invited onto the working floors until the proposed project has been set in motion. Because faithful Muslims pray five times a day, you will need to adjust your schedules to accommodate their needs. Usually, prayers are given upon awakening and at noontime, midday, dusk, and before retiring; this means that twice during the workday there will be time out for prayers. The prayer break usually takes a short ten or fifteen minutes or so, and any quiet area will do. If you accidentally interrupt a Muslim during his prayers, just walk quietly away; there's no need for complicated explanations or apologies. Most organizations have prayer rooms set aside, with carpets. In addition, devout Muslims will not work on Friday (the Muslim Sabbath), and in fact begin to end work early on Thursday, before sundown. The official work week is Saturday through Thursday, 9 A.M. to 4 P.M. Oftentimes, because of the heat, many businesspeople work into the night (with a break for lunch—sometimes at home—in the afternoon); do not be surprised if an early evening office meeting is scheduled.

Management Styles

Because of the rigid rank and hierarchy orientation, titles are very important; the highest ones (e.g., vice president) are usually reserved for very senior, executive-level positions, and should not be used as casually as they are in the United States. Any criticism of Arab workers must be done very carefully, even privately. Deference is shown by subordinates to their seniors; paternalistic concern is often shown by executives to their subordinates. Superiors are very sensitive to inquiring about their subordinate's opinions; however, once a decision is made by superiors, the superiors are followed, often unquestioningly. If you are doing business with the correct person, things will probably move quickly; it is essential, therefore, to have a good and trustworthy contact in the Arab world (this "sponsor," in fact, is legally required in Saudi Arabia and other Gulf states) who can make the necessary contacts for you. Let this person take the time he needs to take to do this for you, for if you pressure him into making contacts sooner, he may connect you to someone who is not as useful as the one he was originally waiting for: this will not serve you. Again, be patient. Never use time as a means of pressure.

Boss-Subordinate Relations

The decision-making system usually works from the top on down, with key decisions often coming from individuals in high positions of power. Superiors are expected to provide clear and fully informed sets of instructions: that is their responsibility, and it is the responsibility of subordinates to carry out those instructions. Consequently, "management-by-objective" and other egalitarian and individually empowered management styles often may not work in this environment: without clear instruction from above, subordinates often will do nothing. They also lose respect for the manager for not making the decisions he should be making.

Conducting a Meeting or Presentation

At your first meeting in Saudi Arabia, you will probably be received in a very comfortable waiting area, which may or may not be where most of the meeting is conducted between you and your Saudi colleague (an equally good place to host a meeting would be in a meeting room of one of the international hotels you will inevitably be staying at). If this is the case, you are merely being sized up, and your colleague is a gatekeeper. There will be much hosting by your Saudi contacts with tea/coffee/tea. When serving any refreshments in the office, be sure they are served in porcelain, glass, or silver tea sets: the use of paper or Styrofoam shows disrespect and is very bad form. There may be several people in the room with you and your Arab contact whom you may or may not be introduced to. These "ghost people" are probably trusted friends or relations of your Arab colleague, and he will no doubt want their input after the meeting. If you are not introduced to them, do not ask to be: acknowledge them with a smile and a nod, and proceed with your meeting. If you are meeting with a decision maker, the discussions will probably be direct, forthright, and businesslike. If you do not know the decision-making authority of the person you are with, assume that you will need to meet with many people, and perhaps repeat much of the same discussions each time with different people. There may be many interruptions throughout the meeting; stay calm and flexible. If this is just the beginning of a business relationship, expect to spend most of the time sharing information about your organization with different individuals, or repeating the same things to the same individual. This may feel frustrating, but it is really okay; it means your plans are advancing to the right people in the organization, that those you have previously met with have approved you and moved you on, and that you are building a personal trust with the key decision maker. Business is very personal throughout the region: decision makers have got to know your face. Patience and third-party connections are key.

Negotiation Styles

At first, expect no decisions from your Arab colleagues at the table, and be willing to provide copious amounts of information, to the degree that you can, in response to their questions and in anticipation of their needs. Presentations should be well prepared and simply propounded. Details are best left to questions and backup material, which should be available in both English and Arabic, and left behind. Such materials need to look attractive and professional, and even if only in English should have an attractive "back" cover (since Arabs read from right to left). Ideally, you should present your material to your Arab colleagues for study, along with a proposed agenda, prior to the meeting. Have extra copies available, as you might meet more people than you expect. Should you come with other team members, make sure that your roles are well coordinated. Never disagree with each other in front of Arabs or appear uncertain, unsure, not authorized to make a decision, or out of control in any way.

Most Arabs love to bargain and see this process as a way of getting to know you: it does not imply insincerity to offer one price and then change your mind later (as it often does with Pacific Rim cultures). In fact, avoiding this process will generate suspicion. Final terms must be fair to all (win-win). Contracts and contract law are well known and understood; expect and insist on

well-executed documents to finalize an agreement, but the final document needs
to be short and simple, and may not be the all-inclusive tome that Western contracts tend to be. Remember, the deal should be sealed with a celebratory meal.
Keep communications open, especially when at a distance, and stay in touch
often with your Saudi associates: share more information than you normally
would, not less; and be prepared to make many trips, as needed. Nothing much
will happen without you or someone from your group on site (therefore, try to
have a contact on the ground in the region who can always keep you informed
of what is really going on, if you can).

Written Correspondence

Your business letters should be very formal and respectful of rank and hierarchy. Given names usually are written in uppercase; dates are given using the
day/month/year format (with periods in between, not slashes) if using the Western calendar, or year/month/day format if using the Islamic calendar (the *Hijrah;*
subtract 622 years from the Western date, and add A.H.—"after the hajj"—to
the date. To be safe and respectful, put both Islamic and Western dates on all
correspondence. When writing names, an honorific plus the title is as common
as an honorific plus the last name. You should write your e-mails, letters, and
faxes in a formal, precise way: use a brief but warm personal introduction, then
get down to business. Keep it simple, however, and bulletpoint and outline all
important matters. You may use either the Western format (name, position, company, street address, city, state/province, country, postal code) or the Asian format (company name, individual name, position, country and country code, state/
province, street address) for the addresses.

KUWAIT

*Note: Refer to the preceding section on Saudi Arabia for information about
general Gulf Arab and Arab cultural behaviors; the material that follows
describes country-specific variations on general Gulf Arab and Arab customs.*

Kuwait in many ways is similar to Saudi Arabia, in that it is essentially very
wealthy, due to oil, and has rigid class lines that define its society. Until oil was
discovered, however, Kuwait's economy was derived mainly from pearls and
trading, and historically, Kuwait struggled to define itself independently of Saudi
Arabia and Iraq. Kuwaitis, therefore, have a long tradition of being shrewd traders
and negotiators, and will be equally with you, if you come to Kuwait on business. Today, the wealthy classes (constituting the bulk of national Kuwaitis) run
all aspects of the country, with Palestinians and Pakistanis as foreign workers
doing much of the employed labor (almost 50 percent of the entire population)—although since the Gulf War in the 1990s women have been slowly taking up more of the roles that foreign workers occupied. Subsequently, many
Westerners have presumed a perceived arrogance on the part of native Kuwaitis,

especially in terms of their self-perception vis-à-vis non-Kuwaitis (this includes others in the region, such as Iraqis, Palestinians, and Pakistanis, as well as Westerners). While they are intensely Islamic, life is not as fundamentalist as in Saudi Arabia (Saudi Wahibbism is not practiced in Kuwait), and foreigners are tolerated, if not understood (many Kuwaitis are educated in Europe and the United States, and English competency is high among most businessmen). As in Saudi Arabia, Kuwaiti time is very flexible: do not push for decisions, do not push the discussion, do not make more than one appointment per day; go with the flow of conversation and take your cues about what and when to talk about substantive issues from your Kuwaiti colleagues. Women and men, unlike in Saudi Arabia and the rest of the Gulf region, can work together in Kuwait, although women do not hold significant decision-making roles outside of the home. Unlike in Saudi Arabia, a business meeting will probably seem a little more austere, and coffee will be served only at the beginning and the end of the meeting. As a way of bringing the discussions to a peaceful close, Kuwaitis may light some incense and talk about incidental things. Kuwaitis call the man's long flowing robe the *dishdasha,* and the woman's, the *thoub* (their design makes them more or less formal). Kuwait's National Day is February 25.

OMAN

Oman is probably the most "liberal" of the Gulf States: women, in fact, often join men in social situations, and alcohol is actually consumed in public in some circles (it is still not common, however). Instead of the Saudi headdress, Omanis wear a scarf, plus the *dishdasha.* National Day in Oman is November 18. The Sultan is a Western-educated leader, and his birthday in November is a national holiday, celebrated with camel and horse races in and around Musqat, the port capital. As is the case with all Gulf States, status and rank are highly regarded. Put all your educational degrees on your business cards, as you would in Kuwait and Saudi Arabia. Until recently, Oman, which is the second largest country on the Arabian peninsula, was mainly an agricultural country, and relatively isolated from the world beyond Gulf Arabia and neighboring Asia. Consequently, there is not as much familiarity with the West, and English competency may not be as strong, even among the business class, although Oman is developing into a media center for the region.

QATAR

Like Saudi Arabia, Qatar is a very fundamentalist country. It is run by a small royal family which has complete control over all aspects of life. While there is no drinking of alcoholic beverages, there is much coffee, and it is traditionally drunk from the same cup in a group of people. The cup is passed around, so be sure to finish all the coffee in your cup when it is handed to you as soon as you can, so it can be refilled and passed on to the next person. Qatar's national holiday is Independence Day (September 3); another national holiday occurs on the anniversary of the Accession of the Sheik Khalifa (February 22).

BAHRAIN

As residents of an island nation, Bahrainis have always been trading with foreigners, so they understand non-Islamic ways, although they generally do not subscribe to them. There is a liberalism in people's attitudes toward Westerners and Bahraini women that makes Bahrain a more comfortable place for Western businesspeople, including women. If you are entertained, by the way, at someone's "garden," you will be taken to the family's weekend "retreat"; it may not be elaborate, but the picnic lunch you will be served surely will be. Bahrain's national day is Ruler's Ascension Day (December 16).

UNITED ARAB EMIRATES

Each of the seven emirates that make up this federation has its own way of doing things, but there is nonetheless significant cooperation between them. They currently thrive on world trade, and the more prominent Dubai and Abu Dhabi, for example, have a legacy of being more flexible when dealing with Westerners and adapting to some Western ways more easily than some of their more fundamentalist Arab neighbors; for example, in Abu Dhabi, alcoholic consumption is allowed for Westerners.

YEMEN

Yemen is a time warp: it is "Old Arabia." It still operates mainly according to family agrarian models based on traditional Islamic law and Arab customs. Greet people with the honorific *qadi* (judge), or, for more formality, *faqih* (religious scholar); they are both used before the given name. Do not use the family (last) name in addressing people. Women, after greeting other women, may stroke each other's cheek, as an extra sign of sincerity. Often women have their hands and feet decorated with henna artwork (especially for special occasions, like weddings) by female artisans. The designs are quite beautiful, and a definite mark of Gulf Arab women.

Qat, a mildly stimulating narcotic, is unique to the Yemeni diet. You may be invited to "a chew": you buy your *qat* at the market, take it with you to the gathering, and chew away. The proper technique is to take just a little from the purchased wad at a time, ball it your hand, and put some in your mouth by your cheek. After a few minutes, the bitter juice should be spit out (follow the lead of one of your Yemeni colleagues). There is a sense of heightened awareness, and then euphoria; finally, there is a "crash," during which the chewer becomes very tired. Yemenis do most of their business over *qat* chews. Join in if you want to do business in Yemen. Accompanying the *qat* is usually a water pipe and water for drinking (you won't want to eat, but you will become thirsty—don't worry, *qat* is not physiologically addictive, but people can develop a psychological need for it). You usually sit on cushions when you have a *qat* chew.

Curiously, bargaining is *not* a way of life in Yemen as it is elsewhere in almost all the rest of the Arab world. Yemeni men usually wear a small dagger as part of their daily dress (it is symbolic of their membership in tribes that made their living keeping pirates away from the Yemeni coast).

Dining in Yemen is a little different as well, as meals do not constitute the formal hosting events they are elsewhere in the Arab world. Meals typically occur between prayer times, and as is the case elsewhere in the Arab world, most conversation occurs before the meal, not during and certainly not after it (when it is time to go home). Typically, after you finish your meal, you get up to wash your hands (remember, you've probably eaten with your fingers), and then go into the salon for coffee. If you are in a restaurant, you can summon the waiter by clapping your hands together once or twice.

Yemeni dress codes require that women wear pants underneath their dresses; and men, for modesty's sake, if dressed in Western clothes, often carry a scarf they can put in their laps when they sit down. In Yemen, you must treat everyone as equal, especially in business. The people tend to get right down to business, and there is a much more matter-of-fact approach to getting together to talk business (which is another Yemeni anomaly, in relation to the behaviors in much of the rest of the region). There were once a great many Jews in Yemen, but today it is mainly a Muslim nation. In addition, the region of Eastern Yemen, along the coast, known as the Hadraumat, has a distinctly business and trading culture that goes back millennia, as Hadraumatis often controlled the sea commerce between the Red and Arabian Seas. Even today, Hadraumatis speak a distinctly different language, and are seen as a unique group by themselves and other Yemenis. Holidays in Yemen include Labor Day (May 1), Correction Movement Day (September 26), National Day (October 14), and Independence Day (November 30).

<table>
<tr><td>CHAPTER
TWO</td><td>The Arab Levantine Cultures:
Lebanon, Syria, and Jordan</td></tr>
</table>

Note: Refer to the preceding section on Saudi Arabia for information about general Arab cultural behaviors; the material that follows describes country-specific variations on general Arab customs.

LEBANON

This is a very fractured country, having only recently emerged from decades of civil war. Over 70 percent of the population is Muslim, about evenly split between Sunnis and Shiites, while the remaining 30 percent is mainly (though not only) Christian (Maronite Christian, or deviations of the Maronite order, who established themselves in Lebanon), who traditionally held the wealth and power in the country. This is the source of much of the country's political and economic difficulties. Its diversity, in good times, made Lebanon a fairly Westernized place, something that many more fundamentalist Muslims often objected to, and that many Europeans came to support (in fact, Beirut, its capital, was often referred to as the Paris of the Middle East). It is generally understood that Syria controls the Arab majority politically and militarily in Lebanon, while Israel warily maintains a presence along Lebanon's southern frontier, in part in response to both Syria's role and terrorist activity; these and other factors have in the past reduced Lebanon's national legitimacy to that of a client state of its neighbors. Nevertheless, today Lebanon is returning somewhat to its role as a diverse secular nation, but the people's loyalties are to their political and religious affiliations, clans, and membership groups first, and not to the nation. This makes the difficult task of rebuilding the nation and developing a national cultural identity that much more problematic. Appropriate behaviors are dependent upon, therefore, the membership group that your individual colleague is associated with; the difficulty here will be identifying this and keeping different behaviors separate and appropriate. Westernized women, of which there are many, do play a role in government and business; these women are generally unveiled. The second language after Arabic is French (as the French once had a protectorate over Lebanese territory).

SYRIA

Syria is a study in opposites: it is a modern authoritarian state superimposed upon an ancient religious and cultural crossroads. About 90 percent of the population is Muslim; however, the group that rules is the *Alawite* sect, which represents only about 15 percent of the population. Therein is the reason for the oppressive clamp the government has on all aspects of Syrian life. The remaining 10 percent of Syrians are a mixture of Christians, Druze, Jews, and other groups. Syrians are, compared to their Levant Arab cousins (Palestinians, Jordanians, Lebanese Arabs, and Iraqis), generally well educated and worldly (the French colonial period exposed many to Western ways), although very suspicious of the outside world, particularly the West (the colonial period is reviled as a time of oppression that prevented the flowering of Syrian and Arab identity, a position the government uses to justify both its current internal and external policies). Although they identify with pan-Arabism, the closed Alawite nature of life in Syria prevents Syrians from full cooperation with their neighbors. Be aware that because of the government involvement in day-to-day life, many Syrians may be hesitant to express their views fully, but are, in fact, quite knowledgeable and friendly. Women can play some roles in the workforce, but mainly as teachers and medical personnel. Women are generally not veiled. The second language after Arabic is French (the French once had a protectorate over Syrian territory).

JORDAN

Jordan is a monarchy, but a progressive one, in which the king has traditionally demonstrated a paternalistic concern for his people, who are primarily Bedouin (a nomadic tribe indigenous to the Levant, Gulf Arabia, and Northern Africa) and Palestinian. Because of the British rule over the Transjordan area prior to the nation receiving its independent status in 1946, English is the second language after Arabic. Because the country only officially became independent after World War II, the Jordanian people still have strong connections with their roots, usually Saudi, Bedouin, or Palestinian. The country has a peace agreement, as does Egypt, with Israel, and there is a trend toward modernization. The challenge is to accomplish this without sacrificing its Islamic traditions while modernizing, while at the same time resisting the rising tide of fundamentalism. Remember that the last queen of Jordan was an American: there is much between the two countries that links them, and this is a good point of conversation between Jordanians and Americans.

Before a meal (or sometimes as a simple between-meals snack), many small appetizers may be offered: these are *mezzes* and can include grape leaves, hummus and bread, and other treats. If you have been invited to someone's house for dinner, don't fill up on the *mezzes:* this is just the beginning. The *mensaf,* a traditional Bedouin feast, usually features a freshly slaughtered sheep, and many side dishes, served with rice. The *mensaf* is usually done in honor of an important event (your arrival, a wedding, etc.).

Jordanian secular holidays include Tree Day (January 15), Labor Day (May 1), Independence Day (May 25), Arab Army Day (June 10), King Hussein's Accession to the Throne Day (August 11), and King Hussein's Birthday (November 14).

CHAPTER THREE

The Judaic Levantine Cultures: Israel

Note: As Israeli culture incorporates many Levantine cultural attributes, this chapter will identify only those cultural behaviors that may be different from general Levantine culture; specific emphasis is placed on Jewish customs and traditions in Israel, many of which have their roots in the Middle East and Europe.

Some Introductory Background on Israel, the Israelis, and the Jews

The country of Israel, as is much the case for all countries in the region, is a new one in an ancient land. Originally the home of the Jews in biblical times, the country suffered through numerous historic invasions, and its original inhabitants were forced to leave and live in exile (the Diaspora) over several millennia. It wasn't until after World War II that the State of Israel was born. European Zionists—those who were philosophically and politically dedicated to establishing a Jewish homeland in the area that had been the Land of Israel— propelled this idea forward in the twentieth century. Given the Arab experience with the West up to that point, a Westernized state among Arabs on what Arabs believed to be Palestinian soil (appropriated without their consent) was cause for an immediate war, and Israeli-Arab tensions have been great ever since.

Today, the secular state of Israel is caught in a constant debate about what its future should be: should it remain a secular state, or should it become a Jewish religious state, an Orthodox Jewish state, a secular Jewish state? On these issues, the numerous and powerful Orthodox Jews (Hasidim) clash not only with non-Jewish Israelis (of which there are many) and their Arab neighbors, but also with many secular Israeli Jews (there are more secular Jews in Israel than Orthodox). Jews make up about 80 percent of the population of Israel, many having immigrated just before and after the Holocaust. Most Jews in the Zionist movement were from eastern and central Europe. Jews from these areas (including the new wave of immigrants from Russia and the former Soviet Union) are referred to as Ashkenazi. The other great group were Oriental Jews, mainly from other parts of the Middle East and southern Europe (Spain and Portugal primarily), referred to as Sephardim. There is tension between these two groups, and other Jews who have sought identity and new lives in Israel (the Ethiopian, or African, Jews, for example, who are treated poorly by both

Ashkenazi and Sephardim). Arab Israelis are primarily Palestinians, and there are Christian Palestinians and Israelis, as well; there are also myriad other groups, representing just about every possible expression of religious faith, including Eastern Orthodox, Baha'i, Buddhism, and Hinduism. Native-born Jewish Israelis are referred to as *sabras,* the Hebrew word for a cactus fruit (it's hard and prickly on the outside, but, if you can get it to open up, soft and tasty on the inside). As the Jews are a people besieged throughout history, and as Israelis in particular are still under constant pressure and threat, this defensiveness and "no-time-for-fooling-around-or-make-believe" attitude of the Israelis is understandable. In addition, Israelis have a high tolerance for situations that are constantly in flux, no doubt a necessary requirement for survival by the Jewish people throughout history. The Israelis are an informal, no-nonsense, defiant, sometimes challenging people who will tell you just what they think about you or what you are talking about, or anything else that is on their mind . . . if they decide you are worth the discussion.

The two halves of the Israeli psyche find expression in the country's two great cities. Jerusalem, inland and up in the hills, is the conservative and religious-oriented city—as well as the capital of Israel—while Tel Aviv, on the Mediterranean coast, is the modern, secular, business-oriented, and Westernized side of Israel, and the two cities appear to be drifting further and further apart.

An Area Briefing

Politics and Government

Today, the country is a secular republic with a government built on the British parliamentary model, with a unicameral legislature, the Knesset, and a president and a prime minister. There are many political parties in Israel, but Labor and Likud are the two major parties. Palestinians pose the greatest moral and political dilemma for all Israelis, as Israelis struggle to provide them with sovereign land in exchange for security and peace. In addition, neighboring Arab lands, such as Syria and Iraq and Islamic fundamentalist splinter groups in Lebanon and elsewhere, still do not recognize the State of Israel, and guerrilla violence, in the form of Hezbollah, Hamas, and other radical Islamic fundamentalists, threatens to destabilize daily life through terrorism.

Fundamental Cultural Orientations

Israeli Jews are extremely individualistic: they each have their own ideas, opinions, and beliefs, and are difficult to organize into a cohesive team. The value orientation is, within and among other similar Jews, to be extremely individualistic; but when faced with members of other groups, Israeli Jews can act with unquestioning unity. This means that secular Jews, for example, are generally individualistic among themselves, but when faced with Orthodox Jews or other groups further outside, such as Muslim Palestinians, they will generally act with unity. Arab Israelis, on the other hand, are fairly group conscious, and generally harmony oriented, but have difficulty remaining unified, and can become fractious and individualistic when faced with the challenge of others from outside their group. For Jewish Israelis, hierarchy, status, rank, and the symbols of such are usually of secondary importance: it is an extremely egalitarian and "flattened" society (second only to Australia, in fact), and people act accordingly. Relationships usually determine action, however, so whom you know is important, and the situation, which is always debated, is ultimately what determines decisions, often over existing rules or processes. In this society, rules and processes, while valued as part of the heritage from the West, may only be momentarily useful, and therefore are often of secondary importance when decisions need to be made.

Things change very fast in Israel, and one must be ready to seize opportunities quickly when and where they arise. In this sense, Jewish Israelis, while having a monochronic preference, can also be markedly polychronic. Things happen, unexpected events occur, and more important people suddenly show up: this is normal, and people and schedules need to adjust. It is a very risk-taking culture; Jewish Israelis do not shy away from possibilities, nor do they shy away from conflict and confrontation: they seem, in fact, to thrive on it. They can be very direct, and will demand that you prove yourself and your product as better than the competition before they will feel comfortable. At the same time, while they may seem to haggle and disagree endlessly, when they have developed a comfort level with you, they may just as suddenly change tack and finalize an agreement: it is as if they have decided that enough is enough, and it is time to cooperate.

While Israelis are proud of their ancient traditions, they are always looking forward to a possibly finer tomorrow, and for ways to get there. Israelis, particularly those from European Jewish backgrounds, understand Western traditions and can think very conceptually and linearly; but such thoughts must never conflict with national ideals, Jewish goals, or sometimes even personal efforts. It is an extremely informal culture, where there simply is no time to waste on appearances, formalities, or superficial niceties: who knows, you may not be here tomorrow. This is what can make Israelis so frustrating to outsiders, but also what makes them, like the inside of the prickly pear, such good friends and devoted colleagues, once a deep relationship is established.

Greetings and Introductions

Language and Basic Vocabulary

The main language is Hebrew, which is the ancient language of the Israelites, and which virtually died out as a spoken language with the Diaspora, although it continued to be used as a liturgical and literary language. Hebrew was resurrected as a spoken language by the Zionists at the time of Israel's rebirth, and is a source of immense pride among Jewish Israelis. It is related to Arabic in structure, and many Israeli Arabs also understand Hebrew. Most Israeli businesspeople also speak English (certainly the Ashkenazi, but not necessarily African or Oriental or Russian Jews who immigrated recently), and English is the learned second language of Israeli Jews and Arabs (but not each other's language). There are not as many words in Hebrew as one needs to survive in the modern world, so new ones are always being created. Remember, both Arabic and Hebrew are written right to left (so translated materials should be designed to begin "at the back"). Yiddish is also spoken by older Eastern European Jews, as well as other languages from other immigrant groups, such as Russian.

Here are some basic Hebrew phrases and their English meanings:

shalom	hello / peace / good-bye
boker tov	good morning
erev tov	good evening
layla tov	good night
lehitraot	see you later
Ma shlomkha?	How are you?
slikha	pardon me
bevakasha	please / you're welcome
todah	thank you
ken	yes
lo	no

Plurals are created by adding the suffix *-im* in Hebrew: for example, Sephard becomes Sephardim.

Honorifics for Men, Women, and Children

Most Hebrew speakers will use the first name very quickly, sometimes with the honorific Mr. or Mrs. If the last (family) name is used, as in the West, it will most certainly be accompanied with the appropriate honorific, because it is unusually formal (most Israelis will probably switch to the first name very soon). The honorifics are *mar* (Mr.) and *gveret* (Mrs./Miss/Ms.).

As in the West, most modern married women take their husband's family name, or hyphenate their family name with their husband's.

The What, When, and How of Introducing People

If you are not introduced quickly to others in a group, it is perfectly all right to introduce yourself; in fact, if you don't, you may never get to know anyone else. While Israelis appreciate that you notice seniors first and show respect for the elderly, such attention is not codified in Israeli introductions. In fact, most greetings occur quickly and informally. Please note that this is not the case with Arabs.

Physical Greeting Styles

As is the case with Arabs, Israeli Jews can be extremely demonstrative, and greet each other with hugs and kisses—between the same sex and the opposite sex, as well. Please be advised, however, that Orthodox Jews do not follow this pattern. The custom for Orthodox Jews is for men and women never to touch a member of the opposite sex in public other than their spouses and close female relatives, and this means that women are rarely introduced to men. If they are, they will not extend their hand, and you should not take their hand, in this case. Handshakes are the common greeting between most Israeli Jews, and it is often a firm grasp.

Communication Styles

Okay Topics / Not Okay Topics

Okay: anything that reflects your personal interest in Israel—its food, people, history, Jewish traditions, and so on. *Not okay:* your opinions at first about the Muslim-Jewish or the Palestinian-Israeli conflict. If you are American, do not talk immediately about U.S.-Israeli relations: you will be disappointed at the negative image Israelis have of Americans and their policies and behaviors toward Israel. There is much misunderstanding between American and Israeli Jews (if you are Jewish, you will be asked why you haven't made the *aliyah,* or emigration to Israel). The goal of conversation, at first, between Israeli Jews is not necessarily to establish harmony (as it is with the Arabs), but to establish trust: a trust built not necessarily on agreement and similarities, but on respect for fundamental individualism and an ability to rely on you.

Protocol in Public

Israelis can be animated and loud at a business meeting, on the street, or in a restaurant. However, as a foreigner, you should not respond in kind. There is little use of silence as a communication device. There can be much nonverbal behavior and gesturing. While Arabs do not appreciate being touched on the head, this holds no special meaning for Jews, except for the fact that observant Jewish men wear a *kipa* or *yarmulke,* which is a skullcap on the top of their heads, and observant women usually wear a shawl or head covering of some sort (Orthodox women shave their hair, and wear a wig in public). The bottom of the shoe holds no special meaning either for Jews, but many do avoid using the left hand. Synagogues may be visited, but head coverings are usually required, and modest dress is essential. In most Orthodox synagogues, men and women worship in separate areas. The Jewish Sabbath begins on Friday night and lasts until sundown on Saturday, and most stores, restaurants, and public services shut down. Elevators may be set to stop automatically on all floors during the Sabbath, since observant Jews are not permitted to work on the day of rest, and therefore do not operate elevators. The "thumbs-up" sign is considered to be obscene throughout the Middle East, for both Arabs and Jews, while holding the fingers together with the palm facing up and shaking the hand up and down is a sign for "patience, please." There are more and more no-smoking areas in Israel, but they are still not as common as in the West. Jewish women (with the exception of Orthodox women) are free to travel on their own, and can conduct business; Western businesswomen should have no problems with their authority being accepted in Israel.

Dress

Secular Jews in Israel dress just like Western Europeans and Americans: they are style conscious, and business suits and jeans are everywhere, and worn at the same appropriate times. However, when Israeli businessmen dress, they often leave the shirt collar open, without a tie, and sometimes take their jackets off. Short-sleeved shirts, due to the hot weather, are also common in business settings. Orthodox Jews, however, dress much more modestly; women must have their arms covered to below the elbow and their torsos covered up to the neckline, and their dresses must go below the knee (they do not wear pants); clothes must never be revealing. Many Orthodox men (the Hasidim in particular) wear the old dress of the European shtetl (village), which is a fur-rimmed, black dress hat, a black business suit (often with a long jacket), a white shirt, and a subdued, dark tie. These men often wear a ritual undergarment that has long fringes, which are allowed to extend outside the outer garments. Orthodox men typically sport beards and mustaches that they do not cut, and Orthodox boys may follow the Orthodox tradition of wearing long sideburns with shaved heads.

Dining and Drinking

Mealtimes and Typical Foods

The Jewish diet may or may not be kosher, depending upon whether the home or restaurant is observant. Kosher laws can be quite complex. Some basics involve the absolute prohibition against pork and pork products, shellfish, and the mixing of dairy products and meat at the same meal. In addition, all meats need to be slaughtered according to specific rabbinical requirements in order to be kosher. Additional special laws (Parve) exist for Passover, during which no leavened food products can be served, or even be present in the house, in any form (typically, the house is scrubbed to remove any crumb of bread from the premises just prior to Passover). Observant homes usually have four sets of dishes and cutlery—one for meat and one for dairy for daily use, and another two sets specifically for Passover—and they must *never* be mixed up. Although there is no prohibition against alcohol, curiously, most Israelis do not drink much alcohol. Beer may or may not accompany a meal; wine is more often used ceremonially at religious celebrations.

Table Manners / Use of Utensils / Toasting

The traditional toast is *l'chayim* ("to life"). Western utensils are used throughout Israel, and dining is done the Continental way, with fork in the left hand and knife in the right. The host sits at the head of the table, with the honored guest seated next to the host. In Orthodox homes, men and women may dine in separate areas, or at different times. If you are invited into an Israeli's home, you may or may not need to remove your shoes (check to see if shoes are lined up at the door: that's your cue to remove your shoes, if they are). As for the food, although it is generally similar to the food of the entire region, there is considerable influence of the cuisines of the immigrants, so be ready to sample foods from eastern Europe, Russia, Africa, and India, as well.

Gift Giving

In general, gift giving is not that common for social occasions or business situations, but when visiting a close friend, or staying at someone's home, you are expected to bring something useful and nice from abroad. This can be a household item—a vase, a tray, some personal bath accessories. Flowers are fine for social visits, but avoid calla lilies, for they are used at funerals. Chocolates are much appreciated (make sure they and any other foodstuffs, such as gourmet nuts and dried fruits, you bring as a gift are kosher, if necessary). Electronic goods, which are very prized, may not work in Israel; it is best to avoid giving them.

Special Holidays and Celebrations

Major Holidays

In addition to the Islamic holidays mentioned in previous chapters for the Arabs, Christians also celebrate Christmas and Easter (Orthodox and Roman). However, the majority of the religious holidays are Jewish, and are based on the lunar calendar, which changes their Western calendar dates each year.

Secular

January 1	Bank holiday
May 10	Independence Day
August 10	Bank holiday

Religious

March	Purim: celebrates the rescue of Persian Jews through the shrewdness and wisdom of Queen Esther. Special *hamantashen,* or "Haman cakes" (usually three-sided, with a fruit filling), commemorate her triumph over the Persian king's minister, Haman, who intended to execute the Jews.
April	*Tu B'Shvat* (Arbor Day): celebrates the planting of trees (especially in Israel)
March/April	Pesach (Passover): celebrates the Exodus of the Jews from Egypt: it is a celebration of freedom, and the special feast (seder) features symbolic foods that represent the struggles of the Jews against the Egyptians: bitter herbs dipped in salt water symbolize the tears shed by the people when they were slaves; a hard-boiled egg represents rebirth; parsley represents spring plantings and new birth and sustenance; and matzoh, the unleavened bread that the Jews, in their haste to escape, had to eat because they did not have time for the bread to rise. Four cups of wine are drunk throughout the meal as the story of the Exodus is recounted.
May/June	*Shavuot* (Feast of the Weeks): celebrates God's gift of the Torah to the Jewish people. The Torah is the compilation of laws, writings, and thoughts of the Jewish people; it comprises the first five books of the Old Testament.
July/August	Tishah-b'Ab: commemorates the fall of the Temple in Jerusalem.
September	Rosh Hashanah (Jewish New Year): celebrated for two days with prayers in the temple, and a special feast to welcome in a good and healthy New Year.
September	Yom Kippur (Day of Atonement): following Rosh Hashanah by one week, it is the holiest of Jewish holidays, wherein the

	observant pray for forgiveness for past sins, and hope to be entered into the Book of Life for another year. Observant Jews fast for the twenty-four-hour period.
September/October	Sukkoth (Festival of the Booths): follows five days after Yom Kippur, and commemorates the harvest and God's generosity in providing sustenance and shelter to his people. A shelter made of reeds and other items is built in the backyard of most observant homes in remembrance of the nomadic lives lived by the Israelites after the Exodus. It is also a harvest celebration, and observant Jews eat their meals in the shelter.
December	Hanukkah (Festival of Lights): celebrates the rededication of the Temple in 164 B.C. after its desecration by the Syrian king and the miracle of the oil that kept the Temple lamps burning for eight days (symbolized by the eight-armed candleholder, the Menorah). Children play with dreidels (toy tops) and get gifts of money (gelt); special foods fried in oil (try latkes, or potato pancakes) are eaten in celebration of the event.

Business Culture

The official work week is 9 A.M. to 4 P.M., Sunday through Thursday (9 A.M. to noon, Friday). However, businesses really slow down after Thursday night. Consider that Christians (Roman Catholic and Orthodox, and others) maintain their Sabbath on Sunday, and Muslims on Friday. As Jerusalem is a holy center for all three religions, the city has observances throughout the week, depending upon the religious affiliation.

Management styles between bosses and subordinates can be extremely egalitarian and direct. As a foreigner, you will be treated with respect, and hosted well, but in business negotiations, you will be bargained with, questioned, prodded, and expected to prove why your product is better than the competition's. Israelis love to bargain, and will expect all sorts of concessions; they will also be surprised if you do not drive an equally hard bargain in return. They can demonstrate all sorts of emotions around these issues, but do not take the show too seriously, if you know the terms of the sale are fair and reasonable. In the end, and the end may suddenly appear sooner than you think, they will generally settle for what is reasonable and good for both parties most of the time. You are building a long-term relationship the Israeli way, and that is what is important. It is interesting to note that Israel has developed a significant role in the computer and semiconductor industry, and is known as the Silicon Valley of the Middle East.

Written Correspondence

Your business letters should be matter-of-fact and informal. If you have a personal relationship with your Israeli colleague, be friendly and warm, and inquire about his personal health and his family's in general terms. Use the Western format for the addresses. The abbreviation C.E. after a year means "common era," and is the equivalent of the Gregorian Western calendar abbreviation A.D. (*anno Domini*).

PART TWO

North Africa

The Dry Sea

An Introduction to the Region

In Paleolithic times, scientists tell us, this region that today stretches from the Red Sea in the East to the Moroccan coast in the West was the seabed of a continuous ocean connecting what is today the Atlantic to the Indian. But by biblical times, the water had receded, exposing and transforming this great underwater landmass into an equally vast and challenging desert, interspersed with rare, fertile valleys in which great civilizations flourished. In the East, the Nile Valley supported the development of the ancient Kingdoms of Upper (in the south) and Lower Egypt (in the north) almost five thousand years ago, and the powerful and still relatively unknown ancient Kingdom of Kush (centered in what is now southeastern Egypt and northern Ethiopia); the Nile also supported the Nubians to the south of Egypt in the Sudan, and the flowering of the ancient Kingdom of Axum, which later became the center of the great Ethiopian civilization. These civilizations came and went, but their cultural identities, though transformed through history, live on. Modern Egyptians look back with pride to their Pharoanic forebears and Ethiopians have fiercely retained their biblical roots, including their own unique African Christian Church. Other groups in the Horn of Africa dealt with each other and invading Muslims and Europeans in their own unique ways, and Sudanese struggle today with an identity that is not solely Egyptian, Islamic, Christian, African, or indigenous. The three great historical events that still powerfully influence the daily lives of most Africans—indigenous African cultural development (what we refer to as "Africanism" or "Africanicity"), the Muslim invasion, and European colonialization—transformed the ancient trading kingdoms of Carthage, Mali and Songhai, Ghana, and Tuat of the Central and Western parts of the Sahara and the Sahel (that border area that is neither totally desert nor fertile field that stands between the dry sea to the north and the tropical and fertile agricultural lands of the Africa of the Atlantic and the West African Gulf) into the modern nation states of today. These great civilizations, mightier in their time than those of the Europeans who were about to challenge them, controlled the north-south trans-Sahel commerce between the Atlantic Gulf and the northern Maghreb (the Mediterranean Sahara region), and the east-west trade between Nubia and Egypt in the Nile Valley and the Gambia, Atlantic Gulf, and coastal civilizations.

More than half of all Africans live in northern Africa. These northern Hamitic peoples—as some ethnographers refer to them in order to distinguish them from their southern Black African cousins—have a unique history, but they also participate in the shared cultural heritage of the continent. This theme of regional uniqueness and continental similarities forms the lens through which we can better view both the need for and the challenges facing pan-African identity: often Africans act as one, when facing the rest of the world (primarily Europeans), but Africans often act against Africans, country against country and group against group, when facing each other.

Getting Oriented

North Africa, for our purposes, consists of the following macrocultural groups:

- The classical North African Arab heartland of Egypt, Sudan, and Chad
- The Maghreb of the Sahara and Sahel, consisting of Morocco and Algeria, Tunisia and Libya, Mali, Mauritania, and Niger
- The Horn of Africa, consisting of Ethiopia, Djibouti and Eritrea, and Somalia

Let's begin with perhaps the oldest and most essential, if not influential, culture in the region: Egypt.

The Classical North African Arab World: Egypt, Sudan, and Chad

EGYPT

Some Introductory Background on Egypt and North Africans

Egypt's long traditions of ancient civilizations and involvement with classical and modern European cultures (recall Marc Anthony and Cleopatra, and, in more recent times, the British takeover of Egypt after World War I and the French Protectorate and the subsequent Egyptian Revolution of the 1950s) make Egypt one of the more liberal and secular of all Arab states. For example, women, for the most part, are not veiled, work is not proscribed on Friday (the Muslim Sabbath), there is a significant non-Muslim population (mainly Coptic Christians), and alcohol is available. Although daily life is significantly influenced by Islam, the government remains fiercely committed to secularity and Western objectivist ideas. In fact, the degree to which Islam—under pressure from a rising tide of fundamentalism—is integrated formally into the government and society is hotly debated in Egypt today, and represents a major concern, along with the economy, the population, and relations with its neighbors, including Israel.

Because there is no oil in Egypt (unlike its Gulf Arab neighbors), and other natural resources are slim (unlike its southern African neighbors), Egypt struggles, as much of continental Africa does, with the challenges of the developing world: massive population (Cairo alone has approximately 15 million people, but it is impossible to get an accurate formal count) and the attendant difficulties of unemployment and a lack of quality education, health care, and civil representation in government. Nevertheless, Egypt, relative to many of its neighbors on the continent, has been successful in a number of these and other areas, and is admired by many Arab and non-Arab African nations, as well. The Egyptian people, while living in a poorer, more difficult world than their Gulf Arab cousins, have a reputation for being open, warm, and friendly, with a historical legacy that is extraordinary by any measure.

Some Historical Context

Egypt's Pharoanic heritage today is a source of pride for many Egyptians (today's Coptic Christians are the direct descendants of the ancient Egyptians), as is the fact that many of the remaining works of Classical Greece and Rome were protected and stored in Alexandria when both European empires crumbled and Europe was plunged into the dark ages. Not only was Egypt intimately familiar with both the Greeks and the Romans, but it became one of the main entry points for Islam into the continent: from the beginning of the Muslim invasion in A.D. 642, Egypt played the singular role of being the primary bearer of the new faith to the rest of the continent. It was from Egypt that Islam spread across North Africa and down into the south, due in no small part to the difficulties that the Coptics experienced with both Rome and Constantinople (making the people receptive to a new liberating faith from the East). Ottomans, Mamluks, and Seljuks vied for influence in Egypt; it eventually fell into the Ottoman camp, only to fall victim to European politics (Napolean invaded). Under the Europeans, Viceroy Muhammad Ali modernized Egypt, but it wasn't until Gamal Abdel Nasser succeeded in the revolution that ousted the European-supported king and established the first Republic in Egypt's history that Egypt became a modern Republican nation. Today, Egypt is faced with the challenge of finding ways to integrate its ancient Egyptian, Islamic, and modern Western traditions. Because of these three powerful influences, if we understand the Egyptian culture, and associated Egyptian behaviors, we will be able to modify our behaviors accordingly when dealing with other nations in the classical North African Arab region.

An Area Briefing

Politics and Government

Today, the Arab Republic of Egypt is a parliamentary democracy, made up of twenty-six governates (similar to states). There is a president, a less powerful prime minister, and a bicameral legislature consisting of the People's Assembly (the lower house), and the Shura Council (the upper house). The legal system seeks to integrate Islamic ideas without sacrificing the Napoleonic Code traditions upon which it is based. It is interesting to note that political parties based on religious ideas—including Islam—are illegal, forcing Islamic-based political movements underground.

Schools and Education

All schooling is free, including university education for those who qualify; girls and boys are educated, and, in fact, about 50 percent of all university students are women. Primary school education is mandatory, and most do complete it, so the literacy rate in Egypt is growing (approximately 70 percent). Nevertheless, the challenges of a developing nation make school attendance spotty in many areas, and there is always a lack of teachers, supplies, and infrastructure. There is a knowledge and awareness of the West and its ways among the younger

Egyptians, and many speak English, although most Egyptians on the street do not (the second language in Egypt is French, with English running a close third, and this is true for most businesspeople, as well).

Religion and Demographics

Egypt is 90 percent Sunni Muslim, with the majority of the remaining population being Coptic Christian. Coptics were followers of the Apostle Mark, and had a stormy relationship with both Rome and Constantinople. Eventually, the Coptic Church became autocephalic, with its own authority centered in Egypt. Needless to say, the rise of Islamic fundamentalism is perceived as a major threat by most Coptics, and acts of violence against Coptics by Islamic fundamentalists are not unheard of.

The majority of the people live in the Nile Valley and Cairo and Alexandria, and most are *fellahin* (peasants); there is a small, but growing, middle class. It is a challenge (many feel frustrated with the lack of opportunities within a developing nation) and a strength (the energy and optimism of the young present great possibilities for Egypt's future) that almost 80 percent of the people are under thirty years of age. Bedouins (nomadic desert tribes) and Nubians (Southern Egyptians whose descendants are from Sudan) constitute about 2 percent of the population.

Islam is the youngest of the West's three great religious traditions, beginning with Judaism and Christianity. As a Western religion, it is linked to the Judeo-Christian belief system and rejects Hinduism and Buddhism as "pagan," and not "of the book," or codified. Incorporating both Judaism and Christianity into its system of beliefs, Islam claims that it is the final revelation of a monotheistic God, as revealed to the world through the prophet Muhammad, and that previous "messiahs," such as Jesus and Moses, were merely prophets, along with Muhammad, proclaiming the word of God. Muslims do not follow Muhammad (therefore, they are not Muhammadans, a very derogatory term created by Westerners who did not understand Islam); they believe in Allah, which is the Arabic name for the same God worshipped by Christians and Jews. Muhammad and his followers wrote down the law of God as revealed to them in the Qu'ran (or Koran), the Islamic holy book. It does not negate the Old or New Testaments: it merely provides, in the eyes of Muslim faithful, the final required text. Muhammad received his revelations from God in Medina; prior to Islam, the nomadic tribes of the region believed in a variety of pagan ideas, but with the notion of one God, and the laws under which people were to behave, Muhammad was able to unify the peoples of the Gulf Arab peninsula into the beginnings of a single Arab culture. Islam spread rapidly into Egypt, gaining acceptance through its powerful message, and unifying many non-Coptics against the spreading Coptic ideas under the banner of a religion of Arabs. Islam underwent a serious split almost immediately following Muhammad's death (two major camps emerged, the Shia and the Sunni, in an effort to decide how to continue the faith); Egypt joined the Sunni camp. Sunni Muslims believe that the caliphs, or religious leaders, subsequent to Muhammad are legitimate; Shiite Muslims believe that the caliphs subsequent to Muhammad are usurpers, and therefore do not believe in Sunni authority (and there is a related argument between the two camps revolving around the legitimacy of the caliphs based on their genealogical connection to Muhammad). All Muslims must abide by five basic tenets, or Pillars of Faith:

- Proclaim the supremacy of the one true God, Allah, above all others
- Pray to Allah five times daily
- Observe Ramadan, the holy month, the ninth month of the Islamic calendar, which is essentially a celebration of the first time God revealed his word to Muhammad
- Give alms to the poor and needy
- Perform the hajj, or spiritual (and physical) journey to Mecca, at least once in their lifetime if they are capable of doing so

Specific codes of conduct have developed over time, and have been codified into Islamic law, known as the Shari'a. The degree to which one follows these scriptures often determines how devoutly one applies the Islamic ethical code in day-to-day life; in Egypt, the enforcement of these codes sometimes runs counter to the interests of the secular government, challenging the legitimacy of both. Islamic leaders and secular leaders in Egypt vie for the loyalty of the people.

Because of the understanding, if not acceptance, of Western ways in Egypt, depending upon the individual you are working with (whether they are Western-oriented or fundamentalist Muslim), it can be easier or more difficult for Western women to do business in Egypt today.

Fundamental Cultural Orientations

1. What's the Best Way for People to Relate to One Another?

OTHER-INDEPENDENT OR OTHER-DEPENDENT?   There is a combination of deep concern for family, clan, and other membership groups (such as work and religion), that defines an individual and individual expression. Egyptians, like all Arabs, are deeply connected first to their clan and their families: this is an intensely private life (and therefore, one needs to be very careful about inquiring about the family, among other things). However, individual pride, and how one is seen by others, is perhaps the most important aspect of Arab culture that non-Arabs need to be sensitive to. It is not a heightened sense of individualism separate from others; in fact, it is the opposite. Because of one's intricate relationships with others (there is an old saying that an Arab has one thousand close relatives), one is always keenly aware of how one is being perceived and of one's obligations to others. It is very important that you always show great respect for your Egyptian colleague. Arab pride must be supported and respected.

HIERARCHY-ORIENTED OR EGALITY-ORIENTED?   As Muslims, all people are technically equal in their submission to Allah and his will; however, Arabs structure the secular world with clearly assigned roles, so that Allah's will can be fulfilled effectively. Additionally, Egyptian secular life is rigidly stratified, from the *fellahin* to shopkeepers to government officials, and hierarchy and rank define one's position in society. It is critical that everyone show respect for elders and devout Muslims, and men for women, sons for fathers, older brothers for younger brothers, and so on. All individuals have a role to play in this hierarchy, and are responsible to others and the greater Arab community to fulfill their role. There is a saying in Arabic, "The eye cannot rise above the eyebrow": it means that people must know their station and position in life, and make the best of it. Women and men are different and perform different roles, more or less: in Egypt a woman typically may go out in public alone, but she will probably prefer to go with other female friends or relatives.

RULE-ORIENTED OR RELATIONSHIP-ORIENTED? While many Egyptians have had experience with and in the West, the tension that exists between the application of universal rules over reliable and dependable relationships is palpable. This leads for many to a high dependence on power, authority, and subjective decision making based on the situation and the relationships between the individuals involved. Ultimately, face-to-face knowledge of the individuals involved in any interaction is the basis upon which final decisions are often made.

2. What's the Best Way to View Time?

MONOCHRONIC OR POLYCHRONIC? Egypt is essentially very polychronic, due to the influence of both agrarian and religious traditions. The clock is definitely not the determinant of action; it plays a role most certainly, particularly in the larger, more modern urban areas, and there is an acceptance of Western organizational ideas (westerners should not be late, for example). Nevertheless, there is forgiveness for the inevitable delays (like maddening Cairo traffic!), and understanding when things don't go as planned or scheduled; people may or may not show up at invited events, things may or may not happen as planned. Schedules tend to be loose and flexible. Because who (relationships) is more important than what (tasks) or when (time), there can be many interruptions during a meeting, and people's obligations to other people, who may come and go, are more important than doing things according to schedules. If you are being kept waiting, or are ignored because of someone else's needs, it is an indication of your importance, or lack thereof, relative to the other person, and expressing frustration over being kept waiting only diminishes your importance.

RISK-TAKING OR RISK-AVERSE? Egyptians, and most Arabs, are prone to taking risks when in positions of authority, but avoiding them when they are not. Within organizations, the decision makers can be bold, even reckless, but subordinates generally are not, and take action only when instructed to do so. Therefore, comfort with uncertainty, in general, is low, and much information may need to be exchanged with different people before decisions can be made. Even when decisions are made at the top, the concern for others in the group requires decision makers to consult with subordinates before making decisions. There will be much discussion with trusted others about what you, as a foreigner, bring to the table, *after* you leave the meeting.

PAST-ORIENTED OR FUTURE-ORIENTED? There is a distinct and inherent fatalism in regard to the effect of human action, fundamentally because only Allah determines what and when things will happen. Nevertheless, those empowered by virtue of their position are expected to make the decisions that keep the world running, and by so doing, are fulfilling Allah's will. Therefore, future benefits often do not motivate Egyptians; doing nothing or doing things for the here and now is sometimes more important, and if things do not work out, that is to be expected—no mortal controls the universe, and all is ultimately determined. There is a deep belief that things will take the time they need to take, and that only Allah knows what that is (this has often been summarized as the "IBM" of the Arab world: I for *inshallah*—as and only if Allah wills it; B for *buqrah*—things will take the time they take; and M for *ma'alesh*—loosely translated as, "don't worry," "don't sweat it," "it'll turn out okay; you may not see it now, but it's all for the best").

3. What's the Best Way for Society to Work with the World at Large?

LOW-CONTEXT DIRECT OR HIGH-CONTEXT INDIRECT COMMUNICATORS? Arabs are very context-driven communicators. They will speak in metaphors, and use stories or codified phrases; they will employ analogies, Islamic precedent, and much nonverbal behavior to convey true meaning. They generally avoid confrontation, and are honor-bound to do everything possible to make strangers like and honor them (they are lavish hosts). They will avoid unpleasant discussion as long as possible, and it is precisely because they shun unpleasantness in discussions that anger, often expressed as an insult to pride, can blow fast and hard when disagreements can no longer be avoided.

PROCESS-ORIENTED OR RESULT-ORIENTED? Islamic law, and the complex study of Islam that developed in the Muslim world into its own field of scholastic inquiry, is fundamentally different from Western Greco-Roman philosophies of knowing. In Islam, interpretation and truth are dependent upon "analogous" reasoning, while in the West, such inquiry is based more on "argument" (proving and disproving). Decisions and actions therefore may be the result of reasoning that is not directed at a determination of truth, but rather context-based "correctness" based on similar experiences, often with the strict Islamic code as the only context. Combine this with a tendency to rely also on subjective experience, and the traditional Arab mind is processing information, for the most part, in a different way than the Western mind. Nevertheless, because of the familiarity with the West, there is an openness to new ideas and new ways of thinking in Egypt, but things will always be judged according to their subjective benefit, and the degree to which they support or challenge both personal beliefs and Islamic ideas.

FORMAL OR INFORMAL? Arab society is formal and ritualized, and each group has its own way of honoring the hierarchies, establishing respect and deference, and following (or not following) through on their responsibilities. They are even more formal when one is an outsider, which is always the case with non-Muslims.

Greetings and Introductions

Language and Basic Vocabulary

"Arab" describes the people; "Arabian" describes the culture; "Arabic" describes the language. Arabic is the language of the Qu'ran, and therefore, by extension, is the language of God. As a Semitic language, Arabic is very different from other Asian and European languages, and is written from right to left in a flowing script. Written vowel sounds are assigned to consonant letters with diacritical marks, with words changing tense, agreement, and meaning based on the addition of suffixes and prefixes to the root or stem words.

Words and language have a power all their own in the Arab world; in fact, it has been said that the expression of a feeling or action can sometimes replace the feeling or the action itself. Therefore, the expression of anger, which may involve statements of violence, in fact may be a way of precluding the act of violence. Be extremely sensitive to the meaning of words, the emotion behind them, how they are used, and how you use them. Speech can be flowery, overblown, hyperbolic, and rich in texture; this is meant to both honor the speaker and the person to whom one is speaking. Arabs will tend to overemphasize, reassure, insist that they can do something, know something, or solve the problem, whether or not they actually can; this is not meant to be deceiving, but to indicate their hope for a mutually positive experience. Words more often indicate what Arabs desire more than what might actually be. Many religious phrases are added onto everyday statements (e.g., "_____, *inshallah*"—"if God wills"; or "_____, *mash'allah*"—"what God wills," usually said after speaking about someone's health; or "_____, *alhamdu lillah*"—"thanks be to God," spoken as a way of giving thanks for something that has happened, or that you hope to happen). Never use religious references disrespectfully—it is assumed that all people are religious in some way, even if not Muslim—and be very careful never to use "God" in any way other than in the most respectful sense. There are many forms of Arabic throughout the world, and in Egypt, the Arabic is different from that of Gulf Arabia. Most people speak a more popular Cairene dialect of the Egyptian/Sudanese Arabic; there is also the classical Arabic of Gulf Arabia, Levantine, and North Africa (the Maghreb). All three are mutually intelligible to one another. Coptic, as language, is spoken by a small minority in Egypt.

Finally, it is worth noting that one of the characteristics of Egyptian/Sudanese Arabic is its playfulness with words and the cleverness of the wordplay of the language; Egyptians revel in it.

Here are some basic Arabic phrases and their meanings in English:

marhaba, or *marhaba alan*	hello
marhabtayn, or *marhabtayn alan*	hello (response)
ahlan wasahlan	welcome
ahlan beek	thanks (response)
sabah alkayr	good morning
sabah annoor	good morning (response)

assalamu 'alaykum	peace be with you (general greeting)
wa'alaykum assalam	and upon you, peace (response)
min fadleek	please
aesef	sorry, excuse me
ma'a ssalama (go with safety)	good-bye
allah yisallimak (may God make you safe)	good-bye (response)
shukran	thank you
'afwan	you're welcome

English is taught in schools, so young people often speak and understand some English; businesspeople generally speak some English, and many older ones speak French. Most people on the street, however, speak little English; you may be luckier trying French.

Honorifics for Men, Women, and Children

Names are Arabic in content and structured according to fairly complex and sometimes differing traditions.

Most people have several names, but the order of the names is similar to that of the West, with the given name first, and the family name last. Other names used may refer to one's role in the family (such as son) or an honorary association with an important or meaningful person (often a reference to an important person in Islamic history). It is important to address Arabs by their given (or first) names, because that is really their only true name (the other names being indications of genealogy or relationship). Several common relationship forms found in names are:

- *Bin* or *ould* (North African and Levantine), or *ibn* (Gulf Arab), meaning " . . . son of": for example: Abdel Azziz ibn Mubarrak (Abdel, son of Mubarrak); or Muhammad ould Haidalla (Muhammad, son of Haidalla)
- *Bint* or *binte,* meaning " . . . daughter of": for example, Fatima bint Mubarrak (Fatima, daughter of Mubarrak)
- *Bou* (North African mainly), meaning " . . . father of": for example, Habib bou Guiba (Habib, father of Guiba)

The honorifics Mr., Mrs., Miss, etc., are placed before the surname; and you should always use titles, if they are known (doctor, professor, etc.) before the surname, as well: for example, Dr. Habib, Professor Muhammad, Princess Asma, Sheikh Abdullah ("sheikh" is an indication of importance, and a term most often used in Gulf Arabia; it is not as common in Egypt or North Africa).

- *Al-* + family name: usually indicates "house of" as the family (final) name: for example, Muhammad ibn Abdallah al-Ahmar (Muhammad, son of Abdallah, house of Ahmar). It is not in any way related to the English nickname, "Al," short for Alan.
- Sometimes grandfathers, and male forebears even further back, are acknowledged in the string of names, so that there may be several *ibn* + name groupings within the name: for example, Muhammad ibn Abdallah ibn Muhammad al-

Ahmar (Muhammad, son of Abdallah, son of Muhammad, of the House of Ahmar). Usually, after several generations, the most distant names are dropped. Arabs usually do not give their sons the same first name as the father, but commonly use the grandfather's name, so the first and third name are often the same.

- A woman does not typically take her husband's family name when she marries: she keeps her family name, and is addressed as "Mrs. + her first name."
- Hyphenated names usually represent an attribute plus the name: for example, Abdel-Allah Muhammad ibn Kamal ibn Muhammad al-Tawil (Servant of God Muhammad, son of Kamal, son of Muhammad, of the house of Tawil)
- Muslim males who have made the hajj often use the honorific *hajji* as a title before the surname and any other honorifics; for example, Hajji Dr. Abdel-Allah Muhammad ibn Kamal ibn Muhammad al-Tawil. Muslim females who have made the hajj often use the honorific *hajjah* as a title before the surname, and before any other honorifics.
- Women retain all male references to genealogy in their name after their given female surname: for example, Hajja Dr. Asmah bint Muhammad ibn Kamal ibn Muhammad al-Tawil (a devout, educated sister of the above Abdel-Allah Muhammad who has made the hajj).
- Remember that vowel sounds in Arabic are often indicated with diacritical marks rather than with specific letters. Therefore, translating words, especially names, into English is not an exact science; the same name may be spelled with different vowels (e.g., Mohammed, Muhammad, and M'hamad).

Single women traveling in the region may want to consider wearing a wedding band; it can help avoid a myriad of difficult questions and problems.

Finally, sometimes (especially in the Levant and Egypt), the honorifics *um* (mother) and *abu* (father) may be used in front of the given name, or replace a name completely. This is an affectionate way of referring to someone you may know well and personally.

The What, When, and How of Introducing People

Egyptians may, upon greeting you, call you by your last or first name, with or without your title. Always wait to be introduced to a stranger; never take that responsibility upon yourself, as doing so is considered inappropriate most of the time. Egyptians, and Arabs in general, are most comfortable with third-party introductions, and because business is very personal, you will need an individual to introduce you to the required people. Never presume to seat yourself at a gathering: if possible, wait to be told where to sit. The seating arrangements have usually been carefully worked out in advance, and in most cases reflect the status of the individuals in the group and the honor that is being accorded the guests. When departing, it is important to say farewell to every individual present: the American group wave is not appreciated. Once you greet someone you will encounter later that day in the same circumstances (e.g., at the office), you do not need to greet them when you see them again. Seniors, or those who are obviously the oldest in a group, are greeted first, seated first, and allowed to enter a room first (usually at the center of a group, however, and in most cases preceded by their younger aides).

Physical Greeting Styles

Close associates and businesspeople of the same sex who have developed work-ing relationships often greet each other warmly, with hugs and kisses. Wait until your Egyptian host initiates this behavior before initiating it yourself. Typically, women kiss each other on both cheeks, and men shake hands and touch the other person's shoulder with their left hand. Very close family and friends may also kiss on the forehead. Muslim women and men do not touch or shake hands (unless the woman is Westernized, and you will know if she extends her hand). The handshake may be soft, almost limp sometimes. This does not mean insin-cerity; rather, it is an accommodation to the Western fashion while remaining humble and considerate.

The traditional business introduction also includes the exchange of busi-ness cards. Always take a large supply of business cards with you: you should give one to every new person you are introduced to (there is no need to provide another business card when you are meeting someone again unless information about you has changed, such as a new address, contact number, or position). Be sure your business cards are in fine shape: they are an extension of you as a per-son, and must look as good as possible. Embossed cards are extremely impres-sive, especially with logos in green (the color of Islam). Never hand out a dirty, soiled, bent, or written-on card, and always handle business cards with your right hand only. You should translate your business card into Arabic on the reverse.

When presenting a business card, give it to your colleague so that it is read-able for him as you hold it (he will, in turn, present his card so that it is read-able for you). Do not worry too much about who receives and gives his business card first: the exchange is very quick, and because you would probably not be introduced to that person in the first place if you were not already seen as hav-ing an equivocal rank, there is no need to show deference. There is also no need for bowing.

Smiling and other nonverbal forms of communication may accompany the card exchange. Information about each other's status is the most important information to be exchanged, and this is provided directly on the business card, as well as indirectly through a number of high-context indicators, such as gen-der, age, and the number of people surrounding and assisting the other person. Should you meet more than one individual at a reception, you will have a hand-ful of cards when the greetings are over.

As the business card exchange usually precedes a sit-down meeting, it is important to arrange the cards you have received in a little seating plan in front of you along the top of the desk or table at your seat, reflecting the order in which the people who gave you the cards are seated. This will help you connect the correct names with the correct individuals throughout the meeting. Do this even if you are just meeting one person. During the meeting, it is important never to play with the business cards (do not write on them—ever!); and when the meeting is over, never put them in your back pants pockets: pick them up carefully and respectfully, and place them neatly in your cardholder (a nice looking brass card case would be perfect), then place the cardholder in the left inside jacket pocket of your suit (nearest your heart) or briefcase, if a man, or in your purse or briefcase, if a woman.

Do not photograph people without asking their permission, ever, and do not videotape freely. In some of the countries in the Arab world, videotaping is illegal, and traditionally in Islam, images of people and the human form are considered sacrilegious.

Communication Styles

Okay Topics / Not Okay Topics

Okay: anything that reflects your personal interests and hobbies, religion, and your sincere appreciation of and curiosity about things Egyptian and native to the Arab world. Egyptians love and excel at soccer, and it is a national passion; expressing interest in Egyptian soccer teams is very definitely a positive. Horseback riding is popular, as well (but not betting). *Not okay:* politics, current events, or any subject that might in any way be controversial needs to be avoided at first. Do not inquire about a person's occupation or income in casual conversation, although it may be inquired of you (if so, this is just a way of getting to know more about your country, and not a personal investigation: answer specifically, and fully, with an explanation as to what things cost at home, why you do what you do, and so forth). Other personal questions may be asked of you ("Why are you not married?" or "Do you have any sons?"); the best responses are those that fit the Egyptian context ("Allah has not blessed me yet; I wait patiently."). Do not inquire about family life, especially spouses, or the role of servants and household help. Do not give your opinions about Israelis (and Anwar Sadat's role with Israel), Jews, foreign workers, poverty, the Sudan, the challenge of Islamic fundamentalism to the secular state, or women's rights. Do not talk about sex or tell dirty jokes: it is in very bad taste. Discussions about your company and its work are very much appreciated, as they give Egyptians a chance to learn more about you and your firm. The goal of all conversation, at least at the beginning, is to create and maintain a harmonious atmosphere, despite the difficult or confrontational nature of the topic being discussed. At first, speak about things that you believe you have in common, so that you can build a personal connection that will go far toward maintaining a harmonious bridge between you. This is appropriate for both individuals and organizations.

Tone, Volume, and Speed

The people of this region generally speak in soft, quiet, and restrained tones. Egyptians, and most Arabs, raise their voices only when it is necessary to display anger—and at that point, it is usually too late in the relationship. They may speak rapidly, but if you, in turn, speak rather slowly, they may get the hint and slow down.

Use of Silence

Passive silence—allowing time to pass simply without words—can be a form of proactive communication and is used as a nonverbal way of avoiding confrontation, disagreement, or an unpleasant subject. If confronted with unexplainable silence, gently coax the conversation in a different direction, one that is more mutually harmonious.

Physical Gestures and Facial Expressions

Westerners are advised to reduce the amount of body language they use, although Egyptians and most Arabs are very comfortable with nonverbal behavior (you just do not want to inadvertently offend). Winking, whistling, and other similar displays are considered very vulgar. Public displays of familiarity and affection with the opposite sex are never expressed. Never touch anyone on his or her head, even a child; this is considered the holiest part of the body. Do not point with or intentionally show the sole of your shoe to anyone: this is considered vulgar, as the bottom of the shoe touches the ground, and is therefore the dirtiest part of the body. Any gesture involving a closed fist or made with the "thumbs-up" sign is considered quite vulgar, although touching all the fingertips of one hand to the tip of the thumb of the same hand and bobbing the hand up and down with the palm facing inward means "take it easy" or "calm down." Standing with your hands on your hips is considered very aggressive and should always be avoided. Yawning in public is considered impolite; you must cover your mouth when you yawn.

For any action or gesture that would naturally be done only with one hand, do not use your left hand as this is considered the unclean hand (the hand used for personal hygiene). Pass all documents, business cards, food, and money with your right hand (if you're a southpaw, you will have to practice this). You must remove your shoes before entering a mosque (and some buildings, as well as homes), and you may need to wash your feet and hands at the entrance fountain provided before entering a mosque as well. Women may be restricted to specific areas and times when visiting mosques. Women entering mosques need to have their heads covered, their legs covered to below the knee, and their arms covered to below the elbow; Western women do not necessarily need to have their faces covered. Smile whenever possible: it smoothes the way with strangers quickly and easily.

Waving and Counting

The thumb represents number 1, the pinkie represents the number 5, with everything in between ordered from the thumb down; however, instead of raising the fingers when counting, the whole hand is exposed, and each finger is depressed as the counting is done. It is very insulting to beckon someone with the forefinger (instead, turn your hand so that the palm is facing down and motion inward with all four fingers at once). If you need to gesture for a waiter, very subtly raise your hand or make eye contact. Waving or beckoning is done with the palm down and the fingers moving forward and backward in a kind of scratching motion. It may seem as if the person making the gesture is saying good-bye to you, when in fact you are being summoned over. If you need to point to something or someone, close your fingers, open your palm and face it upward, and pass your hand in the direction you want to indicate.

Physicality and Physical Space

Egyptians and most Arabs stand closer than most North Americans are accustomed to; resist the urge to step back. Many Arabs are comfortable at a distance where they can feel the warmth of the breath of the other person. Never speak with your hands in your pockets: keep them always firmly at your side when standing. If men and women must cross their legs when they sit, it must never be ankle over knee (for women, the preferred style is to cross ankle over ankle; but the bottom of the shoes must not show to the other person). Remember, even in public, formal is always better than informal: no gum-chewing, *ever;* don't slouch; and don't lean against things. Arabs are most comfortable when they are next to other people: in a nearly empty bus, movie theater, or restaurant, in most cases, Arabs will tend to sit next to or near the other person present, instead of far away from them.

Eye Contact

Eye contact can be very direct between strangers and once relationships are established. As a Westerner, you may be the object of other people's stares: this is not meant to be impolite, it is mere curiosity. However, rank changes eye contact patterns: interest in what one's supervisor says is often best shown by averting the eyes, not by making eye contact. The eyes are used extensively to convey true feelings in formal situations where it is difficult to express things verbally. Tune up your nonverbal antennae.

Emotive Orientation

Arabs are emotive and demonstrative. There can be much touching (at least between members of the same sex) during even the most casual conversation. Two men or two women often walk hand in hand or arm in arm down the street. Verbal communication often employs effusiveness, exaggeration, and flowery phrases: this is meant to show sincerity, not duplicity.

Protocol in Public

Walking Styles and Waiting in Lines

On the street, in stores, and in most public facilities, people pay little attention to maintaining orderly lines. Due to the volume of passengers on public transportation, there can be much pushing and jostling. This is not to get into a bus ahead of someone else; it is merely to get in! This is not meant to be disrespectful; if it is bothersome, just say so politely, and you will be treated well. If you ask an Arab for directions, he or she will make every effort to show you the way (even if he or she is not that certain!).

Behavior in Public Places: Airports, Terminals, and the Market

Pride will always demand that Arabs provide you with assistance; even if they do not have an answer they will give you one. If you feel as if you are on the outside, or being treated as a stranger, strike up a polite and respectful conversation: you will be treated honorably.

Establish a personal relationship with a shopkeeper and you can expect much assistance as a newcomer; once this is done, you are treated royally. Stores in the cities are open in the evenings and on weekends, as well as during the day, but close during the Muslim Sabbath (Friday) and in preparation for it (Thursday nights), and on all Muslim holidays. A personal verbal thank-you to store owners, waiters, chefs, and hotel managers for their services is important, as it will help establish the relationship you need to get good service. In goods stores, if you buy an item and you have problems with it, returning the item is usually difficult. Smoking is endemic, and you may have difficulty finding a no-smoking area on public transportation, in restaurants, and in other public places (be sure not to smoke during the day during Ramadan, when Muslims abstain; this is true for eating and drinking during the day during Ramadan when in the presence of observant Muslims, as well). When and if you do smoke, it is critical that you offer a cigarette first to everyone else at the table before you light up, and then offer to light their cigarettes for them. Bathroom facilities can range from Western-style toilets to Asian-style toilets (holes in the floor, with buckets of water or hoses attached to a water line for cleanup instead of paper); be prepared.

Unless they are in the company of other women, or close male relatives, women generally do not go out in public, especially at night. Western women traveling alone in Egypt will place an unusual burden of consideration on the behavior of others toward them: many people won't know what to do or how to act toward them; some other women will want to assist them, and certain men, no doubt, will try to take advantage of them. Traveling alone is not a good idea in any part of the Arab world, including Egypt, for women.

Never bring anything into the countries of the Arab world that can be construed as pornographic or challenging to Islam in even the slightest way: videotapes, books, and magazines that are deemed inappropriate may subject you to harassment. When answering a telephone, say "Hello" or just your given name. Cell phones are ubiquitous.

Bus / Metro / Taxi / Car

Driving is on the left, and whether in the country or the city, being in a car can be hazardous to your health. The roads are not necessarily in good repair in the developing Arab world (although this is *not* the case in Saudi Arabia), and this most definitely includes Egypt; they may not be marked or where maps say they are. Driving in Cairo can be an exercise in madness, with people, cars, buses, trucks, and all manner of animal transport vying for positions on unfathomably crowded and ancient streets. Traveling alone is not a good idea in Egypt, and in other parts of the Arab world it may be dangerous in towns where you are not known.

The best way to catch a cab is at designated taxi stands (hotels are good places, but often charge more for the same ride: a hotel surcharge is added to the meter fare, in some cases). When a taxi has been hailed, negotiate the price. Whenever possible, have the address you need to get to written down on a piece of paper (or use the business card of the person you are going to see, if you can) before you hail the cab.

Tipping

Tipping (the ubiquitous *baksheesh*) is universally required throughout the Arab world, and then some. It is traditional to always give a little something to someone who has helped you out. The offer may be refused in some cases, but if you insist, it will be graciously accepted and appreciated. Tips in restaurants run about 10 percent, and are typically not included in the bill (but double-check to be sure); a tip is not necessary if you have negotiated the fare for the taxi ahead of time and already figured in the tip. For everything else, a few coins are all that is needed, but you should always have a lot of spare change handy to see you through the day.

Punctuality

Punctuality is valued, but not required. You should be on time, but you may be kept waiting for quite awhile: patience and good humor are required. Never get upset over time. If you are late, making a general comment about the traffic is all you need to do to get off the hook for being late. It will be understood.

Dress

The Egyptian native dress for men and women is the *galabbiyah* (a simple white robe); all women should have a scarf ready to cover their heads when necessary (e.g., when entering a mosque). Egyptian women usually are not veiled. It is *not* appropriate for non-Egyptians to dress in traditional Egyptian clothes; Westerners should dress in conservative business clothes (as will most Egyptian businessmen), but may find it more comfortable to wear items that are as loose fitting as possible (the weather is hot, and you may be required to sit cross-legged from time to time on cushions). In all cases, for men and women, most of the body needs to be covered, including arms down to the wrists, torso up to the neck, and legs down to the ankles. (Men must not wear neck jewelry, even if it is not visible underneath clothing.) Clothes must not be tight-fitting or revealing in any way, for men or women. If you're dressing casually, your shirt must be buttoned up to the neck. Women should not wear pantsuits, as they reveal too much of the shape of the legs. Any clothing that is different from the prescribed norm, for men or women, will engender stares from more fundamentalist Muslims. For adults, sneakers, shorts, and T-shirts are only for the gym, or around the house.

Seasonal Variations

In Egypt, most months of the year are dry and hot (January and February may be cooler). Air conditioning, however, can be frigid, and it is in most modern facilities, so be prepared with a shawl or cover-up.

Colors

Neutral and muted, whenever possible.

Styles

For visitors, wear Western conservative clothes.

Accessories / Jewelry / Makeup

Western women should avoid wearing too much makeup. Egyptians appreciate men and women who smell good. There can be a liberal use of cologne among men at work during the day; and if you visit an Egyptian's home, a tray of perfume is sometimes provided at the entrance, for women to use freely as they come and go. At the end of a special meal, incense is often burned and passed around as an extra sensory touch. Colognes and perfumes are typically not made with alcohol (alcohol is generally prohibited in Islam).

Personal Hygiene

In Egypt, cleanliness is associated with purity. Washing both hands and feet more than once a day is very common. Do not blow your nose in public: it is considered very rude. Spitting does occur on the street, but is also regarded as rude. Muslim men may sport facial hair, usually in the form of a mustache and beard (when accompanying traditional dress, usually a sign of a devout Muslim). At the end of a meal, if you use a toothpick, you must cover the "working" hand with the other hand, so that others cannot see your mouth. Remember that Arabs consider dogs very unclean; therefore, do not refer to them or bring them (or pictures of them) along with you.

Dining and Drinking

Mealtimes and Typical Foods

The typical Egyptian diet is rich in grains, breads, fresh vegetables, and fruits. Meats are not that common but can include lamb, goat, and chicken. The national dish of Egypt is *molochaia,* or chicken cooked with herbs, tomatoes, and spices, and a favorite dish is *foul,* or fava beans prepared with olive oil and lemon; stuffed grape leaves are a popular appetizer in Egypt, as is *f'teer,* a kind of pizza filled with meat and vegetables. North African cuisine includes dips made of eggplant (baba ghanoush), and hummus (a chickpea and sesame paste). Olive products are varied, and there is liberal use of fruits (fresh and dried, especially figs, dates, raisins, and pomegranates) and nuts. Breads can be the pocket-type pitas and leavened or unleavened breads, and are served with practically every meal (*aish* is the name for Egyptian bread). Foods can be spicy, but are not necessarily hot. Although they are familiar with Western food, Egyptians and Arabs in general love their food, and most enjoy a fine local meal (if you are hosting them in your country, unless they directly express an interest in trying a local cuisine, take them to the best local Middle Eastern restaurant you can find, and tell the restaurant manager that you are hosting Arab guests: the restaurant management will usually go out of their way to make the meal very fine for you).

If you are serving a meal at home, be sure you do not use alcohol or pork in any of the dishes; and if you do, labeling the dish and serving it separately will still make your Arab guest uncomfortable—simply don't do it. You, as a guest in the more rural regions, may be rewarded with favored parts of the animal, such as the goat's eye or head: this is an honor that needs to be acknowledged before the food is consumed or rejected (if you cannot bring yourself to partake, acknowledge the honor, and suggest that while you will always hold the honor in your heart, you in turn will bestow it on someone who can also appreciate it in their belly: then pass the honored dish on to an Egyptian colleague).

Most meals begin with tasty appetizers of dips and vegetables, and *aish,* and are served buffet or family style, so there is much for everyone. The amount of food at a meal at which you are a guest in the region can be overwhelming; guests must be treated with great respect and honor. It is far better to return for more than to load up your plate at once and not be able to eat any more later.

Breakfast is served from about 7 to 8 A.M., and usually consists of tea and coffee, breads, jams, cheese, and olives. Tea is usually drunk with milk or sugar. Yogurt and fruit drinks are sometimes served for breakfast. The coffee is rich, dark, often very sweet, and served in small cups, usually without milk. It is often flavored with sweet spices, such as cardamom or cinnamon.

Lunch is traditionally the main meal of the day, and even today, in busy cities, lunch can still be an elaborate affair with several courses—or it can be a simple snack prepared and eaten in a matter of minutes. Lunch is served from about noon to 2 P.M. Lunch consists of meat, fish, and/or vegetables, with rice or yogurt, and can be in a stewlike vegetable sauce. The drinks served with lunch and dinner are usually soft drinks, fruit juices, and/or tea, with Arabic coffee after the meal.

Dinner is served from 8 P.M. on, with 9 P.M. the customary late time. Even if the main meal of the day was lunch, dinner is only slighter lighter—this is often the case with families at home. The dinner menu is often similar to that of the more formal lunch; dinner drinks are similar to those served at lunch. When you come to an Egyptian home, even for just a brief visit, you will be served some sweet delicacy plus a cool drink (usually iced water, lemonade, or fruit juice) and/or tea and coffee. The sweet is not a dessert; you will get that at the end of the meal as well. Desserts can be very sweet, such as honeyed pastries, not unlike baklava, with puddings made of sweetened yogurts, nuts, rosewater, and eggs.

Regional Differences

Remember, Islam prohibits the use of pork, and most meats of any kind for Muslims need to be prepared *halal* (meat slaughtered according to Islamic prescriptions). A staple grain is couscous, cooked in a thousand different ways with many different ingredients. Do not eat in front of your Muslim colleagues, or invite them to join you for a meal, during the day during Ramadan, as Muslims typically fast (and refrain from drinking and smoking) during the day, and feast with family and friends at night. Ramadan lasts for a lunar month: this is simply not a good time to do business or go out entertaining in the North African Arab world.

Typical Drinks and Toasting

Tea and coffee are served everywhere, all the time. Sometimes tea or coffee is boiling hot: sometimes it is lukewarm; most of the time tea is served with milk or sugar. Coffee is served in small cups, always without milk; it is strong, black, often intensely presweetened (so taste first before adding sugar!), and sometimes spiced. Coffee is individually brewed: if you want it sweet, it is *zaida;* not too sweet is *mahzbout,* and prepared with no sugar is *sadah.* Always accept the cup of tea and/or coffee, even if you only put it to your lips or just take a few sips. Your cup will always be refilled if it is less than half full. The ceremony of tea/coffee/tea can last hours, as you chat and converse, and do business, and it goes something like this: you will be offered tea; when you are finished, you will be offered coffee; when you are finished, you will be offered tea again, and the whole process can repeat itself. This is an important relationship-building event. Typically, beer and other alcoholic drinks are not served: fruit juices and lemonades, along with tea, may accompany most meals. Because you must never pour your own drink (be it juice, tea, or coffee), you must always be alert throughout the meal as to whether or not your neighbor's cup or glass needs refilling. If it is less than half full, it needs refilling; alternately, if yours is less than half full, your neighbor or host is obliged to refill it. If he or she does not, do not refill it yourself, for this will cause your neighbor or host to lose face; instead, diplomatically indicate your need by pouring a little more drink into your neighbor's glass, even if it doesn't really need it.

If you are the honored guest, you are not expected to make a statement or toast, but if you offer a small compliment, it will be appreciated; you can do this at the end of the meal, just before everyone departs. An appropriate comment would be to wish for the health of the host and all those present, and to the prosperity of the business under discussion. Make it as eloquent and flowery as you like, but always be very sincere.

Avoid drinking tap water anywhere in the region (this means you should brush your teeth with bottled water and not take ice in any of your drinks; drink only bottled water, or brewed tea or coffee or soft drinks, and avoid getting water from the morning shower into your mouth; never eat fresh fruits or vegetables that cannot be peeled first, and ideally cooked later before eating). This is a serious matter: there are some very nasty bugs going around in developing countries. In addition, avoid all dairy products except in the finest hotels, as the required refrigeration may be questionable.

A word about water and its use in the region: consider that most of the region is desert, so despite the graciousness of your hosts, water use is a serious concern in this part of the world. Even if you won't drink tap water, use it judiciously when you do use it. A final note about water caution: outside of the cities, never swim in freshwater lakes, ponds, or rivers (only use recreational swimming pools): you can contract serious parasitic infections from swimming in these waters.

Table Manners and the Use of Utensils

Before meals, as the food is served, guests say, "*Sahtain*" (the equivalent of "bon appetit"), or "*Bismillah*" (in the name of God); when the meal is over, guests should also say, "*Daimah*" ("may there always be plenty at your table").

You may or may not be given Western utensils. Throughout the region, people use spoons, forks, and knives, if necessary, or no utensils at all, depending upon the food being served. Since the spoon is more important than the fork, if you are right-handed, keep the spoon in the right hand, and put it down to switch to the fork if and when you need it. Never use your left hand for eating, especially if you are eating directly with your hands.

What do you do when no utensils are available? Why, eat with your fingers, of course! Many think it makes the experience more fun, maybe because you're adding an extra sense to an already very sensory experience: the sense of touch. A great variety of foods can be eaten with the hands, most of the time using bread like a utensil to scoop up some of the food. Here are some other things to note about eating in Egypt:

- Wash your hands before you sit down to eat if you will not use utensils. Many restaurants have washrooms and sinks out in the open specifically for this purpose. (However, you may want to wash your hands with bottled water at the hotel first since the washing water at the restaurant may be more hazardous to your health than the germs already on your hands!) You will also need to wash your hands again at the end of the meal, especially after eating the saucy dishes, since you've probably got some messy fingers by the end of the meal. Don't worry, it's to be expected.
- Use your right hand when picking up and eating food: never your left hand. Keep your left hand at your side. Do not place your left hand on the table, and do not pass food with your left hand.
- Pork will typically not be on the menu.
- Alcohol will usually not be served with the meal.
- Men and women, in some establishments, may be asked to dine separately.
- If you absolutely cannot eat without some kind of utensil, it's usually perfectly all right to ask for one. The proprietors, or your hosts, are usually more than pleased to accommodate Westerners.

A word about smoking: it is ubiquitous throughout the region. Usually, you do not smoke until the meal is over. In Egypt and the Levant, the *nargilah,* or water pipe, may be offered at the end of the meal (this is filled with tobacco—marijuana and hashish, particularly available in the Maghreb, is illegal, and you do take your risks if you indulge). Fresh mints or caraway seeds may be offered as a special treat just before you go.

Most discussion occurs before the meal, not after, although dining at someone's home will last well into the night. Expect to be told that it is too early to leave the first time you try; stay a while longer, but if the hosts serve some ice water or another cool drink, you should leave soon thereafter.

Seating Plans

The most honored position is at the head of the table, with the second most important person, or the honored guest, seated next to the head of the table. (Spouses are usually not invited to business meals in restaurants. Do not ask if your spouse can join you; it will embarrass your Egyptian colleague. However, your spouse might be invited with you to a meal at home, especially if the spouse of the host will be there, which will probably be the case. The invitation will then be phrased, "My spouse invites your spouse." By the way, invitations, business or social, will almost always be verbal, not written.) Be prepared that in some more traditional homes, you might sit on carpets on the floor at very low tables. Men and women eating at more observant homes may dine in separate areas (and spend the entire evening separated) or at separate times, with the men dining first.

Refills and Seconds

You will always be offered more food. Leave a bit on your plate if you do not want more food. You will be implored to take more two or three times, in the form of a little ritual. The game is as follows: first you refuse, then the host insists, then you refuse again, then the host insists again, and then you finally give in and take a little more. This is known as the *uzooma* (the see-saw dialogue of imploring, rejecting, and finally submitting). If you really don't want anymore, take very little and leave it on your plate. Your host will constantly ask you if you are enjoying yourself, and will implore you to have more. To leave food on your plate is a sign of wealth; to have more food to offer is also a sign of wealth. You may always have additional beverages; drink enough to cause your cup or glass to be less than half full, and it will generally be refilled. A reminder: never refill your own glass; always refill your neighbor's glass, and he or she will refill yours.

At Home, in a Restaurant, or at Work

The honored guest is served first, then the oldest male, then the rest of the men, then children, and finally women. Do not begin to eat or drink anything until the oldest male at the table has been served and has begun. At the end of the meal, it is appropriate to thank the host or hostess for a wonderful meal.

In informal restaurants, you may be required to share a table. If so, do not force conversation: act as if you are seated at a private table. Women should be sensitive to the fact that they may be seated only with other women. Waitstaff may be summoned by subtly raising your hand or by making eye contact; waving or calling their names is very impolite. The business breakfast is unknown in the region, and most business meals are lunches. Business meals are generally not good times to discuss business or make business decisions. Take your cue from your Egyptian associates: if they bring up business, then it's okay to discuss it, but wait to take your lead from their conversation. No gum-chewing, ever, at a restaurant or on the street. It is safer to never host Muslim Egyptians in a nightclub or any establishment where liquor is served (even if they ask about going to a nightclub, they may be doing so for your sake, and it will make them uncomfortable if you actually go). Music may accompany the meal in restaurants, with performance dancing (usually traditional belly dancing) as well.

When invited to a colleague's home for a formal meal, you will be invited to sit anywhere you like at the table; resist the impulse to sit down, and wait until your host gives you further instructions. These will generally come after the host or eldest man is seated, and often you will be placed at his side. It is an honor to be invited into an Egyptian home, but a great obligation as well. (You may, in fact, be invited into a private home sooner than you are taken to a restaurant, as Egyptians want to get to know you). The "salon," where you will be entertained, is a symbol in Arab culture of the honor and responsibility the host has to the guest. Once invited inside, you may need to remove your shoes: this is still a custom in many homes (not in restaurants, however). You will know when you approach the home and see a row of shoes at the door (keep your socks in good shape, and wear comfortable but well-made slip-ons for such occasions). Once inside the home, do not wander around: much of the house is really off-limits to guests. If you move from room to room in an Egyptian home or restaurant, be sure to always allow the more senior members of your party to enter the room ahead of you. Servants and household help are very common in middle- and upper-class homes; do not comment on them, and do not offer to help: they are there to serve.

Being a Good Guest or Host

Paying the Bill

Usually the one who does the inviting pays the bill, although the guest is expected to make an effort to pay. Sometimes other circumstances determine who pays (such as rank). Making payment arrangements ahead of time so that no exchange occurs at the table is a very classy way to host, and is very common. Western businesswomen, if out with men, will have a problem paying the bill at a restaurant; if you want to, make payment arrangements ahead of time, and don't wait for the check to arrive at the table. It may be easiest to do this at one of the international hotel dining rooms (they are rarely as much fun, but they are very convenient, and they do avoid a lot of problems!).

Transportation

It's a very nice idea, when acting as the host, to inquire ahead of time as to whether your guests will require transportation. If necessary, you should arrange for taxi service at the end of the meal. When seeing your guests off, you must remain at the entrance of the house or restaurant, or at the site where you deposited your guests into the car, until the car is out of sight: it is very important not to leave until your guests can no longer see you, should they look back. Guests are seated in cars (and taxis) by rank, with the honored guest being placed in the back directly behind the front passenger seat; the next honored position is in the back behind the driver, and the least honored position is up front with the driver.

When to Arrive / Chores to Do

If invited to dinner at a private home, do not offer to help with the chores: you are a guest, and the servant or household staff performs such tasks. You should not expect or ask to visit the kitchen. Do not leave the table unless invited to do so. When in the home, be careful not to admire something too effusively: Egyptians may feel obligated to give it to you, and in turn, you will be required to present them with a gift of equal value. Instead of saying something like "I love that vase," say something like "Vases that beautiful in my country are only found in museums." Your compliments, while being appreciated, will most likely be dismissed. Remember also that many Egyptians consider it bad luck to have their children praised: it can bring ill fortune to them (comment on the children indirectly, but comment on them positively).

Gift Giving

In general, gift giving is not that common for social occasions, but is common in business situations between trusted colleagues. It is not only done as a gesture of thanks, but as a way of helping to ensure good business relations in the future (be careful not to go overboard here, as a gift that looks like an obvious bribe is not appreciated, and may land you in quite a bit of trouble . . . with the authorities in your home country, more than likely). In business settings, this usually takes the form of a personal gift that symbolically says the correct thing about the nature of the relationship. When going to the region on business, bringing a gift for the key decision maker is usually enough. Your gift does not have to be elaborate or expensive, but it should, whenever possible, be personalized (engraved, or representative of the personalities of the receiver or giver or of an aspect of the relationship). Present your gift when you arrive in the country; before you leave to return home, you will receive a farewell gift, usually at the last meeting. When Egyptians visit your country, they will also bring you a gift, and before they leave, you should give them farewell gifts. Holiday cards are much appreciated by Coptics, and New Year's greetings are generally understood and appreciated by all.

The most appropriate gift for a personal visit to a home, or as a thank-you for dinner, would be a box of fruits, pastries, cakes, cookies, or other sweets, or a thoughtful and practical item that you know the family can use (e.g., a calculator for the kids). A man typically only gives a gift to a man, a woman to a woman; remember, any gift given by a man to a woman must come with the caveat that it is from his wife/sister/mother, or else it is far too personal. Sending a handwritten thank-you note the day after the dinner is a very good idea. If you are staying with a family, an appropriate thank-you gift would be a high-quality item that represents your country and is difficult or expensive to get in Egypt; this is also a good idea for a key business associate. Avoid gifts from or about the United States with political implications (although relations between the United States and some Arab states are good, the politics of the United States in the region are questioned by many Arabs). Do not give alcohol (and this includes perfumes or colognes made with alcohol), pork, art or photographs that depict natural scenes or people (this runs counter to Islamic beliefs that man must not attempt to reproduce what God has made), or cutlery (which symbolizes the severing of a relationship). A fine gift for a Muslim would be a silver compass, so that he will always know which direction to face when he says his daily prayers (Muslims must face Mecca no matter where in the world they are when they say their prayers).

For both giving and receiving gifts, two hands are used always. Gifts may or may not opened by the receiver in front of the giver (this depends upon the nature of the gift, more often than not: foodstuffs meant for dessert, for example, will be opened for all to enjoy); the presenter typically offers the gift humbly and as an incidental aside, then, usually received after some imploring, it is graciously acknowledged, and accepted.

Gifts should be wrapped well. Typically, gifts are wrapped in ordinary paper first then wrapped again in green or other bright colors; white wrapping is perfectly fine.

By the way, if you have a copy of the Qu'ran (received as a gift or not), never place it on the floor or below any object: it must be the highest book on the shelf. Do not give a copy of the Qu'ran as a gift: it is far too significant for a business or social acknowledgment.

Special Holidays and Celebrations

Major Holidays

Avoid doing business the entire month of Ramadan. Many cities have different local holidays as well, so double-check with your Egyptian associates before making final travel plans.

Islamic holidays are the most important holidays throughout the region. Islamic holidays are on the lunar calendar, so the dates change each year, and all holidays begin at sundown the day before.

The most important Islamic holidays are (in order of their usual occurrence):

Ramadan
Eid al Fitr: A multiday (usually two or three) celebration of the end of the
    fast at the end of Ramadan)
Eid al Adha: The Feast of the Sacrifice, celebrating Abraham's willingness
    to sacrifice his son
Hajj: The first day of the annual pilgrimage to Mecca
Birth of the Prophet Muhammad
Islamic New Year (also an official secular holiday)

The secular holidays are:

January 1	New Year's Day
March	Sham el-Nasseem (a celebration of the beginning of Spring)
May 1	Labor Day
June 18	Evacuation Day
July 23	Anniversary of the Revolution
October 6	Armed Forces Day
October 24	Popular Resistance Day

Business Culture

Daily Office Protocols

The traditional Egyptian office can be closed or open, but no matter how the architecture is designed, you can be sure many people will be coming and going. This is not so much a statement on your unimportance as much as it is a statement about the importance of your host: that he is needed by many, and that in the polychronic Egyptian culture, things are handled in order of their importance, and not according to the clock. Be patient. In the Egyptian organization, hierarchy is strictly observed. Executives are usually placed on different floors than the rank and file. You probably will not be invited into the working floors until the proposed project has been set in motion. Because faithful Muslims pray five times a day, you will need to adjust your schedules to accommodate their needs. Usually, prayers are given upon awakening and at noontime, mid-day, dusk, and before retiring; this means that twice during the workday, there will be time out for prayers. The prayer break usually takes a short ten or fifteen minutes or so, and any quiet area will do. If you accidentally interrupt a Muslim during his prayers, just walk quietly away: there's no need for complicated explanations or apologies. Most organizations have prayer rooms set aside, with carpets. In addition, devout Muslims will not work on Friday (the Muslim Sabbath), and in fact begin to end work early on Thursday, before sundown. The official work week is Saturday through Thursday, 9 A.M. to 4 P.M. Oftentimes, because of the heat, many businesspeople work into the night (with a break for lunch—sometimes at home—in the afternoon); do not be surprised if an early evening office meeting is scheduled. Remember to present your business card with the right hand only.

Management Styles

Because of the rigid rank and hierarchy orientation, titles are very important; and the highest ones (e.g., vice president) are usually reserved for very senior, executive-level positions and should not be used as casually as they are in the United States. Any criticism of Egyptian workers must be done very carefully, even privately. Deference is shown by subordinates to their seniors; paternalistic concern is often shown by executives to their subordinates. Superiors are very sensitive to inquiring about their subordinate's opinions; however, once a decision is made by superiors, the superiors are followed, often unquestioningly. If you are doing business with the correct person, things will probably move quickly; it is essential, therefore, to have a good and trustworthy contact in the Egyptian world who can make the necessary contacts for you (in fact, in Egypt, you must have an officially designated "agent" who will assist you in all your business dealings: you can locate these people through consular and/or trade association contacts prior to your trip). Let this person take the time he needs to take to do this for you, for if you pressure him into making contacts sooner, he may connect you to someone who is not as useful as the one he was originally waiting for: this will not serve you. Again, be patient. Never use time as a means of pressure.

Boss-Subordinate Relations

The decision-making system usually works from the top on down, with key decisions often coming from individuals in high positions of power. Superiors are expected to provide clear and fully informed sets of instruction: that is their responsibility, and it is the responsibility of subordinates to carry out those instructions. Consequently, "management-by-objective" and other egalitarian and individually empowered management styles often may not work in this environment; without clear instruction from above, subordinates often will do nothing. They also lose respect for the manager for not making the decisions he should be making.

Conducting a Meeting or Presentation

At your first meeting in Egypt, you will probably be received in a very comfortable waiting area, which may or may not be where most of the meeting is conducted between you and your Egyptian colleague (an equally good place to host a meeting would be in a meeting room of one of the international hotels you will inevitably be staying at). If this is the case, you are merely being sized up, and your colleague is a gatekeeper. There will be much hosting by your Egyptian contacts of tea/coffee/tea. When serving any refreshments in the office, be sure they are served in porcelain, glass, or silver tea sets: the use of paper or Styrofoam shows disrespect and is very bad form. There may be several people in the room with you and your Egyptian contact whom you may or may not be introduced to. These "ghost people" are probably trusted friends or relations of your Egyptian colleague, and he will no doubt want their input after the meeting. If you are not introduced to them, do not ask to be: acknowledge them with a smile and a nod, and proceed with your meeting. If you are meeting with a decision maker, the discussions will probably be direct, forthright, and businesslike. If you do not know the decision-making authority of the person you are with, assume that you will need to meet with many people, and perhaps repeat much of the same discussions each time with different people. There may be many interruptions throughout the meeting; stay calm and flexible. If this is just the beginning of a business relationship, expect to spend most of the time sharing information about your organization with different individuals, or repeating the same things to the same individual. This may feel frustrating, but it is really okay; it means your plans are advancing to the right people in the organization, that those you have previously met with have approved you and moved you on, and that you are building a personal trust with the key decision maker. Business is very personal throughout the region: decision makers have got to know your face. Patience and third-party connections are key.

Negotiation Styles

At first, expect no decisions from your Egyptian colleagues at the table, and be willing to provide copious amounts of information, to the degree that you can, in response to their questions and in anticipation of their needs. Presentations should be well-prepared and simply propounded. Details are best left to questions and backup material, which should be available in both English and Arabic, and left behind; such materials need to look attractive and professional, and even if only in English, should have an attractive "back" cover (since Egyptians read from right to left). Ideally, you should present your material to your Egyptian colleagues for study, along with a proposed agenda, prior to the meeting. Have extra copies available, as you might meet more people than you expect. Should you come with other team members, make sure that your roles are well-coordinated. Never disagree with each other in front of Egyptians, or appear uncertain, unsure, not authorized to make a decision, or out of control in any way.

Most Egyptians love to bargain and see this process as a way of getting to know you: it does not imply insincerity to offer one price and then change your mind later (as it often does with Pacific Rim cultures). In fact, avoiding this process will generate suspicion. Final terms must be fair to all (win-win). Remember to confirm what might sound like agreement with multiple inquiries: Arabic communication patterns include hyperbole and reassurance, when in fact, they may not be completely in agreement with you. Contracts and contract law are well known and understood; expect and insist on well-executed documents to finalize an agreement, but the final document needs to be short and simple, and may not be the all-inclusive tome that Western contracts tend to be.

Remember, the deal should be sealed with a celebratory meal. Keep communications open, especially when at a distance, and stay in touch often with your Egyptian associates: share more information than you normally would, not less, and be prepared to make many trips, as needed.

Written Correspondence

Your business letters should be very formal and respectful of rank and hierarchy. Given names usually are written in uppercase; dates are given using the day/month/year format (with periods in between, not slashes) if using the Western calendar, or year/month/day format if using the Islamic calendar (the Hijrah; subtract 622 years from the Western date, and add A.H.—"after the hajj"—to the date). In Egyptian business correspondence, unless you know you are writing to an observant Muslim, it is appropriate to use Western dates and business writing styles. When writing names, an honorific plus the title is as common as an honorific plus the last name. You should write your e-mails, letters, and faxes in a formal, precise way: use a brief but warm personal introduction, then get down to business. Keep it simple, however, and bulletpoint and outline all important matters. Use the Western format (name, position, company, street address, city, state/province, country, postal code) for the addresses.

SUDAN

Note: Refer to the previous section on Egypt for information about general North African Arab cultural behaviors; the material that follows describes specific Sudanese variations on general North African Arab customs.

Some Historical Context

Sudan has had a long and tumultuous history; its current condition represents a nadir of what once was the territory of the great and ancient Nubian civilization and the kingdom of Kush. Historically, Sudan (and it is not "the" Sudan) has struggled for a unified identity in the face of forces that continuously—and continue today to—pull it apart in basically two different directions: either coming under domination from the north (beginning with the Ancient Egyptians, the Kush, and then the Islamists) or domination from the south (the indigenous peoples of Nuba, the Dinka, the Funj, the Shilluk, the Nuer, and other African peoples), or the Christians of the east (originating with the Ethiopians and their ancient kingdom of Axum). Sudanese and Egyptians are historical enemies, with outside groups historically aligning themselves with either northern or southern Sudan to advance their own interests in the region. Today, a long-simmering civil war between north and south has reduced the country to devastating poverty for most of its 35 million inhabitants, and one must distinguish between northern and southern Sudanese behaviors when discussing the culture of the country. The north is primarily Muslim, Islam having advanced south into Sudan from Egypt. But Sudan always struggled, prior to Islam, to keep the mighty northern Egyptian civilization at bay; at one point, the Kushites (of what is now northern Sudan and southern Egypt) ruled both Egypt and Sudan, but when their civilization fell to the Egyptians, Sudan struggled once again against its former northern nemesis, turning to the early advancing Christians from Ethiopia for help. Sudan remained Christian well into the fifteenth century until Egypt, this time a province itself of the Ottoman Empire, ruled it as a semi-autonomous region. By the mid-1800s, Ottoman rule was deeply entrenched, until Muhammad Ahmad Abdullah led a successful revolt against the Egyptians. At the same time, European colonization was expanding on the continent, and when the Ottoman Empire fell at the end of World War I, the British stepped in to Sudan (as they did in Egypt and other parts of the region). When Britain granted Sudan independence, the old simmering rivalries between northern Muslims and southern Christians and Africans came to the surface again, and since that time Sudan has faced a succession of political coups and endless civil war; the accompanying bouts with natural disasters (mainly droughts and famine and the flooding of the Nile rivers—there are two, the Blue and White, that converge in northern Sudan to form the Nile itself) are, under these circumstances, that much more devastating.

An Area Briefing

Politics and Government

Today, the government in Khartoum, the capital, is Islamic, and Islamic law (*shari'a*) governs the country; nevertheless, the Christian and African animist south refuses to acknowledge this government, and Khartoum struggles to provide a certain legal autonomy to the south while maintaining a unified Islamic nation. Recognize that the difficult political and economic situation of the country has made all essential services—roads, telecommunications, transportation, education, and health services, for example—poor to nonexistent. As is the case throughout Africa and the world when faced with such trying conditions, you must remain on the alert and be flexible, calm, and prepared for living in constant uncertainty and unpredictability. It will quickly direct your behavior, and you will come to learn one of the great lessons of Africa: how such terrible histories can make such beautiful people.

Religion and Demographics

Muslims constitute about 50 percent of the total population; of the remaining 50 percent, about 10 percent are Christian, with the rest being African animist in their beliefs; there is small group of Mahdists (followers of the religious sect founded by Muhammad Ahmad Abdullah), which began a tradition of linking religious movements with political parties, alive still today.

There is a small Nubian minority in the northeast; there are also the Nuba Mountain people, a small indigenous people in the south (who are not related to Nubians). Most of the African indigenous tribes previously mentioned live in the south. In addition, there are several million refugees from the Ethiopian and Eritrean conflict in the eastern Sudan.

Greetings and Introductions

Language and Basic Vocabulary

Since the government is Islamic, Arabic is the official language, but is generally spoken only by the Arab population in the north. In addition to Arabic, there are hundreds of local languages and dialects, the most prominent, in the south, being Bari.

Here are a few phrases in southern Bari that can be used in most places throughout southern Sudan:

do pure	good morning
do parana	good afternoon
gwon ada?	how are you?

Communication Styles

Physical Gestures and Facial Expressions

Throughout Sudan, one nods the head down once to indicate "yes," and up to indicate "no." In the south, men and women do greet each other with a simple handshake.

Emotive Orientation

Northern Muslim Sudanese have a reputation for being conservative, quiet, and polite; southern Christian and African animist Sudanese are generally perceived as being more open, warm, and expressive. All concerns related to Islam as mentioned in previous sections of this book need to be considered when working with northern Sudanese. In the south, there is a much more relaxed attitude toward women and men greeting each other, or working and socializing together.

Dress

In the north, the traditional dress is the *jalabia* (a long, white, robelike garment), plus an *imma* (turban) for men, and the traditional neck-to-ankle *hijab* for women (some women may also wear the *tarha,* or veil). Modern and southern Sudanese wear conservative Western business clothes.

Dining and Drinking

Mealtimes and Typical Foods

Because of the difficult agricultural, political, and economic conditions, food is a major concern: most people eat only two meals a day, and malnutrition and starvation are common. Even in the south, men and women typically eat apart from each other; food is usually eaten with the hands (one reason for the custom of washing hands before and after every meal), and all Sudanese eat with only the right hand. Food, when available, usually consists of grains, vegetables, and fruit. Some Sudanese specialties include *kisra* (like a bread made of many fine layers of flour dough), *fatta* (a dish of chickpeas, cheese, lentils, vegetables, and bread), and *aseeda,* a version of the mush or porridge that is ubiquitous throughout northern Africa. Southerners will sometimes prepare and drink a beer made of sorghum called *marisa* (alcohol is officially banned by Khartoum). As is the case with all agriculturally dependent economies, most business, whatever its nature, is conducted in the morning, and by mid-afternoon, things begin to slow down significantly. Concurrently, because business and socializing are often one and the same, visiting people usually occurs in the mid-morning or late afternoon, and visiting, whether announced or not, at someone's home or place of work is a major way to socialize and do business.

Special Holidays and Celebrations

Major Holidays

National holidays in Sudan, in addition to local African traditional celebrations (mainly in the south) and Islamic holidays (mainly in the north) are:

North

January 1	Independence Day
March 3	Unity Day
May 1	Labor Day

South

January 1	New Year's Day and Independence Day
December 25	Christmas (celebrated by both Christians and animists)

CHAD

Note: Refer to the previous sections on Egypt and Sudan for information about general North African and Arab cultural behaviors; the material that follows describes specific Chadian variations on general North African and Arab customs.

On the opposite end of the spectrum from Egypt (and certainly from the Gulf Arab states) is Chad, one of the world's poorest nations. Landlocked, with the expanding Sahara in the west, adversarial Libya in the north, and a mosaic of sometimes hostile and disparate peoples at its center and in the south, Chad is a culture and country in name only, a European creation carved out of the desert and *sahel* by the French and Italians at the end of the nineteenth century (Libya went to the Italians, and Chad to the French). The same patterns we saw in Sudan repeat themselves in Chad, but with the additional complexity of many more local and indigenous groups, customs, and hostile histories. There is, in fact, no one group that dominates the country today. Prior to the Muslim invasion, which was introduced by Arab traders who were crossing the territory, there were many ancient civilizations, mainly based on trade and commerce, which linked the Mediterranean and the south and west with the east, such as the Sao civilization in southern Chad, and the great thirteenth-century competing trading kingdoms of Bornu, Ouaddi, and Kanem.

An Area Briefing

Religion and Demographics

Prior to the Europeans, the territory was inhabited mainly by nomadic tribes, which either retained their African animist beliefs (mainly in the south, about 25 percent today), adopted Christianity (about 25 percent, again mainly in the south), and Muslim (about 50 percent, mainly in the north).

From the ancient Sao people today we have the Sara people, who further break down into major ethnic groups such as the N'gambaye, the Sara Maj Ngai, the Goulaye, and the Sara-Kibba. Other southern groups include the Moundang, Mbourm, Moussai, and Massa; Arab or northern Chadians include the Toubou, Hadjerai, Kotoko, Janembou, Maba, and the indigenous Saharan nomads of Chad, the Zakawa and the Gorane (the Fulani and Mbororo from the south are nonindigenous Saharan nomads that traverse Chad). The animosity between northern and southern groups can be extreme, and the Sao kingdom came to an end after being conquered and overrun by Muslims from the north. Christianity, Islam, and African animist beliefs all influence one another in Chad, so Muslims are known to buy *gris-gris* (local charms) and seek the advice of local animist healers and leaders, and there is a strong belief throughout every group in the power of witchcraft and magic.

Greetings and Introductions

Language and Basic Vocabulary

Because of the complexity of the ethnic groups, there is an equally complicated linguistic and religious story: Arabic and French are the two official languages, but people in the south often speak their own local language, as well. Children often speak several languages by the time they reach their teens, with many young people also eager to study and learn English. Chadian Arabic is the particular Arabic spoken by most people in the country, and it is infused with influences from all the local indigenous languages plus phrases that have been transported into Chad by the traders from nearby countries, such as Fulani from the south.

A few basic greetings in local Sara are:

lafia ngai	hello (use at any time of day)
i baii?	how are you?
aw lafia	good-bye

Honorifics for Men, Women, and Children

Elders are addressed as "mother" or "father" whether or not one is directly related. Children often address their own parents as mother or father plus the name of the family's eldest child. Remember, many Muslims can have several wives, as Islam permits a man up to four, as long as he can prove he can take care of them and the children; this results in, among other things, many children living together in extended families.

Physical Greeting Styles

Greetings must follow the appropriate forms of the different groups; see the previous sections on Islamic and Arabic greetings for northern Chadians and Arabs. Most Chadians, and certainly in the south and with non-Islamic Chadians, greet each other by saying "lale," and shaking hands (or waving, to a large group). There is much physical contact: friends often hold hands during an entire discussion, and when in the presence of an elder or someone one needs to show particular respect to, Chadians will often bow or kneel dramatically while shaking or holding the other person's hand. Sometimes the handshake is done with the left hand supporting the elbow of the right hand that is doing the shaking as a sign of extra sincerity.

Communication Styles

Physical Gestures and Facial Expressions

People greet each other mainly through socializing and visiting, and announce themselves at each other's homes by clapping their hands at the front door. There are some specific Chadian gestures: agreement is indicated by thrusting the chin forward and clicking the tongue; children in school raise their hands and snap their fingers for attention; if you are outside and speaking with someone, twisting a palm from facedown to faceup is a way of asking someone whose eyes you catch, "Hey, what's up?" Sometimes a *ssssppps* sound is used to get someone's attention (usually a person of lower rank, like a subordinate or a waiter); don't do this.

Dress

Dress is representative of the different religious group affiliations: Most women, especially in the north, wear the ankle-length wraparound dress known as the *pagne* (if a woman is married, she wears an extra pagne cloth on the front of the dress). Women wear short-sleeved, brightly patterned shirts and a head wrap; Muslim women wear a top that covers their arms to their wrists, often a veil, and braided hair. Tattoo-type patterns of henna designs are sometimes pricked into the skin around the chin and lips of northern women. Southern Chadians, men and women, often wear Western-style clothes, if they can get them: men wear the *complet* (like a suit, but really a tunic top and baggy pants). Muslim men traditionally wear the *bou-bou* (the long, ankle-length robe that is worn over trousers), often with a dagger tucked into the sleeve, and a turban. Most Chadians wear flip-flops or sandals. Non-Muslim southerners may also sport tattoos or scars representative of their particular ethnic group.

Dining and Drinking

Mealtimes and Typical Foods

Food consists mainly of grains; meat and fish are expensive. The ubiquitous north African porridge in Chad is known as *boule* (usually served dipped in a sauce, which can be made of spices and peanuts). Sometimes it is flavored with sugar and lemon for a different taste. Special occasions call for *tan kul* in the south (a kind of sauce served over fish or meat and beans) or *nashif* in the north (usually meat plus a spicy tomato sauce). Arabs throughout the country eat *esh* (boiled flour with a sauce, called *moulah*); nomads rely on the dairy products from their herds, including yogurt and milk, often combined with butter and sweet spices; and women—especially market women—often make *bili-bili,* a local beerlike brew. Lunch is the main meal, and is usually prepared over a three-rock fire made on the ground or over charcoal.

At Home, in a Restaurant, or at Work

If you do visit a Chadian home, you will always be welcome, and since visits are often unannounced or unarranged (due to the lack of telecommunications and transportation systems), be sure not to intentionally come at mealtimes. Nevertheless, you will be given hot water, or tea if they have some, and you will be regarded as particularly important. Sometimes local *hadjilidj* nuts will also be served. Especially honored guests will be given special gifts when they leave, such as the leftover food, eggs, or, on rare occasions, a live chicken. Most meals are taken seated on a mat on the floor, and eaten with the right hand. Men and women eat separately in most cases throughout the country. When seated on the ground, be sure your feet (do not wear shoes) do not point at other guests or at the food: tuck them to your side or under your buttocks. In most cases, the men will be served meat (with guests being offered the best parts—usually the organs), and children will be served what the guests and men leave over; women usually eat after the children. Be especially considerate of the limited size and range of the food being offered, and of the great sacrifice that is being made in your honor. Refuse the food several times before accepting it, and then take small portions, and only what you will certainly eat. Do not begin eating until the host has signaled to do so. (There are also food taboos, such as never giving eggs to children lest they grow up to be thieves, and limiting the amount of food pregnant women receive so that they do not deliver babies that are too fat—and hence difficult to deliver.) Mentioning to someone that they look fat is a compliment.

Gift Giving

When visiting, both socially and for business, you must exchange gifts, and the best gifts to bring are practical, nonelectrical items.

Special Holidays and Celebrations

Major Holidays

Local Chadian holidays are a mix of local African religious celebrations, Islamic holidays, and Christian holidays (mainly Christmas and Easter); in addition, the national holidays are:

January 1	New Year's Day
March 8	International Women's Day
May 1	Labor Day
August 11	Independence Day
November 28	Proclamation of Independence Day
December 1	President Deby Day

The Maghreb and Sahel: Morocco, Algeria, Tunisia, Mali, Mauritania, and Niger

Note: Refer to the previous sections on Egypt, Sudan, and Chad for information about general North African Arab cultural behaviors; the material that follows describes country-specific variations on general North African Arab customs.

MOROCCO

Some Historical Context

The Maghreb, in general, describes the North African region that was originally settled by the Imazighen, or Berber, people, and whose landscape is primarily Saharan and Sahel.

The Imazighen throughout Moroccan history have had to deal with invaders from across the Gibraltar Straits, the Mediterranean, and the Sahara—Phoenicians, Romans, Vandals, Visigoths, Greeks, and eventually Arabs (the Umayyad dynasty of North Africa) in the seventh century, bringing Islam and changing the way of life for all Moroccans forever. Although the Imazighen at first fought the Arabs (they did manage to establish, in fact, two of their own mighty kingdoms from the eighth to the thirteenth centuries), the Alaouite Dynasty finally took control in the fifteenth century and, claiming to be direct descendants of the Prophet Muhammad, established Islam as the basis for the new Arab-led Morocco. With the European colonization of the eighteenth century came the French, who made Morocco a protectorate; when the French gave Morocco its independence in the twentieth century, the old monarchy was restored. Today, Morocco is a constitutional monarchy, and the king is generally well respected.

Throughout the Maghreb, cities are usually arranged in medina ("old town"), casbah (the old town fort area), and "new town." As you move from one area to the other, recognize that the neighborhoods change dramatically: you can get very lost in the medina and casbah. It is, in many ways, a symbol of the need to have personal relationships in order to make your way through life in this part of the world: whether in the casbah or the desert, you need to rely on others to survive.

An Area Briefing

Religion and Demographics

The official and only recognized religion is Islam (many Moroccans, particularly Berbers, practice Sufiism, a sect of Islam that emphasizes personal revelation and spirituality); there is also a small group of Moroccan Jews native to the country, and Christians from Europe. In Morocco, the indigenous Berbers account for approximately 40 percent of the current population—and they refer to themselves as Imazighen, or Amazigh in the singular; Arabs and African Muslims—or Haratin (mainly in the south)—make up the bulk of the balance, along with Europeans and others. There is a small Spanish-speaking group in the south, near the Spanish Sahara border, an area that Morocco has annexed (or liberated from Spain as the Moroccan perceive it, as it once was a Spanish colony: the inhabitants of the Saharan Arab Democratic Republic, as guerilla liberation fighters in Western Sahara prefer to refer to their country, are mainly nomadic desert Bedouins). There are essentially three classes: the royal family and the educated elite, the middle class (one of the largest in the Arab world) of merchants, and the poor and agrarian workers (including the nomadic peoples, or Bedouin). There is a strong familiarity with Western ways in the major cities, but the people in the country are fiercely conservative and relate first to their local indigenous groups.

Greetings and Introductions

Language and Basic Vocabulary

French, Berber, and Arabic are all spoken, although the Arabic that is spoken is the *derija* (literally "dialect") Arabic, and although intelligible to other North African Arabic speaking people, it is different enough from classical Arabic to make it unintelligible to many classical Arabic speakers, such as Gulf Arabs. Additionally, the Imazighen speak numerous dialects of their own language, depending upon which Imazighen group one is a member of (Irifin, for example, are Berbers who live in the Rif area of Morocco and speak Tarifit, a Berber language unrelated to Arabic). In addition to the traditional Arab greetings previously mentioned, the word *labess* is used both as a greeting and as a response: generally, it means "Hi."

Physical Greeting Styles

Greetings are important, and generally follow the prescribed Arab greetings mentioned in earlier chapters, with some local adaptations. For one thing, because of urban Moroccans' familiarity with the West, a soft handshake is all that is required. Bringing the right hand back to touch one's heart after the handshake is an extra sign of sincerity. Traditionally, children kiss the right hand of the parent, elder, or honored guest when greeting them. Very close friends or relatives, particularly two women, might brush the cheek of the other upon leaving.

Communication Styles

Men and women typically socialize separately, with men commonly going to coffee bars, and women meeting in homes. In addition to previously mentioned okay and not okay topics for conversation in Arab countries, in Morocco do not give your opinions about the conflicts with Algeria or Spanish Sahara, or the relations between Arabs, Berbers, and Haratin.

Dress

Both men and women wear the traditional garment, the *djellaba,* which is a hooded caftan or robe, often worn with slippers; women do cover their heads. Conservative Western clothing is common, particularly in the cities. More traditional Berber women may have intricate designs tattooed onto their lips and chin.

Personal Hygiene

Consider going to a *hammam,* or public bath, when in Morocco or anywhere in the Maghreb. It is a custom that is still adhered to, even among those who have private plumbing, for the tradition and the camaraderie. Men and women are separated. Bring a bucket, soap, and a loofah with you: when you enter you will get a towel. Attendants will wash you from your bucket, and you may be expected to scrub someone (and someone may scrub you!).

Dining and Drinking

If you are invited into a home, you will no doubt be served refreshments, which might include mint tea (the national drink) or some fruit (usually dates), nuts (pistachios or almonds), and a cool drink, sometimes milk. Dining is traditionally done on a carpet or mat on the floor, around a large communal plate, and you eat from the portion of the communal plate that is closest to you. Remember, since most of the time you will be eating with your hands, never put your hand into your mouth, as you will use it again to touch the communal food (unless you are not having any more). Couscous is the local grain, and there are many local and national dishes, especially *tajine* (Moroccan stew). Usually, a mound of couscous is placed on a tray, an indentation is made in the center of the mound; and the tajine is placed in the center. You eat it with your right hand, and you can have a hot pepper dipping sauce on the side, if you like. If there are bones in the *tajine,* you will be expected to suck out the marrow: if you don't want to, don't take the bone. Pigeon is a special and favorite dish, usually served in a pastry.

Tea is usually served minted, and very sweet. Tea is prepared in a unique way in Morocco: it is mixed with sugar in the pot and boiled (mint may or may not be added at this time), and more sugar, mint, and tea may be added for a second or third boil, sometimes after the mixture has been poured into a glass and back into the pot again (for aeration, which many believe improves the flavor).

When the tea is ready to be served, the teapot is held high in the air, so that as the tea is poured into the glass, a little ring of bubbles forms around the surface (the *fez*): this is proof of proper aeration. Tea is usually served in glasses, and mint stems are also usually left in the glass. As the guest of honor, you might be invited to prepare and pour the tea. By the way, during Ramadan, a special dish, called the *harira,* is served at the beginning of the evening meal as a special way of breaking the daily fast: it is like a spicy chicken soup.

Special Holidays and Celebrations

Major Holidays

In addition to the traditional Islamic holidays mentioned in previous chapters that are observed in Morocco, there are myriad *moussems,* or local religious festivities, in various towns throughout the year; additionally, market days at the local souks are often centerpieces for town gatherings. Secular holidays in Morocco are:

January 1	New Year's Day
March 3	Feast of the Throne
May 1	Labor Day
July 9	Youth Day
November 6	Green March
November 18	Independence Day

Business Culture

Businesses may close during the day for about three hours around lunchtime, for people to eat, rest, and avoid the intense midday heat; subsequently, many businesses stay open later into the cool of the early evening (although this is not the pattern for government offices).

ALGERIA

Some Historical Context

Algeria is an enormous but sparsely inhabited country (most of the territory is barren Sahara, with the majority of the population living along the coast). The indigenous peoples are the Imazighen (or Berbers), and they struggled through-out history with invaders from Europe and the Middle East (Phoenicians, Greeks, Romans, Vandals, Arabs—in the form of the Umayyad Dynasty, who brought Islam with them—and finally the French in the twentieth century). Today, most

Berbers and Arabs are indistinguishable, with the exception of certain mountain and nomadic groups, who maintain a fierce independence.

There is periodic instability in Algeria, due to its efforts to emerge out of a rigid legacy of French colonialization, and due to powerful forces of fundamentalism that challenge its efforts to establish its own secular sovereignty. (French is definitely the second language—and in some cases, the preferred language— but knowing the limits and with whom to be "Western" or "fundamentalist" is a serious and important skill in Algeria today.) Algeria is perhaps the most conservative and fundamentalist of the Maghreb countries, so your behaviors should reflect this.

Communication Styles

Algerians have a reputation of being cordial and open, but perhaps a bit more standoffish with non-Algerians than their Tunisian or Moroccan neighbors—at least at first. Be careful, when building your relationship with Algerians, not to give opinions casually about Algeria's relationship to the West, France, its neighbors, or the continuing struggle between secular government and Islamic fundamentalism. But feel free to bring up soccer, which is a national passion.

When greeting each other, some Algerians hold onto the right hand after shaking, as a sign of sincerity; the older French custom of kissing both cheeks survives; and young people when greeting elders usually refer to them as either aunt or uncle. When greeting someone you recognize at a distance, clasp your two hands together and give them a little shake.

Dress

A uniquely Algerian traditional dress includes a skirt and top for women that is covered with a long overdress, the color of which is an indication of the region that the individual comes from (for example, the overdress in the east is dark-colored, but in central Algerian towns, it is white, and in the west it can be many different bright colors). Many Imazighen women throughout the Maghreb wear considerable jewelry—gold bracelets, necklaces, and rings—as this is a sign of wealth (and indeed may constitute the bulk of the personal fortune of the individual). Almost all Algerian men sport a moustache and some have a beard.

Dining and Drinking

Many European traditions have infiltrated Algerian customs, including the preparation of food, even native dishes (often elaborate, French-styled sauces are used). Some Algerian specialties (in addition to the Maghreb *tajine* and couscous) are *makrout* (a dessert pastry filled with fruits) and *chorbo* (a European-style soup).

Special Holidays and Celebrations

Major Holidays

Algeria celebrates all Islamic holidays. The major secular holidays are:

January 1	New Year's Day
May 1	Labor Day
June 19	Coup d'Etat de H. Boumedienne (in honor of the leader of the recent government)
July 5	Independence Day
November 1	Revolution Day

TUNISIA

Some Historical Context

Tunisia is the country in the Maghreb to have retained its French traditions most strongly. French is spoken as much as (or more than) Arabic, and many French, in fact, vacation in Tunisia. However, this affiliation with France and the West in general does not negate the strong Islamic influence, and one needs to follow the recommendations made throughout this and previous chapters. (Most of the population is Muslim, but there are minority populations of Jews and Christians, as well.) Due no doubt in part to its geographic location, Tunisia was coveted by many invaders, and was the site of Carthage, the center of the great Phoenician Empire of 800 B.C. (Carthage fell after three Punic Wars with Rome, and there are many Roman ruins to be found in Tunisia today.) When Islam came through, Tunisia became a particularly important center of Islamic culture in North Africa (in fact, the majority of Muslims in Tunisia are Sunni, following the particular *Malikite* sect, which was a force for defining Sunni traditions for much of the Sunni world, emphasizing the importance of group consensus as a way of life, in opposition to the more rigid Shi'ite perspective of following the dictates of individuals who are direct descendants of Muhammad). After the end of the Ottoman Empire, the French made Tunisia a protectorate. Once granted its independence, Tunisia took a more moderate path, with President Bourgiba ruling and advancing women's rights, modernization, education, and health care. Although culturally influenced by Islam, religion-based political parties are illegal, and the government maintains a strictly secular nature.

Communication Styles

Greeting and socializing with Tunisians will be familiar, as they are so familiar themselves with Western ways; just be sure to greet everyone when you meet them, to be sincere, and to take the time to build and honor Arab pride.

Dress

The traditional Tunisian garment is the *safsari,* a long piece of cloth that completely covers the dress underneath. Like their neighbors, Amazighen women can be tattooed around their lips and chin, use kohl (a form of mascara) around their eyes, and on special events use henna to make beautifully elaborate designs on their hands and feet (mainly for weddings). In the evening, men and women sometimes wear jasmine in their hair.

Dining and Drinking

Mealtimes and Typical Foods

During mealtimes, you will be seated at a low table on the floor (a *mida*). Some unique Tunisian dishes (in addition to the ubiquitous Maghreb tajine and couscous, which, by the way is a special treat, to be admired for its fluffiness and myriad of styles of preparation), are *breek* (fried dough stuffed with vegetables, eggs, and fish), and *tabuna* (Tunisian round bread). Sometimes at a meal there will be a communal water glass: be sure it contains mineral water, and pass it around after you have sipped from it; if you do not want to drink from it, you do not have to.

Special Holidays and Celebrations

Major Holidays

Tunisia celebrates all Islamic holidays. Secular holidays are:

January 1	New Year's Day
January 18	Revolution Day
March 20	Independence Day
April 9	Martyr's Day
May 1	Labor Day
June 1–2	Victory and Youth Day
July 25	Republic Day
August 13	Women's Day
September 3	Memorial Day
October 15	Evacuation Day
November 7	Second Revolution Day

MALI

Some Historical Context

Mali's greatest moment was in the fourteenth century, when it was the richest and most successful of all the West and North African Empires, having Timbuktu as its capital and great center of Islamic learning; by the fifteenth century, however, the Songhai replaced the Malian Empire in the region, and by the nineteenth century, the French had firmly colonized the region (French West Africa, or in Mali's individual case, Western Sudan). Perhaps because of the complex diversity within the country, compounded with the tenets of Islam, and the challenging environment, Malians have learned the value of nonconfrontation and living life one day at a time; they are seen as a gentle and polite people, who go the extra mile to keep things calm and in harmony, especially between indigenous groups (the same cannot be easily said about the attitude among some of Mali's neighbors regarding internal diversity). For example, one particular mode of speech employed in Mali is the joking cousin remark, which is a joke or sarcastic way of referring to a Malian and a situation outside of one's group: its main goal is to deal with someone or something in a lighthearted way, in order to avoid a confrontation. Nevertheless, there are inevitable tensions and class distinctions between the larger northern light-skinned and southern dark-skinned Malians.

An Area Briefing

Religion and Demographics

The country is divided into the arid, Saharan north, and the savannah-like sahel in the south (there is a small, riverine area around the Senegal river, where most of the agriculture for the country is based). These two major geographical divisions also divide the people who, although 90 percent Muslim, see themselves as light-skinned northern Malians and dark-skinned southern Malians. In reality there are many different indigenous groups that make up these two divisions: the Bambara (who speak a language of the same name) are the largest group (about one-third of the population), in the center and south of the country, and the Malinke, the second largest group in the west. Numerous smaller groups, such as the Songhai (descendants of the great Songhai Empire of Central Northern Africa in the fourteenth century) and the Dogon can be found along the Senegal river. Throughout the country, one can find the nomadic Tuareg, from the north, who have fought for their own independent status in Mali and neighboring countries. Although the official language is French, due to Mali's recent incarnation prior to independence as a colony of France, Arabic is spoken, along with Bambara (Bambara, like many of the other indigenous languages, is an oral language: the Griots are a special group of people in Mali culture who are charged with the responsibility of passing down oral history in Bambara).

Greetings and Introductions

Greetings are similar to those mentioned in previous chapters, except that Malians will sometimes also greet someone by clasping their own hands together and bowing slightly. Always greet someone with his or her first name. In Bambara, the greetings are:

i Ni Ce	hello
i somogo be di wa?	how are you and your family?
here tilena wa?	how is your day going?

Use French if you know it (English is not well-understood almost everywhere in the country). If you are introduced to a *marabout* (the Islamic teacher of the village) or *dugutigi* (village chief), it is important not to speak directly to him, but to a third-party intermediary.

Dress

Wearing modest Western clothes, as we have seen in all these countries, is appropriate, but traditional Malian dress for men is the *boubou* (the long flowing robe), and long wraparound skirts for women (please note that non-Muslim women may omit blouses in their daily dress).

Dining and Drinking

When visiting a Malian home, you will be hosted with tea, nuts, and other small food items. Older people enjoy enormous respect; always avert your eyes when speaking with an elder. The most appropriate gift to bring with you is some food. Dining is done around a communal dish or bowl, but people are separated into discreet groups around different bowls; for example, older men share one bowl, women share another, children yet another. Always and only eat with your right hand and take food only from your side of the bowl.

At a Malian meal, you will no doubt eat *to,* the national dish of porridge, sometimes dipped in a particular sauce (very popular is *tiga diga na,* peanut and tomato sauce). Remember, food is scarce at different times of the year, and malnutrition is rampant: as a guest, act accordingly and respectfully.

Special Holidays and Celebrations

Major Holidays

All Islamic holidays and local animist holidays are observed; in addition, the secular holidays are:

January 1	New Year's Day
January 20	Army Day
May 1	Labor Day
September 22	Independence Day

MAURITANIA

Some Historical Context

The name comes from "Maur" in French, or "Moor" in English, and refers to the fact that this is the land of the nomad and the caravan. For much of Mauritania's history, the people were nomadic traders, criss-crossing the Sahara from north to south, bringing slaves and goods from the fertile riverine region in the south, across the drier sahel, and eventually to the Saharan north and Morocco, in exchange for Moroccan and western goods to bring back south. Before Islam came to the region, the great Ghanian Empire of the tenth century ruled the area (throughout much of the region, the trading Ghanian Empire was followed by the Malian of the fourteenth, and then the Songhai of the fifteenth, and so on).

An Area Briefing

Religion and Demographics

The people of Mauritania reflect its three topographical regions. In the north are two groups of "Moors" (Moors call themselves *Bidhane*—Bedhouin): White Moors, who are essentially Arabs and light-skinned, and Black Moors, who are descended from the sub-Saharan African slaves of the White Moors (slavery has been a powerful tradition in Mauritania—only legally outlawed in 1980—and one that was tapped into successfully by the arriving Europeans in the nineteenth century), and in the south Black (sub-Saharan) Africans, made up of many smaller indigenous peoples, such as the Wolof, Pular (or Fulani), Soninke, and Halpular (or Toucouleur, who once had a very successful Empire in the riverine region). All speak their own language, each claims a local economic niche (for example, Pulaar are cattle people and Halpular are farmers), and tension between Black Mauritanians and the Moors in the north (as well as between White and Black Moors) can erupt from time to time. Islam and the Arabic spoken as a national language throughout the country, Hassaniya, serve to unite these groups from time to time. The differences, however, can be palpable: Moors, for example, tend to be a bit standoffish and independent, while Black Africans are more warm, open, and demonstrative. Among the Moors, social stratification is indelible, with the *Marabouts* (or religious leaders) being at the top of the ladder.

Greetings and Introductions

Language and Basic Vocabulary

Some greetings are:

iyak labass (Hassaniya)	hello (literally, "I wish you no evil")
an moho (Soninke)	
nanga def (Wolof)	
m'bda (Fulani)	
labass (Hassaniya)	Response to above greeting
jam (Soninke)	
jam rekk (Wolof)	
jam tan (Fulani)	

You might hear a clicking sound while you are speaking: this is an indication that the person making the clicking is listening, so just continue speaking.

If Mauritanians disagree with you, they may suck air in through their teeth or lips, making a kind of hissing sound.

Physical Greeting Styles

Some unique Mauritanian gestures: when greeting any elder, sometimes the elder's right hand is taken by the greeter and placed on the top of the greeter's head, while lowering themselves in front of the elder, as a sign of respect.

Dress

Traditional dress for Moorish men includes the *boubou* (the long white robe, sometimes referred to as the *dara'a* when it is blue), plus a turban; Black African men wear much more colorful clothes, often of conservative Western style. Moorish women wear the *moulafa* (one large cloth wrapped around the entire body) plus a head covering; Black African women typically wear a wrap-around skirt with a *boubou* and a head wrap. Women, as they do throughout the region, wear all their jewelry as a sign of wealth, especially gold, and are often decorated with henna "tattoos."

Dining and Drinking

When visiting or hosting, Mauritanians serve both *zrig* (a mixture of milk, water, and sugar) and tea. Tea is served in a little ceremony that mirrors different aspects of life: you will be served first a small cup of tea without sugar representing the difficulty that life is; then you will be served a second cup sweetened and minted, indicating that life gets better when one marries; and a third cup follows that is usually highly sweetened and minted, an indication of the sweet condition of life when one has children. Typical foods mainly revolve around various preparations of couscous and porridge. Be sure not to give your opinion about the tensions that exist between the ethnic groups in the country, and the difficulties that Mauritania has had with Morocco (both countries at one time claiming Western Sahara) and with Senegal (originally home to many Black Africans of the south and Black Moors of the north).

Special Holidays and Celebrations

Major Holidays

Islamic and animist holidays are celebrated; in the north, the Feast of Getna is celebrated, when the dates are harvested. National holidays include:

January 1	New Year's Day
March 8	International Women's Day
May 1	Labor Day
November 28	Independence Day

NIGER

An Area Briefing

Religion and Demographics

Pronounced, as in French, the national language, "Nee-jair" (and the people are "Nigerien," to distinguish them from Nigerian), this is the land of the Hausa (the country was historically referred to as Hausaland) although the Hausa are mainly in the southeast, while the indigenous Djerma are in the southwest and around the capital. Hausa comprise over 50 percent of the population, while Djerma comprise 25 percent, and the rest of the population is broken up into many smaller indigenous groups, including the light-skinned nomadic Tuaregs who, as is the case throughout the entire North African region, have resisted (and continue to resist) affiliation with the local nation-states. About 10 percent of the population are Fulani, who were the first to establish Islam in the region. Because of the mix of ethnicities, Hausa, Fulani, and Arabic are spoken, and dress and language typically distinguish people: for example, Tuareg women usually are unveiled (most other women in the country, despite their indigenous origins, are veiled); Fulanis wear black *boubous,* while Tuareg men wear white embroidered *boubous* and green or blue turbans; non-Tuareg women wear *pagnes* (long, wraparound skirts of many colors), with married women wearing an extra cloth on the pagne (which often doubles as a baby-carrier on their back).

Greetings and Introductions

Some unique aspects of greetings in Niger: it is important to always make the greetings long and involved inquiries into the health, family, and extended family (sometimes including the livestock!) of the person whom you are greeting; responses to these and other questions are typically always in the positive (if there is some negative information or news to come, it is revealed in the conversation after the greeting). The actual greetings are themselves inquiries. In Hausa, the greetings are:

> *ina kwana?*   good morning (literally, "How did you sleep?")
> *ina ini?*   good afternoon, good evening ("How did your day go?")

and the appropriate response is:

> *lahiya lau*   Well (literally, "healthily")

Local indigenous groups in the east of the country greet each other by shaking a raised fist at eye level and saying, *"Wooshay, wooshay!"* (literally, "Hi!").

Communication Styles

Nigeriens do not refer to each other by name, either first or last; instead, they call each other by position or relationship (e.g., old mother, young friend, or fish seller), or a nickname, if they know each other. It is absolutely taboo for a woman to speak the name of her husband, and for anyone to speak the name of a deceased relative or friend. In-law parents never speak directly to their in-law children.

Physical Gestures and Facial Expressions

Never indicate the number 5 by raising all five fingers of one hand at once: this is very insulting; instead, bring the fingertips of one hand together at once so they touch the top of the thumb. Malian and Mauritanian gestures are used in Niger as well.

Dining and Drinking

The tea ceremony as previously discussed for Mauritanians is also practiced in Niger, and to leave before drinking all three cups is insulting. Millet, and food-stuffs made with millet, form the basis of the Nigerien diet, and may be added to all sorts of food (for example, when added to fermented milk with hot peppers, it is a daily drink called *hura*; when added to a tomato sauce, it is called *tuwo*).

Special Holidays and Celebrations

Major Holidays

All Islamic holidays are celebrated, as Islam is particularly important in Niger. Secular holidays are:

January 1	New Year's Day
April 24	Reconciliation Day (celebration of the truce between rebels and the government)
August 3	Independence Day
December 18	Proclamation of the Republic Day

CHAPTER SIX

The Horn of Africa: Ethiopia, Eritrea, Somalia, and Djibouti

Note: Refer to the previous sections on Egypt and the Maghreb and Sahel for information about general North African cultural behaviors; the material that follows describes country-specific variations on general North African customs.

ETHIOPIA

Some Historical Context

The two most significant cultural considerations when discussing Ethiopia are that it is a mainly non-Muslim country in a Muslim world and that it is the oldest continuously independent country on the continent.

Ethiopia traces its history back to the romantic union of Sheba, then queen of Abyssinia (as Ethiopia was known in biblical times), and Solomon, king of Judea (resulting in a Solomonic Dynasty that lasted almost until the tenth century A.D. Ethiopia spent much of the next thousand years fighting off Muslims and then Europeans (Italy, in two brief expansionist and colonialist periods—one at the end of the nineteenth century, and again under Mussolini in the twentieth—attempted to make Ethiopia a colony), ultimately succeeding both times. Most recently, African politics plunged Ethiopia into a deadly civil war, mainly with the Tigrean ethnic minority in the north, and then into a war with the newly independent nation of Eritrea, with the resulting all-too-familiar African pattern of devastation, displacement, poverty, famine, corruption, and anarchy.

This last bit of political history was a replaying of one of the great plagues of Ethiopia: along with locusts and unpredictable rainfall, Ethiopia, despite the official power of the Ethiopian Orthodox Church, has struggled historically to keep its many disparate indigenous peoples—who cooperate with one another cautiously, at best—united. When the British returned the exiled Emperor Haile Selassie I to the throne at the end of World War II, the emperor was able for a time to give Ethiopia a center, until corruption and ethnic tensions overcame the subsequent regimes after his death.

An Area Briefing

Religion and Demographics

The major ethnic group in the country, the Oromo, live mainly in the center, around and near the capital, Addis Ababa; there are Somalis in the east (about 8 percent), Tigreans in the north (12 percent—before Eritrea was independent, this percentage was much higher, as most Eritreans are Tigrinya or Tigrean), and Amhara in the northwest (about 30 percent).

The fact that Ethiopia is not an Islamic country does not mean that it has not been influenced by Islam or the political pressures that history has imposed, and continues to impose, on Africa: Almost 40 percent of Ethiopians are Muslim. Another 45 percent are Christian (specifically, members of the Ethiopian Orthodox Church, closely related to Roman Catholicism—not Eastern Orthodoxy—making them Coptic, like Egyptian Copts, except that Egyptian Copts are most closely aligned with Eastern Orthodoxy), with the remaining percentages of the population being a combination of other denominations of Christianity, animists, and Jews, most of whom have emigrated recently to Israel.

Westerners need to appreciate the position, and hence the tradition, of the Ethiopian Orthodox Church in Ethiopia: It prides itself on having maintained a Christian presence in North Africa for over one thousand years; in addition, Ethiopian Copts will remind Westerners that Ethiopia officially adopted Christianity as its religion long before many European nations did. In fact, many Ethiopians claim that the original Lost Ark of the Covenant is secretly held near Axum, the ancient capital of Abyssinia during biblical times, and during many religious festivals throughout the year, local Ethiopian Orthodox Churches take out their own arks of the covenant, similar to the ancient Jewish tradition. The country's biblical roots express themselves today in the beliefs, politics, and daily life of its many peoples.

Greetings and Introductions

Language and Basic Vocabulary

Amharic is the official language in Ethiopia today. Amharic is a Semitic language, like Hebrew and Arabic, and along with Tigrinya, the base language for both Tigreans and Tigrinyas, Amharic is written in an ancient Sabian script. Compare this to the spoken language of the major Oromo group, Oromifaa, which is written in a Latin script, and you begin to see the lines that separate the groups in Ethiopia; in fact, the government has drawn local state boundaries within Ethiopia according to these ethnic divisions, which has pleased some of the groups and, of course, angered others. In addition to Amharic, and the local major and minor languages spoken by the various groups, the Ethiopian Orthodox Church uses the ancient Sabian language Ge'ez in its services and scripture. Although English is taught in secondary schools, few Ethiopians know it.

Here are some typical greetings:

Amharic:	*endemin neh?*	how are you? (spoken to a male)
	endemin nesch?	how are you? (spoken to a female)
	tena yistilin	how are you? (more formal, for either sex)
Oromifaa:	*akam jirta?*	how are you?

Tigrinya: *kamelaha?*   how are you? (spoken to a male)
            kamelehee?   how are you? (spoken to a female)

Honorifics for Men, Women, and Children

People are addressed by their title or relationship (doctor, mother of ———, Mr., Miss, and so forth) plus their first, or given, name (not their last, or family, name, as there really are none in Ethiopia—the last name is merely the first name of the father, and is not used when addressing an individual).

Physical Greeting Styles

Ethiopians tend to have a demeanor of calm and quiet. They may appear stoic at times, but exude a warmth and softness of speech that indicates a desire always for harmonious relations. Along with the greeting styles already outlined in previous sections on North Africa (minus the Arabic), Ethiopians will shake hands with one another softly when greeting, but will also bow when introduced to an elder or senior (in fact, children, when greeting elders, typically bow down and kiss the elders' knees, while the elders kiss the foreheads of the children). Eye contact, especially between juniors and seniors, is to be avoided.

Communication Styles

Physical Gestures and Facial Expressions

Trilling the tongue with a sharp high-pitched tone indicates pleasure and excitement. And a word of caution: when Ethiopians slowly nod their head up and down as you speak, they may not be indicating agreement: more likely, it is merely a way of saying, "I am listening, go on"; when they agree, they will say so, or nod their head up and down more vigorously.

Dining and Drinking

Dining customs are similar to those in the rest of the region—you will be offered food from a communal plate, and are expected to eat with your right hand from the area of the plate that is directly in front of you. Ethiopians will host you ceremoniously with their coffee, which is considered some of the finest in the world. First the coffee is roasted and ground, sometimes in your presence; the grinds are then boiled, and coffee is served heavily sweetened, black, and in small cups without handles. Typically, you drink three cups, and fresh popcorn is often served with it. Common foods include the ubiquitous north African porridge, often served with butter (and eaten, in this case, with a wooden spoon). *Kitfo* is a kind of raw meat preparation, served with cheese and cabbage, and *koocho* is a kind of bread made from a local plant (not wheat flour). A very popular Ethiopian bread, used with many meals and dishes, is *injera,* which is made from a local grain, *teff.* It has a slightly sour taste and is often served with a stew of meats and vegetables called *wat;* you break off a piece of the *teff* and use it like a utensil. Interestingly, in Ethiopia, Orthodox Christians, as is the case with observant Muslims, do not eat pork, or any meat on Wednesdays and Fridays.

Special Holidays and Celebrations

Major Holidays

Muslims in Ethiopia observe all major Islamic holidays outlined in previous chapters; Orthodox Coptics observe the following Christian holidays:

January 7	Christmas
January 20	Epiphany
March/April	Holy Week and Easter

National holidays are:

March 2	Victory of Adwa Day (the day Ethiopians defeated the first Italian invasion)
May 5	Victory Day
May 28	Downfall of the Communist Regime Day
September	Ethiopian New Year (lunar calendar)

Additionally, at the end of September, all faiths celebrate *Meskel,* an ancient pre-Islamic and pre-Christian holiday (known today as Finding the True Cross) that celebrated the end of winter and the beginning of spring (remember, the seasons in biblical times in this region were reversed). Each group in Ethiopia has a different way of celebrating *Meskel,* but a common custom is for every individual to place a tree branch vertically into the ground; the group dances around the branches, and an elder is given the honor of lighting the pyre, which burns all night: in the morning, a great feast is usually had by the entire community.

Ethiopia follows the Coptic calendar (which has twelve thirty-day months and a thirteenth month of five or six days, each year); this results in a seven-year difference between Coptic and Gregorian—or Western—calendars, but business is typically done according to the Western calendar. Also, Coptic daily time is calculated on a twenty-four-hour clock that begins at sunrise (using 6 A.M. as the start time), not midnight, so 9 A.M. is three o'clock.

ERITREA

Some Historical Context

Until the end of the twentieth century, Eritrea was a territory incorporated into the northeast section of Ethiopia: today it is an independent nation. Although Britain made Eritrea a protectorate, it advocated Eritrea's reestablishing itself into a federation with Ethiopia after World War II, which, for a short time, Eritrea did. Shortly after Haile Selassie's death, however, ethnic tensions grew, and the Eritrean freedom movement exploded as a force in the Ethiopian civil war. Italy may not have been successful in its efforts to colonize Ethiopia at the end of the nineteenth century, but it did successfully colonize Eritrea, and today, the capital, Asmara, has the distinct look and feel of a Western-designed city (Asmarans enjoy the broad Italian boulevards and some of the remaining Mediterranean traditions, such as socializing in distinctly Western-style cafes and coffee shops). The combination of indigenous Tigrean and Tigrinya traditions and the influence of the West and Islam have given Eritreans some unique characteristics, one of the most impressive being their ability to form a national identity out of this diversity, which is adopted by all: Eritreans have created what some refer to as the African miracle after their war with Ethiopia. Through hard work and a pulling together for the sake of one nation, Eritreans, mainly without Western aid, have created a nation, relative to its neighbors, that is economically, politically, and socially successful, a major example of which is the distinct lack of crime and devastating poverty that accompanies so many developing nations. Eritreans are universally known for their self-sufficiency, optimism, and strong work ethic, and even among the Muslim population, both women and men are expected to work as equals.

An Area Briefing

Religion and Demographics

Eritrea's population of mainly Tigreans and Tigrinyas (both speaking dialects of basically the same language, with Tigreans being a more nomadic people) are basically equally split along religious lines, with approximately 50 percent of the country being Christian (Eritrean Orthodox Church, closely aligned to the Ethiopian Orthodox Church), and the other half being Muslim. While always closely aligned to Ethiopia, Tigreans and Tigriny as always saw themselves as separate, and often oppressed by the Oromo majority in Ethiopia.

Communication Styles

Greetings are similar to those noted in Ethiopia. When an Eritrean waves his or her hand back and forth sideways with palm facing front, this indicates disagreement. In opposition, snapping fingers is a sign of agreement.

Dress

Eritreans may be distinguished from Ethiopians in their dress: women usually wear their hair, for example, tightly braided in the front but free in the back, and only Muslim women will be veiled. Muslim women also wear dresses covered with another cloth, called a *luiet,* and Christian women often wear brightly colored, patterned dresses. Most all women use henna as a dye for both skin decorations and hair. Muslim men wear the traditional *jalabiya* (a long white gown over trousers) plus a turban; Christian men wear a long white shirt over trousers.

Dining and Drinking

Local foods and eating customs are similar to those discussed in the section on Ethiopia, but there is a national dish called *shuro,* which is a bean flour mixed with spices, often served with lentils, spices, and other vegetables, and sometimes meats.

Special Holidays and Celebrations

Major Holidays

National holidays are:

January 1	New Year's Day
March 8	International Women's Day
May 24	Independence Day
June 20	Martyr's Day
September 1	Anniversary of the Beginning of the Armed Struggle

Orthodox Christian holidays are:

January 7	Christmas
January	*Timket* (the baptism of Jesus)
March/April	*Fasika* (Easter)
September	*Meskel* (finding of the True Cross)

All Islamic holidays are celebrated by Muslims, as outlined in previous chapters.

SOMALIA

Some Historical Context

The long and noble history of the Somali people is unfortunately not reflected in the political realities of today. Today, Somalia is a divided and anarchic place, ruled by no central government. It is, in many ways, the sad outcome of a people with long traditions of clan relationships who were exploited by outsiders, first Arabs (mainly Omanis from the Arabian Gulf region across the straits from Somalia who, in fact, married into many of the leading Somali clans and became leaders of those clans themselves), and then Europeans, mainly British, Italian, and French, who carved up Somalia into three different sections: British Somaliland in the north, French Somaliland in the far north, and Italian Somaliland in the south. Somalis are highly sensitive to colonialism, and almost any foreign involvement in the country is viewed suspiciously as a cover for colonial exploitation. Throughout much of Somalia's struggles with outsiders, Somalis fiercely protected their interior lands from the invading foreigners, who often settled along the coasts. When the Europeans finally left, Italian and British Somaliland were united into one independent country, Somalia, while French Somaliland became Djibouti. However, the deeper clan traditions quickly destabilized the fragile and new country, and the country was plunged into anarchy. Today, northern Somalia has declared itself independent (although Somaliland, the name chosen for the northern region, remains unrecognized by most of the international community), and is, relatively speaking, economically and politically stable. The south, however, is mired in clan warfare, fueled (literally with guns and figuratively with competing philosophies) by allegiances formed with the various clans by outside countries, including all of Somalia's neighbors, disparate Muslim fundamentalists, and the major international players during the cold war. In addition to the disintegration in the south, and the claim for independence in the north, northeastern clans have banded together in a claim for independence of their region, known as Puntland (land of frankincense; indeed, Somalia was trading with the rest of Arabia and Asia for millennia, providing the entrepot through which much of the largesse of Africa would be traded with the rest of the world).

An Area Briefing

Religion and Demographics

Somalis are tall, slender people, and easily distinguishable from their Ethiopian neighbors. They are extremely self-reliant, and build relationships and friendships only after mutual respect and equality is established, and this is certainly tested with outsiders, be they non-Somalis, or non-clan members.

The clan tradition in Somalia needs to be appreciated for its cultural and social significance over Somali behavior. All of Somali society is organized into massive clan structures, sometimes numbering millions of people, and each clan is highly stratified. Each clan has its own dialect and traditions, and an individual's identification with a particular clan, and his or her status within that clan, is something that needs to be immediately determined upon greeting. Some of the larger clans are the Isaak, the Darod, the Hawiye, the Dir, the Digil, and the Rahanwayn. There is inter- and intraclan fighting, as each claims territory and allegiances. Nearly 100 percent of all Somalis, of whatever clan, are Sunni Muslim, and follow all Islamic traditions and beliefs (with the typical Horn of Africa adjustment for the role of women, wherein they can and do manage and own business and property, and in work situations are viewed as being significantly more equal with men than their Gulf Arabian cousins).

Greetings and Introductions

Language and Basic Vocabulary

Somali, a language that is rooted in the older Cushite languages (originating form the ancient Kush kingdom of Sudan), is spoken by all clans, but there are three distinct dialects of Somali that are not really mutually intelligible. Originally, any version of Somali was an oral language, although in the twentieth century, there has been an effort to create a written language based on Latin script.

Two typical Somali greetings are:

nabad	peace (very common)
maha le shegay?	hi, how are you?

Communication Styles

Physical Gestures and Facial Expressions

Somali gestures include the broad use of hand and arm movements when speaking (often accompanied with fluttering fingers): putting both index fingers parallel to each other indicates "the same," or agreement; the opposite is conveyed by quickly twisting an open hand from left to right. Placing the thumb underneath the chin indicates that you have eaten enough; snapping the fingers means "please go on" or "continue."

Dress

Somali men traditionally dress in long, flowing skirts, like kilts, called *ma'awiis,* plus shirts and shawls, and a colored turban (or *koofiyad,* like a cap); oftentimes, the *ma'awii* is replaced by a wraparound cloth that begins below the knees and ends up slung over the shoulder, doubling as a top and a shawl. Women traditionally wear the *direh,* a long dress, or their version of the wrap, the *guntino.*

Personal Hygiene

There is a long tradition of cleanliness among Somalis; they often bathe in the morning and then again before retiring at night, and they polish their teeth several times a day with local preparations. Women use henna to color their hair and decorate their skin.

Dining and Drinking

Somali socializing and dining patterns are, in general, similar to those in the rest of the region, with some influence from across the straits. For example, the Yemeni tradition of having a *khat* (as *qat* is referred to in Somalia) chew in the afternoon is common among Somali men, often as a prelude to a *shir* (a gathering of decision makers from a clan: today, *shirs,* often using the shari'a as their basis for consideration, make up the foundation of whatever governing agency exists in Somalia).

DJIBOUTI

Djibouti was originally a small territory that encompassed the home of the Afar, a trading people on the coast. Djiboutis are very familiar with Western ways, due to their history as a seafaring people who traded first with Arabs from across the straits that separated them from the Arabian peninsula, and then with European colonialists (mainly in the form of the French, who used the port area as a staging ground for their colonial exploits in the region and who administered the area as the French protectorate of Northern Somaliland until granting Djibouti independence after World War II). Today, Djibouti continues its business and trade traditions by providing Ethiopia an outlet to the sea through its port. Djiboutis are primarily Muslim, and the primary languages are Arabic and French. Djibouti, formerly French Somaliland, was granted independence when Italian Somaliland and British Somaliland were united into one independent country.

PART THREE

West Africa

The Ancient Traders

Introduction to the Region

From the tenth century A.D. through the fifteenth century, the great kingdoms of Mali, Ghana, and Songhai vied for supremacy over the vast West African region not only with each other, but with the invading armies of Islam (mainly in the form of the Almoravids) that eventually insinuated themselves into the fabric of daily life, both regal and peasant, for many of the peoples of this region. At the time, these kingdoms surpassed the civilizations of Europe, which was mired in the Dark Ages. But in another three hundred years or so, the kingdoms would be defeated and colonized by those same Europeans, and the people sacrificed to an expanded slave trade as the conquerors pursued the exploitation and development of what would become known as the New World in the Americas. This region, south of the sahel, fertile with canopy rainforest and rivers, exposed on the west and south to the vast Atlantic Ocean, was essentially very different from the Sahel and Sahara to the north. For one thing, its peoples were more diverse, more numerous, and living with a topography that kept them always near but always separated from each other; this was very different from the experience of the nomadic peoples of the north, living in isolation from one another strewn across a great desert. For another, the West Africans were Black Africans, while the northern desert people were lighter-skinned Moors. Here in the West African Guinean forests, single indigenous groups could exist almost independently of one another, although such independence often bred hostility, especially when in competition for the great trading routes and the commodities that traveled over them. The northern, lighter-skinned Arabs and the Almoravids, while bringing Islam to these peoples, did not penetrate these forest areas as thoroughly or easily as they did the vast open desert in the north; therefore, there is much that, even today, is retained there from the ways of the past, and the Islam that did take hold was one much changed by the local traditions themselves. These local groups managed to maintain their own beliefs and ways of life, resulting in cultures that today combine the traditions of various groups (the Yoruba, the Fulani, the Nok, the Malinke, the Mande) and those of the external

Islamic and European forces that impacted them. As empires grew, in Ghana (tenth century), Mali (fourteenth century), and Central or Songhai—what is now Nigeria and Burkina Faso—sections of the region (sixteenth century), these peoples came in contact with one another, clashed, and exchanged new ways of life with each other. Today, many of the political, social, and economic realities of daily life in the countries we will explore in this region are the result of the European conquest, the impact of Islam, and the struggle to maintain indigenous customs and traditions in the face of being vanquished and sometimes enslaved. These countries, with a few exceptions (Côte d'Ivoire, Senegal, and Nigeria), are among the poorest in the world: even the most basic infrastructures often do not exist, and most people live difficult lives of patient and extraordinary simplicity, if not beauty and nobility, focused mainly on providing for themselves and their loved ones the essential requirements of life.

Getting Oriented

The region is best explored by looking first at the Atlantic Coast cultures, moving from north to south, of Senegal and Gambia, Guinea and Guinea-Bissau, Sierra Leone and Liberia, and Côte d'Ivoire (Ivory Coast). Then we will look at the West African Gulf countries, altering our north-south direction just a little in order to refer to cultures that need to be spoken of together, such as Ghana and Nigeria, Benin and Togo, and Burkina Faso. As we move through this complicated and vast region, we will discover the complexity of ethnic groups and patterns of language, social organization, and religion that reveal the lasting impact of Islam and European colonization. (It is important to avoid the term tribe: when used by non-Africans, it is often seen as insulting and has strong colonialist overtones. If Westerners do not describe their ethnic groups as tribes, neither should they use the term to describe Africa's ethnic groups. Nevertheless, ethnic pride in Africa can be very strong, and members of any particular ethnic group may themselves have no problem describing themselves and their group as members of a particular tribe.) For example, moving south along the coast from Senegal in the northwest to Nigeria in the southeast, for the sake of comparison (and acknowledging that in each country there are many other influences), we can make these broad distinctions:

	Predominant Religion	*Official Language*	*Predominant Ethnicity*
Senegal	Islam	French	Wolof
The Gambia	Islam	English	Mandinka
Guinea-Bissau	Islam	Portuguese	mixed
Guinea	Islam	French	Mandinka, mixed
Sierra Leone	Islam/Christian	English/Crio	Mende/Temne
Liberia	Christian	English	African-American
Côte d'Ivoire	Animist	French	mixed
Ghana	Animist/Christian	English	Ashanti/Akan
Togo	Animist	French	Ewe, mixed
Benin	Animist	French	Fon, mixed
Nigeria	Islam/Christian	English	Yoruba, Ibo, Hausa, Fulani

The European influence in Africa can be seen most profoundly in the distinction that we also need to make when looking at the urban/rural divide in Africa today. In most cases, the rural experience still reflects many of the indigenous customs and attitudes of the local indigenous cultures, while the urban experience in most of developing Africa today reflects the powerful influence of the West. There is an increasing disparity between "traditional" and "modern" behaviors in the countries of the region (and throughout Africa), in both rural and urban areas. For example, throughout most of this region, marriages were prearranged, and this custom is still very strong among rural folk, in most any country; however, in most of the capital cities of these countries, young people today are more often choosing their own partners and moving out of large communal extended family living arrangements to seek independent lives in their own apartments.

Finally, taking a closer look at the impact of Europe on Africa, it is important to consider, beginning in this region and extending on to much of the rest of Africa (beyond North Africa), the different legacies resulting from French and English colonization in Africa. Specifically, the French colonized Africa with the express intent of making their colonies extensions of France and French life; in turn, this meant superimposing and insinuating French culture onto and into local culture, and making local peoples into French citizens in Africa. The degree to which local culture was considered in this process was only insofar as it was necessary to accomplish the goals of Francification. French colonial administrative systems were rigid, bureaucratic, and, while designed perhaps with the intent of "civilizing" an otherwise un-French world, emphasized exclusionary criteria for attaining any measure of such "civilization." The education system in most of the colonies in what was known as French West Africa provides a good example: instruction was to be in French. (Even today, French is used in the schools, even though most children arrive at school with no knowledge of French; this is done more often so that no one indigenous language has to be selected as a national language, which could create the perception of ethnic favoritism in many former French colonies that are, in fact, ethnically diverse.) Coupled with a rigid and inflexible European grading and classification system that was (and in many cases still is) irrelevant to the day-to-day needs of the students and their families, this system ensured that only a select few could actually graduate to becoming citizens, as the French defined it. The French ruled over their colonies directly and in a very centralized way, and as if the colonies were merely extensions of France in Africa.

British colonization followed a different path: indirect rule, without the underlying notion that Africans even could or would ever become British citizens. There was little in the British colonial experience to even suggest that the Briton in Africa was on a mission (with certain notable exceptions) to bring Africans into a more British world; instead, the goal was to achieve mercenary success by providing infrastructure and direction, imposed from above, but regulated and controlled by Africans themselves. This was indirect and decentralized rule. The result in Africa today can be seen in the very different ways that former French and British colonies structure their worlds, in everything from notions of individual empowerment to business organization, to political party development, to education systems. Of course, countries other than France and Britain were active during the period of European colonization, including Belgium (the Congo), the Netherlands (South Africa), and Portugal (Guinea, Angola, and other areas)—even Germany and Italy, to a lesser degree—and their methods were reflective of their cultures. For example, Belgium ruled through the Church, and the Portuguese, the first Europeans to explore and colonize Africa, were the last Europeans to grant independence to their African colonies: in fact, in Guinea-Bissau, they were "exploring" the interior until well into the 1950s. Nevertheless, the greatest impact by Europe in Africa was made by France and Britain, and we can see these respective legacies beginning in the countries that lie along the West African coast.

The Atlantic Cultures: Senegal, The Gambia, Guinea-Bissau, Guinea, Sierra Leone and Liberia, and Côte d'Ivoire

CHAPTER SEVEN

SENEGAL

Some Introductory Background on Senegal and the Senegalese

Today, Senegal is one of the most Westernized of all West African nations, no doubt due in part to a long history of European involvement, its traditional association with indigenous trading empires, and its special relationship with the Americas. The indigenous people of this country were Black Africans, and many Senegalese are descendants of the great Mandinke (a Mali-related Empire) and Serahule (a coastal trading group) empires.

Islam entered into the Senegambia region from the north and east, across the desert, with Arab merchants, but the Europeans—the Dutch, the English, and finally the French—came from the sea. Ultimately, Senegal became the single most important entrepot for slaves to North America from West Africa; today, the auction site on Goree Island off the Senegalese coast—the departure point for most of the slaves sold to North America from West Africa—is a pilgrimage site for African-Americans, many of whom are descended from slaves sold in Senegal.

The Senegambia today is made up primarily of two countries, Senegal and The Gambia (which is surrounded by Senegal on three sides), which once were one. North of the Gambia River, which runs horizontally through the Senegambia, and serves as the lifeline for both The Gambia and Senegal, Senegal is flat and *sahel*-like; south of the river, it is more Guinean canopy rainforest. The people are different, too, and there is a separatist movement in southern Senegal that challenges the government in Dakar, the capital. Tourism is a major source of revenue, as is peanuts (brought into Senegal during the slave trade), and because of the familiarity with the West, there is a clear distinction between secularized Senegalese (typically the young, urban elite) and more traditional Senegalese (who typically live in rural areas). Despite this division, Senegal has been a relative success story in Africa, with a growing economy (at a rate second only to Côte d'Ivoire in West Africa), and a certain amount of stability.

Some Historical Context

It's important to appreciate that Senegal lies at a critical cultural dividing line in Africa: that between the northern Arab world and the southern Black African world. Although it incorporates many of the Islamic beliefs and customs of the north, life in Senegal is essentially Black African, with a broad awareness of European and Western ways. Consequently, there has been friction between Senegalese and their Moorish neighbors to the north in Mauritania. Having been independent from France only since 1960, Senegal feels lingering resentment toward and ambivalence about their former colonial ruler. Finally, the special role that Senegal played in the slave trade with the Americas places a unique burden on Senegalese in regard to their African-American relations: they are challenged to bridge the distance that many African-Americans unexpectedly find between themselves and the Senegalese culture (it is, after all, a Senegalese culture and not an African-American one).

An Area Briefing

Politics and Government

The country is divided into ten regions, with a parliamentary government that includes a president and a prime minister. The legislature is called the National Assembly, and there are two major political parties; however, most people feel far more connected to the issues that affect them directly in their local towns and villages rather than to the federal government, and the decisions of local chiefs and religious leaders (called *marabouts*) are far more influential and affect individual lives far more profoundly.

Schools and Education

As is the case throughout all of West Africa, schooling for children is spotty and difficult to mandate. Beyond the lack of teachers, resources, supplies, and infrastructure, many people feel that schooling is irrelevant to their lives and the lives of their children, that it is much more important for the children to be available to help out at home, in the fields, and in the market. In addition, those who are able to send their children to school prefer that the children attend an Islamic school rather than one run by the secular government (there is a distrust by many of secular education when compared to religious upbringing). Compounding this is the French administration of the school system that for better (it obviates ethnic rivalries) or for worse (most children do not speak French when they enter school, and this makes learning extremely difficult) results in an excessive dropout rate. Finally, it must be noted that most of the indigenous languages spoken in West Africa, including Senegalese, are oral languages, making the concept and achievement of literacy first dependent upon the development of an accepted script for the spoken language. In Senegal, sometimes Arabic script is used to write local languages, sometimes an adapted Latin alphabet. There is a knowledge and awareness of the West and its ways among the younger Senegalese, and some urban youth speak English, although most Senegalese, including businesspeople, do not.

Religion and Demographics

Ninety percent of the people are Sunni Muslim, with the majority of the remaining population being Christian and animist. Even so, animist beliefs pervade both Islam and Christianity (for example, many people believe in genies, spirits, and zombies, and many people wear charms—*grigri*—usually in the form of amulets containing written prayers, incantations, or special ingredients to ward off evil). As mentioned, the *marabout,* or Muslim holy men, are powerful people in Senegal, having played a decisive role in the country's struggle for independence against the French, and are respected and consulted at all levels. (*Mourides,* or followers of a special form of Islam unique to Senegal, have blended many animist ideas and Muslim beliefs together.) There is a small, but growing, middle class. It is a challenge (to provide opportunity) and a strength (the optimism and energy of the majority of the population) that, as is the case throughout much of Africa, the majority of the population is under thirty years of age.

Islam is the youngest of the West's three great religious traditions, beginning with Judaism and Christianity. As a Western religion, it is linked to the Judeo-Christian belief system and rejects Hinduism and Buddhism as "pagan," and not "of the book," or codified. Incorporating both Judaism and Christianity into its system of beliefs, Islam claims that it is the final revelation of a monotheistic God, as revealed to the world through the prophet Muhammad, and that previous "messiahs," such as Jesus and Moses, were merely prophets, along with Muhammad, proclaiming the word of God. Muslims do not follow Muhammad (therefore, they are not Muhammadans, a very derogatory term created by Westerners who did not understand Islam); they believe in Allah, which is the Arabic name for the same God worshipped by Christians and Jews. Muhammad and his followers wrote down the law of God as revealed to them in the Qu'ran (or Koran), the Islamic Holy book. It does not negate the Old or New Testaments: it merely provides, in the eyes of Muslim faithful, the final required text. Muhammad received his revelations from God in Medina. Prior to Islam, the nomadic tribes of the region believed in a variety of pagan ideas, but with the notion of one God, and the laws under which people were to behave, Muhammad was able to unify the peoples of the Gulf Arabian peninsula into the beginnings of a single Arab culture. Islam spread rapidly into Senegal, gaining acceptance through its powerful message, and unifying many non-Coptics against the spreading Coptic ideas under the banner of a religion of Senegalese. While Islam underwent a serious split almost immediately following Muhammad's death (two major camps emerged, the Shia and the Sunni, in an effort to decide how to continue the faith), Senegal joined the Sunni camp. Sunni Muslims believe that the caliphs, or religious leaders, subsequent to Muhammad are legitimate; Shi'ite Muslims believe that the caliphs subsequent to Muhammad are usurpers, and therefore do not believe in Sunni authority. All Muslims must abide by five basic tenets, or Pillars of Faith:

- Proclaim the supremacy of the one true God, Allah, above all others.
- Pray to Allah five times daily.
- Observe Ramadan, the holy month, the ninth month of the Islamic calendar, which is essentially a celebration of the first time when God revealed his word to Muhammad.
- Give alms to the poor and needy.
- Perform the hajj, or spiritual (and physical) journey to Mecca, at least once in their lifetime if they are capable of doing so.

Specific codes of conduct, which have developed over time and have been codified into Islamic law, are known as the *shari'a*. One example of such laws that affect life in West Africa and Senegal powerfully is the acceptance of polygamy, as polygamy is also a social condition that is tolerated by many of the indigenous ethnic groups of the region. In Islam, however, a man may typically have only up to four wives, and only if he can support them all equally, and, at least in the case of Senegal, only if all wives agree. The degree to which one follows Islamic scriptures often determines how devoutly one applies the Islamic ethical code in day-to-day life; in Senegal, the Shari'a is enforced with significant consideration for how it "plays" with the local indigenous beliefs.

Because of the understanding, if not acceptance, of Western ways in Senegal, depending upon the individual you are working with (whether they are Western-oriented or fundamentalist Muslim), it may or may not be difficult for Western women to do business in Senegal today.

The predominant ethnic group in Senegal is the *Wolof,* and that is also the name of the language that is spoken by the majority of the people in the country. Other important ethnic groups include the Fulani, or Peul—throughout the West African region—who played a major role in bringing Islam to Black Africa (about 20 percent), and the Serer, the Toucouleur, the Diola and the Mandingo (about 10 percent each). Finally, it is worth noting that there is a significant Lebanese community in Senegal (and elsewhere throughout West Africa—mainly of Shi'ite Muslims), the Lebanese having been successful traders in the region for several centuries.

Fundamental Cultural Orientations

1. What's the Best Way for People to Relate to One Another?

OTHER-INDEPENDENT OR OTHER-DEPENDENT? There is a combination of deep concern for family, clan, and other membership groups (such as work and religion) that defines an individual and individual expression. Senegalese, like all Africans, have a hierarchical sense of loyalties, beginning with their family, and then, in descending order of importance, their ethnic group, their religion, their home village, their country, their region, and their continent. Senegalese are deeply connected first to their clan and their families: for that reason, it is critical that one inquire about the health of all family members. How one performs his or her role vis-à-vis others is judged in Africa, and individuals do nothing without careful consideration for how their actions will be perceived, and for the impact their actions will have on their family and their community. Consequently, individual empowerment and decision making are rare, and consensus-building and confirming group agreement is critical. Sharing, concern for others, humility, and an acceptance—without anger, remorse, or hostility—of one's role are all hallmarks of West African and Senegalese culture.

HIERARCHY-ORIENTED OR EGALITY-ORIENTED? As Muslims, all people are technically equal in their submission to Allah and his will; however, Senegalese structure the secular world with clearly assigned roles, so that Allah's will can be fulfilled effectively. Additionally, Senegalese secular life is rigidly stratified, with three or four generations of the extended family traditionally living together (this is not necessarily the case in the cities); individuals within this highly stratified social structure play their roles—children, women, and men in relation to each other, hosts in relation to guests, religious leaders and other elders in relation to the community. Defining one's rank, therefore, is important, as are status symbols (for example, the jewelry that women wear and the nature and amount of embroidery on one's *boubou,* or robe). It is critical that everyone show respect for elders and devout Muslims. Women and men are different and perform different roles: in Senegal a woman typically may go out in public alone, but she will likely prefer to go with other female friends or relatives). She need not be in the company of a close male relative (husband, father, son, or brother), and she generally will not wear a veil.

RULE-ORIENTED OR RELATIONSHIP-ORIENTED? While many Senegalese have had experience with and in the West, the tension that exists between the application of universal rules over reliable and dependable relationships is palpable. This leads to a high dependence on power, authority, and subjective decision making based on the situation and the relationships between the individuals involved. Ultimately, face-to-face knowledge of the individuals involved in any interaction is the basis upon which final decisions are often made.

2. What's the Best Way to View Time?

MONOCHRONIC OR POLYCHRONIC? Senegal is essentially very polychronic, due to the influence of both agrarian and religious traditions (although less so in Dakar). There is forgiveness for the inevitable delays and unexpected events that define life in Africa, and understanding when things don't go as planned or scheduled; people may or may not show up at invited events, things may or may not happen as planned. Schedules tend to be loose and flexible. Because who (relationships) is more important than what (tasks) or when (time), there can be many interruptions during a meeting, and people's obligations to other people, who may come and go, are more important than doing things according to schedules. If you are being kept waiting, or are ignored because of someone else's needs, it is an indication of your importance relative to the other person, and expressing frustration over being kept waiting only diminishes your importance.

RISK-TAKING OR RISK-AVERSE? Senegalese, and most West Africans, are prone to taking risks when in positions of authority, but avoiding them when they are not. Within organizations, the decision makers can be bold, even reckless, but subordinates generally are not, and take action only when instructed to do so. Therefore, comfort with uncertainty, in general, is low, and much information may need to be exchanged with different people before decisions can be made. Even when decisions are made at the top, the concern for others in the group requires decision makers to consult with subordinates before making decisions. There will be much discussion with trusted others about what you, as a foreigner, bring to the table, *after* you leave the meeting.

PAST-ORIENTED OR FUTURE-ORIENTED? There is a distinct and inherent fatalism in regard to the effect of human action, fundamentally because only Allah determines what and when things will happen, and because the way the world has worked for the indigenous groups is the way the world is expected to work. Nevertheless, those empowered by virtue of their position are expected to make the decisions that keep the world running, and by so doing, are fulfilling Allah's will. Therefore, future benefits often do not motivate Senegalese; doing nothing or doing things for the here and now, is sometimes more important, and if things do not work out, that is to be expected—no mortal controls the universe, and all is ultimately determined. There is a deep belief that things will take the time they need to take, and that it is always more important to maintain smooth interpersonal relationships than to satisfy personal desires.

3. What's the Best Way for Society to Work with the World at Large?

LOW-CONTEXT DIRECT OR HIGH-CONTEXT INDIRECT COMMUNICATORS? Senegalese are very context-driven communicators. They will speak in metaphors, and use stories or codified phrases; they will employ analogies, Islamic precedent, and much nonverbal behavior to convey true meaning. They generally avoid confrontation, and are honor-bound to do everything possible to make strangers like and honor them (they are lavish hosts). They will avoid unpleasant discussion as long as possible, and they shun unpleasantness—especially the expression of anger—in discussions: it is seen as immature and selfish.

PROCESS-ORIENTED OR RESULT-ORIENTED? Islamic law, and the complex study of Islam that developed in the Muslim world into its own field of scholastic inquiry, is fundamentally different from Western Greco-Roman philosophies of knowing. In Islam, interpretation and truth are dependent upon "analogous" reasoning, while in the West, such inquiry is based more on "argument" (proving and disproving). Decisions and actions therefore may be the result of reasoning that is not directed at a determination of truth, but rather context-based "correctness" based on similar experiences, often with strict Islamic code as the only context. Combine this with a tendency to rely on subjective experience, and the Senegalese mind is processing information, for the most part, in a different way than the Western mind. In fact, because of their negative experience with Western exploitation, it can be a struggle sometimes for most Africans—West, Senegalese, or otherwise—to even be open to Western ideas.

FORMAL OR INFORMAL? West African society is basically formal and ritualized, and each group has its own way of honoring the hierarchies, establishing respect and deference, and following (or not following) through on their responsibilities. There are formal ways that guests (outsiders) and hosts (insiders) must act toward one another, in order to preserve the honor of all groups and individuals.

Greetings and Introductions

Language and Basic Vocabulary

French is the "official" language, used in business and government, but Wolof is the most spoken language in the country (spoken, in fact by many non-Wolofs, as well). Sometimes Arabic is used as a lingua franca (most people know only limited Arabic, however). English is not well-known or used, even among the business classes, although young people are eager to learn it and pick it up where they can. Each groups speaks its own indigenous language, as well, which may or may not be understood by other groups, and most indigenous languages are oral. Most of the time, in an effort to keep things positive and to avoid an unpleasant confrontation, Senegalese will tend to reassure, insist that they can do something, know something, or solve the problem, whether or not they actually can; this is not meant to be deceiving, but to indicate their hope for a mutually positive experience. Words more often indicate what they desire than what might actually be. Never use religious references casually or disrespectfully—it is assumed that all people are religious in some way, even if not a Muslim—and be very careful never to use "God" in any way other than in the most respectful sense.

Honorifics for Men, Women, and Children

As is the case throughout most of West Africa, people usually greet each other by title or relationship (e.g., Dr., Mr., Mrs., aunt, mother, cousin) plus the first, or given, name (unless the individuals involved are Westernized, in which case, the standard Western greeting of honorific plus last name would be appropriate). If names are not known, sometimes stating the individual's position as a title is sufficient (e.g., Mr. Engineer or Miss Fish Seller). Children typically refer to their parents as "mother of" or "father of" plus the name of the oldest sibling, and refer to elders in general as either "aunt" or "uncle." Nicknames are very common, and most people are referred to by their nickname, sometimes with an honorific preceding it.

The What, When, and How of Introducing People

Senegalese may, upon greeting you, call you by your last or first name, with or without your title. Always wait to be introduced to strangers; although if you are not introduced after a few minutes, it is appropriate to introduce yourself. As is the case throughout the region, it is critically important to take time when you greet someone to make many inquiries into their health and the health and condition of the lives of their relatives and close friends (even livestock, if appropriate!). It is considered very rude not to take a considerable amount of time when meeting someone to make these inquiries and express understanding of their responses; he or she will do the same in kind. You must acknowledge people you know when you pass them on the street, and you should acknowledge strangers when eyes meet in passing. Never presume to seat yourself at a gathering: if possible, wait to be told where to sit; you will be seated in a spot appropriate to your position and gender. Typically men, women, and children (even boys and girls) are seated separately. Because you will never be refused, and because guests are always welcome (as is the case in much of Africa, because of the lack of communication and transportation facilities, people simply drop in "uninvited" often—in fact, this is typically the most common form of entertainment and socializing), it is important that you do not purposefully make a visit unannounced around mealtime; instead, come in the late morning or early evening. When arriving at someone's home, you will generally announce yourself by tapping on the front gate, or clapping your hands in the front of the house.

When departing, it is important to say farewell to every individual present: the American group wave is not appreciated. Seniors, or those who are obviously the oldest in a group, are always greeted first, seated first, and allowed to enter a room first (usually as the center of a group, however, and in most cases preceded by their younger aides).

Physical Greeting Styles

Close associates and businesspeople of the same sex who have developed working relationships often greet each other warmly, with hugs and kisses, and sometimes, in the French tradition, with two or three kisses. Wait until your Senegalese host initiates this behavior before initiating it yourself. Typically, the greeting involves kissing on both cheeks, and between men, handshakes, and putting one's left hand on the other person's shoulder. Very close family and friends may also kiss additionally on the forehead. Muslim women and men do not touch or shake hands (unless the woman is Westernized, and you will know if she extends her hand). The handshake may be soft, almost limp sometimes. This does not signify insincerity; rather, it is an accommodation to the Western fashion while remaining humble and considerate. Until such familiarity is established, a simple Western-style handshake is appropriate between men, and between Westernized women and men. Obvious juniors (such as children and young relatives) sometimes bow (or curtsy, for girls) in front of elders. If your hand is dirty or you are holding something that cannot be put down, you may extend your wrist, or even elbow, in place of the right hand.

The traditional business introduction also includes the exchange of business cards. Always take a large supply of business cards with you: you should give one to every new person you are introduced to, and they are much appreciated (there is no need to provide a business card when you are meeting someone again, unless information about you has changed, such as a new address, contact number, or position). Be sure your business cards are in fine shape: they are an extension of you as a person and should look as good as possible. Embossed cards are extremely impressive, especially with logos in green (the color of Islam). Never hand out a dirty, soiled, bent, or written-on card, and always handle (give and take) business cards with your right hand only. You should translate your business card into French on the reverse side.

When presenting a business card, you give it to your colleague so that it is readable for him as you hold it (he will, in turn, present his card so that it is readable for you). You may not receive a card in return. Smiling and other nonverbal forms of communication usually accompany the card exchange. Should you meet more than one individual at a reception, you may have a handful of cards when the greetings are over.

As the business card exchange usually precedes a sit-down meeting, it is important to arrange the cards you have received in a little seating plan in front of you along the top of the desk or table at your seat, reflecting the order in which people are seated. This will help you connect the correct names with the correct individuals throughout the meeting. Do this even if you are just meeting one person: it is expected. During the meeting, it is important never to play with the business cards (do not write on them), and when the meeting is over never put them in your back pants pockets: pick them up carefully and respectfully, and place them neatly in your cardholder or inside jacket pocket.

Do not photograph people without asking their permission, ever, and do not videotape freely. In some African countries, videotaping and photographing people and certain sites is illegal.

Communication Styles

Okay Topics / Not Okay Topics

Okay: anything that reflects your personal interests and hobbies and your sincere appreciation of and curiosity about things Senegalese and native to the West African world. Senegalese love and excel at soccer and traditional wrestling, as is the case throughout much of the region: expressing interest in Senegalese soccer teams is very definitely a positive. Interest in Senegalese music, folk art, food, and history will always be met with hours of information (if not a personal tour!). *Not okay:* politics, current events, or any subject that might in any way be controversial needs to be avoided at first. It is important to be sensitive to Senegal's unique history and not to give your opinions about any of Senegal's neighbors (especially Mauritania and Guinea-Bissau, with whom Senegal has had recent struggles), poverty, the challenge of Islamic fundamentalism to the secular state, ethnic rivalries, or religious differences. Do not inquire about a person's occupation or income in casual conversation, although it may be inquired of you (if so, this is generally just a way of getting to know more about your country, and not a personal investigation: answer specifically, and fully, with an explanation as to what things cost at home, why you do what you do, etc.). Other personal questions may be asked of you ("Why are you not married?" or "Do you have any sons?"); the best responses are those that fit the Senegalese context ("Allah has not blessed me yet, I wait patiently."). You may be complimented on your portliness (being heavy is a sign of wealth throughout most of the region) or told that you are too thin. Dismiss all compliments humbly but sincerely. Do not talk about sex or tell dirty jokes: it is in very bad taste. Discussions about your company and its work are very much appreciated, as they give Senegalese a chance to learn more about you and your firm. The goal of all conversation, at least at the beginning, is to create and maintain a harmonious atmosphere, despite the difficult or confrontational nature of the topic being discussed. At first, speak about things that you believe you have in common, so that you can build a personal connection that will go far toward maintaining a harmonious bridge between you. This is appropriate for both individuals and organizations. Abounding and humble courtesy is absolutely critical in all circumstances.

Tone, Volume, and Speed

The people of this region generally speak in soft, quiet, and restrained tones. Most Senegalese raise their voices only when it is necessary to display anger—and at that point, it is usually too late in the relationship. They may speak rapidly, but if you, in turn, speak rather slowly, they may get the hint and slow down.

Use of Silence

Passive silence—allowing time to pass simply without words—can be a form of proactive communication, and is used as a nonverbal way of avoiding confrontation, disagreement, or an unpleasant subject. If confronted with unexplainable silence, gently coax the conversation in a different direction, one that is more mutually harmonious.

Physical Gestures and Facial Expressions

Throughout the region, nonverbal behavior is part of the pattern of communication, and most Senegalese are very comfortable with nonverbal behavior. However, they may not understand many of the Western gestures; therefore, limit your own gestures until you are sure they are understood. Winking, whistling, and other similar displays are considered very vulgar. Public displays of familiarity and affection with the opposite sex are rarely expressed beyond holding hands. Never touch anyone on his or her head, even a child; this is considered the holiest part of the body. Do not point with or intentionally show the sole of your shoe to anyone: this is considered vulgar, as the bottom of the shoe touches the ground and is therefore the dirtiest part of the body. Any gesture involving a closed fist or made with the "thumbs-up" sign may be considered vulgar. Standing with your hands on your hips is considered aggressive and should always be avoided. Yawning in public is considered impolite; you must cover your mouth when you yawn (and some people touch the middle of their forehead with their right index finger after a yawn).

For any action or gesture that would naturally be done only with one hand, do not use your left hand, as this is considered the unclean hand (the hand used for personal hygiene). Pass all documents, business cards, food, and money with your right hand (if you're a southpaw, you will have to practice this). You must remove your shoes before entering a mosque (and some buildings, as well as most homes), and you may need to wash your feet and hands if there is an entrance fountain provided before entering a mosque as well. Women may be restricted to specific areas and times when visiting mosques. Women entering mosques need to have their heads covered, their legs covered to below the knee, and their arms covered to below the elbow; Western women do not necessarily need to have their faces covered. Smile whenever possible: it smoothes the way with strangers quickly and easily. Senegalese get someone's attention by snapping their fingers, and/or making a quiet hissing-type sound.

Waving and Counting

The thumb represents the number 1, the pinkie represents the number 5, with everything in between ordered from the thumb down; however, instead of raising the fingers when counting, the whole hand is exposed, and each finger is depressed as the counting is done. It is very insulting to beckon someone with the forefinger (instead, turn your hand so that the palm is facing down and motion inward with all four fingers at once). If you need to gesture for a waiter, very subtly raise your hand or make eye contact. Waving or beckoning is done with the palm down and the fingers moving forward and backward in a kind of scratching motion. It may seem as if the person making the gesture is saying good-bye to you when in fact you are being summoned over. If you need to point to something or someone, close your fingers, open your palm and face it upward, and pass your hand in the direction you want to indicate.

Physicality and Physical Space

Senegalese may stand closer than most North Americans are accustomed to; resist the urge to step back. Never speak with your hands in your pockets: keep them always firmly at your side when standing. If men and women must cross their legs when they sit, it must never be ankle over knee (for women, the preferred style is to cross ankle over ankle; but the bottom of the shoes must not show to the other person). Remember, even in public, formal is always better than informal, and this is essential when in front of elders or superiors of any kind: no gum-chewing, *ever;* don't slouch; men, take off your hat; and don't lean against things. Senegalese are most comfortable when they are next to other people: in a nearly empty bus, movie theater, or restaurant, in most cases, Senegalese will tend to sit next to or near the other person present, instead of far away from them. As is the case throughout the region, needing or wanting to be alone is suspect, and maintaining privacy by insisting on being alone is considered strange and possibly dangerous: Why would anyone want to be alone when he or she could be in the company of friends and family?

Eye Contact

Eye contact is typically not maintained when speaking, especially by subordinates when speaking with superiors, or juniors with elders. It is best to make eye contact at first, and then avert the eyes, as a sign of respect. Typically, one does not make eye contact while eating, and conversation is often kept to a minimum while eating. Tune up your nonverbal antennae.

Emotive Orientation

Senegalese are very warm, sensitive, friendly, and hospitable. They may not, however, be demonstrative, at least at first, as formal rules require a slow process of getting to know each other. Once people do know each other, however, there can be much touching (at least between members of the same sex) during even the most casual conversation. Two men or two women often walk hand in hand or arm in arm down the street. Verbal communication often employs effusiveness, exaggeration, and flowery phrases: this is meant to show sincerity, not duplicity. One should be especially careful not to interrupt others when they are speaking: a more thoughtful approach to conversation, in which you give the other person signals that he or she is being listened to rather than chime in quickly with your own thoughts, is much preferred throughout the entire region.

Protocol in Public

Walking Styles and Waiting in Lines

On the street, in stores, and in most public facilities, people pay little attention to maintaining orderly lines. Due to the volume of passengers on public transportation, there can be much pushing and jostling. This is not to get into a bus

ahead of someone else; it is merely to get in! This is not meant to be disrespectful; if it is bothersome, just say so politely, and you will be treated well. If you
ask a Senegalese for directions, he or she will make every effort to show you
the way (even if he or she is not that certain!).

Behavior in Public Places: Airports, Terminals, and the Market

Pride will always demand that Senegalese provide you with assistance; even if
they do not have an answer they will give you one. If you feel as if you are on
the outside, or being treated as a stranger, strike up a polite and respectful conversation: you will be treated honorably, and this is a wonderful way to start a
relationship (at first, men must only speak to men, and women must only speak
to women).

Establish a personal relationship with everyone you interact with, from
shopkeeper to government official, and you can expect much assistance as a
newcomer. Often this is one of the purposes for bargaining in the market: when
you do bargain, consider that your money is, in most cases, going to the upkeep
of entire families who live at susbsistence levels. When bargaining, keep in
mind also that it is generally considered good luck to be the first or last shopper
in a store or at a stall, so you might get a better price if you can manage to be
the first to arrive when they open or the last when they close. Stores in the cities
are open in the evenings and on weekends, as well as during the day, and market stores and stalls usually determine their own hours; government offices in
Senegal, however, and throughout the region, often open early (around 7 or
8 A.M.) and close early (around 3 or 4 P.M.). Many stores close during the Muslim Sabbath (Friday) and in preparation for it (Thursday nights), and on all
Muslim holidays. A personal verbal thank-you to store owners, waiters, chefs,
and hotel managers for their services is important, as it will help establish the
relationship you need to get continuing good service. Shopping doubles as a
social event, so plan to socialize as well as shop. Smoking is popular, for sure,
though not necessarily endemic, and you need not look for "no-smoking" areas,
as such formal rules can rarely be enforced (be sure not to smoke during the
day during Ramadan, when Muslims abstain; this is true for eating and drinking
during the day during Ramadan, as well, when in the presence of observant
Muslims). When and if you do smoke, it is critical that you offer a cigarette first
to everyone else at the table before you light up, and then offer to light their
cigarettes for them. Bathroom facilities are rare or nonexistent (with the exception of new Western-style hotels, and then only when the plumbing, electricity,
and other associated infrastructural requirements work, including telephones,
which may or may not be the case): be prepared (take toilet paper with you as
you travel about).

Unless they are in the company of other women, or close male relatives,
women generally do not go out in public alone, especially at night; Western
women traveling alone in Senegal will generally not have a problem but should
be prepared for the fact that this behavior is not typical in the region: some people won't know what to do or how to act toward them, some other women will
want to assist them, and certain men, no doubt, may try to take advantage of
them.

Bus / Metro / Taxi / Car

There are a few well-paved roads, mainly between the major cities; most transportation is by public bus (which is known by any number of different names in different countries throughout Africa) or private driver, for the elite, if they can afford to hire one. Do not attempt to drive alone in Africa. Driving almost anywhere is nearly impossible and subjects you to all sorts of dangers—civil, natural, and unnatural—and driving at night is suicide. Private cars are virtually unknown. Driving may be officially on the left or right (depending upon whether the country was influenced by the British or French during the colonial times), but more practically, such distinctions are irrelevant because cars are driven wherever they can be. Some trains do exist in certain areas, and planes are the best forms of transportation over long distances. Be prepared for chaotic and unplanned circumstances at almost all public transport facilities, including rail stations, bus depots, and airports. Most locals get around by bus, truck, or animal cart, or on foot. And remember, as is the case throughout the region, when the infrastructure doesn't work, rely on people: the best way, for example, to get a message through sometimes, is simply to pass it along to travelers, drivers, and others who are going in the direction of the person you want to communicate with.

The best way to catch a cab (which exist only in the capital city of Dakar) is at designated taxi stands (hotels are good places, but often charge more for the same ride: a hotel surcharge is added to the meter fare, in some cases). When a taxi has been hailed—and you do so in Senegal by holding out your arm—negotiate the price before you get in. Whenever possible, have the address you need to get to written down on a piece of paper (or use the business card of the person you are going to see, if you can) before you hail the cab.

Tipping

Tipping (the ubiquitous *baksheesh*—or *dash,* as it is more commonly referred to throughout West Africa) is universally required throughout the region, as a way to help get things done, and as a way of thanking people and being appreciative of the help they offer: it is more commonly a social gesture. Typically, it is a way of taking care of people; when abused, it is a form of graft that in some countries in the region represents a rampant form of corruption. It is traditional to always give a little something to someone who has helped you out. The offer may be refused at first in some cases, but if you insist, it will be graciously accepted and appreciated. Tips in restaurants run about 10 percent, and are typically not included in the bill (but double-check to be sure); a tip is not necessary if you have negotiated the fare for the taxi ahead of time, and already figured in the tip. For everything else, a few coins is all that is needed, but you should always have a lot of spare change handy to see you through the day. United States currency is generally greatly appreciated throughout the region; the Senegal currency is the CFA Franc.

Punctuality

Punctuality is valued, but not required. Consider timeliness a target. You should be relatively on time, but you may be kept waiting for quite awhile: patience and good humor are required. Never get upset over time. If you are late, you need not have an explanation. It will be understood.

Dress

The Senegalese native dress for men is the *boubou,* a long robe worn over baggy pants, and a loose-fitting shirt; the traditional dress for women is a long, wrap-around dress known as a sarong, plus a head wrap. The colors of the clothing can range from a single bright color or white to myriad patterns of bright colors. Senegalese women usually are not veiled, but if they have made the hajj, they often wear a white headcovering; such a symbol commands great respect. It is not appropriate for non-Senegalese to dress in traditional Senegalese clothes; Westerners should dress in conservative business clothes (as will many Senegalese businessmen) but may find it more comfortable to wear items that are as loose fitting as possible (the weather is hot). Never wear (and this is the case throughout most of Africa) anything that could be interpreted as a military uniform. Urban youth and Westernized people wear casual Western clothes (often secondhand from Europe or the United States). Men should not wear neck jewelry, even if it is not visible underneath clothing, although women often wear their wealth in the form of jewelry. Clothes must not be tight-fitting or revealing in any way, for men or women. If you're dressing casually, your shirt must be buttoned up to the neck. Western women should not wear pantsuits, as they reveal too much of the shape of the legs. Shoes are traditionally sandals or flip-flops. Westerners should avoid wearing any expensive clothes or jewelry: not only does it make you a potential mark for thieves, but it is ostentatious and can be seen as a sign of selfishness and colonialist exploitation.

Personal Hygiene

In Senegal, cleanliness is associated with purity, and most Senegalese bathe at least twice a day if they can. Washing both hands and feet more than once a day is very common, and one must wash hands before and after eating every meal. Senegalese enjoy perfumes and henna skin designs. Do not blow your nose in public: it is considered very rude. Spitting does occur on the street, but also is regarded as rude.

Dining and Drinking

Mealtimes and Typical Foods

The typical Senegalese diet is rich in grains—usually rice—breads, fresh vegetables, and fruits. Meats are not that common but can include lamb, goat, and chicken; fish is more likely as a source of animal protein. Each ethnic group has its own specialties and preferences, and remember, Muslims will not eat pork or drink alcohol (although it is available). Typically, dishes revolve around rice with a sauce of vegetables, fish, or meat, or combinations thereof. *Yassa,* for example, is a popular dish made of rice and chicken in a spicy sauce; *thiebou dien* is a fish and rice stew (mainly eaten as a luncheon dish). The national Wolof dish is *mbaxal-u-saloum* (peanuts, fish, tomatoes, and spices over rice). Foods can be spiced, but are not necessarily hot. The peanut, introduced by

Western colonialists, and better known in West Africa as the "ground nut," is a major crop in Senegal and a staple ingredient in much of the cuisine.

A note on hosting and dining with Muslims: If you are serving a meal at home, be sure you do not use alcohol or pork in any of the dishes. If you do, labeling the dish and serving it separately will still make your Muslim guest uncomfortable: simply don't do it. You, as a guest in the more rural regions, may be rewarded with the opportunity to dine first or be offered the favored food, such as the meat: please consider that this may mean that others in the family do not eat this. If you are offered something you cannot eat or drink, acknowledge the honor, and suggest that while you will always hold the honor in your heart, you in turn will bestow it on someone who can also appreciate it in his or her belly: then pass the honored dish on to a Senegalese colleague. Alternately, you may say thank you but that you have just eaten or drunk. You will never be denied food if it is available, but consider the dire malnutrition and difficulty in obtaining adequate nourishment in this part of the world.

Breakfast is served from about 6 to 9 A.M., lunch from 12 to 2 P.M., and dinner from 8 to 10 P.M., although at the "hungry times" of the year (usually just before the harvest), many people make do with just two meals per day. Traditionally, children, women, and men dine separately, and men are offered the best parts first, women next, and children typically last.

It is very important to remove your shoes before entering a Senagalese home, and when seated to always make sure that your toes and feet are not pointing to the food or to others at the meal. Desserts usually consist of fruit, with or without some milk, honey, or yogurt.

Regional Differences

Remember, Islam prohibits the use of pork, and most meats of any kind for Muslims need to be prepared *halal* (meat slaughtered according to Islamic prescriptions). Do not eat in front of your Muslim colleagues, or invite them to join you for a meal, during the day during Ramadan, as Muslims typically fast (and refrain from drinking and smoking) during the day, and feast with family and friends at night. Ramadan lasts for a lunar month: this is simply not a good time to do business or go out entertaining in the Muslim world. If you visit a Senegalese home, you may be invited to share a kola nut: it has a mild stimulant, like caffeine, and sharing one is a common way of passing the time.

Typical Drinks and Toasting

Tea and coffee are available in most places. When you come to a Senegalese home, even for just a brief visit, you will most likely be served tea, usually in a round of three cups: typically, the first is unsweetened, the second with some sugar, and the third one very sweet, mirroring the development of the friendship as you get to know each other. Always accept the cup of tea and/or coffee, even if you only put it to your lips or just take a few sips. Your cup will always be refilled if it is less than half full. Typically, beer and other alcoholic drinks are not served: fruit juices and lemonade, along with tea, may accompany meals (but at most meals it is considered impolite to drink and eat at the same time: first you eat, then you drink). You must never pour your own drink; wait patiently to be served.

If you are the honored guest, you are not expected to make a statement or toast, but if you offer a small compliment, it will be appreciated (and then dismissed as unnecessary); you can do this at the end of the meal, just before everyone departs. An appropriate comment would be to wish for the health of the host and all those present; always be humble.

Avoid drinking tap water anywhere in the region. This means you should brush your teeth with bottled water and not take ice in any of your drinks; drink only bottled water, or brewed tea or coffee or soft drinks; and avoid getting water from the morning shower into your mouth. Never eat fresh fruits or vegetables that cannot be peeled first, and ideally cooked later before eating. This is a serious matter: there are some very nasty—and sometimes deadly—bugs going around in developing countries. In addition, avoid all dairy products except in the finest hotels, as the required refrigeration may be questionable. Do not swim in freshwater lakes, ponds, or rivers (the Guinea worm is a particular problem in this region, along with many other parasitic infections).

Table Manners and the Use of Utensils

Before meals, you must wash your hands, and wash them again when the meal is over. Traditionally, one eats with one's right hand from a communal plate or bowl (or set of plates and/or bowls). Never use your left hand unless you are eating something that clearly requires two hands; occasionally you may be offered a spoon or fork, which also must be held in the right hand. Keep your left hand off of any bowls or serving items. If there is only one communal bowl, it is appropriate for the youngest person present to hold the lip of the bowl with the thumb and index finger of their left hand while the elders partake first (men first, women second, children last). Eat only from the part of the communal plate or bowl that is directly in front of you. Some people may dip their index finger into the food first and taste it: this is an old tradition of making sure that the food is safe to eat and has become a replacement for saying a small prayer before eating. You may be seated either on the floor or on low stools. Do not smoke in the same area where the food is being served, and wait to smoke until after the meal is finished (women do not smoke). At the end of the meal, a small burp signifies satisfaction, after which some praise to the cook and thankfulness to Allah for the food is a welcome gesture.

Seating Plans

The most honored position is next to the host. Most entertaining is done in people's homes: in fact, except for very high-level government or corporate (usually multinational) events, restaurants are considered inappropriate and too "cold" for getting to know each other well enough to build a relationship (and maybe do business). The home, the market, or a local café is where people meet, socialize, and get things done, including business (although business is not easily done in the market). Your spouse might be invited with you to a meal at home, especially if the spouse of the host will be there, which will probably be the case. The invitation will then be phrased, "My spouse invites your spouse," and women and men will eat separately. By the way, invitations, business or social, will almost always be verbal, not written.

At Home, in a Restaurant, or at Work

The honored guest is served first, then the oldest male, then the rest of the men, then women, and finally children. Do not begin to eat or drink anything until the oldest male at the table has been served and has begun. At the end of the meal, it is appropriate to thank the host or hostess for a wonderful meal.

In informal restaurants, you may be required to share a table. If so, do not force conversation: act as if you are seated at a private table. Women should be sensitive to the fact that they may be seated only with other women. Waitstaff may be summoned by subtly raising your hand or by making eye contact; waving or calling their names is very impolite. Since business and socializing in this part of the world is usually one and the same, business is often discussed over meals, once individuals know each other well enough to talk terms. Take your cue from your Senegalese associates: if they bring up business, then it's okay to discuss it, but wait to take your lead from their conversation.

Once inside the home, do not wander around. If you move from one area to another in a Senegalese home or restaurant, be sure to always allow more senior members of your party to enter the room ahead of you.

Being a Good Guest or Host

Paying the Bill

Usually the one who does the inviting pays the bill. Thanks and compliments are not easily given or received, since it is believed that there is no need to say such things between trusted friends and family; nevertheless, it is important to state humble thanks, and to accept thanks graciously.

Transportation

It's important to make sure that guests have a way to return from where they came, if they are visiting; by the same token, you want to be sure not to put your host out by not having made such arrangements ahead of time for yourself, if and when you visit. If invited into a home, you may also be invited to spend the night, and if so, you must be careful to keep a low profile and use as few resources as possible. If cars are arranged, it will typically be at very high-level government functions, and in such cases, when seeing your guests off, you must remain at the entrance of the house or restaurant, or at the site where you deposited your guests into the car, until the car is out of sight: it is very important not to leave until your guests can no longer see you, should they look back. Guests are seated in cars (and taxis) by rank, with the honored guest being placed in the back directly behind the front passenger seat; the next honored position is in the back behind the driver, and the least honored position is up front with the driver.

When to Arrive / Chores to Do

If invited to dinner at a private home, do offer to help with the chores or in any other way you can. Do not leave the meal area unless invited to do so. When in the home, be careful not to admire something too effusively: Senegalese may feel obligated to give it to you, and doing so might represent a great sacrifice. Your compliments will most likely be dismissed. Remember also that Senegalese consider it bad luck to have their children praised: it can bring ill fortune to them (comment on the children indirectly, but comment on them positively).

Gift Giving

In general, gift giving is not that common for social occasions, but is common in business situations between trusted colleagues. It is not only done as a gesture of thanks, but as a way of helping to ensure good business relations in the future (be careful not to go overboard here, as a gift that looks like an obvious bribe may land you in quite a bit of trouble . . . with the authorities in your home country, more than likely). In business settings, this usually takes the form of a personal gift that symbolically says the correct thing about the nature of the relationship. When going to the region on business, bringing a gift for the key decision maker is enough. Your gift does not have to be elaborate or expensive, but it should, whenever possible, be personalized (representative of the personalities of the receiver or giver or of an aspect of the relationship). Present your gift when you arrive in the country; before you leave to return home, you will receive a farewell gift, usually at this last meeting. When Senegalese visit your country, they will also bring you a gift, and before they leave, you should give them farewell gifts.

The most appropriate gift for a personal visit to a home, or as a thank-you for dinner, would be a box of fruits, coffee, or nuts, and something for the children, such as a toy, picture books, or school supplies (paper and writing utensils and calculators, with a supply of batteries, are very valued). A man typically only gives a gift to a man, a woman to a woman; remember, any gift given by a man to a woman must come with the caveat that it is from his wife/sister/ mother, or else it is far too personal. Do not give alcohol (and this includes perfumes or colognes made with alcohol), pork, art or photographs that depict natural scenes or people (this runs counter to Islamic beliefs that man must not attempt to reproduce in an image what God has made), or cutlery (which symbolizes the severing of a relationship). A fine gift for a Muslim would be a silver compass, so that he will always know which direction to face when he says his daily prayers (Muslims must face Mecca no matter where in the world they are when they say their prayers).

For both giving and receiving gifts, two hands are used always. Gifts may or may not be opened by the receiver in front of the giver (this depends upon the nature of the gift, more often than not: foodstuffs meant for dessert, for example, will be opened for all to enjoy); the presenter typically first offers the gift humbly and as an incidental aside, then, usually received after some imploring, it is acknowledged and accepted.

Gifts should be wrapped, but special gift-wrapping is not necessary (nor readily available; it will probably be used again for some additional purpose). By the way, if you have a copy of the Qu'ran (given or received as a gift or not), never place it on the floor or below any object: it must be the highest book on the shelf. Do not give a copy of the Qu'ran as a gift: it is far too significant for a business or social acknowledgment.

Special Holidays and Celebrations

Major Holidays

Avoid doing business during the entire month of Ramadan. Some towns have different local holidays as well, so double-check with your Senegalese associates before making final travel plans.

Islamic holidays are celebrated by most Muslims. Islamic holidays are on the lunar calendar, so the dates change each year, and all holidays begin at sundown the day before.

The most important Islamic holidays are (in order of their usual occurrence):

Ramadan	
Korite	The celebration of the end of the fast at the end of Ramadan
Tabaski	The Feast of the Sacrifice, celebrating Abraham's willingness to sacrifice his son
Hajj	The first day of the annual pilgrimage to Mecca
Mawloud	Birth of the Prophet Muhammad
Tamkharit	Islamic New Year (also an official secular holiday)

Secular and additional holidays:

January 1	New Year's Day
March/April	Easter
April 4	Independence Day
May 1	Labor Day
June	Ascension
August	Whitmonday
November 1	All Saints' Day
December 25	Christmas

Business Culture

Daily Office Protocols

The Senegalese office may be a modern office in an urban building or a traditional stall near the market, but no matter where it is, you can be sure there will be many people coming and going. This is not so much a statement about your unimportance as much as it is a statement about the importance of your host: that he is needed by many, and that in the polychronic culture, things are handled in order of their importance, and not according to the clock. Be patient. In the Senegalese business organization, hierarchy is strictly observed. Because faithful Muslims pray five times a day, you will need to adjust your schedules to accommodate their needs. Usually, prayers are given upon awakening and at noontime, midday, dusk, and before retiring; this means that at least twice during the workday, there will be time out for prayers. The prayer break usually lasts a short ten or fifteen minutes, and any quiet area will do. If you accidentally interrupt a Muslim during his prayers, just walk quietly away: there's no need for complicated explanations or apologies. Most organizations have prayer rooms set off to the side, with carpets. In addition, devout Muslims will not work on Friday (the Muslim Sabbath), and in fact begin to end work early on Thursday, before sundown. The official workweek is Saturday though Thursday, 9 A.M. to 4 P.M. Remember to present your business card with the right hand only.

Management Styles

Titles and education are very important, and the highest ones (e.g., vice president) are usually reserved for very senior, executive-level positions, and should not be used as casually as they are in the United States. Any criticism of Senegalese workers must be done very carefully, even privately. Deference is shown by subordinates to their seniors; paternalistic concern is often shown by seniors to their subordinates. Superiors are very sensitive to inquiring about their subordinate's opinions; however, once a decision is made, the superiors are followed, often unquestioningly. If you are doing business with the correct person, things will probably move quickly; it is essential, therefore, to have a good and trustworthy Senegalese contact who can make the necessary contacts for you (you can locate these people through consular and/or trade association contacts prior to your trip). Let this person take the time he needs to do this for you, for if you pressure him into making contacts sooner, he may connect you to someone who is not as useful as the one he was originally waiting for: this will not serve you. Again, be patient. Never use time as a means of pressure.

Boss-Subordinate Relations

The decision-making system usually works from the top on down, with key decisions often coming from individuals in high positions of power. Superiors are expected to provide clear and fully informed sets of instructions: that is their responsibility, and it is the responsibility of subordinates to carry out those instructions. Consequently, "management-by-objective" and other egalitarian and individually empowered management styles often may not work in this environment: without clear instruction from above, subordinates often will do nothing. They also lose respect for the manager for not making the decisions he should be making.

Conducting a Meeting or Presentation

There will be much hosting by your Senegalese contacts of tea, coffee, and soft drinks. When serving any refreshments in the office, be sure they are served in porcelain, glass, or silver tea sets: the use of paper or Styrofoam shows disrespect and is very bad form. There may be many more people at the meeting than you were expecting: this is typically because there are many more people who need to be consulted about the decision regarding you and your business; in most cases, you will be introduced to everyone. If you are not introduced to them, do not ask to be: acknowledge them with a smile and a nod, and proceed with your meeting. If you are meeting with a decision maker, the discussions will probably be direct, forthright, and businesslike. If you do not know the decision-making authority of the person you are with, assume that you will need to meet with many people, and perhaps repeat much of the same discussions each time with different people. There may be many interruptions throughout the meeting; stay calm and flexible. Business is personal throughout the region: decision makers have got to know your face. Patience and third-party connections are key.

Negotiation Styles

At first, expect no decisions from your Senegalese colleagues at the table, and be willing to provide copious amounts of information, to the degree that you can, in response to their questions and in anticipation of their needs. Presentations should be well-prepared and simply propounded. Details are best left to questions and backup material, which should be available in French, and left behind. Such materials need to be simple, to the point, and interesting to look at. Unless you already have a well-established relationship, agendas need to be very broad and very flexible: everything unexpected will occur, and everything you did not plan to discuss will be brought up. Should you come with other team members, make sure that your roles are well-coordinated. Never disagree with each other in front of Senegalese or appear uncertain, unsure, not authorized to make a decision, or out of control in any way.

Most Senegalese love to bargain and see this process as a way of getting to know you: it does not imply insincerity to offer one price and then change your mind later (as it often does with Pacific Rim cultures). In fact, avoiding this process will generate suspicion. Final terms must be fair to all (win-win). Remember to confirm what might sound like agreement with multiple inquiries: communication patterns often include reassurance, when in fact, your local associates may not be completely in agreement with you. Contracts and contract law are helpful, but ultimately useless: unless you are working with a well-known multinational or high government offices (and even there, contracts will be, in the end, unenforceable), it is better to keep the agreement to a short statement of mutual intent. If possible, the deal should be sealed with a celebratory meal. Keep communications open, especially when at a distance, and stay in touch often with your Senegalese associates: share more information than you normally would, not less, and be prepared to make many trips, as needed.

Written Correspondence

Your business letters should be informal and warm, and reflect the personal relationship you have established. Nevertheless, they must include a recognition of any titles and rank. Given names usually are written in uppercase; dates are given using the day/month/year format (with periods in between, not slashes). In business correspondence with Senegalese colleagues, unless you know you are writing to an observant Muslim, it is appropriate to use Western dates and business writing styles. When writing names, an honorific plus the title is as common as an honorific plus the first name (unless they are Westernized, in which case it is appropriate to use typical Western form). You should write your e-mails, letters, and faxes in an informal, friendly, and warm manner: use a brief and warm personal introduction, and segue smoothly into business. Keep the business issues and language clear and simple, however, and bulletpoint and outline all important matters. Use the Western format (name, position, company, street address, city, state/province, country, postal code) for the addresses.

THE GAMBIA

Note: Refer to the previous section on Senegal for information about general West African cultural behaviors; the material that follows describes country-specific variations on general West African customs.

Some Historical Context

Although the official name of this country is The Gambia (an allusion to its role in the Senegambia region), for convenience purposes, we will simply refer, as is done in the region, to "Gambia" and "Gambians." This tiny, elongated country that straddles the Gambia river was once part of Senegambia, and has had an on-again, off-again relationship with its geographically enveloping neighbor, Senegal. More united and cooperative than combative, these two countries nevertheless do have their differences, mainly historical, despite their overarching similarities. Although the Portuguese were the first Europeans to navigate the West African coast, the British made Gambia their protectorate, until independence was granted in the 1960s. There is a strong European influence still in Gambia, in business and tourism: the beaches are beautiful, and many Europeans vacation there; Gambian familiarity and comfort with non-African visitors is expressed in their term *tarranga,* loosely translated as "the pleasure of hosting guests."

An Area Briefing

Politics and Government

As is the pattern with other countries in the region, the federal government commands the least interest and loyalty of the people: the local chief, or *Alikalo,* has most of the power and is sought when important decisions need to be made. Developing a relationship with the local Alikalo is important if one is attempting business in Gambia.

Religion and Demographics

Most Gambians are Muslim, although about 15 percent are Christian. Most of the various groups within Gambia get along well, but do stay separate in their customs and beliefs. Following most of the Islamic behaviors and codes is the most appropriate expectation, so plan to behave as advised in other Muslim countries. The indigenous Gambian people are far more diverse than those in Senegal. Mainly Black Africans, living mostly in four small groups that had staked out their territorial claims long ago along the Gambia River, they are Mandinkas (descendants of the great Mali empire of the fourteenth century), Fulanis (from the Guinean forests to the southeast), Wolofs (from the Senegambia to the north), and Serrahules (from the coast and the north). There are other smaller ethnic groups as well.

Greetings and Introductions

Language and Basic Vocabulary

As a result of Gambia's history with Britain, English is the official language, although most people speak their local indigenous language as a first language. Wolof is the second language (it is the main indigenous language and the language of business and commerce), and French—necessary for dealing with neighbors—is taught in the upper grades at school. Most of the Gambian languages are oral, although there are efforts to create scripts, mainly in Arabic and Latin, for Wolof and other languages.

Honorifics for Men, Women, and Children

Gambians greet elders by stating their first name, and may then repeat the last name several times. As is the custom throughout the region, mainly only first, or given, names are used in greetings, along with an appropriate honorific, which usually reflects the relationship between the two individuals speaking. Nicknames are very popular, and children commonly refer to an elder as either "aunt" or "uncle," or if close, "mother" and "father," even if they technically are not.

Physical Greeting Styles

Despite the general proscription against using the left hand, it is appropriate when saying good-bye to someone to shake hands with the left hand, as a special way of wishing them a safe journey (it is not a casual or common gesture, and is generally reserved for special good-byes).

Dress

Gambians wear conservative, informal Western dress, and Westerners in Gambia should do the same (do not wear traditional Gambian dress). Traditional Gambian dress for men includes the *chaya* (the loosely fitting pants, usually with a drawstring waist), plus the long robe (*haftan*); women wear the *deppeh* or *dendiko ba* (a long, colorful wraparound dress), plus a head wrap.

Dining and Drinking

Foods are similar to those previously mentioned for the region; the kola nut is a special treat, often shared between friends.

Special Holidays and Celebrations

Major Holidays

Gambians celebrate most major Islamic holidays. The official national holidays are:

January 1	New Year's Day
February 18	Independence Day
March/April	Easter
May 1	Labor Day
July 22	Celebration of President Jammeh's Victory
December 25	Christmas

GUINEA-BISSAU

Some Historical Context

Once united with the nearby Cape Verde Islands, Guinea-Bissau today is an independent nation that struggled fiercely right into the second half of the twentieth century to free itself of its colonial status from Portugal. Consequently, one of the hallmarks of Guinea-Bissaun behavior is a remarkably united and almost nationalistic pride among all the diverse peoples of the country, as Guinea-Bissauans: there may be differences between the many ethnic groups of the country, but they are subordinated to the greater goal of getting along with each other, once united in opposition to the Portuguese. This stands in contrast to patterns in neighboring countries of disintegration into ethnic clashes after independence. There is relatively little crime, begging, or homelessness, despite the desperate poverty of the country; individual families and ethnic groups take care of their own.

An Area Briefing

Religion and Demographics

Guinea-Bissau has been described as the melting pot of West Africa, with all the regional groups—Mandinke, Mande, Fulani, Papel, Bijago, and others—represented; perhaps the largest group are the Balanta people. The religious affiliations are as diverse as the ethnic groups; approximately 30 percent of the people are Muslim, about 10 percent Christian, but the majority of the people are animist. There is a popular animist belief in *Irans,* or local spirits that can be invoked to help one communicate with the greater creator God: praying to and contacting particular Irans on behalf of individuals seeking help and assistance is the responsibility of local religious chiefs.

Greetings and Introductions

Language and Basic Vocabulary

Although Portuguese is the official lingua franca, hardly anyone uses it, and most Guinea-Bissauans speak their indigenous language, or a kind of Creole (or Kriolu as it is known in the country), which is a blend of the main indigenous languages and Portuguese.

Physical Greeting Styles

Greetings must be long and involved, and often people hold each other's hands throughout entire conversations as a sign of sincerity and friendship.

Communication Styles

Physical Gestures and Facial Expressions

Guinea-Bissauan point with their chin or outstretched tongue (they are not insulting you when they put their tongue out!); pointing with fingers or the hand is prohibited. Indicating agreement is often demonstrated by clucking the tongue once or twice, indicating disagreement by making several clicking sounds in the mouth.

Special Holidays and Celebrations

Major Holidays

Official Guinea-Bissauan holidays (in addition to Muslim-celebrated Islamic holidays, and a Christian-celebrated Carnival in mid-February) are:

January 1	New Year's Day
January 20	National Heroes' Day
March 8	International Women's Day
March/April	Easter
May 1	International Workers' Day (Labor Day)
August 3	Martyrs of Colonialism Memorial Day
September 24	Independence Day
November 14	Guinean Background Opportunity Day (celebration of Guinean identity)
December 25	Christmas

GUINEA

Some Historical Context

Today's Guinea is the heartland of black West Africa, and although once part of the greater kingdoms of the region (Upper Guinea was once part of the Ghana, Mali, and Songhai empires), Guinea stands alone as having, relatively recently, established its own great empire in the region.

Samory Touré was the Guinean who, in the mid-1800s, spread Islam throughout Guinea and, in the process, helped to create a united, powerful, and successful society. Although the Fulo (Fulani) who migrated into the Guinean region from the Gulf Atlantic area brought Islam with them in the sixteenth century, it was Samory Touré who, through Islam and his many skills, brought a powerful country together. Additionally, Touré stands as one of the first African "freedom fighters" against the colonialists (in his case, the French). Ultimately, he was captured, and Guinea became just another part of French West Africa. But this legacy of resistance and proud independence remained: Guinea was the only French colony to vote itself out of the developing French community of associated Francophone (French-speaking) African states, and in so doing isolated itself from its neighbors and much of the Western world. The result has been difficult for Guinea, in terms of its development, but the people are united by their history and the resulting strong nationalist identity, and by Islam.

An Area Briefing

Religion and Demographics

Guinea has a complex mix of peoples (about 40 percent Fulo, or local descendants of the greater Fulani group, the Malinke, and the Soussou), speaking many indigenous languages, united in Islam (about 85 percent of the population, the remainder being mainly animist), and French-influenced (France was the main colonial power). Originally, the Malinke (Mandingo) settled in Upper Guinea, the Sousso along the coast, and the Fulo in the interior.

Greetings and Introductions

Language and Basic Vocabulary

French is the official language of government and business, but local people mainly speak their own indigenous languages (Soussou, Pular, Malinke, and others), and Arabic phrases (as greetings, or to give thanks) are used in daily life by many. There is also a significant population of refugees from the civil wars of neighboring Liberia and Sierra Leone, who speak Krio, their version of Creole, and this too has influenced the language spoken by many Guineans.

Special Holidays and Celebrations

Major Holidays

In addition to all major Islamic holidays, national Guinean holidays are:

January 1	New Year's Day
May 1	Labor Day
October 2	Independence Day
November 1	All Saints' Day
December 25	Christmas (the week between Christmas and the New Year is celebrated by all Guineans)

SIERRA LEONE and LIBERIA

Some Historical Context

In contrast to its neighbor Guinea, to the north, one of the great influences on the development of both Liberian and Sierra Leone culture was the role that both of these nations played in the Atlantic Slave trade, and the developing African-American culture of North America (Africans who were sent as slaves to South America mainly came from Angola and South Africa; however, Senegal and Sierra Leone were major slave export stations for North America and the Caribbean). In fact, the Gullah people of the U.S. Carolina coast are descendants of the slaves from Sierra Leone. While Sierra Leone was a British colony (originally explored, however, by the Portuguese, who named the area for the massive cliffs—or "lion mountains"—that rise from the sea along the coast) originally set up to exploit the vast natural resources of the country (mainly diamonds and other mineral wealth), Liberia was established primarily and exclusively as a homeland for returning African-Americans: today, most Sierra Leonians are ethnic Africans; many Liberians are descendants of returned African-Americans.

An Area Briefing

Politics and Government

Liberia was established, uniquely and primarily, as a nation precisely for the repatriation of African-Americans to Africa, in response to the development of the Pan-African movement in the 1800s in North America and Britain (it is important to note that the territory of Liberia was also a slave depot during the slave trade, and Sierra Leone was also a center for the repatriation of European—mainly British—Africans). The unique and unusual histories of both countries have resulted in massive social, political, and economic dislocation. Isolated and often rebuked by its neighbors and the West, Liberia and Sierra Leone have collapsed into violent states of anarchy and what appears to be endless cycles of civil war. Essentially, the influence of the strong British missionary and trade presence in Sierra Leone virtually destroyed most of the preexisting indigenous social fabric, and the U.S. and European Pan-African movements' vision of Liberia as a homeland for repatriated African-Americans was ultimately unsupported by the United States: this resulted in a cultural vacuum for both countries. Essentially, the ruthless colonial mercantilism that replaced indigenous Sierra Leonian culture, and the anarchic vacuum of Liberia, has created a larger culture of warring thugs and gangs, each staking their own claim to both the vast diamond wealth of Sierra Leone, and for Liberian support, of their respective claims. The struggle reveals in bold relief the fact that most of Africa's internecine struggles, while sometimes apparently ethnic-based, are really about power and wealth, and in the case of Sierra Leone, diamonds. In fact, while it is perhaps the worst place in the world to be right now, Sierra Leone has vast potential to be an incredibly wealthy nation: who controls the diamond wealth is the source of the conflict.

Religion and Demographics

There are two major ethnic groups in Sierra Leone: the Mende in the north and the Temne in the south. Most people are either Christian or Muslim (there has been, up until recently, a strong Lebanese business community, mainly Shi'ite, although most Muslims in Sierra Leone are Sunni), and elements of both infuse the other, along with many animist beliefs. Hostility and distrust between the groups, and the overarching culture of civil gangsterism, has reinforced the importance of allegiance and membership to groups on whom one can rely: there is a strong tradition in Sierra Leone and Liberia of secret societies to which most people claim membership (known in Liberia as *Poro* for men, and *Sande* for women).

Greetings and Introductions

Language and Basic Vocabulary

Because of the strong British- and American-influenced culture, English is the official language of both countries, but local indigenous languages (mainly Mende or Temne) are spoken in Sierra Leone, and a kind of Creole, or *Krio,* as it is known, is the major language spoken in Liberia.

Sierra Leonians address friends as *"padi,"* and greet each other with the phrase "I say." Muslim customs have infused daily behavior of both Christians and Muslims, so the proscriptions referred to in earlier sections on interpersonal and communication styles generally apply. When meeting an elder or someone to whom one wants to show particular respect, it is not uncommon to shake hands, supporting one's right elbow with one's left hand. Socializing (or "keeping time" as it is referred to) is done differently by the different groups in both countries, but because of the familiarity with both British and Western ways,

Westerners should not encounter unfamiliar practices. The greatest difficulty for both countries today is day-to-day survival, and visiting, for business or pleasure, is a difficult option in either nation.

Dress

Most people today dress in Western clothes, but there is the traditional Sierra Leonian *lappas,* worn by women, which is a long dress, tied at the waist and worn with a blouse and a head wrap. Men wear traditional *gara* shirts (colorful shirts made from a local cottonlike plant).

CÔTE D'IVOIRE

Some Historical Context

Because Britain and other European countries were already finding their sources for the slave trade elsewhere along the coast, the area that became Côte d'Ivoire was overlooked, and a vacuum was created for the French to eventually move in. When they did, they did so as traders, and after a long and vicious war with the Malinke warrior Samory Toure, they eventually claimed the territory as their own. Côte d'Ivoire was one of Africa's first great post-colonial success stories, through the almost iron will of one man, Félix Houphouët-Boigny, who, by focusing on developing the agricultural sector (a significantly different strategy from that used by neighboring West African countries, where the focus was on developing a manufacturing and industrial base), was able to lift the majority of the population out of poverty and create the independent nation of Côte d'Ivoire peacefully out of the French colony that it was, without alienating France (in fact, by inviting their involvement through investment). In twenty years, Côte d'Ivoire became the world's largest producer of cocoa, and Africa's greatest exporter of coffee, pineapple, palm oil, and cotton. Abidjan, the commercial capital, exploded, fueled by the economy and massive immigration from up-country. Today, the city is known as the Paris of West Africa, and is heavily influenced, architecturally and culturally, by its French traditions. In response partly to the country's newfound wealth, and partly to the admiration engendered by many of his people, and, no doubt, partly to ego, Houphouët-Boigny literally built a new administrative capital, Yamoussoukro, a "castle-city" of bureaucrats and a testament to the power of one single man. However, the shakeout from the collapse of the boom times in the 1980s has resulted in a more subdued atmosphere, replacing what was, for much of the second half of the twentieth century, a sometimes exploding economy, replete with all the excesses, corruption, and social dislocation associated with such growth in a developing nation.

An Area Briefing

Religion and Demographics

Because the indigenous groups in the country primarily emigrated to the region several centuries ago, indigenous is a debatable term. The major groups today are the Krou (from the Liberia and Sierra Leone region), the Akan (from neighboring Ghana), and the Malinke (from the northwest and Guinea); there are many local indigenous subgroups of these major groups (such as the Dan, who live in the upland mountains and are renowned for their carvings, art, and masks). Most Ivoirians speak their local indigenous languages, as well as French, which is the national language; English is spoken by many businesspeople.

Although French patterns of colonialization typically include strong imposition of French culture on day-to-day patterns of life, Catholicism never really took root among the people. Today, despite the cathedrals and official remnants of the French colonial past, Catholicism is practiced by about only 15 percent of the population; the rest are Muslim (about 25 percent) and animist, although there is a unique form of Christianity, founded by a Liberian, William Wade Harris, in the 1800s, which is an amalgam of Christian and animist beliefs; unsurprisingly, followers are known as Harristes.

Dining and Drinking

Ivoirian cuisine is a combination of French and local traditions, resulting in the imaginative use of three basic ingredients and the associated local bounty of the country: rice, *foutou* (a dough made of yams, cassava, or plantain, pounded into a sticky pasta), and *attieke* (grated, fluffed cassava, used as a grain, and not unlike couscous). They are served with local vegetables, meats, fish, and any number of incredibly sweet or savory sauces, very French-influenced in some cases. Ivoirians in the cities enjoy dining outside (in the tradition of French cafés) and at local roadside stands known as *maquis* (versions of which can be found throughout all of West Africa). Because of the development of the modern city of Abiajan (yes, there are skyscrapers and high-fashion stores on French-designed boulevards, with Mercedeses purring through the streets!) and the influence of the West (West Africa's most luxurious high-rise hotel, The Ivory, is located here), socializing and business can occur patterned very much after Western ways: nevertheless, it will be influenced by West African traditions and customs, and it is this very Ivoirian combination of a not-too-indigenous indigenous culture and a strong Western influence that makes Côte d'Ivoire slightly different from its neighbors.

The West African Gulf: Nigeria, Ghana, Togo, Benin, and Burkina Faso

NIGERIA

Some Introductory Background on Nigeria and the Nigerians

One of the largest countries in West Africa, Nigeria also claims to have the largest number of diverse peoples in the region, and there is an enormous diversity of beliefs and languages, as well as a large and growing population. It is precisely this fact that gives Nigeria its unique identity: it wasn't one single country, or even a unified region, until after it received its independence from Britain in the 1960s. Even when Britain made it a protectorate of the United Kingdom, the protectorate was defined as only the region along the coast and around what has now become the commercial center of Lagos (the capital of Nigeria is Abuja, but most of the life of the country is centered in Lagos); the rest of what was to become Nigeria was still an amalgam of many different ethnic groups, with varying levels of tensions between them. Nigeria's future success, of course, was based on the discovery of massive amounts of oil offshore and in the Delta region (where the three rivers of the country converge into an outlet onto the Atlantic Ocean). However, independence was new, and democracy even newer, and in the absence of a representative system for all groups in the country the oil boom quickly became a vehicle for corruption; instead of fueling a wealthy economy for all Nigerians, it was used to fuel the goals of one ethnic group over the other. Nigerian corruption became notorious (even today, Western businesses need to be very careful operating in Nigeria, as scams and rip-offs, not to mention real dangers, abound). The degree to which Nigerians can solve their simmering ethnic differences and establish a fair democracy for all will go a long way to solving some of the critical issues facing the country. As it stands, there is still much resentment among the groups, with a growing Islamic fundamentalism in the north increasingly being put forward as the solution to the problems. Nevertheless, Nigeria stands as a powerful symbol of what Africa can be, and the indigenous traditions of some of its remarkable peoples, as we shall see, provide the rest of the world with some interesting African-based solutions to some of the world's most intractable political problems.

Some Historical Context

It's important to appreciate that Nigeria lies at yet another critical cultural dividing line in Africa—that between the West African world of Black Africans of the Malinke, Mali, and Guinean cultures and the Bantu Black African world of equatorial and southern Africa. As we move down the gulf, we will see this line being drawn more distinctly in such places as Cameroon and Gabon. Prior to the British protectorate, the region was ruled by various empires of varying and changing size: in Paleolithic times, the Nok people were indigenous to the region, but the first great modern indigenous empire were the Hausa people (now located in the north of the country): they were the first to convert to Islam in the thirteenth century, and one of their enduring legacies was the creation of a highly stratified and very powerful feudal system, which is still in place today. Along with the Hausa, the Fulani proselytized Islam and created a powerful empire of their own in the 1800s; before their powerful presence, the Yoruba (their kingdom was known as the kingdom of the Oyo) presided over the southwest (and into what is today Togo), and the Ibo of the southeast remained, as they are in many ways today, isolated and very independent (they have attempted to secede in the past and form their own independent Republic of Biafra). When the British came, they quickly associated mainly with the Yoruba, who, along with the Dahomey people of what is now the country of Benin, mastered a well-run slave trade throughout the region. As the slave trade grew, Britain expanded its interests in the area, and the colony of Nigeria was born.

An Area Briefing

Politics and Government

There are thirty-six states in the Federal Republic of Nigeria, with a bicameral legislature, and a president as the executive. Each state has its own governor and legislatures as well, and local politics and authority command the allegiance of the local ethnic groups over which they preside. It is interesting to note that traditional Ibo society was effectively stateless, yet well run, as was the case with many (though far from most) traditional societies in the region; no doubt, there are important ramifications for the rest of the world today to understanding this phenomenon and its elements: in the Ibo's case, one of the factors has to do with the socioreligious institution, found increasingly throughout this region, of oracles and divination, as it allows individuals to take control of their personal lives within the social constraints established by the rest of the community and communicated to individuals through the oracular mediums.

Schools and Education

As is the case throughout all of West Africa, schooling for children is spotty and difficult to mandate. Beyond the lack of teachers, resources, supplies, and infrastructure, many people feel that schooling is irrelevant to their lives and the lives of their children, that it is much more important for the children to be available to help out at home, in the fields, and in the market. In addition, those who are able to send their children to school prefer that the children attend an Islamic school rather than one run by the secular government (there is a distrust by many of secular education when compared to religious upbringing). Compounding this is the British administration of the school system that for better (it obviates ethnic rivalries) or for worse (most children do not speak English when they enter school, and this makes learning extremely difficult) results in an excessive dropout rate in the secondary grades, although most pupils complete primary school. Most students who do graduate secondary school are men; and the literacy rate for girls is significantly lower (it must be noted that most of the indigenous languages spoken in West Africa, and this includes Nigeria, are oral languages, making the concept and achievement of literacy first dependent upon the development of an accepted script for the spoken language). Despite these difficulties, there are a significant number of Nigerian students enrolled in colleges and universities around the world.

Religion and Demographics

The people of Nigeria are about evenly split between Islam and Christianity, with about 10 percent of the population retaining their animist beliefs. Even so, animist beliefs pervade both Islam and Christianity; for example, many people believe in genies, spirits, and zombies—collectively known as *juju*—and many people wear charms (*grigri,* usually in the form of amulets containing written prayers—sometimes in Arabic—or incantations or special ingredients to ward off evil). Animists typically revere a Creator God, and the devout invoke good and evil through the assistance of intermediary spirits; people capable of doing this are usually spiritual leaders practiced in witchcraft. Ancestor worship is a particularly powerful element in animism. Tension is growing throughout the country between Christians and Muslims over the extent to which Muslims, particularly in the north, can impose religious law—known as the *shari'a*—as the legitimate law of the land. It is a challenge (to provide opportunity) and a strength (the optimism and energy of the majority of the population) that, as is the case throughout much of Africa, the majority of the population is under thirty years of age.

Islam is the youngest of the West's three great religious traditions, beginning with Judaism and Christianity. As a Western religion, it is linked to the Judeo-Christian belief system and rejects Hinduism and Buddhism as "pagan," and not "of the book," or codified. Incorporating both Judaism and Christianity into its system of beliefs, Islam claims that it is the final revelation of a monotheistic God, as revealed to the world through the prophet Muhammad, and that previous "messiahs," such as Jesus and Moses, were merely prophets, along with Muhammad, proclaiming the word of God. Muslims do not follow Muhammad (therefore, they are not Muhammadans, a very derogatory term created by Westerners who did not understand Islam); they believe in Allah, which is the Arabic name for the same God worshipped by Christians and Jews. Muhammad and his followers wrote down the law of God as revealed to them in the Qu'ran (or Koran), the Islamic Holy book. It does not negate the Old or New Testaments: it merely provides, in the eyes of Muslim faithful, the final required text. Muhammad received his revelations from God in Medina; prior to Islam, the nomadic tribes of the region believed in a variety of pagan ideas, but with the notion of one God, and the laws under which people were to behave, Muhammad was able to unify the peoples of the Gulf Arabian peninsula into the beginnings of a single Arab culture. Islam was spread rapidly in Nigeria by the Yoruba and Fulani peoples. While Islam underwent a serious split almost immediately following

Muhammad's death (two major camps emerged, the Shia and the Sunni, in an effort to decide how to continue the faith), Nigeria joined the Sunni camp. Sunni Muslims believe that the caliphs, or religious leaders, subsequent to Muhammad are legitimate; Shiite Muslims believe that the caliphs subsequent to Muhammad are usurpers, and therefore do not believe in Sunni authority. All Muslims must abide by five basic tenets, or Pillars of Faith:

- Proclaim the supremacy of the one true God, Allah, above all others.
- Pray to Allah five times daily.
- Observe Ramadan, the holy month, the ninth month of the Islamic calendar, which is essentially a celebration of the first time God revealed his word to Muhammad.
- Give alms to the poor and needy.
- Perform the hajj, or spiritual (and physical) journey to Mecca, at least once in their lifetime if they are capable of doing so.

Specific codes of conduct, which have developed over time and have been codified into Islamic law, are known as the *shari'a*. One example of such laws that affect life in West Africa and Nigeria powerfully is the acceptance of polygamy, as polygamy is also a social condition that is tolerated by many of the indigenous ethnic groups of the region. In Islam, however, a man may typically have only up to four wives, and only if he can support them all equally, and, at least in the case of Nigeria, only if all wives agree. The degree to which one follows Islamic scriptures often determines how devoutly one applies the Islamic ethical code in day-to-day life; in Nigeria, the enforcement of those codes is done with significant consideration for how it "plays" with the local indigenous beliefs.

Because of the understanding, if not acceptance, of Western ways in Nigeria, depending upon the individual you are working with (whether they are Western-oriented or fundamentalist Muslim), it may or may not be difficult for Western women to do business in Nigeria today.

All of the major ethnic groups are extremely proud of their role and their accomplishments, and sometimes, of their supremacy over others. The major ethnic group in Nigeria is the Hausa, mainly in the center of the country, who have the reputation for being in military and political control of the country; the Fulani in the north press the issues of Islam to the foreground; the Ibo in the southeast control some of the oil and are very independent-minded (and bitter about their failed Biafran independence movement and the subsequent catastrophe of the war and famine); and the Yoruba of the southwest are known as controlling the press and finance of the country.

Fundamental Cultural Orientations

1. What's the Best Way for People to Relate to One Another?

OTHER-INDEPENDENT OR OTHER-DEPENDENT?   There is a combination of deep concern for family, clan, and other membership groups (such as work and religion) that defines an individual and individual expression. Nigerians, like all Africans, have a hierarchical sense of loyalties, beginning with their family, and then, in descending order of importance, their ethnic group, their religion, their home village, their country, their region, and their continent. Nigerians are deeply connected first to their clan and their families: for that reason, it is critical that one inquire about the health of all family members. How one performs his or her role vis-à-vis others is judged in Africa, and individuals do nothing without careful consideration for how their actions will be perceived, and for the impact their actions will have on their family and their community. Consequently, individual empowerment and decision making are rare, and consensus-building and confirming group agreement are critical. Sharing, concern for others, humility, and an acceptance—without anger, remorse, or hostility—of one's role, at least within one's group, are all hallmarks of West African and Nigerian culture.

HIERARCHY-ORIENTED OR EGALITY-ORIENTED? Both Nigerian secular life and ethnic group membership (as well as Islamic life for Muslims) are rigidly stratified, with three or four generations of the extended family traditionally living together (this is not necessarily the case in the cities); individuals within this highly stratified social structure play their roles—children, women, and men in relation to one another, hosts in relation to guests, religious leaders and other elders in relation to the community. Defining one's rank, therefore, is important, as are status symbols (for example, the jewelry that women wear, the ritual scarification imposed by the ethnic group, and the pattern used on the traditional robe). It is critical that everyone show respect for elders and devout Muslims. Women and men are different and perform different roles; in Nigeria a woman typically may go out in public alone, but she will probably prefer to go with other female friends or relatives. She need not be in the company of a close male relative (husband, father, son, or brother), and Muslim women generally will not wear a veil; in fact, although all groups are male-dominated, Nigerian women in general do play a more significant role in public life: they work, are represented in the intellectual community, and are active in politics.

RULE-ORIENTED OR RELATIONSHIP-ORIENTED? While many Nigerians have had experience with and in the West, the tension that exists between the application of universal rules over reliable and dependable relationships is palpable. This leads to a high dependence on power, authority, and subjective decision making based on the situation and the relationships between the individuals involved. Ultimately, face-to-face knowledge of the individuals involved in any interaction is the basis upon which final decisions are often made.

2. What's the Best Way to View Time?

MONOCHRONIC OR POLYCHRONIC? Nigeria is essentially very polychronic, due to the influence of both agrarian and religious traditions (although less so in Lagos and the cities). There is forgiveness for the inevitable delays and unexpected events that define life in Africa, and understanding when things don't go as planned or scheduled; people may or may not show up at invited events, things may or may not happen as planned. Schedules tend to be loose and flexible. Because who (relationships) is more important than what (tasks) or when (time), there can be many interruptions during a meeting, and people's obligations to other people, who may come and go, are more important than doing things according to schedules. If you are being kept waiting, or are ignored because of someone else's needs, it may be an indication of your importance relative to the other person, and expressing frustration may only diminish your importance.

RISK-TAKING OR RISK-AVERSE?   Nigerians are prone to taking risks, especially when in positions of authority. Within organizations, the decision makers can be bold, even reckless, but subordinates generally are not. Therefore, comfort with uncertainty, in general, is high, and while much information may need to be exchanged with different people before decisions can be made in large groups, individuals can make decisions quickly. There can be much discussion with trusted others about what you, as a foreigner, bring to the table, *after* you leave the meeting.

PAST-ORIENTED OR FUTURE-ORIENTED?   A distinct and inherent fatalism in regard to the effect of human action is fundamental to both Islamic and indigenous beliefs. Nevertheless, those empowered by virtue of their position (or luck) are expected to make the decisions that keep the world running, and by so doing, are fulfilling either Allah's will or they are at the mercy of the fate of their group. Therefore, future benefits often do not motivate Nigerians; doing nothing, or doing things for the here and now, is sometimes more important, and if things do not work out, that is to be expected—no mortal controls the universe, and all is ultimately determined. There is a deep belief that things will take the time they need to take, and that it is always more important to maintain smooth interpersonal relationships until opportunities come along: when that happens, Nigerians will be sure to seize them!

3. What's the Best Way for Society to Work with the World at Large?

LOW-CONTEXT DIRECT OR HIGH-CONTEXT INDIRECT COMMUNICATORS? Nigerians are very context-driven communicators. They will speak in metaphors, and use stories or codified phrases; they will employ analogies, Islamic precedent, and much nonverbal behavior to convey true meaning. They generally do not avoid confrontation as a primary goal, as do most of their neighbors in the region, and often will be quite frank and direct about what is on their mind. Southern Nigerians have a reputation for being open, direct, and outgoing, while northerners are typically seen as being more conservative, nonconfrontational, quiet, and harmony-oriented. In fact, southern Nigerians can be quite boisterous, aggressive, and loud, and it is important not to interpret this kind of behavior as an expression of anger. When they are angry they can be quite loud and direct about it (or can suddenly become sullen and silent).

PROCESS-ORIENTED OR RESULT-ORIENTED?   Islamic law, and the complex study of Islam that developed in the Muslim world into its own field of scholastic inquiry, is fundamentally different from Western Greco-Roman philosophies of knowing. In Islam, interpretation and truth are dependent upon "analogous" reasoning, while in the West, such inquiry is based more on "argument" (proving and disproving). Decisions and actions therefore may be the result of reasoning that is not directed at a determination of truth, but rather context-based correctness based on similar experiences, often with strict Islamic code as the only context. Combine this with a tendency to rely on subjective experience, for both Muslims and non-Muslims, and the Nigerian mind is processing information, for the most part, in a different way than the Western mind; in fact, because of their negative experience with Western exploitation, it may be a struggle sometimes for most Africans—West, Nigerian, or otherwise—to even be open to Western ideas.

FORMAL OR INFORMAL?   West African society is basically formal and ritualized, and each group has its own way of honoring the hierarchies, establishing respect and deference, and following (or not following) through on their responsibilities. There are formal ways that guests (outsiders) and hosts (insiders) must act toward one another, in order to preserve the honor of all groups and individuals. Nevertheless, and perhaps because of the multiethnic nature of the country, Nigerians have adopted a breezy, informal manner with most individuals— non-Africans included—that has become, in many ways, a defining hallmark of their interpersonal communication style.

Greetings and Introductions

Language and Basic Vocabulary

English is the official language, used in business and government, but Pidgin English is the version most used, as a way to bridge the language gap between groups and individuals. Each indigenous group speaks its own language, as well, which may or may not be understood by others in other groups, and most indigenous languages are oral. Most of the time, Nigerians will tend to reassure, insist that they can do something, know something, or solve the problem, whether or not they actually can; this may or may not be intended to deceive, although words more often indicate what they desire more than what might actually be. Never use religious references casually or disrespectfully—it is assumed that all people are religious in some way, even if not a Muslim—and be very careful never to use "God" in any way other than in the most respectful sense.

Honorifics for Men, Women, and Children

As is the case throughout most of West Africa, people usually greet each other by title or relationship (e.g., Dr., Mr., Mrs., aunt, mother, cousin) plus the first, or given, name (unless the individuals involved are Westernized, or if they are first being introduced, in which case, the standard Western greeting of honorific plus last name would be appropriate). If names are not known, sometimes stating the individual's position as a title is sufficient (e.g., Mr. Engineer or Miss Fish Seller). Children typically refer to their parents as "mother of" or "father of" plus the name of the oldest sibling, and refer to elders in general as either "aunt" or "uncle." Nicknames are very common, and most people are referred to by their nickname, sometimes with an honorific preceding it.

The What, When, and How of Introducing People

Nigerians may, upon greeting you, call you by your last or first name, with or without your title. Always wait to be introduced to strangers; although if you are not introduced after a few minutes, it is appropriate to introduce yourself. As is the case throughout the region, it is critical to take time when you greet someone to make many inquiries into his or her health and the health and condition of his or her relatives and close friends (even livestock, if appropriate!). It is considered very rude not to take a considerable amount of time when meeting someone to make these inquiries and express understanding of his or her responses; he or she will do the same in kind. You must acknowledge people you know when you pass them on the street, and you should acknowledge strangers when eyes meet in passing. Never presume to seat yourself at a gathering: if possible, wait to be told where to sit; you will be seated in a spot appropriate to your position (i.e., a guest, elder, with the men, if a male, and with the women, if a woman). Typically, men, women, and children (even boys and girls) are seated separately. Because you will never be refused, and because guests are always welcome (as is the case in much of Africa, because of the lack of communication and transportation facilities, people simply drop in "uninvited" often—in fact, this is typically the most common form of entertainment and socializing), it is important that you do not purposefully make a visit unannounced around mealtime; instead, come in the late morning or early evening. When arriving at someone's home, you will generally announce yourself by tapping on the front gate or clapping your hands in the front of the house. When departing, it is important to say farewell to every individual present: the American group wave is not appreciated. Seniors, or those who are obviously the oldest in a group, are greeted first, seated first, and allowed to enter a room first (usually as the center of a group, however, and in most cases preceded by their younger aides).

Physical Greeting Styles

Close associates and businesspeople of the same sex who have developed working relationships often greet each other warmly, with hugs and sometimes kisses. Wait until your Nigerian host initiates this behavior before initiating it yourself. Typically, the greeting between men involves a handshake, and putting one's left hand on the other person's shoulder. Very close family and friends may also kiss additionally on the forehead, but each ethnic group has different greetings. Muslim women and men do not touch or shake hands (unless the woman is Westernized, and you will know if she extends her hand). The handshake may be soft, almost limp sometimes; this does not mean insincerity, rather, it is an accommodation to the Western fashion while remaining humble and considerate. Until such familiarity is established, a simple Western-style handshake is appropriate between men and men, and Westernized women. Obvious juniors (such as children and young relatives) sometimes bow (or curtsy, for girls) in front of elders. If your hand is dirty or you are holding something that cannot be put down, you may extend your wrist, or even elbow, in place of the right hand.

The traditional business introduction also includes the exchange of business cards. Always take a large supply of business cards with you: you should give one to every new person you are introduced to (there is no need to provide another business card when you are meeting someone again unless information about you has changed, such as a new address, contact number, or position). Be sure your business cards are in fine shape: they are an extension of you as a person and must look as good as possible. Embossed cards are extremely impressive, especially with logos in green (the color of Islam) in the north. Never hand out a dirty, soiled, bent, or written-on card, and always handle business cards with your right hand only. Your card should be in English.

When presenting a business card, give it to your colleague so that it is readable for him as you hold it (he will, in turn, present his card so that it is readable for you). You may not receive a card in return. Smiling and other nonverbal forms of communication usually accompany the card exchange. Should you meet more than one individual at a reception, you may have a handful of cards when the greetings are over.

As the business card exchange usually precedes a sit-down meeting, it is important to arrange the cards you have received in a little seating plan in front of you along the top of the desk or table at your seat, reflecting the order in which people are seated. This will help you connect the correct names with the correct individuals throughout the meeting. Do this even if you are just meeting one person; it is expected. During the meeting, it is important never to play with the business cards, and when the meeting is over, never put them in your back pants pockets: pick them up carefully and respectfully, and place them neatly in your cardholder or inside jacket pocket. Do not photograph people without asking their permission, ever, and do not videotape freely. In some African countries, videotaping and photographing people and certain sites are illegal.

Communication Styles

Okay Topics / Not Okay Topics

Okay: anything that reflects your personal interests and hobbies, and your sincere appreciation of and curiosity about things Nigerian and native to the West African world. Nigerians love and excel at soccer and traditional wrestling; expressing interest in Nigerian soccer teams is very definitely a positive. Interest in Nigerian music, folk art, food, and history will always be met with hours of information (if not a personal tour!). *Not okay:* Politics, current events, or any subject that might in any way be controversial needs to be avoided at first. It is important to be sensitive to Nigeria's unique history and not to give your opinions about any of Nigeria's neighbors or internal ethnic groups, poverty, the challenge of Islamic fundamentalism to the secular state, ethnic rivalries, or religious differences. Do not inquire about a person's occupation or income in casual conversation, although it may be inquired of you (if so, this is generally just a way of getting to know more about your country, and not a personal investigation: answer specifically and fully, with an explanation as to what things cost at home, why you do what you do, and so forth). Other personal questions may be asked of you ("Why are you not married?" or "Do you have any sons?"); the best responses are those that fit the Nigerian context (I've not been blessed yet, I wait patiently."). You may be complimented on your portliness (being heavy is a sign of wealth throughout most of the region), or told that you are too thin. Dismiss all compliments humbly but sincerely. Do not talk about sex or tell dirty jokes when women are present: it is in very bad taste. Discussions about your company and its work are very much appreciated, as they give Nigerians a chance to learn more about you and your firm. At first, speak about things that you believe you have in common, so that you can build a personal connection that will go far toward maintaining a harmonious bridge between you. This is appropriate for both individuals and organizations.

Tone, Volume, and Speed

Many Nigerians are more animated, loud, and aggressive in tone than their neighbors. This may be especially true of southern Nigerians. They may speak rapidly, but if you, in turn, speak rather slowly, they may get the hint and slow down.

Use of Silence

Passive silence—allowing time to pass simply without words—can be a form of proactive communication and may be used as a nonverbal way of avoiding confrontation, disagreement, or an unpleasant subject. If confronted with unexplainable silence, gently coax the conversation in a different direction, one that is more mutually harmonious.

Physical Gestures and Facial Expressions

Throughout the region, nonverbal behavior is part of the pattern of communication, and most Nigerians are very comfortable with nonverbal behavior. However, they may not understand many of the Western gestures; therefore, limit your own gestures until you are sure they are understood. Winking, whistling, and other similar displays are considered very vulgar. Public displays of familiarity and affection with the opposite sex are never expressed beyond holding hands. Never touch anyone on his or her head, even a child; this is considered the holiest part of the body for Muslims. Do not point with or intentionally show the sole of your shoe to anyone: this is considered vulgar, as the bottom of the shoe touches the ground and is therefore the dirtiest part of the body. Standing with your hands on your hips is considered very aggressive and should always be avoided. Yawning in public is considered impolite; you must cover your mouth when you yawn (and some people touch the middle of their forehead with their right index finger after a yawn) and when you use a toothpick. Pushing your hand forward, palm facing out, fingers spread apart, is a very aggressive and rude behavior.

For any action or gesture that would naturally be done only with one hand, do not use your left hand, as this is considered the unclean hand (the hand used for personal hygiene). Pass all documents, business cards, food, and money with your right hand (if you're a southpaw, you will have to practice this). You must remove your shoes before entering a mosque (and some buildings, as well as most homes), and you may need to wash your feet and hands at the entrance fountain provided before entering a mosque as well. Women may be restricted to specific areas and times when visiting mosques. Women entering mosques need to have their heads covered, their legs covered to below the knee, and their arms covered to below the elbow; Western women do not necessarily need to have their faces covered. Smile whenever possible: it smoothes the way with strangers quickly and easily. Nigerians sometimes get someone's attention by snapping the fingers, and/or making a quiet hissing-type sound.

Waving and Counting

The thumb represents the number 1, the pinkie represents the number 5, with everything in between ordered from the thumb down. It is very insulting to beckon someone with the forefinger (instead, turn your hand so that the palm is facing down and motion inward with all four fingers at once). If you need to gesture for a waiter, subtly raise your hand or make eye contact. Waving or beckoning is done with the palm down and the fingers moving forward and backward in a kind of scratching motion. It may seem as if the person making the gesture is saying good-bye to you, when in fact you are being summoned over. If you need to point to something or someone, close your fingers, open your palm and face it upward, and pass your hand in the direction you want to indicate.

Physicality and Physical Space

Nigerians may stand closer than most North Americans are accustomed to; resist the urge to step back. Never speak with your hands in your pockets: always keep them firmly at your side when standing. If men and women must cross their legs when they sit, it must never be ankle over knee (for women, the preferred style is to cross ankle over ankle; but the bottom of the shoes must not show to the other person). Remember, even in public, formal is always better than informal, and this is essential when in front of elders or superiors of any kind: no gum-chewing, *ever;* don't slouch; men, take your hat off; and don't lean against things. Nigerians are most comfortable when they are next to other people: in a nearly empty bus, movie theater, or restaurant, in most cases, Nigerians will tend to sit next to or near the other person present, instead of far away from them. As is the case throughout the region, needing or wanting to be alone is suspect, and maintaining privacy by insisting on being alone is considered strange and possibly dangerous: Why would anyone want to be alone when he or she could be in the company of friends and family?

Eye Contact

Eye contact is typically not constantly maintained when speaking, especially by subordinates when speaking with superiors, or juniors with elders. It is best to make eye contact at first, however. Typically, one does not make eye contact while eating, and conversation is often kept to a minimum while eating. Tune up your nonverbal antennae.

Emotive Orientation

Nigerians are very warm, sensitive, friendly, and hospitable. They may not, however, be demonstrative, at least at first and in the north, as formal rules require a slow process of getting to know each other. Once they do know each other, however, there can be much touching (at least between members of the same sex) during even the most casual conversation. Two men or two women often walk hand in hand or arm in arm down the street. Verbal communication often employs effusiveness, exaggeration, and flowery phrases: this is meant to show sincerity, not duplicity. In general, one should be especially careful not to interrupt others when they are speaking: a more thoughtful approach to conversation, in which you give the other person signals that he or she is being listened to, rather than where you chime in quickly with your own thoughts, is much preferred throughout the entire region.

Protocol in Public

Walking Styles and Waiting in Lines

On the street, in stores, and in most public facilities, people typically pay little attention to maintaining orderly lines. Due to the volume of passengers on public transportation, there can be much pushing and jostling. This is not to get into a bus ahead of someone else; it is merely to get in! This is not meant to be disrespectful; if it is bothersome, just say so politely, and you will be treated well. If you ask a Nigerian for directions, he or she will make every effort to show you the way (even if he or she is not that certain!).

Behavior in Public Places: Airports, Terminals, and the Market

Pride will always demand that Nigerians provide you with assistance; even if they do not have an answer they will give you one. Be careful with whom you strike up conversations, especially in the cities, as Nigerians have a reputation for conning and scamming. Men must only speak to men, and women must only speak to women.

Establish a personal relationship with everyone you must interact with, from shopkeeper to government official, and you can expect much assistance as a newcomer. Often this is one of the purposes for bargaining in the market: when you do bargain, consider that your money is, in most cases, going to the upkeep of entire families who live at subsistence levels. When bargaining, keep in mind also that it is generally considered good luck to be the first or last shopper in a store or at a stall, so you might get a better price if you can manage to be the first to arrive when they open or the last when they close. Stores in the cities are open in the evenings and on weekends, as well as during the day, and market stores and stalls usually determine their own hours; government offices, however, often open early (around 7 or 8 A.M.) and close early (around 3 or 4 P.M.). Many stores may close during the Muslim Sabbath (Friday) and in preparation for it (Thursday nights), and on all Muslim holidays. A personal verbal thank-you to store owners, waiters, chefs, and hotel managers for their services is important, as it will help establish the relationship you need to get continuing good service. Shopping doubles as a social event, so plan to socialize as well as shop. Smoking is popular, and in some places endemic, and you need not look for "no-smoking" areas, as such formal rules can rarely be enforced (be sure not to smoke during the day during Ramadan, when Muslims abstain; this is true for eating and drinking during the day during Ramadan, as well, when in the presence of observant Muslims). When and if you do smoke, it is critical that you offer a cigarette first to everyone else at the table before you light up, and then offer to light their cigarettes for them. Bathroom facilities are rare or nonexistent (with the exception of new Western-style hotels, and then only when the plumbing, electricity, and other associated infrastructural requirements work, including telephones, which may or may not be the case): be prepared (and bring toilet paper with you as you travel about).

Unless they are in the company of other women, or close male relatives, women generally do not go out in public alone, especially at night; Western women traveling alone in Nigeria will generally not have a problem, but should be prepared for the fact that this behavior is not typical in the region: some people won't know what to do or how to act toward them, some other women will want to assist them, and certain men, no doubt, may try to take advantage of them.

Bus / Metro / Taxi / Car

There are a few well-paved roads, mainly between the major cities; most transportation is by public bus (which is known by any number of different names in different countries throughout Africa) or private driver, for the elite, if they can afford to hire one. Do not attempt to drive alone in Africa. Driving almost anywhere is nearly impossible and subjects you to all sorts of dangers—civil, natural, and unnatural—and driving at night is suicide. Private cars are virtually unknown. Driving in Africa may be officially on the left or right (depending upon whether the country was influenced by the British or French during the colonial times), but more practically, such distinctions are irrelevant because cars are driven wherever they can be. Some trains do exist in certain areas, and planes are the best forms of transportation over long distances. Be prepared for chaotic and unplanned circumstances at almost all public transport facilities, including rail stations, bus depots, and airports. Most locals get around by bus, truck, or animal cart, or on foot (depending upon whether they are in rural or urban areas, and this distinction makes for considerably different ways of life in Nigeria). And remember, as is the case throughout the region, when the infrastructure doesn't work, rely on people: the best way, for example, to get a message through sometimes, is simply to pass it along to travelers, drivers, and others who are going in the direction of the person you want to communicate with.

The best way to catch a cab (in Lagos, for example) is at designated taxi stands (hotels are good places, but often charge more for the same ride: a hotel surcharge is added to the meter fare, in some cases). When a taxi has been hailed—and you do so in Nigeria by holding out your arm—negotiate the price before you get in. Whenever possible, have the address you need to get to written down on a piece of paper (or use the business card of the person you are going to see, if you can) before you hail the cab.

Tipping

Tipping (the ubiquitous *baksheesh*—or *dash,* as it is more commonly referred to throughout West Africa) is universally required throughout the region, as a way to help get things done, and as a way of thanking people and being appreciative of the help they offer: it is more commonly a social gesture. Typically, it is a way of taking care of people; when abused, it is a form of graft that in some countries in the region, Nigeria included, represents a rampant form of corruption. It is traditional to always give a little something to someone who has helped you out. The offer may be refused at first in some cases, but if you insist, it will be graciously accepted and appreciated. Tips in restaurants run about 10 percent, and are typically not included in the bill (but double-check to be sure); a tip is not necessary if you have negotiated the fare for the taxi ahead of time and already figured in the tip. For everything else, a few coins are all that is needed, but you should always have a lot of spare change handy to see you through the day. United States currency is generally greatly appreciated throughout the region; the Nigerian currency is the naira.

Punctuality

Punctuality is valued, but not required. Consider timeliness a target. You should be relatively on time, but you may be kept waiting for quite a while: patience and good humor are required. Never get upset over time. If you are late, you need not have an explanation. It will be understood.

Dress

Many Nigerians in the urban areas wear conservative Western dress, although some of the elite prefer to spice up the Western wardrobe with traditionally vibrant Nigerian colors, designs, and fabrics. Most Nigerians are most comfortable wearing their traditional dress, which is dependent upon the ethnic group. Women generally wear dresses that cover most of their body, with accompanying head wraps. Nigerian attire has a reputation, in general, for being very colorful and highly patterned, often reflecting tribal traditions. It is not appropriate for non-Nigerians to dress in traditional Nigerian clothes; Westerners should dress in conservative business clothes (as will many Nigerian businessmen), but may find it more comfortable to wear items that are as loose fitting as possible (the weather is hot). Never wear (and this is the case throughout most of Africa) anything that could be interpreted as a military uniform. Urban youth and westernized people wear casual Western clothes (often secondhand from Europe or the United States). Men should not in the northern Muslim area wear neck jewelry, even if it is not visible underneath clothing, although women often wear their wealth in the form of jewelry. Clothes should not be tight-fitting or revealing in any way, for men or women. Western women in Muslim areas should not wear pantsuits, as they reveal too much of the shape of the legs. Shoes with traditional dress are typically sandals or flip-flops. Westerners should avoid wearing any expensive clothes or jewelry: not only does it make you a potential mark for thieves, but it is ostentatious and can be seen as a sign of selfishness and colonialist exploitation.

Personal Hygiene

In Nigeria, cleanliness is associated with purity, and most Nigerians try to bathe at least twice a day. Washing both hands and feet more than once a day is very common, and one must wash hands before and after eating every meal. Many Nigerians enjoy perfumes and henna skin designs. Do not blow your nose in public: it is considered rude. Spitting does occur on the street, but is also is regarded as rude.

Dining and Drinking

Mealtimes and Typical Foods

The typical Nigerian diet is rich in rice, yams, and cassava (a root vegetable), plus breads, fresh vegetables, and fruits. Meats are enjoyed when available, as well as fish along the coast and rivers. Each ethnic group has its own specialties and preferences, and remember, Muslims will not eat pork or drink alcohol (although it is available). Typically dishes revolve around rice, with a sauce of either vegetables, fish, or meat, or combinations thereof. The Yoruba, for example, generally like their food hot and spicy, and the Fulani, who are traditional herdsmen, raise cattle and traditionally enjoy dairy and meat products.

A note on hosting and dining with Muslims: If you are serving a meal at home, be sure you do not use alcohol or pork in any of the dishes, and if you do, labeling the dish and serving it separately will still make your Muslim guest uncomfortable. Simply don't do it. You, as a guest in the more rural regions, may be rewarded with the opportunity to either dine first, or to be offered the more favored food, such as the meat: please consider that this may mean that others in the family do not eat this. If you are offered something you cannot eat or drink, acknowledge the honor, and suggest that while you will always hold the honor in your heart, you in turn will bestow it on someone who can also appreciate it in his or her belly: then pass the honored dish on to a Nigerian colleague. Alternatively, you may say thank you but that you have just eaten or drunk. Remember in this region, and throughout much of Africa, you will never be denied food if it is available, but consider the dire malnutrition and difficulty in obtaining adequate nourishment in this part of the world.

Breakfast is served from about 6 to 9 A.M., lunch from 12 to 2 P.M., and dinner from 8 to 10 P.M., although at the "hungry times" of the year (usually just before the harvest), many people make do with just two meals per day. Traditionally, children, women, and men dine separately, and men are offered the best parts first, women next, and children typically last.

It is very important to remove your shoes before entering most Nigerian homes (look to see if other sandals are lined up at the entrance as your cue), and when seated to always make sure that your toes and feet are not pointing to the food or to others at the meal. Typically, conversation while eating is minimal, and most Nigerians avoid eye contact when dining. Desserts usually consist of fruit, pastries, or yogurt.

Regional Differences

Remember, Islam prohibits the use of pork, and most meats of any kind for Muslims need to be prepared *halal* (meat slaughtered according to Islamic prescriptions). Do not eat in front of your Muslim colleagues, or invite them to join you for a meal, during the day during Ramadan, as Muslims typically fast (and refrain from drinking and smoking) during the day, and feast with family and friends at night. Ramadan lasts for a lunar month: this is simply not a good time to do business or go out entertaining in the Muslim world.

Typical Drinks and Toasting

Tea and coffee are available in most places. When you come to a Nigerian home, even for just a brief visit, you will most likely be served tea, usually in a round of three cups: typically, the first is unsweetened, the second with some sugar, and the third one very sweet, mirroring the development of the friendship as you get to know each other. Always accept the cup of tea and/or coffee, even if you only put it to your lips or take just a few sips. Your cup will always be refilled if it is less than half full. Typically, beer and other alcoholic drinks may also be served. Fruit juices and lemonade, along with tea, may accompany meals, but for most traditional meals, it is impolite to drink and eat at the same time: first you eat, then you drink). You must never pour your own drink; wait patiently to be served.

If you are the honored guest, you are not expected to make a statement or toast, but if you offer a small compliment, it will be appreciated (and then dismissed as unnecessary); you can do this at the end of the meal, just before everyone departs. An appropriate comment would be to wish for the health of the host and all those present; always be humble.

Avoid drinking tap water anywhere in the region (this means you should brush your teeth with bottled water and not take ice in any of your drinks. Drink only bottled water, brewed tea or coffee, or soft drinks; and avoid getting water from the morning shower into your mouth. Never eat fresh fruits or vegetables that cannot be peeled first, and ideally cooked later before eating). This is a serious matter: there are some very nasty—and sometimes deadly—bugs going around in developing countries. In addition, avoid all dairy products except in the finest hotels, as the required refrigeration may be questionable. Do not swim in freshwater lakes, ponds, or rivers (the Guinea worm is a particular problem in this region, along with many other parasitic infections).

Table Manners and the Use of Utensils

Modern Lagos has been significantly Westernized, so many of the Western modes of dining are understood and accepted. However, understanding the traditional Nigerian modes of dining behavior will be quite helpful as they are apparent and respected in most places. They vary from group to group, but the following basic suggestions should be considered: Before meals, you must wash your hands, and wash them again when the meal is over. Traditionally, one eats with one's right hand from a communal plate or bowl (or set of plates and/or bowls). Never use your left hand unless you are clearly eating something that requires two hands; occasionally you may be offered a spoon or fork, which also must be held in the right hand. Keep your left hand off any bowls or serving items. If there is only one communal bowl, it is appropriate for the youngest person present to hold the lip of the bowl with the thumb and index finger of their left hand while the elders partake first (men first, women second, children last). Eat only from the part of the communal plates or bowls that is directly in front of you. Some may dip their index finger into the food first and taste it: this is an old tradition of making sure that the food is safe to eat, and has become a replacement for saying a small prayer before eating. You may be seated either on the floor, or on low stools. Do not smoke in the same area where the food is being served, and wait to smoke until after the meal is finished (women do not smoke). At the end of the meal, a small burp signifies satisfaction, after which some praise to the cook and thankfulness for the food is a welcome gesture.

Seating Plans

The most honored position is next to the host. Most social entertaining is done in people's homes (although in Lagos there is business dining in restaurants); with the exception of very high-level government or corporate events, usually of the multinational kind, restaurants are considered by most people as inappropriate and too "cold" for getting to know each other well enough to build a relationship. The home, the market, or a local café is where people meet, socialize, and get things done, including business (although business is not easily done in the market). Your spouse might be invited with you to a meal at home, especially if the spouse of the host will be there, which will probably be the case. The invitation will then be phrased, "My spouse invites your spouse," and women and men may (especially in Muslim areas) eat separately. Invitations, business or social, will most always be verbal, not written.

At Home, in a Restaurant, or at Work

The honored guest is served first, then the oldest male, then the rest of the men, then women, and finally children. Do not begin to eat or drink anything until the oldest man at the table has been served and has begun. At the end of the meal, it is appropriate to thank the host or hostess for a wonderful meal.

In informal restaurants, you may be required to share a table. If so, do not force conversation: act as if you are seated at a private table. Women should be sensitive to the fact that they may be seated only with other women. Waitstaff may be summoned by subtly raising your hand or by making eye contact; waving or calling their names is very impolite. Since business and socializing in this part of the world are usually one and the same, business is often discussed over meals, once individuals know each other well enough to talk terms. Take your cue from your Nigerian associates: if they bring up business, then it is okay to discuss it, but wait to take your lead from their conversation.

Once inside the home, do not wander around. If you move from one area to another in a Nigerian home or restaurant, be sure to always allow more senior members of your party to enter the room ahead of you.

Being a Good Guest or Host

Usually the one who does the inviting pays the bill. If invited to a home or if you are hosted in any way, thanks and compliments are not easily given or received, since it is believed that there is no need to say such things between trusted friends and family; nevertheless, it is important to state humble thanks, and to accept such thanks graciously.

Transportation

It's important to make sure that guests have a way to return from where they came, if they are visiting; equally, you want to be sure not to put your host out by not having made such arrangements ahead of time for yourself, if and when you visit. If invited into a home, you may also be invited to spend the night, and if so, you must be careful to keep a low profile and use as few resources as possible. If cars or taxis are arranged, when seeing your guests off, you must remain at the entrance of the house or restaurant, or at the site where you deposited your guests into the car, until the car is out of sight: it is very important not to leave until your guests can no longer see you, should they look back. Guests are seated in cars (and taxis) by rank, with the honored guest being placed in the back directly behind the front passenger seat; the next honored position is in the back behind the driver, and the least honored position is up front with the driver.

When to Arrive / Chores to Do

If invited to dinner at a private home, do offer to help with the chores or in any other way you can. Do not leave the meal area unless invited to do so. When in the home, be careful not to admire something too effusively: Nigerians may feel obligated to give it to you, and doing so might represent a great sacrifice. Your compliments will most likely be dismissed. Remember also that many Nigerians consider it bad luck to have their children praised: it can bring ill fortune to them (comment on the children indirectly, but comment on them positively).

Gift Giving

In general, gift giving is common for social occasions, and in business situations between trusted business colleagues. It is done not only as a gesture of thanks, but as a way of helping to ensure good business relations in the future (be careful not to go overboard here, as a gift that looks like an obvious bribe may land you in quite a bit of trouble . . . with the authorities in your home country, more than likely). In business settings, this usually takes the form of a personal gift that symbolically says the correct thing about the nature of the relationship. When going to the region on business, bringing a gift for the key decision maker is enough. Your gift does not have to be elaborate or expensive, but it should, whenever possible, be personalized (engraved, or representative of the personalities of the receiver or giver or of an aspect of the relationship). Present your gift when you arrive in the country; before you leave to return home you will receive a farewell gift, usually at the last meeting. When Nigerians visit your country, they will also bring you a gift, and before they leave, you should give them farewell gifts.

The most appropriate gift for a personal visit to a home, or as a thank-you for dinner, would be some fruit, coffee, or nuts, and something for the children, such as a toy, picture books, or school supplies (paper and writing utensils and calculators with a supply of batteries are very valued). A man typically only gives a gift to a man, a woman to a woman; remember, any gift given by a man to a woman must come with the caveat that it is from his wife/sister/mother, or else it is far too personal. Gifts to avoid giving Muslims include alcohol (and this includes perfumes or colognes made with alcohol), pork, art or photographs that depict natural scenes or people (this runs counter to Islamic beliefs that man must not attempt to reproduce in an image what God has made), or cutlery (which symbolizes the severing of a relationship). A fine gift for a Muslim would be a silver compass, so that he will always know which direction to face when he says his daily prayers (Muslims must face Mecca no matter where in the world they are when they say their prayers).

For both giving and receiving gifts, two hands are used always. Gifts may or may not be opened by the receiver in front of the giver (this depends upon the nature of the gift, more often than not: foodstuffs meant for dessert, for example, will be opened for all to enjoy); the presenter typically first offers the gift humbly and as an incidental aside, then, usually received after some imploring, it is acknowledged and accepted.

Gifts should be wrapped, but special gift-wrapping is not necessary (and in some cases may not be readily available). If you own a copy of the Qu'ran (given or received as a gift or not), never place it on the floor or below any object: it must be the highest book on the shelf. Do not give a copy of the Qu'ran as a gift to a Muslim: it is far too significant for a business or social acknowledgment.

Special Holidays and Celebrations

Major Holidays

Avoid doing business during the entire month of Ramadan. Some towns have different local holidays as well, so double-check with your Nigerian associates before making final travel plans.

Islamic holidays are celebrated by most Muslims. Islamic holidays are on the lunar calendar, so the dates change each year, and all holidays begin at sundown the day before. The most important Islamic holidays are (in order of their usual occurrence):

Ramadan
Idul Fitr   The celebration of the end of the fast at the end of Ramadan
Idul Adha   The Feast of the Sacrifice, celebrating Abraham's willingness
              to sacrifice his son
Hajj   The first day of the annual pilgrimage to Mecca
Maulid an-Nabi Birth of the Prophet Muhammad
Islamic New Year (also an official secular holiday)

Secular and additional holidays:

January 1	New Year's Day
March/April	Easter
May 1	Labor Day
October 1	National Day
December 25	Christmas
December 26	Boxing Day

Business Culture

Daily Office Protocols

The Nigerian office may be a modern office in an urban building or a traditional stall near the market, but no matter where it is you can be sure there will be many people coming and going. This is not so much a statement about your unimportance as much as it is a statement about the importance of your host: that he is needed by many, and that in the polychronic Nigerian culture, things are handled in order of their importance and not according to the clock. Be patient. In the Nigerian business organization, hierarchy is strictly observed. Because faithful Muslims pray five times a day, you will need to adjust your schedules to accommodate their needs. Usually, prayers are given upon awakening and at noontime, midday, dusk, and before retiring; this means that twice during the workday, there will be time out for prayers. The prayer break usually takes a short ten or fifteen minutes or so, and any quiet area will do. If you accidentally interrupt a Muslim during his prayers, just walk away quietly: there's no need for complicated explanations or apologies. Most organizations have prayer rooms set off to the side, with carpets. In addition, devout Muslims will not work on Friday (the Muslim Sabbath), and in fact begin to end work early on Thursday before sundown. The official workweek is Monday through Friday, 9 A.M. to 4 P.M. (remember, the Muslim Sabbath is on Friday, beginning Thursday evening at sunset; the Muslim workweek therefore often includes Saturday and Sunday), and sometimes a half day Saturday morning.

Management Styles

Titles and education are very important, and the highest ones (e.g., vice president) are usually reserved for very senior, executive-level positions, and should not be used as casually as they are in the United States. Any criticism of Nigerian workers must be done very carefully, even privately. Deference is shown by subordinates to their seniors; paternalistic concern is often shown by seniors to their subordinates. Superiors are not typically sensitive to inquiring about their subordinate's opinions, and once a decision is made, the superiors are followed, often unquestioningly. If you are doing business with the correct person, things will probably move quickly; it is essential, therefore, to have a good and trustworthy Nigerian contact who can make the necessary contacts for you (you can locate these people through consular and/or trade association contacts prior to your trip). Let this person take the time he needs to do this for you, for if you pressure him into making contacts sooner, he may connect you to someone who is not as useful as the one he was originally waiting for: this will not serve you. Again, be patient. Never use time as a means of pressure.

Boss-Subordinate Relations

The decision-making system usually works from the top on down, with key decisions often coming from individuals in high positions of power. Superiors are expected to provide clear and fully informed sets of instructions: that is their responsibility, and it is the responsibility of subordinates to carry out those instructions. Consequently, "management-by-objective" and other egalitarian and individually empowered management styles often may not work in this environment: without clear instruction from above, subordinates often will do nothing. They also lose respect for the manager for not making the decisions he should be making.

Conducting a Meeting or Presentation

There will be much hosting by your Nigerian contacts with tea, coffee, and soft drinks. When serving any refreshments in the office, be sure they are served in porcelain, glass, or silver tea sets: the use of paper or Styrofoam shows disrespect and is very bad form. There may be many more people at the meeting than you were expecting: this is typically because there are many more people who need to be consulted about the decision regarding you and your business; in most cases, you will be introduced to everyone. If you are not introduced to them, do not ask to be: acknowledge them with a smile and a nod, and proceed with your meeting. If you are meeting with a decision maker, the discussions will probably be direct, forthright, and businesslike. If you do not know the decision-making authority of the person you are with, assume that you will need to meet with many people, and perhaps repeat much of the same discussions each time with different people. There may be many interruptions throughout the meeting; stay calm and flexible. Business is personal throughout the region: decision makers have got to know your face. Patience and third-party connections are key.

Negotiation Styles

At first, expect no decisions from your Nigerian colleagues at the table and be willing to provide copious amounts of information, to the degree that you can, in response to their questions and in anticipation of their needs. Presentations should be well prepared and simply propounded. Details are best left to questions and backup material, which should be available and left behind; such materials need to be simple, to the point, and interesting to look at and can generally be in English. Unless you already have a well-established relationship, agendas need to be very broad and very flexible: everything unexpected will occur, and everything you did not plan to discuss will be brought up. Should you come with other team members, make sure that your roles are well-coordinated. Never disagree with each other in front of Nigerians or appear uncertain, unsure, not authorized to make a decision, or out of control in any way.

Most Nigerians love to bargain and see this process as a way of getting to know you: it does not imply insincerity to offer one price and then change your mind later (as it often does with Pacific Rim cultures). In fact, avoiding this process will generate suspicion, whether in the office or the market. Final terms need not be fair to all: in fact, Nigerians may bargain and negotiate with the expectation that in order for them to get something, you need to lose something. If you suspect something is too good to be true, or feel you are being manipulated, you are probably right in both cases. Remember to confirm what might sound like agreement with multiple inquiries: communication patterns often include reassurance, when in fact, your local associates may not be completely in agreement with you. Contracts and contract law are helpful, but ultimately useless. Unless you are working with a well-known multinational or high-government offices (and even there, contracts will be, in the end, unenforceable), it is better to assume the agreement will be unenforceable; nevertheless, put everything in writing that you can and insist on the same from your Nigerian associates. If possible, the deal should be sealed with a celebratory meal. Keep communications open, especially when at a distance, and stay in touch often with your Nigerian associates: share more information than you normally would if you can, not less, and be prepared to make many trips, as needed.

Written Correspondence

Your business letters should be informal and warm, and reflect the personal relationship you have established. Nevertheless, they must include a recognition of any titles and rank. Given names usually are written in uppercase; dates are given using the day/month/year format (with periods in between, not slashes)—in Nigerian business correspondence, unless you know you are writing to an observant Muslim, it is appropriate to use Western dates and business writing styles. When writing names, an honorific plus the title is as common as an honorific plus the first name (unless they are Westernized, in which case it is appropriate to use typical Western form). You should write your e-mails, letters, and faxes in an informal, friendly, and warm manner: use a brief and warm personal introduction, and segue smoothly into business. Keep the business issues and language clear and simple, however, and bulletpoint and outline all important matters. Use the Western format (name, position, company, street address, city, state/province, country, postal code) for the addresses.

GHANA

Note: Refer to the previous section on Nigeria for information about general West African cultural behaviors; the material that follows describes country-specific variations on general West African customs.

Some Historical Context

The great Ghanaian civilization extended far beyond the borders of the current nation of Ghana today. Originally known as the Gold Coast in colonial times, the nation of Ghana was granted its independence from Great Britain in 1957, becoming the first Black African colony to gain independence from the United Kingdom: this is a source of great national pride in Ghana, and one should know this and comment on it. (Also, evidencing any knowledge of the great Ghanaian Empire of the tenth century will be especially useful, and help you gain the reputation of being a knowledgeable and enlightened Westerner.) When the British arrived, they exploited the area for its natural mineral wealth, especially gold, and clashed with the local indigenous peoples, mainly the powerful Ashanti. Although the Ashanti were defeated, their king was allowed to remain in power, and the social structures of Ashanti life were upheld; to this day the Ashanti king in Ghana has many regional and autonomous powers. (Compare this British decentralized form of colonialization with the French centralized form seen in many of the neighboring countries. One should note that neither approach was implemented out of any sense of compassion; they merely represent two different approaches to efficient colonial exploitation.) Kwame Nkrumah, the first president of Ghana, is credited as having moved the country from a colony to an independent nation, but his form of socialism impoverished the nation; the leader most credited with Ghana's economic success (and relative to many of its neighbors, Ghana is an economically and politically stable country) is Jerry Rawlings, who led Ghana at the end of the twentieth century.

An Area Briefing

Religion and Demographics

Today's Akan represent the largest ethnic group in the country, inhabiting the central and eastern areas of the country; they are related to the Ashanti (who are in the south-central area). In addition, there are the Ewe in the east, the Fante along the coast, and many other smaller groups throughout the country. Because there are some tensions between the groups from time to time, special zones called *zongos* in some cities have been set up as residential areas for people who are not indigenous to the area. About 50 percent of the people are Christians, of some denomination, with 20 percent Muslim, and the remaining 30 percent animist; as is the case throughout the region, animist ideas and beliefs pervade all religions.

Greetings and Introductions

Language

English is the official language, although each ethnic group speaks its own indigenous language, which, ironically, makes English all the more popular as the lingua franca. In the south of the country, the Twi dialect spoken by the Akan people is more commonly used as a language between groups, and in the north, Hausa, the language of the neighboring Hausa people, is used as the common interethnic language of communication.

Like their Nigerian cousins, Ghanaians tend to be loud, very warm, friendly, boisterous, and outgoing, and this differs from the typical pattern of interpersonal communication and relationships among the people of many of Ghana's neighbors in West Africa.

Physical Greeting Styles

When men greet each other, good friends sometimes grasp each other's hands, and shake while simultaneously slowly pulling the palms away; before the hands are separated, each man grasps the other's middle finger with their thumb and forefinger, and snaps it (you may see versions of this greeting throughout the West African Gulf). Knocking the sides of both hands together as they are held out in front of you means "please" or "thank you," depending upon the context.

Dress

Dress can be casual Western-style dress, or the traditional Ghanaian (really Asante—the traditional spelling of Ashanti) dress of the kente-cloth (colorful woven strips of cloth that are draped over the body) for men and the traditional wraparound long dresses for women. Muslims wear the more traditional robes and head turban (but usually, as is much of the clothing in Ghana, more colorful).

Dining and Drinking

Ghanains generally like their food highly spiced. Some specialties include *fufu* (that dough-and-vegetable combo seen in other parts of the region), *ampesi* (root vegetables such as yams or plantains boiled up and served with a sauce), and the Ghanaian form of the ubiquitous West African porridge called *tuo zaafi* (commonly referred to as *teezee*) in Ghana.

Special Holidays and Celebrations

Major Holidays

All Muslim and Christian holidays are celebrated by the faithful in Ghana; national holidays are:

January 1	New Year's Day
March 6	Independence Day
March/April	Easter
July 1	Republic Day
December 25	Christmas
December 26	Boxing Day

TOGO

Some Historical Context

Once a part of Ghana, Togo, during colonial times, was the German colony of Togoland for a short period of time, and then was divided between France and Britain after Germany lost its African territories after World War I. Britain took the smaller western portion as part of its Gold Coast territory (later to become Ghana), and France took the eastern portion (to become what is Togo today). Originally, the peoples of this country were the Adja-Ewe, but the artificial European borders that divide the many peoples of the larger Togolese region make the country a nation in name only; in fact, most Togolese have more in common ethnically with people in neighboring countries than they have with each other within Togo. Perhaps for this reason, tolerance and a self-reliant attitude prevails among most people, without the inclination to seek dominance over others within the country.

An Area Briefing

Religion and Demographics

Some of the ethnic groups in the country include the Fon (who are, in fact, the dominant group in neighboring Benin), the Ewe, the Losso, the Kabye, and many others. In both Togo and neighboring Benin, we begin to see a cultural split along north/south lines, which continues in Nigeria; in Togo, this split takes the form of northern peoples being more from the Sudan and of Hamitic roots, and the southern groups being more Equatorial African, with Bantu roots. The majority of Togolese are animists, 30 percent are Christian, and 10 percent are Muslim: all groups have infused the others with their beliefs, creating unique forms of the religions in Togo.

Greetings and Introductions

Language and Basic Vocabulary

The official language is French, but as is the case in many of the countries in the region, most indigenous languages are preferred, and certain ones are used more commonly as the language for intergroup communication: in the case of Togo, the Mina language is the preferred language. English greetings, curiously, are common, at least among Ewe and other peoples in the south, in addition to their own language, usually in the form of a kind of Pidgin English.

Physical Greeting Styles

Men when shaking hands sometimes release the shake and snap their thumb and middle finger together; when in the presence of an elder, juniors often bow, and the elder claps as an indication of acknowledgment.

Dining and Drinking

When finished eating, it is polite to make a slight burp to indicate satisfaction, and if meat is served, it is important to break the bones and suck on the marrow: nothing must be wasted.

Special Holidays and Celebrations

Major Holidays

All Islamic and Christian holidays are celebrated by the faithful. National holidays are:

January 1	New Year's Day
January 13	Liberation Day
April 27	Independence Day
May 1	Workers' Day
June 21	Togolese Martyrs' Day

BENIN

Some Historical Context

A strip of land wedged between Togo and Nigeria, Benin (whose name changed from its colonial name of Dahomey when it gained independence) is the homeland of the mighty Fon people. The Fon ruled their kingdom of Danhomey for several centuries until the French came to colonize the area, and were known throughout the region as fierce warriors and shrewd businesspeople: they excelled in a number of areas, including the slave trade. Before the Europeans came, the

Fon were conquering and enslaving nearby groups (sometimes selling them to Arab traders who were coming inland from the eastern coasts); when the French arrived on the scene, the French also participated in the slave trade to a certain degree, and in so doing effectively ended the Fon rule. Today, having gotten over the bumps of the initial transition to independence, Benin is a model of effective democracy in Africa, as it has recently experienced little of the civil strife so common among emerging developing nations (in part the result of a quick and effective reversal from a short-lived attempt to create a communist system once the Soviet Union collapsed in the 1990s).

An Area Briefing

Religion and Demographics

If there is a blemish on Benin's relative success, it is the difficulty and tension that exists between southern Beninese and northern Beninese. While the Fon is the largest ethnic group in the country, there are many other smaller groups represented, including two rather large groups, the Yoruba and the Bariba. The Fon in the south often refer to their northern cousins derisively as "Somba," meaning savages or primitives, while the Beriba and others in the north, with equal derision, see their southern cousins as manipulatively clever, and too shrewd to be trusted. This division probably has its source in the historical experience of local ethnic groups with the expanding Fon, and the fact that southern Fon were exposed to Europeans first, while interior groups were not. Southerners, consequently, are seen as more open, outgoing, and direct, while northerners are seen as more conservative, withdrawn, and cautious.

Most Beninese are animists, no matter their indigenous group, and ancestor worship, divination, voodoo (local Fon deities who assist individuals to communicate with the great Creator-God, Mahu), Orisha (local Yoruba deities who assist individuals to communicate with the great Creator-God, Olorun), and other expressions of animist belief are common. There are Muslims, mainly in the north, and about an equal number of Christians throughout the country, but even these beliefs are heavily infused with animist ideas and customs.

Greetings and Introductions

Language and Basic Vocabulary

Because the French colonized the country, French is the official language, but as is the case throughout the region, local indigenous languages are spoken by the people, resulting in people who, as adults, usually speak several languages. Essentially, Yoruba and other languages are spoken in the north, and Fon and its related Adja-Fon group of languages are spoken in the south.

It is important to note that while people who are similar in rank greet each other with first names, and sometimes first names and titles, it is disrespectful to greet someone senior to you with his or her first name: in this case, it is best to simply address the person with his or her title, and use no name at all (if you must use a name, use his or her family name if you know it, although you may not be provided with that information). Once individuals of the same sex know each other, they often greet each other with several kisses, ending with a light kiss on the lips. Hitting the side of one's thigh with one's hand is an expression of frustration and disagreement.

Dining and Drinking

When you are a guest, it is common for your Beninese host to pour you a drink and take a sip before handing you the cup or glass. In turn, you take a sip and spit a little on the floor before drinking: your host is showing you that the drink, essentially, is safe, and you are demonstrating a remembrance of the dead before participating in an essential act of the living.

And when it comes to food, consider that much of it in Benin is highly spiced. There is the basic West African mixture of vegetables and rice, and the ubiquitous porridge made of different grains (corn flour makes *wo,* yam flour makes *amala,* and ground cassava makes *gari*). Meat is rarely available, and if it is served remember that no part of the animal is wasted: you eat everything, bones included.

Special Holidays and Celebrations

Major Holidays

In addition to the local animist holidays, the official Beninese holidays are:

January 1	New Year's Day
March/April	Easter
May 1	International Workers' Day
August 1	Independence Day
December 25	Christmas

BURKINA FASO

Some Historical Context

In colonial days, as part of French West Africa, Burkina Faso was known as Upper Volta. While an inland country and therefore technically not an Atlantic Gulf country, Burkina Faso was originally the home of several powerful and competing kingdoms from the eighth century to the eleventh century, related to and part of the cultures of the surrounding region. There is a strong tolerance among all Burkinabe for all ethnic groups within the country, and most Burkinabe, while identifying first with their family and ethnic group, are equally proud of their nation, and will be quick to tell outsiders about their nation's achievements: you will no doubt be regaled with stories of Thomas Sankara, the Burkinabe leader who led the nation to independence. The capital of Burkina Faso, Ouagadoughou, is more familiarly referred throughout the country simply as Ouaga.

An Area Briefing

Religion and Demographics

The Burkinabe (as they refer to themselves) are a combination of many ethnic subgroups of the central North African Voltaic peoples, the largest of which are the Mossi; others include Fulani, Senoufo, Bobo, Bwaba, and Gurma. French is the official language, but Moore, the language of the Mossi, is the most commonly spoken language, while Dioula is the most popular language for intergroup communication (it developed over the centuries specifically as a language for commerce between the ethnic groups in the Voltaic region). Greetings may be in French or local languages, or a combination. The population is about equally split between Islam, Christianity, and animist beliefs, and each religion infuses the other significantly.

Special Holidays and Celebrations

Major Holidays

Islamic and Christian holidays are observed by the faithful. The Burkina Faso national holidays are:

January 1	New Year's Day
January 3	Fête du 3 Janvier
March 8	International Women's Day
May 1	Labor Day
August 4	Revolution Day
August 5	Independence Day
December 25	Christmas (the period between Christmas and the New Year is a special holiday time for all Burkinabe)

PART FOUR

Central and Eastern Africa

The Equatorial Heart

An Introduction to the Region

The equator is more than just a geographical feature that runs horizontally through the heart of Africa: it is also, roughly, a megacultural dividing line between the Hamitic Africa of the north and the Black Africa of the south. Although there is great variation along this line (sometimes for considerable distances in either direction), it is not incorrect to observe that the linguistic, social, religious, and cultural roots of Black Africa lie here, while those of the north lie, as we have already seen, elsewhere. Here is the great division between the Bantu civilizations of the south (from Congo down to the Cape) and the Guinean and North African civilizations of the north; the great division between religions (animist in the south, Muslim in the north); and the great division between languages (Bantu and Swahili-based in the south; Hamitic, Arabic, and indigenous West African in the north). The countries that lie along this line typically reveal influences of both, but as we move south into the equatorial heart of Africa, we experience more clearly the world of the Black African, who speaks Bantu, practices animism and Christianity, and shares with the rest of Africa the sad and difficult legacy of the colonial experience, primarily, but not exclusively, at the hands of Western Europeans.

While equatorial Africa (and, as we shall see in part five, South Africa as well) struggled with the French, British, and Belgians (not to mention the Germans and Portuguese), East Africa additionally, and much earlier, struggled with Arabs—mainly in the form of Omanis and other Gulf Arabs—who also came to East Africa to exploit, and in some cases, enslave. If there is a horizontal line that geographically and culturally divides north and south Africa, there is also a vertical line, mirroring the great topographical feature of this region, the Rift Valley, which runs north-south, and which separates the vast plains in the east from the canopied rain forests of the center and west. And the peoples, of course, and their cultures, on either side of this line, are different too.

Today, these regions struggle in their own unique ways with these colonial legacies, and cultures on all sides of these dividing lines express the resulting tensions through struggles with each other. It is difficult, for example, to understand the tragic collapse of Congo—clearly in the equatorial center of Africa—without also understanding the politics of East Africa, most specifically, the vicious ethnic histories between the Tutsi and Hutu peoples, and the sad national and sometimes personal self-interests of the past and current centuries which have fanned and continue to inflame these rivalries.

This is the land of immense natural resources, of histories so ancient their pasts have not yet been measured, of proud and patient people caught in desperate circumstances beyond the understanding of many non-Africans. It is an irony that on the same plains where human life began, the twentieth century has experienced one of the world's great genocides; that in the same equatorial rainforests where the diversity of life explodes, some of the world's most horrific diseases, such as HIV and Ebola, have emerged; and where people have organized themselves into some of the oldest social systems on earth, they suffer under the scourge of maniacal dictators and their minions. Yet, it is perhaps exactly in the enormity of the challenges that face the region that the world can find its own redemption, and perhaps this is the great opportunity and lesson that Africa presents to us all: to save the environment and redefine our human relationships, both personal and social; in a sense, to create an ecology of living.

Getting Oriented

This equatorial region, for our purposes, can be divided into its central heart and the east. Right in the middle of the heart is the cultural center of gravity for the entire region, Congo, or more accurately, Congos, as the traditional "Kongo" cultures of the region today are represented by the Democratic Republic of the Congo (formerly Zaire, and in colonial times, the Belgian Congo, itself an immense amalgam of myriad distinct cultures, many of which struggle today for political independence) and the Republic of the Congo. However, culturally the two are so similar that they can be treated as one. Surrounding the Congolese cultures are the countries that straddle the great African equatorial divide, and therefore reveal cultures that are more a mix of both north and south: Cameroon, Gabon, and the Central African Republic.

As we move east, we explore the great plains cultures of Kenya and Tanzania, and the complex cultural identities of Uganda, Rwanda, and Burundi, and their impact on each other, the equatorial center, and Africa and the world at large.

The Center: Cameroon, the Central African Republic, Gabon, and Congo

As many of the cultural behaviors of Cameroon, the Central African Republic, and Gabon are related to those of the West African Gulf countries, the information below represents country-specific variations from the information on West African Gulf countries provided in the previous section. Congo and Congolese culture will be treated separately at the end of this chapter.

CAMEROON

Some Historical Context

Cameroon ("The" Cameroons is no longer an accepted name, as it is more a colonialist designation of a particular region, and not the appropriate description of an independent country) has been described as "Africa's Crossroads" because it straddles, and therefore incorporates, the complexity of the cultures of both north and south Africa; as such, it is an appropriate country to start us on our journey into equatorial Africa. The original inhabitants of Cameroon were the Aka people, more commonly known in the West as pygmy, and today, many Aka still leave deep in the rain forests of Cameroon. About 1,500 years ago, however, Bantu peoples from the south and Hausa peoples from the north began inhabiting the area (pushing the Aka further into the forests); the Fulani came from the north in the fifteenth century, bringing Islam with them, and soon after came the Portuguese (who named the area after the large prawns—*cameros*, in Portuguese—that they discovered in the rivers along the coast). Already the divisions within the country became apparent, as southern Cameroonians participated in the slave trade (which was mainly to Europe), while northern Cameroonians developed the culture of Islam in the interior. For a time, Germany had stewardship over the north and south, but after losing World War I, Germany divided Cameroon between the French and the British (the French had the area from the capital, Yaounde, east, and the British took the area west of the capital to the sea). Today there are two major cities in Cameroon reflecting this division, the capital in the east and the major commercial city of Douala in the west. For a time, British Cameroon was administered as part of Nigeria, but when independence came, the two areas were united into one country.

Culturally, however, the two areas are still different, but because differences and divisions are the essence of the country, there is a high level of tolerance among most Cameroonians.

An Area Briefing

Religion and Demographics

The largest ethnic groups in the country today are the Fulani in the north, the Bamileke in the west, and the Beti (or Pahouin as they are also known) in the south, plus the Aka of the interior. There are many other smaller groups throughout the entire country, and all together, there are more than two hundred different languages spoken in Cameroon. About 50 percent of the people are Christian, a combination of Catholic (a result of the French influence) and Protestant (a result of the British influence), plus about 25 percent Muslim, and the rest animist; nevertheless, as is the case throughout the region, animist ideas infuse the practice of both Christianity and Islam.

Greetings and Introductions

Language and Basic Vocabulary

French and English are the official languages, and most city dwellers can speak enough of both; most other people speak a little of one or the other, and use their native language mostly. French is spoken mainly in the Francophone section of the country, and English, and its related Pidgin English, is spoken in the Anglophone section of the country. (Pidgin English is also used as a language of trade more or less throughout the country.)

Honorifics for Men, Women, and Children

Perhaps one of the strongest unifying hallmarks of Cameroonian behavior is the exceptionally strong emphasis placed on the importance of rank and hierarchy, and the consequent respect for formality and obligations that individuals have toward one another. For example, the most common way to greet someone is simply with their title, whether it is Dr., Mr., cousin, or mother. Most of the time, names, whether given or family, are simply not used, and this is especially true between people who are first being introduced to each other. Titles help individuals to identify (and be identified by) their status, which is demonstrated in many nonverbal ways, as well.

For example, the amount, kind, and degree of embroidery and design that one has on their traditional clothing is an indication of rank and status. Wealth, as a reflection of status, is demonstrated through numerous symbols: scarification and henna skin designs, as well as hairstyles (particularly among women) all indicate status and rank.

Physical Greeting Styles

When being introduced to someone new, individuals will often bow slightly; this is certainly the case for juniors when they meet elders, even if they know each other. Occasionally, juniors, when speaking with seniors, will touch their right arm with their left hand during the handshake as an extra sign of respect. It is not uncommon for women to curtsy in front of elders, their husbands, and others. (In Anglophone regions of the country, there may be less deference shown to positions and rank, and more formality in Francophone sections.) The West African "snap" handshake is done, but usually only among peers and generally with young people, wherein they snap the middle and thumb finger together as the hands are pulled apart, and it is only among peers and young people of the same gender and age that people refer to each other by name (and in this case, it is the first or given name, or more often a nickname, that is used).

You will hear the common phrase "*Ha na?*," which is Pidgin English for "How are you?" Answer in any local language, French, or English, if appropriate.

Communication Styles

Physical Gestures and Facial Expressions

As is the case in some other parts of the region, one avoids pointing with the index finger, and instead indicates direction with the nose, chin, or by puckering the lips in the direction needing to be indicated. Following some of the typical Muslim protocols, such as not showing or pointing the sole of the shoe, not using the left hand, and not touching the top of the head of another individual, are all important for Muslims and non-Muslims alike. Nodding the head quickly up and down while audibly sucking in air is an indication of agreement, while "no" is often indicated simply by shrugging the shoulders. When approaching a Cameroon home, it is important to remove one's shoes, and if approaching the home of someone with significant status, it is very respectful to remove one's shoes several yards away before one even gets near the house. Because group orientation is so powerful, people with obligations and responsibilities to each other, such as family or clan members, typically share whatever they may have with each other (for example, if someone gets a job, wages are often distributed among others in the family), and holding the hand out with the palm slightly cupped and facing upward is a nonverbal sign that you need to share what you have.

Dining and Drinking

The main meal of the day is in the evening. As a guest, you must taste everything (never sniff at the food, that is very insulting) that is presented, but if there is something you cannot or choose not to eat, you need simply to say that you have just eaten. Food is similar to that of neighboring countries previously mentioned (*fufu,* porridge, *garri,* and stews made of vegetables and spices). Because of the abundance of flora and fauna in the rainforest, when meat is available, it may be from many different kinds of animals. Food can be spicy. While Muslims will avoid alcohol, many Cameroonians enjoy local beers (and, of course, the ubiquitous soft drinks), and palm and banana wines. In such a group-oriented culture, it may be surprising to know that guests typically do not bring food as a gift when they go to others' homes for a meal: in Cameroon, it would be implying that the host cannot provide; instead, bring a gift for the family or, better yet, the children.

Special Holidays and Celebrations

Major Holidays

Muslim and Christian holidays are celebrated by the faithful. National holidays in Cameroon are:

January 1	New Year's Day
February 11	Youth Day
March/April	Easter
May 1	Labor Day
May 20	Unification Day
August 15	Assumption
December 25	Christmas

THE CENTRAL AFRICAN REPUBLIC

Some Historical Context

Conveniently referred to as the CAR, the Central African Republic is a twentieth-century construction imposed on an ancient area where northern and southern African civilizations converged, clashed, and merged over the centuries. As is the case with neighboring Gabon and Cameroon, the indigenous people of the area were most likely the Aka or pygmies, and when the French came to the region, what is the CAR was merely a section of the greater territory known as French Equatorial Africa.

An Area Briefing

Religion and Demographics

The predominant ethnic groups in the country are the Gbaya and Banda, each comprising about 30 percent of the population. There are many other smaller ethnic groups in the CAR, including the Aka and the itinerant Mbororo (descendants of the Fulani, who are migratory herders throughout the region, and do not consider themselves citizens of the CAR or, like the Tuaregs of North Africa, any other country of the region through which they pass). There is also a significant population of Mediterranean Europeans (mainly in the cities as a small merchant class) and refugees from neighboring Chad, which, at one time, was part of French Equatorial Africa, as well. About 50 percent of the population is Christian, the result of significant missionary effort in the nineteenth century, with the rest being animist and Muslim. As is the case throughout the region, animism infuses all religious practices.

Greetings and Introductions

Language and Basic Vocabulary

There are two official languages, French and the Bantu language, Sango, which is understood by many of the various ethnic groups within the country, and which serves, far more than French, as a language for intergroup communication and commerce throughout the country.

Some Sango greetings are:

bara ala	hello
tonga na nyen?	how are you doing?
ala yeke senge?	are you doing okay?

Central Africans greet people individually when in small groups; when in a larger group, it is okay to raise both hands, with the palms facing the group, and greet everyone with "Bara ala kwe!" (Greetings to all!).

Communication Styles

Central Africans (a term used by citizens of the CAR to describe themselves; when in the CAR it is important, therefore, to use this term carefully, as it is meant to refer only to citizens of the CAR and not as a generic term to describe inhabitants of central Africa) are viewed by their neighbors as extremely warm and friendly people, who have a deep and abiding loyalty to their family, clan, and friends.

Physical Gestures and Facial Expressions

Central Africans often indicate agreement by raising the eyebrows and making a quick clicking sound. Holding the arm out and flipping the hand palm up, palm down several times is a way to ask, "How are things going?" Central Africans sometimes make a kind of hissing sound when they need to get someone's attention. Making the U.S.-style "okay" sign with the thumb and forefinger has no negative connotation, but simply means "nothing," or "zero," as it does in France. Throughout the central African region, when children fold their arms over their stomachs, it is a sign of respect, typically shown when they are in the presence of their parents or elders.

Dining and Drinking

Along with the foods we have already discussed that are common to the region, in the CAR there are two daily staples that make up the traditional meal: *ngunza,* a very thick sauce made from cassava leaves, peanut butter, and tomatoes, and *gozo,* boiled dried cassava and flour: you scoop up the *ngunza* with a piece of *gozo.* Vegetables and meats are offered in addition when available.

Special Holidays and Celebrations

Major Holidays

Islamic and Christian holidays are celebrated by the faithful, and the national holidays in the CAR are:

January 1	New Year's Day
May 1	Labor Day (Fête du Travail)
May	Fête des Mères (Mothers' Day)
August 13	Independence Day
December 1	Declaration of Independence from France Day

GABON

Some Historical Context

Like its neighbors, the original inhabitants of Gabon were the pygmie, who were replaced by immigrating Bantu people around A.D. 1000. Much of Gabon was part of the larger and very powerful Bantu Bakongo Empire (one of the many Congo cultures that emerged in the region at the time). When the French came, Gabon became a major center for the export of slaves and natural resources, such as timber, rubber, and animals. As in much of French Equatorial Africa, the borders of Gabon were set according to French territorial expectations, and not according to the indigenous ethnic groups within its borders: consequently, many Gabonese have more in common with their cousins in other neighboring countries than they do with other Gabonese. Nevertheless, and despite the more than forty different ethnic groups within Gabon, ethnic differences are generally well tolerated.

An Area Briefing

Religion and Demographics

The largest group are the Fang people, about 30 percent of the population, although most groups in the country define themselves as Bantu. There is a large contingent of Western workers in Gabon managing many of the export industries on behalf of Western multinationals. French is the official language, and although Fang is spoken by the Fang, it is not generally well-known among other groups; most people speak their own indigenous language and French, more or less.

Because of the significant French influence, more than half the population is Catholic, but the Catholicism practiced in Gabon is heavily infused with local animist traditions; an additional 20 percent are Protestant, with a small Muslim minority.

Communication Styles

One of the defining characteristics of Gabonese, at least when compared with their neighbors, is their frank and direct outspokenness. They are perceived by other, more nonconfrontation-oriented neighbors, to be aggressive, combative, and sometimes disrespectful. In fact, this is more a reaction to the fact that in Gabon, it is not expected for anyone to say "please" and "thank you," since Gabonese believe that such statements are insincere and unnecessary between friends and individuals who have an obligation to provide for each other. The more direct, frank style of interpersonal communication may also be the result of the powerful French influence in the country at large. It has been said that the Gabonese are to their region of Africa what Nigeria and Ghana are to West Africa. Be that as it may, Gabonese are courteous and friendly people who shake hands and sometimes employ the typical French greetings when meeting colleagues and associates. A smile always accompanies the greeting, and Gabonese are always on the lookout for a laugh and a joke. In Fang, the universal greeting is "Mbolo" ("hello"), and a combination of French and Fang phrases will be used when greeting people. It is customary to use a title in place of, or sometimes in addition to, the first name.

Physical Gestures and Facial Expressions

The "thumbs-up" sign, which is not necessarily a good sign in northern Africa, means "okay" in Gabon and throughout most of central Africa. Making a fist with the left hand, raising it slightly, and hitting the top of it with the palm of the right hand indicates agreement. Agreement is also indicated by placing the thumbnail against the inside of the center of the top row of teeth and snapping it forward. Holding the fingers together and shaking the wrist quickly indicates enthusiasm and excitement. Most of the other previously discussed gestures throughout the region apply in Gabon as well.

Dining and Drinking

Socializing, as is the case throughout the region, is the main form of entertaining (and doing business), and is typically done in one's home. Typical foods that are served have been deeply influenced by the French; beignets (doughnuts) and brochettes (skewered meats and vegetables) are very popular. Cassava (or manioc) is the main root vegetable, and is used with and on everything in a variety of forms. Meats, when available, are often dried or smoked (the preferred methods of preserving them in rural areas), and fish is available along the coast. Stews, porridge, and spicy sauces often accompany many of the dishes. A popular fruit in the region is the *atanga,* which is a hard fruit that once boiled is often used as a spread on breads (sometimes referred to as bush butter). Also popular is *odika,* used to make a sauce called *chocolat* because of its color (it is made from the mango pit). Urban Gabonese often dine Western-style, with spoons, the main meal of the day being in the evening. In most Gabonese homes, food is prepared in one area and served in another: the cooking and eating is done by the women in the *cuisine,* and eating, for men and guests, is done in the salon, or eating area.

Special Holidays and Celebrations

Major Holidays

Muslim and Christian holidays are celebrated by the faithful, and local animist festivals are held throughout the country, town by town. Official holidays in Gabon are:

January 1	Jour de l'An (New Year's Day)
March/April	Pâques (Easter)
May 1	Fête du Travail (Labor Day)
August 17	Fête Nationale (Independence Day)
November 1	Toussaint (All Saints' Day)
December 25	Noël (Christmas)

CONGO

Some Introductory Background on Congo and the Congolese

The Democratic Republic of the Congo, or DRC, is an enormous country, about half the size of the United States, rich in history, natural resources, cultures, promise, and a remarkable diversity of people with Bantu roots. What a sad irony then, that this great center of equatorial Africa, at the time of this writing, has imploded into a destructive anarchy, with gangster-like clans vying for control over the greatness that Congo can be. There are few non-Africans in the DRC today, and when it will be safe to return is currently unknown. The Republic of the Congo is a separate state, nestled between the western boundary of the DRC and Gabon, Cameroon, and the CAR; it represents, at least in the hindsight of history, the ability of a former Congolese province to secede successfully from the rest of the mother country as it slid into chaos. It is not the only Congolese province to seek independence: Katanga, for example, has been strongly separatist from the very beginning of Congo's independence from Belgium. And there are others, some aligned with Congo's neighbors, both benefiting and suffering from such alliances and alignments. The roots of this current catastrophe can be found in several areas: the awful colonial legacy of King Leopold of Belgium, who in the 1800s essentially turned Congo into a personal slave state; the greed and stupidity of recent leaders; the independent, vying interests of neighboring states; and the interests of the larger superpowers, particularly during the Cold War. Together, these elements virtually ensured the collapse of Congo. But Congo has been around, as a mosaic of unique and powerful Bantu cultures in the center of Africa, for millennia, and no doubt will rise to its promise again. When and how is the question.

Until that time, the purpose of looking at Congo is not to discuss it as a destination for tourism or business (it clearly isn't), but rather because by understanding some of the elements of Congolese culture, we can better understand the powerful influence it has had on its neighbors, many of which can and should be visited. The interplay between Congolese culture, the country of Congo, and the countries and cultures of its neighbors are inextricably bound together; in order to know one, we must know the other, and there is no root culture more important in central equatorial Africa than Congolese culture.

Some Historical Context

King Leopold's initial vision may have been to form a trading company to exploit Congo's riches, but in the end, he reduced the country and its people to a plundered and enslaved vassal state, and in so doing, set a precedent for vast and awful exploitation as a way of life. Looking back one can see that he was just the first of many, Congolese included, who ruled Congo for their own personal enrichment, at the expense and suffering of its people. When Congo achieved its independence from Belgium after World War II, Patrice Lumumba led the country as a socialist state; the challenge of holding this immensely diverse nation together began to weigh, and pressure from secessionist groups grew rapidly. Different groups aligned themselves with the different political and economic agendas of the superpowers: the West, which was suspect of Lumumba and his socialist policies, supported some of the rebels, while the Soviet Union supported Lumumba. This set the stage for phase one of the collapse: Katanga seceded, civil war ensued, and factions formed within and outside of Congo. Lumumba was murdered, and Mobutu Sese Seko took control. Mobutu ruled as a dictator, claiming that his undemocratic control was necessary until stability returned (not an uncommon argument in fractured developing nations); unfortunately, for more than twenty years, he became used to the power and excess that he created for himself. Through his policy of "Africanization," he changed the name of the country to Zaire (taking the name the Portuguese gave to the River Congo when they first explored the region several centuries before, and revealing perhaps more than he meant to about how much his success was a result of this colonial legacy) and amassed a personal fortune, like King Leopold, at the expense of his people and the country. The United States made him an ally, adding to the size of his bank account, until the bubble burst in the 1990s. It had been too much for too long, and rebels began to tip the balance of power in Congo. The economy plunged the country into chaos; soldiers broke ranks and formed themselves into armed private militias, each aligned with different interests; secessionist movements grew; and the remains of what was Congo became ripe for the political catastrophe that was developing just outside the eastern borders of Congo in Rwanda and Uganda: the murderous ethnic violence of Tutsis versus Hutus. Phase two of the collapse was about to begin.

The war in Rwanda between Hutus (the majority) and Tutsis (the ruling minority) exploded. For centuries these two groups had been at each other's throats, with clan-like enmities going back centuries. When the Rwandan civil war exploded, more than 1 million Hutu refugees spilled across the border into Zaire. However, Tutsis and Hutus can be found throughout the region, as the states that were created in central equatorial Africa by the European colonial powers were often not drawn in consideration for local ethnic borders. Hutu refugees in Zaire, paranoid that they were still at the mercy of Tutsis in Zaire, began slaughtering the Tutsis there. Rwanda sent Tutsi troops into Zaire, ostensibly to protect them, but also to advance its own interests in the vacuum that was the collapsed Congo. Rwandan Tutsis defeated the Congolese and the Hutus—bringing the ethnic conflict into Zaire—repatriated the Hutus back into Rwanda to be slaughtered on their home turf, and aligned themselves within Congo with the new Congolese rebel leader, Laurent Kabila.

In phase three, Kabila led an armed struggle against Mobutu and other splinter groups; the country was plunged into a new round of civil war. In 1997, Mobuto was ousted, Kabila took control, and in a repeat of Congolese historical precedent, banned most democratic processes. Older political allies turned, and neighboring states aligned once again to push their own interests in the fractured state (the current scramble is mainly over control of the diamond mines, as Congo is the world's largest producer of diamonds, and this wealth is fueling the fighting on both sides): anti-Kabila rebels joined with Tutsis in the east, eager to get back at Hutus and the Congolese government, and neighboring countries lined up. Hutus and Tutsis came pouring into Zaire from other neighboring countries to fight each other, supported by either the rebels or the Kabila government. Angola, Zimbabwe, and Namibia in the south sent troops to Kabila, and Rwanda and Uganda backed the rebels in the north and east. The United Nations stepped in with peacekeeping troops. As of this writing, the fighting continues, the ethnic rivalries remain inflamed, and the greed of individuals and nations keeps the specter of oppression alive, transformed yet undiminished, in Congo.

An Area Briefing

Politics and Government

Since the struggle for political control is undetermined, it is difficult to describe a political system in Congo today. The president has broad powers over all three nominal branches of the government; there is no functioning legislature; all political parties are banned; there is no functioning constitution; and the eastern provinces are controlled by various rebel factions, each beholden to particular outside interests and neighboring states, each in a war against both the government in Kinshasa and each other.

Schools and Education

As is the case throughout all of West Africa, schooling for children is spotty and difficult to mandate under the best circumstances; under the current circumstances, it is, in some cases, nonexistent. Beyond the lack of teachers, resources, supplies, and infrastructure, many people believe that schooling is irrelevant to their lives and the lives of their children, that it is much more important for the children to be available to help out at home, in the fields, and in the market. Compounding this is the complexity of languages spoken in Congo, which makes administering any kind of unified education system difficult at best. The educated elite has, for all intents and purposes, left the country, adding to the problems already being experienced in the realm of education.

Religion and Demographics

Congo is mainly Christian (about 80 percent), due to the historical presence of European missionaries: today, about 50 percent of the Christian population is Roman Catholic and 20 percent is Protestant (observers of Kimbanguism, a uniquely Congolese sect of Protestantism established early in the twentieth century); 10 percent of the population is Muslim, and the rest animist. Even so, animist beliefs pervade both Islam and Christianity (for example, many people believe in genies, spirits, and zombies—collectively known as *juju*—and many people wear charms—*grigri,* usually in the form of amulets containing written prayers, incantations, or special ingredients to ward off evil). Animist beliefs typically revere a Creator God, and the devout invoke good and evil through the assistance of intermediary spirits; people capable of doing this are usually spiritual leaders practiced in witchcraft. Ancestor worship is a particularly powerful element in animism. Religion, of whatever kind, plays a powerful role in the daily lives of most of the people. It is a challenge (to provide opportunity) and a strength (the optimism and energy) that, as is the case throughout much of Africa, the majority of the population is under thirty years of age. The current devastation means that there is no effectively functioning formal economy; most exchanges occur through barter or with foreign currency. The official unemployment rate is almost 80 percent. The role of women in Congo has been severely impacted by current events; since the present economy is an informal one, women play a vital role in whatever business there is on a daily basis: in the market, or in town, they often are responsible for the daily business of life. In western Congo, society is structured along matriarchal lines, where a wife's brother has more authority than the wife's husband (this system is traditional among many of the indigenous Bantu people of that area); in eastern and northern Congo, society is more patrilinear, being more influenced by Islam, and can also be polygamous.

The Congolese people are mainly of Bantu origin, with more than two hundred subethnic groups, the four largest being the Mongo, the Luba, the Kongo, and the Mangbetu-Azande; together they make up about half the total population of Congo. The remaining 50 percent is a vast mix of many different groups, including Hutu, Tutsi, pygmy (Aka), Sudanese, and other eastern and northern African groups. There are vast numbers of refugees from neighboring countries as well, and a small merchant class of Lebanese and Indians.

Fundamental Cultural Orientations

1. What's the Best Way for People to Relate to One Another?

OTHER-INDEPENDENT OR OTHER-DEPENDENT? There is a combination of deep concern for family, clan, and other membership groups (such as work and religion) that defines an individual and individual expression. Congolese, like all Africans, have a hierarchical sense of loyalties, beginning with their family, and then, in descending order of importance, their ethnic group, their religion, their home village, their country, their region, and their continent, and the current circumstances only serve to emphasize the distinctions between "in" and "out" groups. Congolese are deeply connected first to their clan and their families: for that reason, it is critical that one inquire about the health of all family members. How one performs his or her role vis-à-vis others is judged in Africa, and individuals do nothing without careful consideration for how their actions will be perceived and for the impact their actions will have on their family and their community. Consequently, individual empowerment and decision making are rare, and consensus-building and confirming group agreement are critical. Sharing, concern for others, humility, and an acceptance—without anger, remorse, or hostility—of one's role, at least within and for one's group, are all hallmarks of Central African and Congolese culture.

HIERARCHY-ORIENTED OR EGALITY-ORIENTED? Both Congolese secular life and ethnic group membership (as well as Islamic life for Muslims) is rigidly stratified, with three or four generations of the extended family traditionally living together (this is not necessarily the case in the cities); individuals within this highly stratified social structure play their roles—children, women, and men in relation to one another, hosts in relation to guests, religious leaders and other elders in relation to the community. Defining for others one's rank, therefore, is important, and status symbols (for example, the jewelry that women wear, the ritual scarification imposed by the ethnic group, or the pattern used on the traditional robe) are traditionally important. It is critical that everyone show respect for elders and the devout, and, in the current circumstances, the politically powerful. Women and men are different and perform different roles: in Congo, a woman typically may go out in public alone, but she will probably prefer to go with other female friends or relatives. She need not be in the company of a close male relative (husband, father, son, or brother), and Muslim women generally will not wear a veil; in fact, although all groups are male-dominated, Congolese women in general do play a significant role in public life, especially in the western part of the country.

RULE-ORIENTED OR RELATIONSHIP-ORIENTED? While many Congolese have had experience with and in the West, the tension that exists between the application of universal rules over reliable and dependable relationships is palpable, especially under current circumstances, where legitimacy for the imposition of rules is challenged. This leads to a high dependence on power, authority, and subjective decision making based on the situation and the relationships between the individuals involved. Ultimately, face-to-face knowledge of the individuals involved in any interaction is the basis upon which final decisions are often made.

2. What's the Best Way to View Time?

MONOCHRONIC OR POLYCHRONIC? Congo is essentially very polychronic, due to the influence of agrarian and religious traditions, and the current unpredictable situation of daily life. There is forgiveness for the inevitable delays and unexpected events that define life in Africa, and understanding when things don't go as planned or scheduled; people may or may not show up at invited events, things may or may not happen as planned. Schedules tend to be loose and flexible. Because who (relationships) is more important than what (tasks) or when (time), there can be many interruptions during a meeting, and people's obligations to other people, who may come and go, are more important than doing things according to schedules. If you are being kept waiting, or are ignored because of someone else's needs, it is an indication of your importance relative to the other person, and expressing frustration over being kept waiting only diminishes your importance.

RISK-TAKING OR RISK-AVERSE?   Congolese are prone to taking risks when in positions of authority, but avoiding them when they are not. Within organizations, the decision makers can be bold, even reckless, but subordinates generally are not, and take action only when instructed to do so. Therefore, comfort with uncertainty, in general, is low, and much information may need to be exchanged with different people before decisions can be made. Even when decisions are made at the top, the concern for others within the group requires decision makers to consult with subordinates before making decisions. There will be much discussion with trusted others about what you, as a foreigner, bring to the table, *after* you leave the meeting.

PAST-ORIENTED OR FUTURE-ORIENTED?   There is a distinct and inherent fatalism in regard to the effect of human action when considering day-to-day life. Nevertheless, those empowered by virtue of their position are expected to make the decisions that keep the world running, and by so doing are either fulfilling their destiny, however their religious beliefs define it, or that of their group. Therefore, future benefits often do not motivate Congolese; doing nothing, or doing things for the here and now, is sometimes more important, and if things do not work out, that is to be expected—no mortal controls the universe, and all is ultimately determined. There is a deep belief that things will take the time they need to take, and that it is always more important to maintain smooth interpersonal relationships until opportunities come along: when that happens, Congolese will be sure to seize them!

3. What's the Best Way for Society to Work with the World at Large?

LOW-CONTEXT DIRECT OR HIGH-CONTEXT INDIRECT COMMUNICATORS? Congolese are very context-driven communicators. They can speak in metaphors, and use stories or codified phrases; they will employ analogies, precedent, and much nonverbal behavior to convey true meaning. They generally do not avoid confrontation as a primary goal, as do many of their neighbors in the region, and often will be quite frank and direct about what is on their mind. Congolese have a reputation for being open, direct, and outgoing, quick with a laugh and a joke, boisterous, aggressive, and loud (at least as viewed by others who are less so!).

PROCESS-ORIENTED OR RESULT-ORIENTED?   The interpretation of events and the determination of truth and right and wrong in Congolese society are context-bound, and not a philosophical search for absolutes. Decisions and actions therefore may be the result of reasoning that is not directed at a determination of truth, but rather context-based "correctness" based on similar experiences. Combine this with a tendency to rely on subjective experience, and the Congolese mind is processing information, for the most part, in a different way than the Western mind. In fact, because of their negative experience with Western exploitation, it may be a struggle sometimes for most Africans—Congolese or otherwise—to even be open to Western ideas.

FORMAL OR INFORMAL?   Central African society is basically formal and ritualized, and each group has its own way of honoring the hierarchies, establishing respect and deference, and following (or not following) through on their responsibilities. There are formal ways that guests (outsiders) and hosts (insiders) must act toward one another, in order to preserve the honor of all groups and individuals. Nevertheless, and perhaps because of the multiethnic nature of the country, Congolese are quick to adopt a breezy, informal manner with most individuals—non-Africans included—once a relationship has been established.

Greetings and Introductions

Language and Basic Vocabulary

English may become the official language, as the government seems to be moving in that direction, but in the past, French was the official language. However, even then, only a small percentage of the people used it, preferring instead to use their own indigenous language, or Lingala, the most widely used indigenous language (especially in the west). Lingala is a Bantu language, as is Kikongo (spoken mainly in the southwest), Tshiluba (spoken mainly in central and southern Congo), and Swahili (spoken mainly in the east). Westerners need to remember that the English that is used is in most cases highly influenced by the local languages, resulting in a kind of Pidgin English. Each group speaks its own indigenous language, as well, which may or may not be understood by others in other groups, and most local indigenous languages are oral. Most of the time, Congolese will tend to reassure, insist that they can do something, know something, or solve the problem, whether or not they actually can; this may or may not be intended to deceive, although words more often indicate what they desire than what might actually be.

Using English or French when greeting people, especially in the cities, is usually appropriate, but the Lingala "*Mbote*" ("hello") or "*Sango nini?*" ("How are things?"), or the Swahili "*Jambo*" ("Hi!"), are much more common. Part of what has contributed to the perception that Congolese can be abrupt and direct is the fact that pleasantries such as "please" and "thank you," for many ethnic groups in this part of the world, are not expressed (in fact, there may not be such words in the language): this is typically because there is such an overriding sense of group obligation to others that to have to make such requests and statements seems unnecessary and implies the possibility that one might not in fact do what is being requested. Be careful not to misjudge this speech pattern: Congolese will typically demonstrate their thankfulness through action, not words.

Honorifics for Men, Women, and Children

As is the case throughout most of central Africa, people usually greet each other by title or relationship (e.g., Dr., Mr., Mrs., aunt, mother, cousin) plus the first, or given, name (unless the individuals involved are Westernized, or if they are first being introduced, in which case, the standard Western greeting of honorific plus last name would be appropriate). If names are not known, sometimes stating the individual's position as a title is sufficient (e.g., Mr. Engineer or Miss Fish Seller). Children typically refer to their parents as "mother of" or "father of" plus the name of the oldest sibling, and refer to elders in general as either "aunt" or "uncle." Nicknames are very common, and most people are referred to by their nickname, sometimes with an honorific preceding it.

The What, When, and How of Introducing People

Always wait to be introduced to a stranger, although if you are not introduced after a few minutes, it is appropriate to introduce yourself. As is the case throughout the region, it is critical to take time when you greet someone to make many inquiries into their health and the health and condition of the lives of their relatives and close friends (even livestock, if appropriate!). It is considered very rude not to take a considerable amount of time when meeting someone to make these inquiries and express understanding of his or her responses; he or she will do the same in kind. You must acknowledge people you know when you pass them on the street, and you should acknowledge strangers when eyes meet in passing. Never presume to seat yourself at a gathering. If possible, wait to be told where to sit; you will be seated in a spot appropriate to your position. Typically, men, women, and children (even boys and girls) are seated separately. Because you will never be refused, and because guests are always welcome (as is the case in much of Africa, because of the lack of communication and transportation facilities, people simply drop in uninvited often—in fact, this is typically the most common form of entertainment and socializing), it is important that you do not purposefully make a visit unannounced around mealtime; instead, come in the late morning or early evening. When arriving at someone's home, you will generally announce yourself by tapping on the front gate, or clapping your hands in the front of the house; do not enter until invited in. When departing, it is important to say farewell to every individual present: the American group wave is not appreciated unless the group is unusually large. Seniors or those who are obviously the oldest in a group are always greeted first, seated first, and allowed to enter a room first (usually as the center of a group, however, and in most cases preceded by their younger aides).

Physical Greeting Styles

Close associates and businesspeople of the same sex who have developed working relationships often greet each other warmly, with hugs and sometimes three kisses. Wait until your Congolese host initiates this behavior before initiating it yourself. Typically, the greeting between men involves a handshake or touching the temples of the other person three times with the index finger of the right hand. Very close family and friends may also kiss additionally on the forehead; each ethnic group has different greetings. Muslim women and men do not touch or shake hands (unless the woman is Westernized, and you will know if she extends her hand). The handshake may be soft, almost limp sometimes; this does not mean insincerity, rather, it is an accommodation to the Western fashion while remaining humble and considerate. Rural people may greet each other by clapping their hands softly a few times and bowing slightly. Children and young relatives sometimes bow (or curtsy, for girls) in front of elders. If your hand is dirty or you are holding something that cannot be put down, you may extend your wrist, or even elbow, in place of the right hand.

The traditional business introduction sometimes includes the exchange of business cards. If you have business cards, use them, but don't expect the Congolese to have them for you. Always take a large supply of business cards with you: you should give one to every new person you are introduced to (there is no need to provide another business card when you are meeting someone again unless information about you has changed, such as a new address, contact number, or position). Be sure your business cards are in fine shape: they are an extension of you as a person and must look as good as possible. Embossed cards are extremely impressive. Try not to hand out a dirty, soiled, bent, or written-on card, and always handle business cards with your right hand only. Your card should be in English.

When presenting a business card, give it to your colleague so that it is readable for him as you hold it. You may not receive a card in return. Smiling and other nonverbal forms of communication usually accompany the card exchange. Should you meet more than one individual at high-level receptions, you may have a handful of cards when the greetings are over.

As the business card exchange usually precedes a sit-down meeting, it is important to arrange the cards you have received in a little seating plan in front of you along the top of the desk or table at your seat, reflecting the order in which people are seated. This will help you connect the correct names with the correct individuals throughout the meeting. Do this even if you are just meeting one person; it is expected. During the meeting, it is important not to play with the business cards (do not write on them without asking permission to do so), and when the meeting is over, never put them in your back pants pockets: pick them up carefully and respectfully, and place them neatly in your cardholder or inside jacket pocket. Do not photograph people without asking their permission, ever, and do not videotape freely. In some African countries, videotaping and photographing people and certain sites are illegal.

Communication Styles

Okay Topics / Not Okay Topics

Okay: anything that reflects your personal interests and hobbies and your sincere appreciation of and curiosity about things Congolese and native to the Central African world. Congolese love and excel at soccer: expressing interest in Congolese soccer teams is very definitely a positive. Interest in Congolese music, folk art, food, and history will always be met with hours of information (if not a personal tour!). *Not okay:* Politics, current events, or any subject that might in any way be controversial needs to be avoided at first. It is important to be sensitive to Congo's unique history and not to give your opinions about any of Congo's neighbors or internal ethnic groups, poverty, the challenge of Islamic fundamentalism to the secular state, ethnic rivalries, or religious differences. Do not inquire about a person's occupation or income in casual conversation, although it may be inquired of you (if so, this is generally just a way of getting to know more about your country and not necessarily a personal investigation: answer specifically, and fully, with an explanation as to what things cost at home, why you do what you do, and so forth). Other personal questions may be asked of you ("Why are you not married?" or "Do you have any sons?"); the best responses are those that fit Congolese context ("I've not been blessed yet; I wait patiently."). You may be complimented on your portliness (being heavy is a sign of wealth throughout most of the region), or told that you are too thin. Dismiss all compliments humbly but sincerely. Do not talk about sex or tell dirty jokes when women are present: it is in very bad taste. Discussions about your company and its work are very much appreciated, as they give Congolese a chance to learn more about you and your firm. At first, speak about things that you believe you have in common, so that you can build a personal connection that will go far toward maintaining a harmonious bridge between you. This is appropriate for both individuals and organizations.

Tone, Volume, and Speed

Many Congolese are more animated, loud, and aggressive in tone than some of their neighbors. They may speak rapidly, but if you, in turn, speak rather slowly, they may get the hint and slow down.

Use of Silence

Passive silence—allowing time to pass simply without words—can be a form of proactive communication, and is used as a nonverbal way of avoiding confrontation, disagreement, or an unpleasant subject. If confronted with unexplainable silence, gently coax the conversation in a different direction, one that is more mutually harmonious.

Physical Gestures and Facial Expressions

Throughout the region, nonverbal behavior is part of the pattern of communication, and most Congolese are very comfortable with nonverbal behavior. However, they may not understand many of the Western gestures; therefore, limit your own gestures until you are sure they are understood. Winking, whistling, and other similar displays with the opposite sex are considered vulgar. Public displays of familiarity and affection with the opposite sex are not expressed beyond holding hands. Never touch anyone on his or her head, even a child: this is the holiest part of the body for Muslims. Do not point with or intentionally show the sole of your shoe to anyone: this is considered vulgar, as the bottom of the shoe touches the ground, and is therefore the dirtiest part of the body. Any gesture involving a closed fist or made with the "thumbs-up" sign may be considered vulgar by some. Yawning in public is considered impolite; you must cover your mouth when you yawn, and when you use a toothpick. To indicate that something is complete or full, make a fist in the left hand, and tap it with the palm of the right hand a few times.

For any action or gesture that would naturally be done only with one hand, do not use your left hand, as this is considered the unclean hand (the hand used for personal hygiene). Pass all documents, business cards, food, and money with your right hand (if you're a southpaw, you will have to practice this). You must remove your shoes before entering a mosque (and some buildings, as well as most homes). Smile whenever possible: it smoothes the way with strangers quickly and easily. Congolese sometimes get someone's attention by snapping the fingers and/or making a quiet hissing sound.

Waving and Counting

The thumb represents the number 1, the pinkie represents the number 5, with everything in between ordered from the thumb down. It is very insulting to beckon someone with the forefinger (instead, turn your hand so that the palm is facing down and motion inward with all four fingers at once). If you need to gesture for a waiter, very subtly raise your hand or make eye contact. Waving or beckoning is done with the palm down and the fingers moving forward and backward in a kind of scratching motion. It may seem as if the person making the gesture is saying good-bye to you, when in fact you are being summoned over. If you need to point to something or someone, close your fingers, open your palm and face it upward, and pass your hand in the direction you want to indicate.

Physicality and Physical Space

Congolese may stand closer than most North Americans are accustomed to; resist the urge to step back. Never speak with your hands in your pockets: always keep them firmly at your side when standing. If men and women must cross their legs when they sit, it must never be ankle over knee (for women, the preferred style is to cross ankle over ankle; but the bottom of the shoes must not show to the other person). Remember, even in public, formal is always better than informal, and this is essential when in front of elders or superiors of any kind: no gum-chewing; don't slouch; men, take your hat off; and don't lean against things. Congolese are most comfortable when they are next to other people: in a nearly empty bus, movie theater, or restaurant, in most cases, Congolese will tend to sit next to or near the other person present, instead of far away from them. As is the case throughout the region, needing or wanting to be alone is suspect, and maintaining privacy by insisting on being alone is considered strange and possibly dangerous, especially in current circumstances: Why would anyone want to be alone when he or she could be in the company of friends and family?

Eye Contact

Eye contact may not typically be maintained when speaking, especially by subordinates when speaking with superiors, or juniors with elders. It is best to make eye contact at first, and then avert the eyes from time to time. Typically, one does not make eye contact while eating, and conversation is often kept to a minimum while eating. Tune up your nonverbal antennae.

Emotive Orientation

Congolese are warm, sensitive, friendly, and hospitable. Once they know each other, there can be much touching (at least between members of the same sex) during even the most casual conversation. Two men or two women often walk hand in hand or arm in arm down the street. Verbal communication often employs effusiveness, exaggeration, and flowery phrases: this is meant to show sincerity, not duplicity. One should be especially careful not to interrupt others when they are speaking: a more thoughtful approach to conversation, in which you give the other person signals that he or she is being listened to, rather than chime in quickly with your own thoughts, is much preferred throughout the entire region.

Protocol in Public

Walking Styles and Waiting in Lines

On the street, in stores, and in most public facilities, people pay little attention to maintaining orderly lines. Due to the volume of passengers on any kind of transportation, there can be some gentle pushing and jostling. This is not to get in ahead of someone else; it is merely to get in! This is not meant to be disrespectful; if it is bothersome, just say so politely, and you will be treated well. If you ask a Congolese for directions, he or she will make every effort to show you the way (even if he or she is not that certain!).

Behavior in Public Places: Airports, Terminals, and the Market

Pride will usually demand that Congolese provide you with assistance; even if they do not have an answer they will give you one. Be careful with whom you strike up conversations, especially in the cities (men must only speak to men, and women must only speak to women).

Establish a personal relationship with everyone you interact with, from shopkeeper to government official. Often this is one of the purposes for bargaining in the market: when you do bargain, consider that your money is, in most cases, going to the upkeep of entire families who live at subsistence levels. When bargaining, keep in mind also that it is generally considered good luck to be the first or last shopper in a store or at a stall, so you might get a better price if you can manage to be the first to arrive when they open or the last when they close. Stores in the cities are open in the evenings and on weekends, as well as during the day, and market stores and stalls usually determine their own hours; government offices in Congo, however, often open early (around 7 or 8 A.M.) and close early (around 3 or 4 P.M.). Some Muslim stores may close during the Muslim Sabbath (Friday) and in preparation for it (Thursday nights), and on all Muslim holidays. A personal verbal thank-you to store owners, waiters, chefs, and hotel managers for their services is important, as it will help establish the relationship you need to get continuing good service. Shopping doubles as a social event, so plan to socialize as well as shop. Smoking is popular, and in some places, endemic, and you need not look for "no-smoking" areas, as such formal rules can rarely be enforced (be sure not to smoke in front of Muslims during the day during Ramadan, when Muslims abstain; this is true for eating and drinking during the day during Ramadan, as well, when in the presence of observant Muslims). When and if you do smoke, it is critical that you offer a cigarette first to everyone else at the table before you light up, and then offer to light their cigarettes for them. Bathroom facilities throughout the region are rare or nonexistent: be prepared. This is also the case for most infrastructural basics, including transportation, electricity, water, and food.

Unless they are in the company of other women, or close male relatives, women generally do not go out in public alone, especially at night; in the current circumstances, this is equally true for men.

Bus / Metro / Taxi / Car

There are a few well-paved roads, mainly between the major cities; most transportation is by foot or with animals. There is no driving, nor is there any workable public transportation system anywhere. Private cars are virtually unknown. Be prepared for chaotic and unplanned circumstances at almost any public transport facilities, including rail stations, bus depots, and airports. Most locals get around by animal cart or on foot (depending upon whether they are in rural or urban areas, and this distinction makes for considerably different ways of life in Congo). And remember, as is the case throughout the region, when the infrastructure doesn't work, rely on people: the best way, for example, to get a message through, sometimes, is simply to pass it along to travelers, and others who are going in the direction of the person you want to communicate with.

Tipping

Tipping (the ubiquitous *baksheesh*—or *dash,* as it is more commonly referred to in central Africa) is universally required throughout the region, as a way to help get things done, and as a way of thanking people and being appreciative of the help they offer: it is more commonly a social gesture. Typically, it is a way of taking care of people; when abused, it is a form of graft that in some countries in the region, Congo included, can be a rampant form of corruption. In most daily circumstances, it is traditional to always give a little something to someone who has helped you out. The offer may be refused at first in some cases, but if you insist, it will be graciously accepted and appreciated. Tips in restaurants run about 10 percent, and are typically not included in the bill (but double-check to be sure); a tip is not necessary if you have negotiated the fare for a car or any kind of transport for a fee ahead of time, and already figured in the tip. For everything else, a few coins is all that is needed, but you should always have a lot of spare change handy to see you through the day. United States currency is generally greatly appreciated throughout the region; the official Congo currency is the franc congolais.

Punctuality

Punctuality is valued, but not required. Consider timeliness a target. You should be relatively on time, but you may be kept waiting for quite a while: patience and good humor are required. Never get upset over time. If you are late, you need not have an explanation. It will be understood.

Dress

Many Congolese in the urban areas wear conservative Western dress, although some of the elite prefer to spice up the Western wardrobe with traditionally vibrant Congolese colors, designs, and fabrics. Most Congolese are most comfortable wearing their traditional dress, which is dependent upon the ethnic group. Women generally wear dresses that cover most of their body (the ubiquitous *pagne*), with an accompanying head wrap. Congolese attire has a reputation, in general, for being very colorful and highly patterned. It is not appropriate for non-Congolese to dress in traditional Congolese clothes; Westerners should dress in casual conservative business clothes (as will many Congolese businessmen), but may find it more comfortable to wear items that are as loose fitting as possible (the weather is hot). Never wear (and this is the case throughout most of Africa) anything that could be interpreted as a military uniform. Urban youth and Westernized people wear casual Western clothes (often secondhand from Europe or the United States). Men should not in the northern Muslim area wear neck jewelry, even if it is not visible underneath clothing, although women often wear their wealth in the form of jewelry. Clothes should not be tight-fitting or revealing in any way, for men or women. Shoes with traditional dress are typically sandals or flip-flops. Westerners should avoid wearing any expensive clothes or jewelry: not only does it make you a potential mark for thieves, but it is ostentatious and can be seen as a sign of selfishness and colonialist exploitation.

Personal Hygiene

In Congo, cleanliness is associated with purity, and most Congolese bathe at least twice a day when they can. Washing both hands and feet more than once a day is very common, and one must wash hands before and after eating every meal. Many Congolese enjoy perfumes, henna skin designs, and identifying ritual scarification. Do not blow your nose in public: it is considered very rude. Spitting does occur on the street, but also is generally regarded as rude.

Dining and Drinking

Mealtimes and Typical Foods

The typical Congolese diet is rich in rice, yams, and cassava (a root vegetable), plus breads, fresh vegetables, and fruits. Meats are enjoyed when available, and fish along the coast and rivers. Each ethnic group has its own specialties and preferences, and remember, Muslims will not eat pork and generally avoid alcohol (although it is available). Typically, dishes revolve around rice, with a sauce of either vegetables, fish, or meat, or combinations thereof. Consider that the availability of food is a serious issue during the current circumstances. Malnutrition and starvation are endemic in parts of the country.

A note on hosting and dining with observant Muslims: If you are serving a meal at home, be sure you do not use alcohol or pork in any of the dishes, and if you do, so labeling the dish and serving it separately will still make your Muslim guest uncomfortable. Simply don't do it. You, as a guest in the more rural regions, may be rewarded with the opportunity to either dine first, or be offered the more favored food, such as the meat: please consider that this may mean that others in the family do not eat this. If you are offered something you cannot eat or drink, acknowledge the honor, and suggest that while you will always hold the honor in your heart, you in turn will bestow it on someone who can also appreciate it in his or her belly: then pass the honored dish on to a Congolese colleague. Alternately, you may say thank you but that you have just eaten or drunk. When offered food, it is important to at first refuse; it as appropriate to join your host at the table only after several rounds of being implored to do so. Remember, in this region, and throughout much of Africa, you will never be denied food if it is available, but consider the dire malnutrition and difficulty in obtaining adequate nourishment in this part of the world.

Breakfast is served from about 6 to 9 A.M., lunch from 12 to 2 P.M., and dinner from 8 to 10 P.M., although at the "hungry times" of the year (usually just before the harvest), many people make do with just two meals per day. Traditionally, children, women, and men dine separately, and men are offered the best parts first, women next, and children typically last. Dinner is the main meal of the day.

It is very important to remove your shoes before entering most Congolese homes (look to see if other sandals are lined up at the entrance as your cue), and when seated to always make sure that your toes and feet are not pointing to the food or to others at the meal. Typically, conversation while eating is minimal, and most Congolese avoid eye contact when dining.

Regional Differences

Most meats of any kind for Muslims need to be prepared *halal* (meat slaughtered according to Islamic prescriptions). Do not eat in front of your Muslim colleagues, or invite them to join you for a meal, during the day during Ramadan, as Muslims typically fast (and refrain from drinking and smoking) during the day, and feast with family and friends at night. Ramadan lasts for a lunar month: this is simply not a good time to do business or go out entertaining in the Muslim world.

Typical Drinks and Toasting

Tea and coffee are available in most places. When you come to a Congolese home, even for just a brief visit, you will most likely be served tea or a cool drink. When it is offered, refuse and wait to be implored, then accept graciously. Your cup will typically be refilled if it is less than half full. Typically, beer and other alcoholic drinks may also be served: fruit juices and lemonades, along with tea, may accompany meals, but for most traditional meals, it is impolite to drink and eat at the same time: first you eat, then you drink. You should never pour your own drink; wait patiently to be served.

If you are the honored guest, you are not expected to make a statement or toast, but if you offer a small compliment, it will be appreciated (and then dismissed as unnecessary); you can do this at the end of the meal, just before everyone departs. An appropriate comment would be to wish for the health of the host and all those present; always be humble.

Avoid drinking tap water anywhere in the region (this means you should brush your teeth with bottled water and not take ice in any of your drinks; drink only bottled water, brewed tea or coffee, or soft drinks; and avoid getting water from the morning shower into your mouth; never eat fresh fruits or vegetables that cannot be peeled first, and ideally cooked later before eating). This is a serious matter: there are some very nasty—and sometimes deadly—bugs going around in developing countries. In addition, avoid all dairy products except in the finest hotels, as the required refrigeration may be questionable. Do not swim in freshwater lakes, ponds, or rivers; many parasitic infections are a particular problem in this region.

Table Manners and the Use of Utensils

Because of the familiarity with the West, many of the Western modes of dining are understood and accepted, especially among the urban elite (such as dining with utensils, and holding knives and forks throughout the meal in the same hands). However, understanding the traditional Congolese modes of dining behavior will be quite helpful as they are apparent and respected in most places. Even though they vary from group to group, the following basic suggestions should be considered: Before meals, you must wash your hands, and wash them again when the meal is over. Traditionally, one eats with one's right hand from a communal plate or bowl (or set of plates and/or bowls). Never use your left hand unless you are clearly eating something that requires two hands; occasionally you may be offered a spoon or fork, which also must be held in the right hand. Keep your left hand off any bowls or serving items. If there is only one communal bowl, it is appropriate for the youngest person present to hold the lip of the bowl with the thumb and index finger of their left hand while the elders partake first (men first, women second, children last). Eat only from that part of the communal plates or bowls that is directly in front of you. Some may dip their index finger into the food first and taste it: this is an old tradition of making sure that the food is safe to eat, and has become a replacement for saying a small prayer before eating for some. You may be seated either on the floor or on low stools. Do not smoke in the same area where the food is being served, and wait to smoke until after the meal is finished: women do not smoke. At the end of the meal, some praise to the cook and thankfulness for the food are a welcome gesture.

Seating Plans

The most honored position is next to the host. Most social entertaining is done in people's homes. The home, the market, or a local café is where people meet, socialize, and get things done, including business (although business is not easily done in the market). Your spouse might be invited with you to a meal at home, especially if the spouse of the host will be there, which will probably be the case. The invitation will then typically be phrased, "My spouse invites your spouse," and women and men may (especially in Muslim areas) eat separately. By the way, invitations, business or social, will almost always be verbal, not written.

At Home, in a Restaurant, or at Work

The honored guest is served first, then the oldest male, then the rest of the men, then children, and finally women. Do not begin to eat or drink anything until the oldest man at the table has been served and has begun. At the end of the meal, it is appropriate to thank the host or hostess for a wonderful meal.

In informal restaurants, you may be required to share a table. If so, do not force conversation: act as if you are seated at a private table. Women should be sensitive to the fact that they may be seated only with other women. Waitstaff may be summoned by raising your hand or by making eye contact; waving or calling their names is very impolite. Since business and socializing in this part of the world are usually one and the same, business is often discussed over meals, once individuals know each other well enough to talk terms. Take your cue from your Congolese associates: if they bring up business, then it's okay to discuss it, but wait to take your lead from their conversation.

Once inside the home, do not wander around. If you move from one area to another in a Congolese home or restaurant, be sure to always allow more senior members of your party to enter the room ahead of you.

Being a Good Guest or Host

Paying the Bill

Usually the one who does the inviting pays the bill. If invited to a home or if you are hosted in any way, thanks and compliments are not easily given or received, since it is believed that there is no need to say such things between trusted friends and family; nevertheless, it is important to state humble thanks, and to accept thanks graciously.

Transportation

It's important to make sure that guests have a way to return from where they came, if they are visiting; equally, you want to be sure not to put your host out by not having made such arrangements ahead of time for yourself, if and when you visit. If invited into a home, you may also be invited to spend the night, and if so, you must be careful to keep a low profile and use as few resources as possible. Seeing your guests off, you must remain at the entrance of the house or restaurant, or at the site where you deposited your guests, until they are out of sight: it is very important not to leave until your guests can no longer see you, should they look back.

When to Arrive / Chores to Do

If invited to dinner at a private home, do offer to help with the chores and to help out in any way you can. Do not leave the meal area unless invited to do so. When in the home, be careful not to admire something too effusively: Congolese may feel obligated to give it to you, and doing so might represent a great sacrifice. Your compliments will most likely be dismissed. Remember also that many Congolese consider it bad luck to have their children praised: it can bring ill fortune to them (comment on the children indirectly, but comment on them positively).

Gift Giving

In general, gift giving is common for social occasions, and in business situations between trusted colleagues. However, it is important not to give a gift when first invited into someone's home, or at the first business meeting: gift giving is typically done only between individuals who have already formed a relationship, and is appropriate only at the second meeting and thereafter. When it does occur, it is done not only as a gesture of thanks, but as a way of helping to ensure good business relations in the future. In business settings, this usually takes the form of a personal gift that symbolically says the correct thing about the nature of the relationship. When going to the region on business, bringing a gift for the key decision maker is enough. Your gift may have to be elaborate and expensive, depending upon the circumstances and the position of the individual you are meeting, and it should, whenever possible, be personalized (engraved, or representative of the personalities of the receiver or giver or of an aspect of the relationship). You present your gift when you arrive in the country; before you leave to return home, you will receive a farewell gift, usually at the last meeting. When Congolese visit your country, they will also bring you a gift, and before they leave, you should give them farewell gifts.

The most appropriate gift for a personal visit to a home, or as a thank-you for dinner, would be some fruit, coffee, or nuts, and something for the children, such as a toy, picture books, or school supplies (paper and writing utensils and calculators with a supply of batteries are very valued). A man typically only gives a gift to a man, a woman to a woman; remember, any gift given by a man to a woman must come with the caveat that it is from his wife/sister/mother, or else it is far too personal. Gifts to avoid giving Muslims include alcohol (and this includes perfumes or colognes made with alcohol), pork, art or photographs that depict natural scenes or people (this runs counter to Islamic beliefs that man must not attempt to reproduce in an image what God has made), or cutlery (which symbolizes the severing of a relationship). A fine gift for a Muslim would be a silver compass, so that he will always know which direction to face when he says his daily prayers (Muslims must face Mecca no matter where in the world they are when they say their prayers).

For both giving and receiving gifts, two hands are used always, and gifts may or may not be opened by the receiver in front of the giver (this depends upon the nature of the gift, more often than not: foodstuffs meant for dessert, for example, will be opened for all to enjoy); the presenter typically first offers the gift humbly and as an incidental aside, then, usually received after some imploring, it is acknowledged, and accepted.

Gifts should be wrapped, but special gift-wrapping is not necessary (and probably not readily available). By the way, if you own a copy of the Qu'ran (given or received as a gift or not), never place it on the floor or below any object: it must be the highest book on the shelf. Do not give a copy of the Qu'ran as a gift to a Muslim: it is far too significant for a business or social acknowledgment.

Special Holidays and Celebrations

Major Holidays

Avoid doing business the entire month of Ramadan in Muslim areas. Some towns have different local holidays as well, so double-check with your Congolese associates before making final travel plans. Islamic holidays are celebrated by most Muslims, although the Christian holidays are celebrated by the majority of the population.

Secular Congolese holidays are:

January 1	New Year's Day
January 4	Commemoration of the Martyrs of Independence
March/April	Easter
May 1	Labor Day
June 30	Independence Day
August 1	Parents' Day
November 17	Veterans' Day
December 25	Christmas

Business Culture

Daily Office Protocols

The Congolese office may be a modern office in an urban building or a traditional stall near the market, but no matter where it is, you can be sure there will be many people coming and going. This is not so much a statement about your unimportance as much as it is a statement about the importance of your host: that he is needed by many, and that in the polychronic culture, things are handled in order of their importance, and not according to the clock. Be patient. In the Congolese organization, hierarchy is strictly observed. Because faithful Muslims pray five times a day, you will need to adjust your schedules to accommodate their needs if working with Muslims. Usually, prayers are given upon awakening and at noontime, midday, at dusk, and before retiring; this means that twice during the workday, there will be time out for prayers. The prayer break usually lasts a short ten or fifteen minutes or so, and any quiet area will do. If you accidentally interrupt a Muslim during his prayers, just walk quietly away: there's no need for complicated explanations or apologies. Most organizations in Muslim areas have prayer rooms set off to the side, with carpets. In addition, devout Muslims will not work on Friday (the Muslim Sabbath), and in fact begin to end work early on Thursday before sundown. The official workweek is Monday through Friday, 9 A.M. to 4 P.M. (remember, the Muslim Sabbath is on Friday, beginning Thursday evening at sunset; the Muslim workweek, therefore, often includes Saturday and Sunday), and sometimes a Saturday morning.

Management Styles

Titles are very important, and the highest ones (e.g., vice president) are usually reserved for very senior, executive-level positions, and should not be used as a title as casually as they are in the United States. Any criticism of Congolese workers must be done very carefully, even privately. Deference is shown by subordinates to their seniors; paternalistic concern is often shown by seniors to their subordinates. Superiors are not typically sensitive to inquiring about their subordinates' opinions, and once a decision is made, the superiors are followed, often unquestioningly. If you are doing business with the correct person, things will probably move quickly; it is essential, therefore, to have a good and trustworthy Congolese contact who can make the necessary contacts for you (you can locate these people through consular and/or trade and business association contacts prior to your trip). Let this person take the time he needs to do this for you, for if you pressure him into making contacts sooner, he may connect you to someone who is not as useful as the one he was originally waiting for: this will not serve you. Again, be patient. Never use time as a means of pressure.

Boss-Subordinate Relations

The decision-making system usually works from the top on down, with key decisions often coming from individuals in high positions of power. Superiors are expected to provide clear and fully informed sets of instructions: that is their responsibility, and it is the responsibility of subordinates to carry out those instructions. Consequently, "management-by-objective" and other egalitarian and individually empowered management styles often may not work in this environment and in fact are often mistrusted: without clear instruction from above, subordinates often will do nothing. They also lose respect for the manager for not making the decisions he should be making, and managers typically are suspicious of subordinates who make independent decisions.

Conducting a Meeting or Presentation

There will be much hosting by your Congolese contacts with tea, coffee, and soft drinks. When serving any refreshments in the office, be sure they are served in porcelain, glass, or silver tea sets: the use of paper or Styrofoam shows disrespect and is very bad form. There may be many more people at the meeting than you were expecting: this is typically because there are many more people who need to be consulted about the decision regarding you and your business; in most cases, you will be introduced to everyone. If you are not introduced to them, do not ask to be: acknowledge them with a smile and a nod, and proceed with your meeting. If you are meeting with a decision maker, the discussions will probably be direct, forthright, and businesslike. If you do not know the decision-making authority of the person you are with, assume that you will need to meet with many people, and perhaps repeat much of the same discussions each time with different people. There may be many interruptions throughout the meeting; stay calm and flexible. Business is personal throughout the region: decision makers have got to know your face. Patience and third-party connections are key.

Negotiation Styles

At first, expect no immediate decisions from your Congolese colleagues at the table and be willing to provide copious amounts of information, to the degree that you can, in response to their questions and in anticipation of their needs. Presentations should be well-prepared and simply propounded. Details are best left to questions and backup material, which should be available and left behind; such materials need to be simple, to the point, interesting to look at, and can be in French or English (as a second-best option). Unless you already have a well-established relationship, agendas need to be very broad and very flexible: everything unexpected will occur, and everything you did not plan to discuss will be brought up. Should you come with other team members, make sure that your roles are well-coordinated. Never disagree with each other in front of Congolese or appear uncertain, unsure, not authorized to make a decision, or out of control in any way.

Most Congolese love to bargain, and see this process as a way of getting to know you: it does not imply insincerity to offer one price and then change your mind later (as it often does with Pacific Rim cultures). In fact, avoiding this process will generate suspicion, whether in the office or in the market. Remember that in the sometimes desperate conditions of African economies, business, whether in the market, on the street, or the office, is often really all about barter; currency is often not part of the final arrangement. Final terms need not be fair to all: in fact, Congolese may bargain and negotiate with the expectation that in order for them to get something, you need to lose something. If you suspect something is too good to be true, or feel you are being manipulated, you are probably right in both cases. Remember to confirm what might sound like agreement with multiple inquiries: communication patterns often include reassurance, when in fact, your local associates may not be completely in agreement with you. Contracts and contract law are helpful, but ultimately useless: unless you are working with a well-known multinational or high-government offices (and even there, contracts will be, in the end, unenforceable), it is better to assume the agreement will be unenforceable; nevertheless, put everything in writing that you can and insist on the same from your Congolese associates. If possible, the deal should be sealed with a celebratory meal. Keep communications open, especially when at a distance, and stay in touch often with your Congolese associates: share more information than you normally would if you can, not less; and be prepared to make many trips, as needed.

Written Correspondence

Your business letters should be informal and warm, and reflect the personal relationship you have established. Nevertheless, they must include a recognition of any titles and rank. Given names usually are written in uppercase; dates are given using the day/month/year format (with periods in between, not slashes)—in Congolese business correspondence, it is appropriate to use Western dates and business writing styles. When writing names, an honorific plus the title is as common as an honorific plus the first name (unless your colleague is Westernized, in which case it is appropriate to use typical Western form). You should write your e-mails, letters, and faxes in an informal, friendly, and warm manner: use a brief and warm personal introduction, and segue smoothly into business. Keep the business issues and language clear and simple, however, and bulletpoint and outline all important matters (in French is best, but English is a second-best option). Use the Western format (name, position, company, street address, city, state/province, country, postal code) for the addresses.

The East: Kenya, Tanzania, Uganda, Rwanda, and Burundi

KENYA

Some Introductory Background on Kenya and Kenyans

The original Kenyans, it is believed, may have been the Dorobo people, a hunting and gathering group; and depending upon how Neolithic one wants to get, the original unknown social groups of what were the foundations of the entire human race sprang from the great Rift Valley of Kenya and Tanzania. But it wasn't until the Sudanese (or Nilitic, people from the Nile) people came down from the north and met the Bantu people coming up from the south that the many various ethnic groups that make up modern Kenyans were created. Kenya (pronounced preferably with the soft "e" as in "hen," as is "Kenyan") today straddles this north/south divide; there are perhaps two east/west divides, as well: a topographical divide between the agriculturally rich west and the more arid east, and a cultural east/west divide between the coast and the rest of the country (it was along the coast that Arabs came and settled and established a powerful trading empire between East Africa and Gulf Arabia and Asia). The massive tourist industry does not exist in Kenya and the rest of the East African region for nothing: Kenya being one of the great plains states, wildlife is spectacularly abundant, if not threatened, and there is a long tradition in Kenya and other parts of the region of respecting and living in harmony with the animals and nature (in fact, when things go wrong, the reason given is often that this is in response to the sacrilegious treatment of animals and the disregard of nature). For much of its post-independence period, Kenyans enjoyed stability, growth, and harmony. Then in the 1990s, ethnic tensions flared, fanned by severe droughts and floods and a soaring inflation rate and unemployment. Things appear to be stabilizing, but there is a ways to go before Kenya returns to its once shining position as a leader among African nations.

Some Historical Context

When the Nilitic people came down from the north, and the Bantu people up from the south, they each, within their own ethnic groups, retained their indigenous cultures, and, most important, their languages. It is the language in East

Africa that is the critical defining characteristic of the various ethnic groups, as there are many cultural similarities beyond linguistic differences. The languages of both the southern Bantus and the northerners mixed to create what is one of the most prevalent languages in Eastern and Southern Africa: Swahili, or what is more correctly locally referred to as Kiswahili. The first Europeans to explore the region were the Portuguese, traveling up the coast after their journeys east and northward around the Cape toward India; soon after, Arabs from Gulf Arabia, primarily in the form of Omanis (ruled by the Sultan of Oman), established themselves all along the East African coast, with their local presence most concentrated on the island of Zanzibar (today, Zanzibar—part of Tanzania—and other coastal regions in East Africa are primarily Muslim, although most of the rest of East Africa is Christian and animist). Arabs not only controlled the trade of goods in and out of East Africa (mainly spices and animals), but also the trade of slaves. When the British came to East Africa in the form of the British East Africa Company, they leased, and then eventually claimed, the land ruled by the Sultan of Zanzibar from him, and hence established the protectorate of British East Africa, which included Kenya, Tanganyika, Zanzibar, Uganda, and other areas. The struggle for independence grew throughout the mid-twentieth century, spurred on, in part, by violent local uprisings of indigenous peoples against British colonists (Mau Mau rebellions). Eventually, Jomo Kenyatta, the national hero, led Kenya to independence.

An Area Briefing

Politics and Government

There are eight provinces in the republic, with a legislature known as the Bunge, or National Assembly. The president is head of state, and there are several political parties active in the country.

Schools and Education

As is the case throughout much of Africa, schooling for children is spotty and difficult to mandate, although in Kenya, most children are enrolled throughout at least primary school. There is a great belief in the value of education, and Kenyans make every effort to ensure that children enroll in school and remain as long as possible. There is an adult literacy rate, in fact, of almost 80 percent. What the government lacks in being able to provide in terms of education is made up by a sophisticated network of self-help, or *harambee,* schools, which bring in talent and funds from various organizations around the world. Schooling is done in the beginning grades typically in local languages (mainly Kiswahili), but then switches to English for the remaining primary grades onward. Kenyans who can afford to go on to receive university educations.

Religion and Demographics

Most Kenyans are Christian, both Catholic and Protestant, the result of the British and European missionary effort in the eighteenth and nineteenth centuries. Nevertheless, animist and local indigenous beliefs permeate Christian practices; Islam is practiced along the coast. It is a challenge and a strength that, as is the case throughout much of Africa, the majority of the population is under thirty years of age.

Because of the understanding, if not acceptance, of Western ways in Kenya, depending upon the individual you are working with (whether they are Western-oriented or fundamentalist Muslim), Western women typically do not experience much difficulty doing business in Kenya; in fact, about one third of the workforce and post-primary student population in Kenya is female, and many urban Kenyan women are opting for nuclear families, education, and careers, instead of the large extended rural family and the prescribed homemaker role that women traditionally play in it.

All of the major ethnic groups are extremely proud of being part of the nation of Kenya: there is perhaps a greater respect for nationhood among the various ethnic groups in Kenya than one typically finds in Africa. The two major divisive ethnic groups are the Kalenjin and Kikuyu, both located west of the Rift Valley; they typically do not get along, as they vie for control over the valuable land in the area; the Kikuyu make up about 25 percent of the population, the Kalenjin about 15 percent. Other groups are the Luhya, the Luo, the Kamba, the Kisii, the Samburu, and others (the Luo and Turkana groups are the modern-day descendants of the Nilitic peoples of the north). Coincidentally, the well-known Maasai people are one of the smaller minority groups in Kenya, although their presence in the society is significant. Most of these groups are distinguished along linguistic lines, and all groups, for the most part, speak their local languages, which are Bantu-based.

Fundamental Cultural Orientations

1. What's the Best Way for People to Relate to One Another?

OTHER-INDEPENDENT OR OTHER-DEPENDENT?   There is a combination of deep concern for family, clan, and other membership groups (such as work, religion, and nation) that defines an individual and individual expression. Kenyans, like all Africans, have a hierarchical sense of loyalties, beginning with their family, and then, in descending order of importance, their ethnic group, their religion, their home village, their country, their region, and their continent. Kenyans are deeply connected first to their clan and their families: for that reason, it is critical that one inquire about the health of all family members. How one performs his or her role vis-à-vis others is judged in Africa, and individuals do nothing without careful consideration for how their actions will be perceived, and for the impact their actions will have on their family and their community. Consequently, individual empowerment and decision making are rare, and consensus-building and confirming group agreement are critical. Sharing, concern for others, humility, and an acceptance—without anger, remorse, or hostility—of one's role, at least within one's group, are all hallmarks of East African and Kenyan culture.

HIERARCHY-ORIENTED OR EGALITY-ORIENTED?   Both Kenyan secular life and ethnic group membership (as well as Islamic life for Muslims) is rigidly stratified, with three or four generations of the extended family traditionally living together (this is not necessarily the case in the cities); individuals within this highly stratified social structure play their roles—children, women, and men in relation to one another, hosts in relation to guests, religious leaders and other elders in relation to the community. Defining for others one's rank is important, and status symbols (for example, the jewelry that women wear, the ritual scarification imposed by the ethnic group, the pattern used on the traditional robe, and, most especially, the property that one owns, which is typically land or livestock) are traditionally important. It is critical that everyone show respect for elders and devout observers. Women and men are different and perform different roles: in Kenya a woman typically may go out in public alone, but she will probably prefer to go with other female friends or relatives. She need not be in the company of a close male relative (husband, father, son, or brother), and Muslim women generally will not wear a veil; in fact, although all groups are male-dominated, Kenyan women in general do play a significant role in public life: they work, are represented in the intellectual community, and are active in politics, and even in the rural areas, it is the woman who is most likely responsible for the agricultural crop of the family.

RULE-ORIENTED OR RELATIONSHIP-ORIENTED? While many Kenyans have had experience with and in the West, the tension that exists between the application of universal rules over reliable and dependable relationships is palpable. This leads to a high dependence on power, authority, and subjective decision making based on the situation and the relationships between the individuals involved. Ultimately, face-to-face knowledge of the individuals involved in any interaction is the basis upon which final decisions are often made, despite the fact that the British legal infrastructure is used as a basis for administering justice on a more universal scale than is typical in many other parts of Africa: this is a distinguishing characteristic of East Africa, in general.

2. What's the Best Way to View Time?

MONOCHRONIC OR POLYCHRONIC? Kenya is essentially polychronic, due to the influence of both agrarian and religious traditions (although less so in Nairobi and the cities). There is forgiveness for the inevitable delays and unexpected events that define life in Africa, and understanding when things don't go as planned or scheduled; people may or may not show up at invited events, things may or may not happen as planned. Schedules tend to be loose and flexible. Because who (relationships) is more important than what (tasks) or when (time), there can be many interruptions during a meeting, and people's obligations to other people, who may come and go, are more important than doing things according to schedules. If you are being kept waiting, or are ignored because of someone else's needs, it may be an indication of your importance relative to the other person, and expressing frustration over being kept waiting only diminishes your importance.

RISK-TAKING OR RISK-AVERSE? Kenyans are prone to taking risks when in positions of authority, but avoiding them when they are not. Within organizations, the decision makers can be bold, even reckless, but subordinates generally are not, and take action only when instructed to do so. Therefore, comfort with uncertainty, in general, is low, and much information may need to be exchanged with different people before decisions can be made. Even when decisions are made at the top, the concern for others within the group requires decision makers to consult with subordinates before making decisions. There will be much discussion with trusted others about what you, as a foreigner, bring to the table, *after* you leave the meeting.

PAST-ORIENTED OR FUTURE-ORIENTED? There is a distinct and inherent fatalism in regard to the effect of human action. Nevertheless, those empowered by virtue of their position are expected to make the decisions that keep the world running, and by so doing, are fulfilling either their destiny or that of those they are responsible for. Therefore, future benefits often do not motivate Kenyans; doing nothing, or doing things for the here and now, is sometimes more important, and if things do not work out, that is to be expected—no mortal controls the universe, and all is ultimately determined. There is a deep belief that things will take the time they need to take, and that it is always more important to maintain smooth interpersonal relationships until opportunities come along: when that happens, Kenyans will be sure to seize them!

3. What's the Best Way for Society to Work with the World at Large?

LOW-CONTEXT DIRECT OR HIGH-CONTEXT INDIRECT COMMUNICATORS? Kenyans are very context-driven communicators. They will speak in metaphors, and use stories or codified phrases; they will employ analogies, precedent, and much nonverbal behavior to convey true meaning. They generally try to avoid confrontation as a primary goal, as do most of their neighbors in the region, and often will go out of their way to maintain smooth personal relationships in the face of difficult circumstances.

PROCESS-ORIENTED OR RESULT-ORIENTED? Decisions and actions may be the result of reasoning that is not directed at a determination of truth, but rather context-based "correctness" based on similar experiences. Nevertheless, there is an equal respect for the rationalist approach to problem solving and decision making. Both methods are used (often reflected by urban/rural experiences) by Kenyans in their thought processes. Kenyans are open to Western ideas, if they "fit" the African reality and African expectations.

FORMAL OR INFORMAL? East African society is basically formal and ritualized, and each group has its own way of honoring the hierarchies, establishing respect and deference, and following (or not following) through on their responsibilities. There are formal ways that guests (outsiders) and hosts (insiders) must act toward one another, in order to preserve the honor of all groups and individuals.

Greetings and Introductions

Language and Basic Vocabulary

English and Kiswahili are the "official" languages, used in business and government (however, Westerners need to remember that the English that is used is a version of British, not American, English). Kiswahili developed fairly recently, as a way for Africans and Arab traders along the coast to speak with each other: it is not, in and of itself, an indigenous language to any one group, nor is it a Bantu language. It is, however, a combination of Bantu, Arabic, and English, making Kiswahili not a difficult language for speakers of any of those languages to pick up. Today, Kiswahili is promoted by most of the governments in the region as an African language, and as the African language to use (thus, solving the perennial problem of which language to use for national communication). English and Kiswahili are also used as the languages for intergroup communication, as most Kenyans will speak both. Never use religious references disrespectfully—it is assumed that all people are religious in some way—and be very careful never to use "God" in any way other than in the most respectful sense.

The traditional universal Kiswahili greeting is *"jambo!"* (you will hear it everywhere)—occasionally, you will also hear the Salama "Habari gani!" ("What's up?"); the traditional response is "Mzuri" ("Everything is okay"), or "Sijambo" ("I'm fine"). Here are some basic Kiswahili phrases and their meanings in English:

tutaonana or *kwa heri*	good-bye
hujambo?	how are you?
shikamoo	hello, elder, how are you? (Use this form when addressing elders; it is more respectful)
marahaba	"I am well" (Elder reply to the above greeting)
ndiyo	yes
hapana	no
tafadhali	please (when making a very important request)
asante	thank you (when you need to express many thanks)
samahani	excuse me
sawa	okay

Honorifics for Men, Women, and Children

People usually greet each other by title or relationship (e.g., Dr., Mr., Mrs., aunt, mother, cousin) plus the last, or family, name if they have never met before; once a relationship is established, honorifics are often still used, but with first or given names; sometimes, the honorific is dispensed with (between peers, usually). If names are not known, sometimes stating the individual's position as a title is sufficient (e.g., Mr. Engineer or Miss Fish Seller). Children typically refer to their parents as "mother of" or "father of" plus the name of the oldest sibling, and refer to elders in general as either "aunt" or "uncle." Children will use the term "younger mother" or "older mother," whichever is appropriate, when addressing a maternal aunt (a paternal aunt is simply called "aunt"); likewise, they will use the term "older father" or "younger father," again, whichever is appropriate, when addressing a paternal uncle (a maternal uncle is simply called "uncle"). Nicknames are very common, and most people are referred to by their nickname, sometimes with an honorific preceding it.

The What, When, and How of Introducing People

Always wait to be introduced to strangers; however, if you are not introduced after a few minutes, it is appropriate to introduce yourself. As is the case throughout the region, it is critical to take time when you greet someone to make many inquiries into his or her health and the health and condition of the lives of his or her relatives and close friends (even livestock, if appropriate!). It is considered very rude not to take a considerable amount of time when meeting someone to make these inquiries and express understanding of his or her responses; he or she will do the same in kind. You must acknowledge people you know when you pass them on the street, and you should acknowledge strangers when eyes meet in passing. Never presume to seat yourself at a gathering: if possible, wait to be told where to sit; you will be seated in a spot appropriate to your position. Typically, men, women, and children (even boys and girls) are seated separately. Because you will never be refused, and because guests are always welcome (as is the case in much of Africa, because of the lack of communication and transportation facilities, people simply drop in "uninvited" often—in fact, this is typically the most common form of entertainment and socializing), it is important that you do not purposefully make a visit unannounced around mealtime; instead, come in the late morning or early evening. When arriving at someone's home, you will generally announce yourself by tapping on the front gate or clapping your hands in the front of the house. When departing, it is important to say farewell to every individual present unless it is a particularly large group: the American group wave is not appreciated. Seniors, or those who are obviously the oldest in a group, are always greeted first, seated first, and allowed to enter a room first (usually as the center of a group, however, and in most cases preceded by their younger aides).

Physical Greeting Styles

Close associates and businesspeople of the same sex who have developed working relationships often greet each other warmly, with hugs and sometimes kisses. Wait until your Kenyan host initiates this behavior before initiating it yourself. Typically, the greeting between men involves a handshake, and supporting the forearm of the hand that is doing the shaking with the left hand on the right elbow: this shows extra sincerity. Very close family and friends may also kiss additionally on the forehead; each ethnic group has different greetings (Maasai children, for example, will bow in front of elders, and the elder will place his or her hand on the top of the head of the child, as an acknowledgment). Muslim women and men do not touch or shake hands (unless the woman is Westernized, and you will know if she extends her hand). The handshake in all cases may be soft, almost limp sometimes; this does not mean insincerity, rather, it is an accommodation to the Western fashion while remaining humble and considerate. Children and young relatives sometimes bow (or curtsy, for girls) in front of elders. If your hand is dirty or you are holding something that cannot be put down, you may extend your wrist, or even elbow, in place of the right hand.

The traditional business introduction also includes the exchange of business cards, at least in the urban centers. Always take a large supply of business cards with you: you should give one to every new person you are introduced to, and they are much appreciated (there is no need to provide a business card when you are meeting someone again, unless information about you has changed, such as a new address, contact number, or position). Be sure your business cards are in fine shape: they are an extension of you as a person and must look as good as possible. Embossed cards are extremely impressive. Never hand out a dirty, soiled, bent, or written-on card, and always handle business cards with your right hand only. Your card should be in English.

When presenting a business card, you give it to your colleague so that it is readable for him as you hold it (he will, in turn, present his card so that it is readable for you); you should hold the card with two hands in the upper corners as you present it, or at the very least with your right hand: the point is never to present it with your left hand. You may not receive a card in return. Smiling and other nonverbal forms of communication usually accompany the card exchange. Should you meet more than one individual at a reception, you may have a handful of cards when the greetings are over.

As the business card exchange usually precedes a sit-down meeting, it is important to arrange the cards you have received in a little seating plan in front of you along the top of the desk or table at your seat, reflecting the order in which people are seated. This will help you connect the correct names with the correct individuals throughout the meeting. Do this even if you are just meeting one person; it is expected. During the meeting, it is important never to play with the business cards (do not write on them without asking permission to do so); and when the meeting is over, never put them in your back pants pockets: pick them up carefully and respectfully, and place them neatly in your cardholder or inside jacket pocket. Do not photograph people without asking their permission, ever, and do not videotape freely. In some African countries, videotaping and photographing people and certain sites are illegal.

Communication Styles

Okay Topics / Not Okay Topics

Okay: anything that reflects your personal interests and hobbies and your sincere appreciation of and curiosity about things Kenyan and native to the East African world. Kenyan love and excel at soccer; expressing interest in Kenyan soccer teams is very definitely a positive. Interest in Kenyan music, folk art, food, history, and prehistory will always be met with hours of information (if not a personal tour!). *Not okay:* Politics, current events, or any subject that might in any way be controversial must be avoided at first. It is important to be sensitive to Kenya's unique history and not to give your opinions about any of Kenya's neighbors or internal ethnic groups, poverty, the challenge of Islamic fundamentalism to the secular state, ethnic rivalries, religious differences, or endangered species problems. Do not inquire about a person's occupation or income in casual conversation, although it may be inquired of you (if so, this is generally just a way of getting to know more about your country, and not a personal investigation: answer specifically, and fully, with an explanation as to what things cost at home, why you do what you do, and so forth). Other personal questions may be asked of you ("Why are you not married?" or "Do you have any sons?"); the best responses are those that fit the Kenyan context ("I've not been blessed yet, I wait patiently."). You may be complimented on your portliness (being heavy is a sign of wealth throughout most of the region), or told that you are too thin (although the physiognomy of many Kenyans is to be tall and thin). Dismiss all compliments humbly but sincerely. Do not talk about sex or tell dirty jokes when women are present: it is in very bad taste. Discussions about your company and its work are very much appreciated, as they give Kenyans a chance to learn more about you and your firm. At first, speak about things that you believe you have in common, so that you can build a personal connection that will go far toward maintaining a harmonious bridge between you. This is appropriate for both individuals and organizations.

Tone, Volume, and Speed

Kenyans typically speak in soft, muted tones, and look down upon boisterous, loud, and aggressive-sounding speech. English is most definitely spoken with a unique Kenyan accent, but it is rarely spoken too quickly; if it is, however, if you, in turn, speak rather slowly, they may get the hint and slow down.

Use of Silence

Passive silence—allowing time to pass simply without words—can be a form of proactive communication, and is used as a nonverbal way of avoiding confrontation, disagreement, or an unpleasant subject. If confronted with unexplainable silence, gently coax the conversation in a different direction, one that is more mutually harmonious.

Physical Gestures and Facial Expressions

Throughout the region, nonverbal behavior is part of the pattern of communication, and most Kenyans are very comfortable with nonverbal behavior. However, they may not understand many of the Western gestures; therefore, limit your own gestures until you are sure they are understood. Winking, whistling, and other similar displays with the opposite sex are considered very vulgar. Public displays of familiarity and affection with the opposite sex are not expressed beyond holding hands. Never touch a Muslim on their head, even a child: this is the holiest part of the body for Muslims. Do not point with or intentionally show the sole of your shoe to anyone: this is considered vulgar, as the bottom of the shoe touches the ground, and is therefore the dirtiest part of the body. Equally, do not touch an elder unless and until you have a close personal relationship. Making the "thumbs-up" sign with both hands is a general sign of approval; equally, Kenyans express displeasure by making a *tsk*-ing sound with their teeth and tongue. Standing with your hands on your hips is considered very aggressive and should always be avoided. Yawning in public is considered impolite; you must cover your mouth when you yawn, and when you use a toothpick. As is the case throughout the region, the height of people is expressed by holding the hand out with the palm facing upward at the approximate indicated height (the height of animals is expressed the same way, but with the palm facing down, and it is important not to confuse the two).

For any action or gesture that would naturally be done only with one hand, do not use your left hand, as this is considered the unclean hand (the hand used for personal hygiene). Pass all documents, business cards, food, and money with your right hand (if you're a southpaw, you will have to practice this). You must remove your shoes before entering a mosque (and some buildings, as well as most homes). Smile whenever possible: it smoothes the way with strangers quickly and easily.

Waving and Counting

The thumb represents the number 1, the pinkie represents the number 5, with everything in between ordered from the thumb down. It is very insulting to beckon someone with the forefinger (instead, turn your hand so that the palm is facing down and motion inward with all four fingers at once); in fact, directions are most often indicated with the chin, the head, or by puckering the lips and motioning with the head in the appropriate direction. If you need to gesture for a waiter, very subtly raise your hand or make eye contact. Waving or beckoning is done with the palm down and the fingers moving forward and backward in a kind of scratching motion. It may seem as if the person making the gesture is saying good-bye to you, when in fact you are being summoned over. If you need to point to something or someone, close your fingers, open your palm and face it upward, and pass your hand in the direction you want to indicate.

Physicality and Physical Space

Kenyans may stand closer than most North Americans are accustomed to; resist the urge to step back. Never speak with your hands in your pockets: keep them always firmly at your side when standing. If men and women must cross their legs when they sit, it must never be ankle over knee (for women, the preferred style is to cross ankle over ankle; but the bottom of the shoes must not show to the other person). Remember, even in public, formal is always better than informal, and this is essential when in front of elders or superiors of any kind: no gum-chewing, *ever;* don't slouch; men, take your hat off; and don't lean against things. Kenyans are most comfortable when they are next to other people: in a nearly empty bus, movie theater, or restaurant, in most cases, Kenyans will tend to sit next to or near the other person present, instead of far away from them. As is the case throughout the region, needing or wanting to be alone is suspect, and maintaining privacy by insisting on being alone is considered strange, and possibly dangerous: Why would anyone want to be alone when he or she could be in the company of friends and family?

Eye Contact

Eye contact is typically not maintained when speaking with elders or people who are obvious seniors; however, when speaking with peers, or when speaking to a junior, maintaining eye contact is very important, as it shows sincerity. Typically, one does not make eye contact while eating, and conversation is often kept to a minimum while eating. Tune up your nonverbal antennae.

Emotive Orientation

Kenyans are very warm, sensitive, friendly, and hospitable. They may not, however, be demonstrative, at least at first, as formal rules require a slow process of getting to know each other. Once they do know each other, however, there can be much touching (at least between members of the same sex) during even the most casual conversation. Two men or two women often walk hand in hand or arm in arm down the street. One should be especially careful not to interrupt others when they are speaking: a more thoughtful approach to conversation, in which you give the other person signals that he or she is being listened to, rather than chime in quickly with your own thoughts, is much preferred throughout the entire region.

Protocol in Public

Walking Styles and Waiting in Lines

On the street, in stores, and in most public facilities, people *do* pay attention to maintaining orderly lines (this is in contrast to much of the rest of Africa); nevertheless, there can be much jostling and some gentle pushing, if due only to the volume of passengers on public transportation. This is not to get into a bus ahead of someone else; it is merely to get in! This is not meant to be disrespectful; if it is bothersome, just say so politely, and you will be treated well. If you ask a Kenyan for directions, he or she will generally make every effort to show you the way (even if he or she is not that certain!).

Behavior in Public Places: Airports, Terminals, and the Market

Pride will usually require that Kenyans provide you with assistance; even if they do not have an answer they will give you one. Be careful with whom you strike up conversations, however, especially in the cities (men typically must only speak to men, and women must only speak to women). Crime is a growing problem in many cities of Central, East, and South Africa.

Establish a personal relationship with everyone you must interact with, from shopkeeper to government official, and you can expect much assistance as a newcomer. Often this is one of the purposes for bargaining in the market: when you do bargain, consider that your money is, in most cases, going to the upkeep of entire families who live at subsistence levels. When bargaining, keep in mind also that it is generally considered good luck to be the first or last shopper in a store or at a stall, so you might get a better price if you can manage to be the first to arrive when they open or the last when they close. Stores in the cities are open in the evenings and on weekends, as well as during the day, as market stores and stalls usually determine their own hours; government offices, however, often open early (around 7 or 8 A.M.) and close early (around 3 or 4 P.M.). Muslim stores along the coast may close during the Muslim Sabbath (Friday) and in preparation for it (Thursday nights), and on all Muslim holidays. A personal verbal thank-you to store owners, waiters, chefs, and hotel managers for their services is important, as it will help establish the relationship you need to get continuing good service. Marketing doubles as a social event, so plan to socialize as well as shop. Smoking is popular, and in some places, endemic, and you need not look for "no-smoking" areas, as such formal rules can rarely be enforced (be sure not to smoke during the day during Ramadan in the presence of Muslims, when Muslims abstain; this is true for eating and drinking during the day during Ramadan, as well, when in the presence of observant Muslims). When and if you do smoke, it is critical that you offer a cigarette first to everyone else at the table before you light up, and then offer to light their cigarettes for them. Bathroom facilities throughout the region are rare or non-existent (with the exception of new Western-style hotels, and then only when the plumbing, electricity, and other associated infrastructural requirements work, including telephones, which may or may not be the case): be prepared (take toilet paper with you as you travel about).

Unless they are in the company of other women, or close male relatives, women generally do not go out in public alone, especially at night; Western women traveling alone in Kenya will generally not have a problem, but should be prepared for the fact that this behavior is not typical in the region: some people won't know what to do or how to act toward them, some other women will want to assist them, and certain men, no doubt, will try to take advantage of them.

Bus / Metro / Taxi / Car

There are a few well-paved roads, mainly within and between the major cities; most transportation is by public bus (which is known by any number of different names in different countries throughout Africa), or private driver, for the elite, if they can afford to hire one. Do not attempt to drive alone in Africa. Driving almost anywhere is nearly impossible and subjects you to all sorts of dangers—civil, natural, and unnatural—and driving at night is suicide. Private cars are virtually unknown except among the very wealthy, and although driving in Kenya is on the left (from the British tradition), the distinction is irrelevant, as cars are driven wherever they can be in most areas. Some trains do exist in certain areas, and planes are the best forms of transportation over long distances. Be prepared for chaotic and unplanned circumstances at almost all public transport facilities, including rail stations, bus depots, and airports. Most locals get around by bus, truck, or animal cart or on foot (depending upon whether they are in rural or urban areas, and this distinction makes for considerably different ways of life in Kenya). And remember, as is the case throughout the region, when the infrastructure doesn't work, rely on people: the best way, for example, to get a message through sometimes, is simply to pass it along to travelers, drivers, and others who are going in the direction of the person you want to communicate with.

The best way to catch a cab in Kenya (and cabs are plentiful) is at designated taxi stands (hotels are good places, but often charge more for the same ride: a hotel surcharge is added to the meter fare, in some cases). When a taxi has been hailed—and you do so in Kenya by holding out your arm—negotiate the price before you get in. Whenever possible, have the address you need to get to written down on a piece of paper (or use the business card of the person you are going to see, if you can) before you hail the cab.

Tipping

Tipping (the ubiquitous *baksheesh*) is universally required throughout the region, as a way to help get things done, and as a way of thanking people and being appreciative of the help they offer: it is more commonly a social gesture. Typically, it is a way of taking care of people; when abused, it is a form of graft that in some countries in the region, Kenya included, can be a rampant form of corruption. It is traditional to always give a little something to someone who has helped you out. The offer may be refused at first in some cases, but if you insist, it will be graciously accepted and appreciated. Tips in restaurants run about 10 percent, and are typically not included in the bill (but double-check to be sure); a tip is not necessary if you have negotiated the fare for the taxi ahead of time, and already figured in the tip. For everything else, a few coins are all that is needed, but you should always have a lot of spare change handy to see you through the day. United States currency is generally greatly appreciated throughout the region; the Kenya currency is the Kenyan shilling.

Punctuality

Punctuality is valued, but not required. Consider timeliness a target. You should be relatively on time, but you may be kept waiting for quite awhile: patience and good humor are required. Never get upset over time. If you are late, you need not have an explanation. It will be understood.

Dress

Many Kenyans in the urban areas wear conservative Western dress, although some of the elite prefer to spice up the Western wardrobe with traditionally vibrant Kenyan colors, designs, and fabrics. Kenyan traditional dress is dependent upon the ethnic group. Women generally wear dresses that cover most of their body, some with accompanying head wraps, and a *kanga,* or long cloth that wraps or drapes over the outfit (it is very useful for carrying babies on the back or groceries, as well). Kenyan attire has the reputation, in general, for being very colorful and highly patterned. It is not appropriate for non-Kenyans to dress in traditional Kenyan clothes; Westerners should dress in conservative business clothes (as will many Kenyan businessmen), but may find it more comfortable to wear items that are as loose fitting as possible (the weather is hot). Never wear (and this is the case throughout most of Africa) anything that could be interpreted as a military uniform. Urban youth and Westernized people wear casual Western clothes (often secondhand from Europe or the United States). Clothes should not be tight-fitting or revealing in any way, for men or women, and sleeveless blouses for women and shorts are not appropriate. Western women in Muslim areas should not wear pantsuits, as they reveal too much of the shape of the legs. Shoes with traditional dress are typically sandals or flip-flops. Westerners should avoid wearing any expensive clothes or jewelry: not only does it make you a potential mark for thieves, but it is ostentatious and can be seen as a sign of selfishness and colonialist exploitation.

Personal Hygiene

In Kenya, cleanliness is associated with purity, and most Kenyans try to bathe at least twice a day. Washing both hands and feet more than once a day is very common, and one must wash hands before and after eating every meal. Do not blow your nose in public: it is considered very rude. Spitting does occur on the street, but is also generally regarded as rude.

Dining and Drinking

Mealtimes and Typical Foods

The typical diet is rich in rice, yams, and cassava (a root vegetable), plus breads, fresh vegetables, and fruits. Meats are enjoyed when available, and fish along the coast and rivers. Each ethnic group has its own specialties and preferences, and remember, Muslims will not eat pork or drink alcohol (although it is available). Typically, dishes revolve around rice, with a sauce of either vegetables, fish, or meat, or combinations thereof. There are various kinds of "bread," made from a variety of grains in different ways: *ugali* is a very stiff dough, *chapati* is the Indian-style flatbread, *mandazi* is a kind of doughnut, and *kitumbua* is a fried bread. Breads are eaten with virtually every meal, which usually consists of some vegetables in a stew, with meats and fish if available. A common dish is *uji,* a form of the ubiquitous African porridge.

A note on hosting and dining with observant Muslims: If you are serving a meal at home, be sure you do not use alcohol or pork in any of the dishes, and if you do so, labeling the dish and serving it separately will still make your Muslim guest uncomfortable: simply don't do it. You, as a guest in the more rural regions, may be rewarded with the opportunity to dine first, or be offered the more favored food, such as the meat: please consider that this may mean that others in the family do not eat this. If you are offered something you cannot eat or drink, acknowledge the honor, and suggest that while you will always hold the honor in your heart, you in turn will bestow it on someone who can also appreciate it in his or her belly: then pass the honored dish on to a Kenyan colleague. Alternately, you may say thank you but that you have just eaten or drunk. Remember, in this region, and throughout much of Africa, you will never be denied food if it is available, but consider the dire malnutrition and difficulty in obtaining adequate nourishment in this part of the world.

Breakfast is served from about 6 to 9 A.M., lunch from 12 to 2 P.M., and dinner from 8 to 10 P.M., although at the "hungry times" of the year (usually just before the harvest), many people make do with just two meals per day. Traditionally, children, women, and men dine separately, and men are offered the best parts first, women next, and children typically last.

It is very important to remove your shoes before entering most Kenyan homes (look to see if other sandals are lined up at the entrance as your cue), and when seated to always make sure that your toes and feet are not pointing to the food or to others at the meal. Typically, conversation while eating is minimal, and most Kenyans avoid eye contact when dining.

Regional Differences

Remember, Islam prohibits the use of pork, and most meats of any kind for Muslims need to be prepared *halal* (meat slaughtered according to Islamic prescriptions). Do not eat in front of your Muslim colleagues, or invite them to join you for a meal, during the day during Ramadan, as Muslims typically fast (and refrain from drinking and smoking) during the day, and feast with family and friends at night. Ramadan lasts for a lunar month: this is simply not a good time to do business or go out entertaining in the Muslim world.

Typical Drinks and Toasting

Tea and coffee (some of the world's best comes from Kenya) are available in most places. When you come to a Kenyan home, even for just a brief visit, you will most likely be served tea, sometimes served English style—with milk and sugar—if available. Many Kenyans really do take the time to have afternoon tea. When offered, always accept the cup of tea and/or coffee, even if you only put it to your lips or just take a few sips. Your cup will always be refilled if it is less than half full. Typically, beer and other alcoholic drinks may also be served: fruit juices and lemonades, along with tea, may accompany meals, but for most traditional meals, it is impolite to drink and eat at the same time: first you eat, then you drink. You must never pour your own drink; wait patiently to be served.

If you are the honored guest, you are not expected to make a statement or toast, but if you offer a small compliment, it will be appreciated (and then dismissed as unnecessary); you can do this at the end of the meal, just before everyone departs. An appropriate comment would be to wish for the health of the host and all those present; always be humble.

Avoid drinking tap water anywhere in the region (this means you should brush your teeth with bottled water and not take ice in any of your drinks; drink only bottled water, or brewed tea or coffee or soft drinks; and avoid getting water from the morning shower into your mouth; never eat fresh fruits or vegetables that cannot be peeled first, and ideally cooked later before eating). This is a serious matter: there are some very nasty—and sometimes deadly—bugs going around in developing countries. In addition, avoid all dairy products except in the finest hotels, as the required refrigeration may be questionable. Do not swim in freshwater lakes, ponds, or rivers due to the possibility of serious parasitic infection.

Table Manners and the Use of Utensils

Modern Nairobi has been significantly Westernized, as many of the Western modes of dining are understood and accepted (many Kenyans, for example, dine with spoon and knife, held, as they are in Europe, in both hands and in the same hands throughout the meal). However, understanding the traditional Kenyan modes of dining behavior will be quite helpful as they are apparent and respected in most places. They vary group to group; the following basic suggestions should be considered: Before meals, you must wash your hands, and wash them again when the meal is over. Traditionally, one eats with one's right hand from the plate. Never use your left hand unless you are clearly eating something that requires two hands; occasionally you may be offered a spoon or fork, which also must be held in the right hand, unless you also have a knife, in which case the knife is held in the right and the spoon or fork in the left. Keep your left hand off any bowls or serving items. If there is one communal bowl offered, eat only from that part of the communal plates or bowls that is directly in front of you. Some may dip their index finger into the food first and taste it: this is an old tradition of making sure that the food is safe to eat, and has become a replacement for saying a small prayer before eating. You may be seated at a table, on the floor, or on low stools. Do not smoke in the same area where the food is being served, and wait to smoke until after the meal is finished (women do not smoke). At the end of the meal, a small burp signifies satisfaction, after which some praise to the cook and thankfulness for the food are a welcome gesture. Typically people stay around for a bit after the meal for some conversation.

Seating Plans

The most honored position is next to the host. Most entertaining is done in people's homes (although in Nairobi there is business dining in restaurants). The home, the market, or a local café is where local people typically meet, socialize, and get things done, including business (although business is not easily done in the market). Your spouse might be invited with you to a meal at home, especially if the spouse of the host will be there, which will probably be the case. The invitation will then typically be phrased, "My spouse invites your spouse," and women and men may (especially in Muslim areas) eat separately. By the way, invitations, business or social, will almost always be verbal, not written.

At Home, in a Restaurant, or at Work

The honored guest is served first, then the oldest male, then the rest of the men, then children, and finally women. Do not begin to eat or drink anything until the oldest man at the table has been served and has begun. At the end of the meal, it is appropriate to thank the host or hostess for a wonderful meal.

In informal restaurants, you may be required to share a table. If so, do not force conversation: act as if you are seated at a private table. Women should be sensitive to the fact that they may be seated only with other women. Waitstaff may be summoned by raising your hand or by making eye contact; waving or calling their names is very impolite. Since business and socializing in this part of the world are usually one and the same, business is often discussed over meals, once individuals know each other well enough to talk terms. Take your cue from your Kenyan associates: if they bring up business, then it's okay to discuss it, but wait to take your lead from their conversation.

Once inside the home, do not wander around. If you move from one area to another in a Kenyan home or restaurant, be sure to always allow more senior members of your party to enter the room ahead of you.

Being a Good Guest or Host

Paying the Bill

Usually the one who does the inviting pays the bill. If invited to a home or if you are hosted in any way, thanks and compliments may be denied; nevertheless, it is important to state humble thanks, and to accept thanks graciously. When visiting a home as a guest for a meal, it is important to bring your gift in a *kiondo* (a woven bag, used all throughout the country for carrying things), and your gift can be some tea, sugar, flowers, or fruits. At the end of the evening, the *kiondo* will be returned to you with something in it for you, as well, often some leftover delicacy.

Transportation

It's important to make sure that guests have a way to return from where they came, if they are visiting; equally, you want to be sure not to put your host out by not having made such arrangements ahead of time for yourself, if and when you visit. If invited into a home, you may also be invited to spend the night, and if so, you must be careful to keep a low profile and use as little of the resources as possible. If cars or taxis are arranged, when seeing your guests off, you must remain at the entrance of the house or restaurant, or at the site where you deposited your guests into the car, until the car is out of sight: it is very important not to leave until your guests can no longer see you, should they look back. Guests are seated in cars (and taxis) by rank, with the honored guest being placed in the back directly behind the front passenger seat; the next honored position is in the back behind the driver, and the least honored position is up front with the driver. If there are no cars involved, hosts typically walk with their guests some distance beyond the house before saying good-bye.

When to Arrive / Chores to Do

If invited to dinner at a private home, *do* offer to help with the chores and to help out in any way you can. Do not leave the meal area unless invited to do so. When in the home, be careful not to admire something too effusively: Kenyans may feel obligated to give it to you, and doing so might represent a great sacrifice. Your compliments will most likely be dismissed although they are appreciated. Remember also that many Kenyans consider it bad luck to have their children praised: it can bring ill fortune to them (comment on the children indirectly, but comment on them positively).

Gift Giving

In general, gift giving is common for social occasions and business situations between trusted business colleagues. It is done not only as a gesture of thanks, but as a way of helping to ensure good business relations in the future (be careful not to go overboard here, as a gift that looks like an obvious bribe may land you in quite a bit of trouble . . . with the authorities in your home country, more than likely). In business settings, this usually takes the form of a personal gift that symbolically says the correct thing about the nature of the relationship. When going to the region on business, bringing a gift for the key decision maker is enough. Your gift does not have to be elaborate or expensive, but it should, whenever possible, be personalized (representative of the personalities of the receiver or giver or of an aspect of the relationship). You present your gift when you arrive in the country; before you leave to return home, you will receive a farewell gift, usually at the last meeting. When Kenyans visit your country, they will also bring you a gift, and before they leave, you should give them farewell gifts.

The most appropriate gift for a personal visit to a home, or as a thank-you for dinner, would be to bring along some fruit, tea, coffee, or nuts, and something for the children such as a toy, picture books, or school supplies (paper and writing utensils and calculators with a supply of batteries are very valued). A man typically only gives a gift to a man, a woman to a woman; remember, any gift given by a man to a woman must come with the caveat that it is from his wife/sister/mother, or else it is far too personal. Gifts to avoid giving observant Muslims include alcohol (and this includes perfumes or colognes made with alcohol), pork, art or photographs that depict natural scenes or people (this runs counter to Islamic beliefs that man must not attempt to reproduce in an image what God has made), or cutlery (which symbolizes the severing of a relationship). A fine gift for a Muslim would be a silver compass, so that he will always know which direction to face when he says his daily prayers (Muslims must face Mecca no matter where in the world they are when they say their prayers).

For both giving and receiving gifts, two hands are used always, and gifts may or may not be opened by the receiver in front of the giver (this depends upon the nature of the gift, more often than not: foodstuffs meant for dessert, for example, will be opened for all to enjoy); the presenter typically first offers the gift humbly and as an incidental aside, then, usually received after some imploring, it is acknowledged, and accepted.

Gifts should be wrapped, but special gift-wrapping is not necessary (and in some cases may not be readily available). By the way, if you own a copy of the Qu'ran (given or received as a gift or not), never place it on the floor or below any object: it must be the highest book on the shelf. Do not give a copy of the Qu'ran as a gift to a Muslim: it is far too significant for a business or social acknowledgment.

Special Holidays and Celebrations

Major Holidays

Christian and Muslim holidays are celebrated by the devout.

Secular Kenyan holidays are:

January 1	New Year's Day
March/April	Easter
May 1	Labor Day
June 1	Mandaraka Day (Kenyan national independence day)
October 10	Moi Day (President's Day)
October 20	Kenyatta Day
December 12	Independence (*Jamhuri*) Day (British assigned)
December 25	Christmas
December 26	Boxing Day

Business Culture

Daily Office Protocols

The Kenyan office may be a modern office in an urban building or a traditional stall near the market, but no matter where it is, you can be sure there will be many people coming and going. This is not so much a statement about your unimportance as much as it is a statement about the importance of your host: that he is needed by many, and that in the polychronic culture things are handled in order of their importance, and not according to the clock. Be patient. In the Kenyan organization, hierarchy is strictly observed. Because faithful Muslims pray five times a day, you will need to adjust your schedules to accommodate their needs if working with Muslims. Usually, prayers are given upon awakening and at noontime, midday, dusk, and before retiring; this means that twice during the workday, there will be time out for prayers. The prayer break usually takes a short ten or fifteen minutes or so, and any quiet area will do. If you accidentally interrupt a Muslim during his prayers, just walk quietly away: there's no need for complicated explanations or apologies. Most organizations have prayer rooms set off to the side, with carpets. In addition, devout Muslims will not work on Friday (the Muslim Sabbath), and in fact begin to end work early on Thursday before sundown. The official workweek is Monday through Friday, 9 A.M. to 4 P.M. (remember, the Muslim Sabbath is on Friday, beginning Thursday evening at sunset; the Muslim workweek therefore often includes Saturday and Sunday), and sometimes a half day Saturday morning.

Management Styles

Titles are very important, and the highest ones (e.g., vice president) are usually reserved for very senior, executive-level positions, and should not be used as casually as they are in the United States. Any criticism of Kenyan workers must be done very carefully, even privately. Deference is shown by subordinates to their seniors; paternalistic concern is often shown by seniors to their subordinates. Superiors are not typically sensitive to inquiring about their subordinates' opinions, and once a decision is made, the superiors are followed, often unquestioningly. If you are doing business with the correct person, things will probably move quickly; it is essential, therefore, to have a good and trustworthy Kenyan contact who can make the necessary contacts for you (you can locate these people through consular and/or trade association contacts prior to your trip). Let this person take the time he needs to do this for you, for if you pressure him into making contacts sooner, he may connect you to someone who is not as useful as the one he was originally waiting for: this will not serve you. Again, be patient. Never use time as a means of pressure.

Boss-Subordinate Relations

The decision-making system usually works from the top on down, with key decisions often coming from individuals in high positions of power. Superiors are expected to provide clear and fully informed sets of instructions: that is their responsibility, and it is the responsibility of subordinates to carry out those instructions. Consequently, "management-by-objective" and other egalitarian and individually empowered management styles often may not work in this environment: without clear instruction from above, subordinates may do nothing or may make decisions independently. They also lose respect for the manager for not making the decisions he should be making. This is not a reflection of their work ethic, as Kenyans can be very tireless workers, but a reflection of their expectations of the responsibilities of superiors to subordinates.

Conducting a Meeting or Presentation

There will be much hosting by your Kenyan contacts with tea, coffee, and soft drinks. When serving any refreshments in the office, be sure they are served in porcelain, glass, or silver tea sets: the use of paper or Styrofoam shows disrespect and is very bad form. There may be many more people at the meeting than you were expecting: this is typically because there are many more people who need to be consulted about the decision regarding you and your business; in most cases, you will be introduced to everyone. If you are not introduced to them, do not ask to be: acknowledge them with a smile and a nod, and proceed with your meeting. If you are meeting with a decision maker, the discussions will probably be direct, forthright, and businesslike. If you do not know the decision-making authority of the person you are with, assume that you will need to meet with many people, and perhaps repeat much of the same discussions each time with different people. There may be many interruptions throughout the meeting; stay calm and flexible. Business is personal throughout the region: decision makers have got to know your face. Patience and third-party connections are key.

Negotiation Styles

At first, expect no immediate decisions from your Kenyan colleagues at the table, and be willing to provide copious information, to the degree that you can, in response to their questions and in anticipation of their needs. Presentations should be well-prepared and simply propounded. Details are best left to questions and backup material, which should be available in English and left behind. Such materials need to be simple, to the point, and interesting to look at. Unless you already have a well-established relationship, agendas need to be very broad and very flexible: everything unexpected will occur, and everything you did not plan to discuss will be brought up. Should you come with other team members, make sure that your roles are well-coordinated. Never disagree with each other in front of Kenyans or appear uncertain, unsure, not authorized to make a decision, or out of control in any way.

Most Kenyans love to bargain and see this process as a way of getting to know you: it does not imply insincerity to offer one price and then change your mind later (as it often does with Pacific Rim cultures). In fact, avoiding this process will generate suspicion, whether in the office or in the market. Remember that in the sometimes desperate conditions of African economies, business, whether in the market, on the street, or at the office, is often really all about barter; currency is often not part of the final arrangement. Final terms need not be fair to all: in fact, Kenyans may bargain and negotiate with the expectation that in order for them to get something, you may need to lose something. If you suspect something is too good to be true, or feel you are being manipulated, you are probably right in both cases. Remember to confirm what might sound like agreement with multiple inquiries: communication patterns often include reassurance, when in fact, your local associates may not be completely in agreement with you. Contracts and contract law are helpful, but ultimately not as important as the relationship, unless you are working with well-known multinational or high-government offices; nevertheless, put everything in writing that you can and insist on the same from your Kenyan associates. There are legal redress procedures available, contrary to patterns in some neighboring countries, if you need them. If possible, the deal should be sealed with a celebratory meal. Keep communications open, especially when at a distance, and stay in touch often with your Kenyan associates: share more information than you normally would if you can, not less; and be prepared to make many trips, as needed.

Written Correspondence

Your business letters should be informal and warm, and reflect the personal relationship you have established. Nevertheless, they must include a recognition of any titles and rank. Given names usually are written in uppercase; dates are given using the day/month/year format (with periods in between, not slashes)—in Kenyan business correspondence, it is appropriate to use Western dates and business writing styles. When writing names, an honorific plus the title is as common as an honorific plus the last name. You should write your e-mails, letters, and faxes in an informal, friendly, and warm manner: use a brief and warm personal introduction, and segue smoothly into business. Keep the business issues and language clear and simple, however, and bulletpoint and outline all important matters. Use the western format (name, position, company, street address, city, state/province, country, postal code) for the addresses.

Note: Refer to the preceding section on Kenya for information about general East African cultural behaviors; the material that follows describes country-specific variations on general East African customs.

TANZANIA

Some Historical Context

Prior to and just after independence, Tanzania was really two countries: Tanganyika (or the British territory of Tanganyika), which is the mainland part of the current country, and Zanzibar, consisting of several small islands off the eastern coast. This duality speaks much about the history and continuing issues facing Tanzania. Herders and migrating farmers originally inhabited the mainland area, but soon after Islam emerged, Arab traders began plowing the coasts, and settled along the eastern shore and on the eastern islands. Arabs mixed with indigenous Bantu peoples, creating the current Tanzanian people. The Arabic traders established a powerful base for themselves on the island of Zanzibar, and, headed by the Sultan of Oman, exercised complete control over the coastal region until the Portuguese came. In the 1800s, Tanganyika became a protectorate of Germany, but after World War I, Germany lost control of its African possessions to France and Britain: Tanganyika and Zanzibar went to Britain. Dar es-Salaam, on the coast, is the major commercial city of the country, mainly Muslim, while Dodoma is the capital, located inland, of mixed Christian, animist, and Muslim population. There is a tension between Muslims on the coast and in Zanzibar seeking more autonomy, and the need for nationalist unity from Dodoma. Economically, both groups need each other, since the sole economic base in Zanzibar is the spice trade (cloves and cinnamon, specifically), and, despite the vast plains of the mainland, agricultural production, the main source of revenue, is limited due to the presence of the tsetse fly (it carries African Sleeping Sickness, and limits the ability to raise cattle). Consequently, the country, as is the case throughout much of the region, struggles economically.

An Area Briefing

Religion and Demographics

Mirroring the religious split on the mainland is the ethnic split of the country: about one-third of the people are Bantu-speakers, of the Nyamwezi-Sukuma Bantu group, with another third being a combination of mainly Nilotic peoples (from the Nile region), Asians and African-Asians, and Khoi-San people (indigenous people from South Africa who came north); there is a small but powerful merchant class of Arabs and Indians. Finally, there are many refugees from neighboring states.

Greetings and Introductions

Language and Basic Vocabulary

Most of the population along the coast and almost 100 percent of the population of Zanzibar are Muslim; most of the rest of the country is split equally among Christianity (a result of the British missionary influence), Islam, and animism, with all religions influencing each other. Almost all of the people speak the national language, Swahili (more accurately known as Kiswahili), and the form of Kiswahili spoken in Tanzania is known in the region as a very pure form called Kiunguju. English is also an official language, but is mainly reserved for the educated elite, business, and government: trade and daily life are conducted in Kiswahili.

As is the case in other parts of East Africa, although the people are extremely humble, warm, and friendly, it is important for Westerners not to misunderstand the lack of the use of Western pleasantries in speech, such as "please" and "thank you": this does not indicate coldness or rudeness; rather, it is a reflection of the fact that such words do not really exist in native Bantu or other local indigenous cultures precisely because the sense of obligation of mutual group support is so strong, to actually make such statements to other individuals implies the need to state such feelings, which is an impossibility in the indigenous cultures.

Parents are sometimes referred to with the first name of the oldest (or the only male) child, after the honorific "mother" or "father," so the father of Peter, Mary, and baby George may be referred to (by everyone he meets and is introduced to) as "Father Peter." While the *tssk* sound that is so prevalent in East Africa as a way of expressing interest or to get someone's attention is used, in Tanzania it is usually an expression of disapproval.

Dining and Drinking

Dining in Tanzania has been less influenced by the West, so there will be more of the traditional East African style of eating, with the right hand, usually on mats on the floor or low stools. There will be more use of one or two communal bowls of food, so all previously mentioned proscriptions and suggestions regarding this style of eating do apply. Typical Tanzanian foods are *ugali,* the stiff East African porridge-bread that is ubiquitous in East Africa, bananas (prepared in dozens of different ways), fruits, and vegetables, plus grains; occasionally meat and fish are available. On the coast, the grain of choice is rice, usually served spiced and mixed with vegetables in a kind of pilaf.

Special Holidays and Celebrations

All Muslim and Christian holidays are celebrated by the faithful. Secular holidays in Tanzania are:

January 1	New Year's Day
January 12	Zanzibar Revolution Day
April 26	Union Day
May 1	Labor Day
July 7	*Saba Saba* (Farmers' Day)
August 8	*Nane Nane* (International Trade Day)
December 9	Independence Day

UGANDA, RWANDA, and BURUNDI

Some Historical Context

This is the home of the once mighty Buganda kingdom of the early 1800s, a well-organized and highly centralized kingdom (the king was known as the *kabaka,* and, in fact, Uganda had a kabaka well into the twentieth century, even as Britain was granting it independence) that imposed its rule over many smaller neighboring kingdoms. By the time Britain did grant its Ugandan protectorate independence, Uganda was actually serving as the indirect administrator for British interests, not only over the Bugandan people in Uganda itself, but also over the kingdoms that the kabaka had established control over one hundred years before. Uganda became, as the British would refer to it, the "Pearl of Africa," not only because it is located in some of the most spectacularly African terrain in the continent but more to their immediate political and economic interests, it served as the model of British indirect colonial rule in Africa, until the mid-twentieth century, when Britain was forced to grant Uganda independent status. The resentment and hostility that existed on the part of the smaller neighboring states over which the Ugandan kabaka ruled, and toward Britain, which in turn ruled over them through him, boiled over several times throughout history, and is, in part, the reason for the creation of the independent neighboring states of Burundi and Rwanda. However, these states were created mainly by withdrawing Europeans, without consideration for the ethnic differences of the peoples within those new, artificially created borders. The historic animosity between Tutsis and Hutus, for example, were hardly considered when Tutsis and Hutus were thrown together in all three states, setting the stage for the genocide of the twentieth century.

Hutu are the original Bantu people, who, as farmers, inhabited the area of the Rift Valley for many centuries. Tutsi are a tall, nomadic people, who most likely came from the north, and because of their social organization, adopted a warrior ethos, and quickly established authority over the Hutu. For many centuries, the minority ruling Tutsi controlled the Hutu majority, in both what is now Uganda, Burundi, and Rwanda, and parts of other areas. When the colonial powers (particularly the Belgians, who administered the area to become Rwanda and Burundi after the Germans lost at the end of World War I) came to Africa, they gravitated in their policies and their preferences toward the Tutsis for a number of reasons, not the least being a racial preference for the taller, more "European" physiognomy of the Tutsis. European policies enabled the Tutsis to maintain and tighten their control over the Hutus, and act, in some cases, as administrative vassals for the European colonialists. This merely aggravated the Tutsi-Hutu relationship to the breaking point, as the Tutsis' control over the Hutus was practically a feudal relationship of master and serf. The tensions finally exploded into an unthinkable genocide in the mid-1990s when the Interahamwe (an extremist Hutu guerilla group) organized the slaughter of more than a million Tutsis, mainly in Rwanda. It needs to be stated that Tutsis in Burundi have also been responsible for the massacres of many Hutus in that state. Because political instability in the region is rampant, the ethnic conflict, far larger than just the artificial boundaries of the states involved, spilled over into many neighboring states, Congo included. Today, Rwanda, the state most affected by the genocide, is dealing with the horrific aftermath: it is now a relatively stable country whose people, in many ways, are still in a state of shock, but recovering. Tensions between the groups and the countries in this small area of the world still remain high.

One of the reasons for the monumental scale of events in such a relatively small area is the topography of this region: it is extremely mountainous, with some of the most spectacular lakes and vistas to be found anywhere in Africa, if not the world. Unlike those of its broad-plains neighbors to the east or its equatorial rainforest neighbors to the west, the countries of this mountain and lake district are high up, making for a more temperate climate, and an attractive area for settlement. It is one of the most densely populated areas of Africa, one of the contributing sparks that ignited the flames of ethnic conflict.

Ugandans are, in part due to their colonial experience, the support they received from the British in the past (the trappings of colonial culture lived on until very recently in Uganda, with perquisites going to Ugandans who helped support the system), and their own indigenous legacy of strong feudal social structures, very sensitive to rank and authority. Status symbols are particularly important, and the wealthy, well-educated, and powerful are enormously respected, and much effort goes into demonstrating such status. For example, in the cities, owning a motorcycle, car, or even a bicycle is very respected; in the rural areas, owning livestock or several wives may be viewed with equal respect. It is with this backdrop that one can begin to appreciate the power and authority that the awful dictator Idi Amin was able to achieve. An example, even in interpersonal relationships, of the role of authority and rank and status can be seen in the way women and men relate: traditional wives more often kneel when speaking with their husbands or other men; even urban women bend their knees when meeting men, and the role of women in relation to men is particularly subordinate.

An Area Briefing

Religion and Demographics

Most Ugandans are Christian, both Catholics and Protestants (in fact, during colonial times, these groups fought with each other for Christian dominance in the country); there are some Muslims and observers of other faiths, as well. There is a similar pattern in Rwanda and Burundi (with the exception that the colonial experience in Rwanda began with Germany—and Germany, mirroring the British pattern of indirect rule established in Uganda, administered through the local Rwandan kings, or Mwami).

The largest group in Uganda are the Buganda people, with other Bantu, Nilotic, Sudanese, and other northern groups also playing a significant role in the population mix of the country. In Rwanda, 80 percent of the population is Hutu and about 20 percent is Tutsi, although the original indigenous group (before the Hutu came, and before the Tutsi established their feudal monarchy over the land) were the Twa.

Greetings and Introductions

Language and Basic Vocabulary

The official language in Uganda is English, but the local languages include Baganda for the Buganda people, and Lugando, Acholi, and Kiswahili are all spoken by many other groups. The official language in Rwanda and Burundi is French, from the Belgian influence, although English is fast becoming used (it is the intergroup language of the refugees), as is Kiswahili. All Rwandans speak their indigenous language of Kinyarwanda, a unique tonal language.

Rwandans have a reputation for being more withdrawn, conservative, and reticent than many of their neighbors; this was a cultural trait prior to the recent genocide, and no doubt the immense shock of that event is contributing to the continued distrust and reticence of these deeply mindful people. Compounding the tragedy of their country is the enormous AIDS epidemic, taking a particularly ravaging toll in Uganda, Rwanda, and Burundi. In fact, with an infection rate of almost one in seven people throughout this part of East Africa, what family units remained after the genocide are being decimated by HIV. When Rwandans meet someone whom they know well, they may embrace twice, once hugging to one side, then the other. It should be stated that Rwanda has made remarkable advances in emerging from the terror of the recent past, and the beauty of the country and the people is beginning to shine through once more.

Special Holidays and Celebrations

Major Holidays

All Christian and Muslim holidays are celebrated by the faithful in all countries, and as is the case throughout all of Africa, seasonal festivals and local traditions are popularly observed. Secular holidays in Uganda are:

January 1	New Year's Day
January 26	Liberation Day
March 8	Women's Day
March/April	Easter
May 1	Labor Day
June 3	Martyrs' Day
October 9	Independence Day
December 25	Christmas
December 26	Boxing Day

Secular holidays in Rwanda are:

January 1	New Year's Day
January 28	Democracy Day
March/April	Easter
April 7	Genocide Memorial Day
May 1	Labor Day
May 21	Ascension Day
July 1	Independence Day
July 4	Liberation Day
August 15	Assumption Day
September 25	Republic Day
October 1	Heroes' Day
October 26	Armed Forces Day
November 1	All Saints' Day
December 25	Christmas

PART FIVE

Southern Africa

The Promise

An Introduction to the Region

When one thinks of modern Africa, and the future potential of Africa, one is often drawn to the phenomenon of South Africa. A few decades ago, this country was struggling to carve an identity out of a horrific history of brutal colonial and indigenous racism, grinding poverty, and ethnic rivalries. Today, despite its challenges, South Africa is the first place that non-Africans tend to think of when reflecting on the promise of Africa. If it will happen at all, it will happen here first, or so it often seems. If Africa will turn, the turning will be here. The irony, of course, is that it is precisely because of South Africa's familiarity with the West, the courageous South African response to Western colonial brutality and inhumanity that South Africans had to live with, and the potential this history provides for change, that makes for this possibility.

Of course, South Africa is more than the Republic of South Africa to which we are referring. Beyond the mosaic that is the republic at the southernmost end of the continent are the neighboring countries to the north, east, and west. Together, this entire region also presents new possibilities and the promise for the African renaissance, but perhaps not to the same degree as the republic itself. It is as if there were a center of gravity for change in Africa, beginning somewhere between the Cape and Pretoria, and as we move out from this center, the possibilities become more problematic. Perhaps it is simply a function of geography: South Africa, after all, need only deal with neighbors mainly to its north, lying as it does at the all-important sea-lanes connecting the Atlantic Ocean (and subsequently the European world) to the Indian Ocean (and subsequently the Asian world), while so many of those neighbors, in fact, must deal with their greater proximity to one another, and the challenges that such nearness brings. South Africa seems to also be the birthplace of the great Southern African Bantu culture itself, which spread northward out from the Capelands almost into the heart of Kenya, creating, along with the Nilitic/Arabic and Guinean/Atlantic cultures, one of the three great African metacultures. The word itself, *Bantu,* is a derivative of the "AbaNtu," which simply meant "the people," as is the case with so many great civilizations (great, no doubt, partly because of their security—granted by the good fortune often of nothing more than grand isolation—in their belief that they were simply the one and only). For over two thousand years, these people spoke a common language, but as they spread and intermingled with others, the Bantu languages broke down into many different dialects, so that today, even though they share a common grammar and word form, many Bantu people in Southern Africa need English or the modern trade language of Swahili in order to communicate with one another. In fact, the Bantu language, and the Bantu people, broke down into two major groups: the first, the Nguni group, further breaks down into such familiar ethnic subgroups as the Zulu, the Xhosa, the Ndebele, the Swazi, and the Tsonga. All Nguni Bantu groups can communicate with one another, for their individual languages are similar enough to allow for common understanding, and all sometimes—though not always—get along with one another. The second Bantu group is called the "Sotho" (pronounced, "Sootoo," as in the country of Lesotho), and they also further break down into the subgroups of the Northern and Southern Sotho and the Tswana (as in the country of Botswana). Together, these peoples make up the framework for all the indigenous peoples of Southern Africa.

But the original people, before the Bantu, from the timeless past, who inhabited the region were the Khoisan, or more accurately, the Khoi and the San, for they were two groups even then (although neither group's ancestors today, and there are many, refer to each other or themselves with this term). The San were better known to the West, when "discovered" as "Bushmen," those "savages" of the land for whom the Western colonialists could find no point of understanding: they were the eternal stewards of the Southern African landscape, the agriculturalists who lived off the land itself, while the Khoi were the nomadic herders of animals who trekked across the land following the ceaseless patterns of nature, weather, and climate. Of course, the Khoi and the San were forever in a pitched battle with each other, making both ripe for being overtaken by the emerging Bantu, and they, in turn, ultimately by the invading Europeans. (The Khoi referred to themselves as "KhoiKhoin," meaning "men of men," but when the Dutch arrived in South Africa, they derisively called the Khoi "Hottentots," because the rhyming pattern of their speech, coupled with the unique "clicking" sounds of their language, sounded to the Dutch as if they were stammering and stuttering, or as the Dutch would say, *"hatern en tatern,"* hence, "Hottentot," by the English translation. Any version of this word, and the European word for the San, "bushmen," is considered very ugly today in the region: use neither.) If there is a significant difference between this region and the rest of Africa, it is in the presence of the European, not only as explorer, exploiter, or missionary, but as immigrant, for it is here in the Southern African countries of South Africa, Zimbabwe, Zambia, and others, that we see the challenge of truly creating, beyond the *multiethnic* challenge faced by the rest of Africa, the *multicultural* Africa: here, Whites and Asians also claim what they see as a legitimate historical stake in these countries.

Getting Oriented

The region is geographically Southern Africa (a major country of which is The Republic of South Africa, or simply for our purposes, South Africa); for our purposes, it can be further broken down into its geographic components of:

- The North, consisting, from north to south, of the countries of Zambia and Zimbabwe, Malawi, and of the two coastal nations of Mozambique and the Malagasy Republic (on the island of Madagascar)
- The South, consisting of the countries of South Africa, Lesotho and Swaziland, Botswana, and Namibia

The North: Zambia and Zimbabwe, Malawi, and Mozambique and Madagascar

Note: Refer to the previous sections on Kenya and East Africa for information about general East African cultural behaviors; the material that follows describes country-specific variations on general East African customs.

ZAMBIA and ZIMBABWE

Almost 99 percent of all Zambians are Bantu peoples, having lived there over the centuries. Although there are many ethnic groups within this broad Bantu group, Zambians view each other as members of "cousin tribes," and the differences do not typically make for problems. One percent of Zambians are "White Zambians," that is, the descendants of European settlers who claimed the lands. Herein lies the dilemma, which has over time repeatedly challenged the country, of land ownership, wealth, and power redistribution. For both Zambia and Zimbabwe, there is a general understanding of the need, on the part of both groups, to provide equal access to these resources, but the question is how to do it practically. Extremists on both sides dig their heels in: simply take the land away from current white owners and parcel it out to the population? Arrange some sort of compensation for land officially appropriated? But who is to pay, and how, and why? The problem is most serious in Zimbabwe, which has the larger percentage of land ownership along ethnic and racial lines.

The history of the problem, of course, lies in the colonial experience: Europeans—specifically the British, under the colonial auspices of Cecil Rhodes—originally settled in the area as missionaries, explorers, and colonialists, and eventually claimed the entire region of present-day Zambia, Zimbabwe, and Malawi as the Central African Federation of Rhodesia and Nyasaland. The federation eventually broke apart, with northern Rhodesia becoming, upon independence in the mid-twentieth century (and not without a difficult and often violent struggle), Zambia, southern Rhodesia becoming Zimbabwe, and eastern Nyasaland becoming Malawi.

An Area Briefing

Religion and Demographics

Eponymous groups include Icibemba, Chitonga, Silozi, in Zambia, just to name a few, and mainly Ndebele and Shona in Zimbabwe (Shona in the west, and

Ndebele, through a number of subgroups, primarily in the rest of the country). It is important in Zimbabwe to recognize the historical difficulties between Shona and Ndebele—Shona mainly were from the north, west, and east, and established a powerful trading empire in Zimbabwe in the fifteenth century, before Ndebele, as Zulus, came up from the south and eventually became dominant. By the time Rhodes and the Europeans came to the area, the fighting between the two groups had weakened both, and both Matabeleland (the home of the Ndebele) and Mashonaland (the home of the Shona), came under British control as part of southern Rhodesia. Even today in Zimbabwe, Shona and Ndebele leaders often split when it comes to politics. In both countries, Christianity is practiced by the majority of the population, but in Zimbabwe, the Roman Catholic Church is more predominant; in Zambia, Christians are more likely to be of a Protestant denomination, and there is a significant Muslim (about 40 percent) population, as well. As is the case throughout the region, in the east in both countries, there is a small but influential Indian (Hindu) merchant community. In all cases, all religions are infused with local beliefs (consulting mediums, seeking advice from oracles, and traditional healers or "witch doctors"— in local language, N'anga—beliefs in totems and charms, etc.) and have influenced each other.

Greetings and Introductions

Language and Basic Vocabulary

In all three countries, English is the official language, but many local Bantu languages are spoken.

In both countries, demonstrating respect for individuals, especially elders, is critical, and the importance of the extended, appropriate greeting cannot be overemphasized. In Zambia, until and only when one has a personal relationship with someone, the last or family name is used in all introductions, along with the appropriate honorific (Mr., Mrs., Miss, Dr., etc.), or just Sir or Madame (or Bwana, when addressing an unrelated superior, like a boss or supervisor) when a title is used without a name. When one has a personal relationship, first or given names, and more often, nicknames, are used.

Physical Greeting Styles

Showing respect is often demonstrated physically: in both countries, kneeling down in front of elders, or women kneeling in front of men, is typical of greetings between individuals (in fact, in Zimbabwe, because physically lowering oneself to someone of greater rank is important, one does not, for example, rise from the table when an elder enters a room: this is precisely the reverse of the Western practice). One typically kneels when presenting a gift, in both countries. Elders are seated first, greeted first, spoken to first, and accorded every opportunity to be treated with special respect. There is a rigid separation of the traditional roles of men and women, and women are clearly subordinate in their day-to-day behaviors vis-à-vis men. It is important to avert the eyes when speaking with elders and superiors. During the ritual handwashing before and after every meal, younger people will pour the water into a basin for the older people.

In both countries, greetings do not typically include physical hugs or kisses, unless one is especially close with the other individual. Instead, sincerity is shown by shaking hands, and supporting the right hand at the elbow or forearm with the left hand. Additionally, in both countries, clapping hands is a very common way of expressing both greetings and emotions: during conversations, people might clap their hands to indicate involvement, understanding, or enthusiasm; people might clap hands to indicate thankfulness or gratitude (in place of the "please" or "thank you," which are typically not expressed verbally in this region). At the end of a meal, for example, it is appropriate to clap your hand softly a few times and state how satisfied you are with the meal. All other physical protocols highlighted in the East African chapters, such as the use of the right hand, apply.

Dining and Drinking

Deference is also shown in the way one eats: in both countries, except for among some young urban elite, dining is typically done on low stools or around a mat on the floor, and individuals are careful to keep their body positions low when dining with elders or superiors. In Zambia, the national dish is called *nsima:* it is the ubiquitous stiff porridge found throughout central and southern Africa, made from any number of grains, and often eaten with a sauce made from vegetables and spices. In Zimbabwe it is called *sadza.* The drink at each meal, and in between, in most cases, is tea or water, although beer, often of the home-brewed variety, is also very popular.

Special Holidays and Celebrations

Major Holidays

In Zambia, the national holidays are:

January 1	New Year's Day
March 19	Youth Day
March/April	Easter
May 1	Labor Day
May 25	African Freedom Day
July	Heroes and Unity Days (celebrated on the first Monday and Tuesday of the month)
August	Farmers' Day (celebrated on the first Monday of the month)
October 24	Independence Day
December 25	Christmas
December 26	Boxing Day

In Zimbabwe, the national holidays are:

January 1	New Year's Day
March/April	Easter
April 18	Independence Day

May 1	Labor Day
May 25	African Freedom Day
August 11–12	Heroes and Defense Forces Day
December 25	Christmas
December 26	Boxing Day

MALAWI

While Malawi shares many basic cultural traits with East Africa and Zambia, it is important to note the special role that Malawi plays in the region: it was here, in 1915, that John Chilembwe led a major revolt against British colonial rule, which has made him not only a national Malawian hero, but a regional, if not a Pan-African, one as well. It serves non-Africans well to express understanding and admiration for Chilembwe and the fact that he lost his life leading what was then one of the first, and certainly earliest, campaigns for freedom and independence in Africa. In the thirteenth century, the Maravi people (Malawi is a derivative of their name) came to the fertile strip of land running to the side of one of the great East African Rift Valley lakes (currently, Lake Malawi); they settled and were very successful agriculturalists who also managed to cooperate successfully with other Bantu ethnic groups entering the valley; the current tradition that Malawians enjoy of being warmhearted, democratic, and cooperative people no doubt has precedence in this history. The Chewa were the main people who entered the valley, along with the Yao from the east, and today, both groups, along with smaller numbers of several smaller groups, constitute the bulk of Malawi's population. Chewa speak Chichewa, the dominant language, although English is the official language and is spoken well throughout the country. Malawians are quite formal in their introductions with new acquaintances: they always use family names, and always use appropriate honorifics. Do not use the U.S.-style "okay" sign (the circle formed by the forefinger and thumb touching): it is highly offensive. Malawian food and diet are quite similar to that of Zambia.

MOZAMBIQUE and MADAGASCAR

Some Historical Context

Both lands of many different peoples, from many different surrounding areas, today Mozambique and Madagascar basically represent Bantu African cultures that have also been heavily influenced, culturally and ethnically, by many other peoples, and it is this influence from places very far away that makes these two countries uniquely different from their neighbors. Therefore, in addition to the considerations already highlighted for countries in the region, one must also consider the influence that these additional "foreign" cultures have exerted on the developing larger Mozambican and Malagasy cultures.

MOZAMBIQUE

Some Historical Context

In Mozambique, the Khoikhoi and the San were the indigenous peoples (as they were throughout most of the region), but were soon displaced by Bantus around A.D. 300. Arabs and Indians soon discovered the treasures of the African coast, and settled up and down the coastal areas of Mozambique. Then the Shone, from inland Zimbabwe, extended their mighty empire eastward into Mozambique, and the northern Maravi (from the Malawi area) entered south. In the eighteenth century, the Tsonga, the Yao, and the mighty Nguni came. By the time the Portuguese discovered Mozambique (remember Vasco da Gama's famous rounding of the Cape on his trip to India), they came in direct contact with the Gaza Kingdom of the Nguni, then the dominant group in Mozambique. Once the Portuguese settled, they displaced the Arabs, and established a successful slave trade with the local African chiefs, primarily to their colony in Brazil. When slavery was outlawed, Portugal shifted control over Mozambique to private companies, many of them British, and created a system of forced labor, a hair short of slavery, called *chibalo*. It was the revolt against chibalo in the mid-twentieth century that set Mozambique on a very hard-fought course for independence, with Portugal finally granting it in 1974. Once independent, Mozambique established, as was not unusual in the area at the time, a Marxist government and economy, which immediately drove those who did not support such policies into what ultimately turned out to be civil rebellion. By the mid-1990s, the civil war ended, and Mozambique began a remarkable period of economic growth and development. Then, the unpredictability of Africa struck: massive floods devastated the country at the end of the century (nearly a third of the country was underwater!), a condition that the people are only now emerging from.

An Area Briefing

Religion and Demographics

The people are a mix of Tsongas in the south, Shona in the middle region, and Makwe-Lomwe people in the north. Most Mozambicans are Roman Catholic, with about 20 percent of the population Muslim along the coast; most all Mozambicans believe devoutly in animist traditions.

Greetings and Introductions

Language and Basic Vocabulary

Each indigenous group speaks its own local language, plus Kiswahili, although Portuguese is well-known, and is the official language for business, government, and most commerce. The north/south split is evident throughout the country, in the way people greet and relate to each other, as well as the way people live their day-to-day lives (in the south, for example, wealth is displayed through livestock ownership, while in the north wealth is more typically displayed through items—bicycles, cars, jewelry, the size of one's house, etc.). In the south, people greet each other with typical Portuguese or European greetings: shaking hands, and close acquaintances (and two women) greeting each other with hugs and kisses on each cheek; however, in the north, typically, people greet each other with the regional soft clapping of hands. In most cases, greetings may be in local language, or Portuguese.

Some Portuguese greetings include:

ola!	hello (used informally among youth)
tudo bem?	how are things going? (informal)
bom dia	good day
boa tarde	good afternoon
boa noite	good evening
¿como esta?	how are you?
estou bem	I am fine
obrigada/o	thank you

Individuals who do not know each other use honorifics (Senhor, Senhora) plus the family name; individuals who know each other typically use first names and/or nicknames, typically without the honorific if they are peers, and with the honorific if they are in a superior/subordinate relationship.

The thumbs-up gesture is typically fine: it is used throughout the country as a sign of approval, particularly among young people.

Dress

The traditional clothing for women is the *capulana* (a long, wraparound skirt, with a matching head wrap for married women: traditionally, a wife gets an additional capulana from her husband each year). Men wear the *balalaica* (a kind of safari-suit) or *goiabera* (the formal open-collared shirt that is worn outside of the trousers) in the cities, or the *bubu* (like the *boubou*—a long, loose-fitting shirt that is worn over the trousers) in much of the country.

Dining and Drinking

Mozambicans eat three meals per day when they can, the main meal being dinner; the staple porridge-paste of the country is *xima,* typically made with rice. Whenever possible, vegetables, meat, and fish are served along with *xima.*

Special Holidays and Celebrations

Major Holidays

National Mozambican holidays are:

January 1	New Year's Day
February 3	Heroes' Day

April 7	Mozambican Womens' Day
May 1	Labor Day
June 25	Independence Day
September 7	Lusaka Accords Day
September 25	Day of the Armed Struggle
December 25	Christmas

MADAGASCAR

Some Historical Context

Madagascar is one of the world's largest islands, and as an island in the Indian Ocean between Africa and Asia, has been a pearl in the eye of many a trader, whether Asian, African, or European. Malagasy refers to the people of this island today, a complex mix of many of the peoples who have sailed by and settled here; Madagascar refers to the country and the land. In fact, the first settlers to the island were probably from Asia, Malays and Indonesians, who brought with them their own Bahasa-based Malay language and culture. By the time Europeans "discovered" Madagascar, the Merina group was well in charge, and although explored by the Portuguese first, the island was influenced both by the French and the British. Eventually, the British gave up control to the French, and the Malagasy people struggled bitterly for half a century to win their independence, which they finally did in 1972 (it is well worth demonstrating knowledge of the uprising against the French in 1947, which cost the lives of almost 100,000 Malagasy people).

An Area Briefing

Religion and Demographics

Bantu Africans from the African mainland and other Asians mixed with the original settlers to form two major ethnic groups on the island: the Merina and the Betsileo, who today make up the majority of the population; additionally, as both groups settled the island, some remained along the coast (known as Cotiers), while others developed a lifestyle suited to the mountainous highlands of the interior; due to the differences between coastal and mountain life, the two groups became quite different. Consequently, there is some resentment even today between highlanders and coastal people, as well as between people who see themselves as more indigenous when compared to others who are seen or may see themselves as more recent descendants from outside groups.

About half the population calls itself Christian (with some Muslim Cotiers along the coast); the other 50 percent practices local animist beliefs, and animism infuses all religious practices. It is important to recognize the power of such faith among the people, especially as an outsider: razana, or ancestor, worship is practiced by most everyone, and fadys, or various taboos and totems, have a power over almost every daily, seasonal and annual activity (there is a good and bad time to do everything and anything, and this will affect your timetable in Madagascar on an almost daily basis).

Greetings and Introductions

Language and Basic Vocabulary

The Malagasy language is a unique blend of Malay, Indonesian, Bantu, and Arabic (it was first written in an Arabic script, but is now written in a Latin script, the result of the European colonization); French is also an official language, and Malagasy has incorporated many French words into daily vocabulary. It is worth noting that there is an oral tradition in Malagasy of speaking sometimes almost totally in proverbs and metaphors; in fact it is highly regarded to be able to say things succinctly, indirectly and with metaphors and sayings (this is known as *kabary,* and was traditionally regarded as an art: it says something for the indirectness and avoidance of disharmony and confrontation that is a major orientation in the culture). Incidentally, Malagasy words are typically long, relative to Western words: for example, the capital city is Antananarivo, but is more commonly known as "Tana."

Honorifics for Men, Women, and Children

People use either first or last names in greetings, preceded by an honorific if they do not know each other, and without an honorific if they do know each other and they are peers (children, for example, must use the relationship honorific before speaking with adults). Nicknames are very common (prior to colonization, Malagasy simply used one nickname in place of both the first and last names).

Dress

The traditional dress includes the wearing of the *lamba,* which is a long cotton wrap, for both men and women: please note that most *lamba* are white, and a red lamba is a sign of status and authority. It is, as is the case throughout the region, inappropriate for Westerners to wear traditional dress.

Dining and Drinking

The national dish is *loaka,* which is a kind of stew or soup in which most of what is available is cooked together; it is eaten, whenever possible, with rice. Rice is the national grain, and almost all meals are accompanied with a bowl of *sakay,* or a spice mixture for seasoning, which includes peppers, ginger, and garlic. The national drink is *ranovola,* a health drink made from water and the leftover rice in the pot. As a guest, you will always be served *hanikotrana,* a snack of sweets and vegetables, and a cool drink or tea when you visit.

Special Holidays and Celebrations

Major Holidays

National holidays in Madagascar are:

January 1	New Year's Day
March 29	Martyrs' Day
May 1	Labor Day
June 26	Independence Day
November 1	All Saints' Day
December 25	Christmas
December 30	Anniversary of the Republic

The South: South Africa, Lesotho and Swaziland, Botswana, and Namibia

SOUTH AFRICA

Some Introductory Background on South Africa and the South Africans

The unique position that the Republic of South Africa holds for the continent is based largely on the fact that the country has both suffered and profited from the colonial experience more than any other Sub-Saharan nation, if not more deeply, than certainly in ways that more profoundly affect the future of more Africans. Essentially, the significant European presence has made for more than a multiethnic society: it has made for a multiracial one, and consequently, all of the inherent challenges and opportunities, along with the wisdom and knowledge that is the result of both the wonderful and terrible experiences that have occurred in South Africa, are available for South Africans to use, either to their mutual benefit or mutual misery. What happens here will in many ways set the path for how or if much of the rest of Africa will follow. The future is still to be determined, but there is no doubt that South Africa takes the lead role in the future of the sub-Saharan region of the continent.

Some Historical Context

The Khoi and San were the two indigenous groups of the country (today, most Khoisan can be located in southern Namibia, as they have effectively been driven out of the mainstream in South Africa). Once the Bantu arrived about two thousand years ago, they broke into two groups in South Africa, the Nguni group (Swazi, Zulu, Xhosa, Ndebele) and the Sotho group (Tswana, northern and southern Sotho). Today, these various groups can be found in specific locations throughout the country. The first Europeans to arrive were mainly Dutch, who settled in the Transvaal region; their descendants are referred to today as White South Africans. They were traditionally farmers (the word in Dutch is "Boers"). Those who first came settled in the Cape region, but as more arrived, they quickly spread across the veld, becoming known as Trekboers (those who were cattle farmers), and Voortrekkers (advancing migrants, pioneers, and other workers who moved further and further inland). Inevitably, Boers clashed with local Xhosa, Zulu, Ndebele, and others; after the discovery of gold, the British arrived as well, and also clashed with local indigenous Africans, whom the Europeans referred to as "Coloureds" (today, there is not the negative connotation associated with "White" or "Coloured" in South Africa that there is in the United States; "Black" refers to indigenous Africans, "White" to descendants of Europeans, and "Coloured" to people of mixed Asian, White, and African blood). Europeans referred to themselves as Afrikaaners, and developed a language, Afrikaans, based on Dutch (with some English) that was unique to them; Boers and Britons fought for their respective territories and the right to claim the rest of the region in what is remembered as the Boer War at the end of the nineteenth century. The Boers were defeated, and Britain consolidated its territories into the Union of South Africa, comprised primarily of the Orange Free State, the Transvaal, the Cape, and the Natal.

We should take a moment to consider the struggle that indigenous peoples put up against both Boers and Britons in the face of the European conquest (known by Nguni and Sotho alike as the *iMfecane,* or "the time of the crushing"). The Zulus, in particular, were known as fierce warriors, and were feared by both Europeans and other groups. The mighty Zulu warrior Shaka, in fact, imposed a very regimented and highly organized militaristic structure on what had become a huge army of fighting Zulu soldiers, who successfully defeated Europeans in several key battles. Nevertheless, the legacy of constant fighting, of coming together to counter the European enemy only to face the power of a neighboring ethnic group, and of ultimately being overcome and having one's land, rights, property, and even traditions and human dignity, taken away, inevitably set ethnic group against ethnic group, with the result being each group struggling against the other and claiming a different area as their own. It should also be noted that Europeans had evolved, in response to this experience, a fairly complex system of responses to the issue of dealing with various indigenous groups, and at the beginning, the response included, in some cases, cooperation. Over time, however, the mistrust and exploitation between and among the groups became overwhelming for all, and ultimately, a system of apartheid was imposed by the ruling British government of the then independent country of South Africa in the mid-1950s, which essentially segregated all communities along racial lines: Black Africans and coloureds were to live in specified "homelands," while White South Africans controlled the country. With this forced segregation came brutal inequalities, which led eventually to armed resistance (and the legacy of Nelson Mandela, and others) and the eventual collapse of the apartheid system and White-minority rule in South Africa in the early 1990s.

An Area Briefing

Politics and Government

Today, South Africa strives to be the multiracial nation of its new constitution: toward that end, there is a bicameral parliament, a president, and a federal judiciary. There are nine provinces, each with its own parliament and local powers, who directly elect members to the Council, or the upper house of Parliament. There are two major political parties, and several smaller ones. The struggle toward independence and the abolition of apartheid was difficult and long, and the legacies do not evaporate overnight; there is still much suspicion between the indigenous groups and between White and Black South Africans, although there is a growing sense that there needs to be a way for all to participate equitably in the new South Africa. Remarkably, through all of this painful transition, South Africa has emerged with undoubtedly the strongest economy in all of Africa: there is a well-defined and fairly efficient infrastructure on all counts, and a judiciary that is trusted by more and more of the people; massive natural wealth continues to fuel the economy, and the economy has managed to hold steady, with low unemployment and inflation. All South Africans are struggling, through urban crime, corruption, and lingering paranoia, to find a way to take these important assets (although the economy is strong and the country the wealthiest in Africa, for example, wealth distribution is highly unequal, and it is the white community that mainly benefits from this strength), and the diversity of the people, and make them work for the greater good of the country and for Africa.

Schools and Education

As is the case throughout much of Africa, schooling for children is spotty and difficult to mandate, although in South Africa, most children are enrolled throughout at least primary school, and attendance is compulsory up to age fifteen. There is a great belief in the value of education, and South Africans make every effort to make sure children enroll in school and remain as long as possible. There is an adult literacy rate, in fact, of almost 80 percent. Schooling is done in the beginning grades typically in local languages, but then switches to English for the remaining primary grades onward, although Afrikaans is also offered as a language option. South Africans who can afford to go on to receive university educations.

Religion and Demographics

Half of all South Africans—including mainly all Whites and most coloureds—are Christian; Afrikaans-speakers generally belong to the Dutch Reformed Church, and English-speaking Whites generally belong to the Lutheran, Anglican, Presbyterian, Methodist, or other Protestant denominational churches. There are small percentages of Muslims and Jews and a slightly larger percentage of Hindus (from the larger Indian population). Black Africans typically belong to any number of the African Independent Churches, the largest being the Zion Christian Church (these more typically combine indigenous animist beliefs with Christian practices, which is not done in the White churches). An additional 20 percent of all Africans follow their local animist beliefs fairly exclusively. It is a challenge (to provide opportunity) and a strength (the optimism and energy) that, as is the case throughout much of Africa, the majority of the population is under thirty years of age, and the significant AIDS epidemic is threatening to destroy a fabric of life between the generations.

Because of the understanding, if not acceptance, of Western ways in South Africa, depending upon the individual you are working with (whether they are white, Western-educated, urban or rural, a member of local ethnic group, Asian, or Muslim), Western women and men typically do not experience much difficulty doing business in South Africa; women, in fact, make up more than a third of the workforce and post-primary student population in South Africa, and many urban South African women are opting for nuclear families, education, and careers instead of the large extended rural family and the prescribed home-maker role that women traditionally play in it.

The majority of the population, by over 70 percent, is black African, made up of basically Nguni and Sotho subgroups, each generally staying within their own area, and speaking their own indigenous language: Zulu (the largest), Xhosa, North Sotho, South Sotho, Tswana, Swazi, Ndebele, Venda. Of the remaining 30 percent of the population, about 10 percent are mixed race combinations of Whites, Blacks, Asians, and Khoikhoi. About 5 percent are Indian, the descendants mainly of a large Indian immigration at the beginning of the twentieth century into South Africa of workers and merchants. Whites constitute just slightly more than 10 percent of the total population, and this includes all Dutch, British, Scottish, Irish, and German descendants. Additionally, there are several million "unofficial" refugees from various neighboring countries.

Fundamental Cultural Orientations

Depending upon the group one is interfacing with, there can be some significant variances in the fundamental cultural orientations of the people. In general, white South Africans hold values that are more similar to traditional European values, and black Africans hold values that are more similar to those typical of much of the rest of Africa. The degree to which there are similarities and differences will be the result of many factors, but in many cases, the differences between the two groups at this level of fundamental value orientations can be significant, and pose a challenge to the creation of a national psyche based on shared values. For the following, we will outline those orientations that are more a description of indigenous South African beliefs.

1. What's the Best Way for People to Relate to One Another?

OTHER-INDEPENDENT OR OTHER-DEPENDENT? There is a combination of deep concern for family, clan, and other membership groups (such as work, religion, and nation) that defines an individual and individual expression among Africans. South Africans, like all Africans, have a hierarchical sense of loyalties, beginning with their family, and then, in descending order of importance, their ethnic group, their religion, their home village, their country, their region, and their continent. South Africans are deeply connected first to their clan and their families: for that reason, it is critical that one inquire about the health of all family members. How one performs his or her role vis-à-vis others is judged in Africa, and individuals do nothing without careful consideration for how others will see it and them, and for the impact their action will have on their family and their community. Consequently, individual empowerment and decision making are rare, and consensus-building and confirming group agreement are critical. Sharing, concern for others, humility, and an acceptance—without anger, remorse, or hostility—of one's role, at least within and for one's group, are all hallmarks of Southern African and South African culture.

HIERARCHY-ORIENTED OR EGALITY-ORIENTED? Both South African secular life and ethnic group membership (as well as Islamic life for Muslims, and Hindu life for Indians) is rigidly stratified, with three or four generations of the extended family traditionally living together (this is not necessarily the case in the cities); individuals within this highly stratified social structure play their roles—children, women, and men in relation to one another, hosts in relation to guests, religious leaders and other elders in relation to the community. Defining for others one's rank is important, and status symbols (for example, the jewelry that women wear, the ritual scarification imposed by the ethnic group, the pattern used on the traditional robe, and, most especially, the property that one owns, which is typically land or livestock) are traditionally important. It is critical that everyone show respect for elders and devout observers. Women and men are different and perform different roles: in South Africa a woman typically may go out in public alone, but she will probably prefer to go with other female friends or relatives. She need not be in the company of a close male relative (husband, father, son, or brother), and Muslim women generally will not wear a veil. In fact, although all groups are male-dominated, South African women in general do play a significant role in public life: they work, are represented in the intellectual community, and are active in politics, and even in the rural areas, it is the woman who is most likely responsible for the agricultural crop of the family.

RULE-ORIENTED OR RELATIONSHIP-ORIENTED?   While many South Africans have had experience with and in the West, the tension that exists between the application of universal rules over reliable and dependable relationships is palpable. This leads to a high dependence on power, authority, and subjective decision making based on the situation and the relationships between the individuals involved. Ultimately, face-to-face knowledge of the individuals involved in any interaction is the basis upon which final decisions are often made, despite the fact that the British legal infrastructure is used as a basis for administering justice on a more universal scale than is typical in many other parts of Africa: this is a distinguishing characteristic of South Africa, in general.

2. What's the Best Way to View Time?

MONOCHRONIC OR POLYCHRONIC?   South Africa is essentially polychronic, due to the influence of both agrarian and religious traditions (although less so in Pretoria, Johannesburg, and other cities). There is forgiveness for the inevitable delays and unexpected events that define life in Africa, and understanding when things don't go as planned or scheduled; people may or may not show up at invited events, things may or may not happen as planned. Schedules tend to be loose and flexible. Because who (relationships) is generally more important than what (tasks) or when (time), there can be many interruptions during a meeting, and people's obligations to other people, who may come and go, are more important than doing things according to schedules. If you are being kept waiting, or are ignored because of someone else's needs, it may be an indication of your importance relative to the other person, and expressing frustration over being kept waiting only diminishes your importance.

RISK-TAKING OR RISK-AVERSE?   South Africans are prone to taking risks when in positions of authority, but avoiding them when they are not. Within organizations, the decision makers can be bold, even reckless, but subordinates generally are not, and take action only when instructed to do so. Therefore, comfort with uncertainty, in general, is low, and much information may need to be exchanged with different people before decisions can be made. Even when decisions are made at the top, the concern for others within the group requires decision makers to consult with subordinates before making decisions. There will be much discussion with trusted others about what you, as a foreigner, bring to the table, *after* you leave the meeting.

PAST-ORIENTED OR FUTURE-ORIENTED? There is a distinct and inherent fatalism in regard to the effect of human action. Nevertheless, those empowered by virtue of their position are expected to make the decisions that keep the world running, and by so doing, are fulfilling either their destiny or that of those they are responsible for. Future benefits may motivate South Africans; however, doing nothing, or doing things for the here and now, is sometimes more important, and if things do not work out, that is to be expected—no mortal controls the universe, and all is ultimately determined. There is a deep belief that things will take the time they need to take, and that it is always more important to maintain smooth interpersonal relationships until opportunities come along: when that happens, South Africans will be sure to seize them!

3. What's the Best Way for Society to Work with the World at Large?

LOW-CONTEXT DIRECT OR HIGH-CONTEXT INDIRECT COMMUNICATORS? South Africans are very context-driven communicators. They will speak in metaphors, and use stories or codified phrases; they will employ analogies, precedent, and much nonverbal behavior to convey true meaning. They generally try to avoid confrontation as a primary goal, as do most of their neighbors in the region, and often will go out of their way to maintain smooth personal relationships in the face of difficult circumstances.

PROCESS-ORIENTED OR RESULT-ORIENTED? Decisions and actions may be the result of reasoning that is not directed at a determination of truth, but rather context-based "correctness" based on similar experiences, often with personal subjective experience being the criteria for decision making. Nevertheless, there is an equal respect for the rationalist approach to problem solving and decision making. Both elements are used, more or less (often reflected by urban/rural experiences), by South Africans in their thought processes. South Africans are open to Western ideas, if they "fit" the African reality and African expectations.

FORMAL OR INFORMAL? Southern African society is basically formal and ritualized, and each group has its own way of honoring the hierarchies, establishing respect and deference, and following (or not following) through on their responsibilities. There are formal ways that guests (outsiders) and hosts (insiders) must act toward each other, in order to preserve the honor of all groups and individuals.

Greetings and Introductions

Language and Basic Vocabulary

Over half the whites speak Afrikaans; some black Africans speak it as well as English, which is the official language used in business and government, and a common, though not universally spoken, language between groups. Most Africans speak a local language based on Nguni, Sotho, Tsonga, or Venda, depending upon the group of which they are a member (some of which have the very unique "clicking" sound and tonality that are associated with South African languages). Few whites speak any of the local African languages, though there is a growing awareness among white South Africans of the need to learn them. Westerners need to remember that the English that is used is essentially a version of British, not American, English.

Here are some of the basic greetings:

English	Afrikaans	Nguni	Sotho
hello/good morning	*goeie more*	*sawubona*	*dumela*
how are things? (informal)	(same)	*kunjani?*	*molo?*
good-bye	*tot siens*	*sawubona*	*sala gashi*

Honorifics for Men, Women, and Children

People usually greet each other by title or relationship (e.g., Dr., Mr., Mrs., aunt, mother, cousin) plus the last, or family, name if they have never met before; once a relationship is established, honorifics are often still used, but with first or given names; sometimes, the honorific is dispensed with (between peers, usually). If names are not known, sometimes stating the individual's position as a title is sufficient (e.g., Mr. Engineer or Miss Fish Seller). Children typically refer to their parents as "mother of" or "father of" plus the name of the oldest sibling, and refer to elders in general as either "aunt" or "uncle." Nicknames are very common, and most people are referred to by their nickname, sometimes with an honorific preceding it.

The What, When, and How of Introducing People

Always wait to be introduced to strangers; although if you are not introduced after a few minutes, it is appropriate to introduce yourself. As is the case throughout the region, it is critically important to take time when you greet someone to make many inquiries into his or her health and the health and condition of the lives of his or her relatives and close friends (even livestock, if appropriate!). It is considered very rude not to take a considerable amount of time when meeting someone to make these inquiries and express understanding of his or her responses; he or she will do the same in kind. You must acknowledge people you know when you pass them on the street, and you should acknowledge strangers when eyes meet in passing. It is not considered appropriate for anyone to publicly display affection (although some urban youth do hold hands in public). Never presume to seat yourself at a gathering: if possible, wait to be told where to sit; you will be seated in a spot appropriate to your position. Typically men, women, and children (even boys and girls) are seated separately. Because you will never be refused, and because guests are always welcome (as is the case in much of Africa, because of the lack of communication and transportation facilities, people simply drop in "uninvited" often—in fact, this is typically the most common form of entertainment and socializing), it is important that you do not purposefully make a visit unannounced around mealtime; instead, come in the late morning or early evening. When arriving at someone's home in rural areas, you will generally announce yourself by tapping on the front gate or clapping your hands in the front of the house. When departing, it is important to say farewell to every individual present, unless it is a particularly large group: the American group wave is not appreciated. Seniors or those who are obviously the oldest in a group are always greeted first, seated first, and allowed to enter a room first (usually as the center of a group, however, and in most cases preceded by their younger aides).

Physical Greeting Styles

Close associates and businesspeople of the same sex who have developed working relationships often greet each other warmly, with hugs and sometimes kisses. Wait until your South African host initiates this behavior before initiating it yourself. Typically, the greeting between men involves a handshake, and supporting the forearm of the hand that is doing the shaking with the left hand on the right elbow: this shows extra sincerity. Very close family and friends may also kiss additionally on the forehead; each ethnic group has different greetings. Muslim women and men do not touch or shake hands (unless the woman is Westernized, and you will know if she extends her hand). The handshake among some indigenous groups is soft, almost limp sometimes; this does not mean insincerity, rather, it is an accommodation to the Western fashion while remaining humble and considerate. Children and young relatives sometimes bow (or curtsy, for girls) in front of elders. If your hand is dirty or you are holding something that cannot be put down, you may extend your wrist, or even elbow, in place of the right hand. Young people sometimes wave farewell by extending the thumb and pinky while keeping the other fingers folded against the palm and moving the hand from side to side.

The traditional business introduction may also include the exchange of business cards, at least in the urban centers. Always take a large supply of business cards with you: you should give one to every new person you are introduced to (there is no need to provide another business card when you are meeting someone again, unless information about you has changed, such as a new address, contact number, or position). Be sure your business cards are in fine shape: they are an extension of you as a person and must look as good as possible. Embossed cards are extremely impressive. Never hand out a dirty, soiled, bent, or written-on card, and always handle business cards with your right hand only. Your card should be in English.

When presenting a business card, give it to your colleague so that it is readable for him as you hold it (he will, in turn, present his card so that it is readable for you). You may not receive a card in return. Smiling and other nonverbal forms of communication usually accompany the card exchange. Should you meet more than one individual at a reception, you may have a handful of cards when the greetings are over.

As the business card exchange usually precedes a sit-down meeting, it is important to arrange the cards you have received in a little seating plan in front of you along the top of the desk or table at your seat, reflecting the order in which people are seated. This will help you connect the correct names with the correct individuals throughout the meeting. Do this even if you are just meeting one person; it is expected. During the meeting, it is important never to play with the business cards (do not write on them without asking permission to do so); and when the meeting is over, never put them in your back pants pockets: pick them up carefully and respectfully, and place them neatly in your cardholder or inside jacket pocket. Do not photograph people without asking their permission, ever, and do not videotape freely. In some African countries, videotaping and photographing people and certain sites are illegal.

Communication Styles

Okay Topics / Not Okay Topics

Okay: anything that reflects your personal interests and hobbies and your sincere appreciation of and curiosity about things South African and native to the South African world. South Africans love and excel at soccer, rugby, and cricket (the last two are more popular with whites, the first with all groups in South Africa): expressing interest in South African soccer teams is very definitely a positive. Interest in South African music, folk art, food, history, and prehistory will always be met with hours of information (if not a personal tour!). *Not okay:* Politics, current events, or recent race relations history, or any subject that might in any way be controversial needs to be avoided at first. It is important to be sensitive to South Africa's unique history, and not to give your opinions at first about any of South Africa's neighbors or internal ethnic groups, poverty, the apartheid years, ethnic rivalries, religious differences, endangered species problems, etc. Do not inquire about a person's occupation or income in casual conversation, although it may be inquired of you (if so, this is generally just a way of getting to know more about your country, and not a personal investigation: answer specifically, and fully, with an explanation as to what things cost at home, why you do what you do, etc.). Do not talk about sex or tell dirty jokes when women are present: it is in very bad taste. Discussions about your company and its work are very much appreciated, as they give South Africans a chance to learn more about you and your firm. At first, speak about things that you believe you have in common, so that you can build a personal connection that will go far toward maintaining a harmonious bridge between you. This is appropriate for both individuals and organizations.

Tone, Volume, and Speed

South Africans typically speak in soft, muted tones, and look down upon boisterous, loud, and aggressive-sounding speech. English is most definitely spoken with a unique South African accent, but it is rarely spoken too quickly. If it is, however, if you, in turn, speak rather slowly, they may get the hint and slow down, as well.

Use of Silence

Passive silence—allowing time to pass simply without words—can be a form of proactive communication, and is used as a nonverbal way of avoiding confrontation, disagreement, or an unpleasant subject. If confronted with unexplainable silence, gently coax the conversation in a different direction, one that is more mutually harmonious. It is not uncommon among certain ethnic groups, but not as common among white South Africans.

Physical Gestures and Facial Expressions

Throughout the region, nonverbal behavior is part of the pattern of communication, and most South Africans are very comfortable with nonverbal behavior. Winking, whistling, and other similar displays with the opposite sex are considered very vulgar. Public displays of familiarity and affection with the opposite sex are not expressed beyond holding hands. Never touch a Muslim on his or her head, even a child: this is the holiest part of the body for Muslims. Do not point with or intentionally show the sole of your shoe to anyone: this is considered vulgar, as the bottom of the shoe touches the ground, and is therefore the dirtiest part of the body. Making the "thumbs-up" sign with both hands is a general sign of approval; do not make the "V for victory" sign with the palms facing in (it is a very vulgar sign done that way; always do it with the palm facing outward). Standing with your hands on your hips is considered very aggressive and should always be avoided. Yawning in public is considered impolite; you must cover your mouth when you yawn, and when you use a toothpick. As is the case throughout the region, the height of people is generally expressed by holding the hand out with the palm facing upward at the approximate indicated height (the height of animals is expressed the same way, but with the palm facing down, and it is important not to confuse the two).

For any action or gesture that would naturally be done with only one hand, avoid using your left hand, as this is considered by many as the unclean hand (the hand used for personal hygiene). Pass all documents, business cards, food, and money with your right hand (if you're a southpaw, you will have to practice this). You must remove your shoes before entering a mosque (as well as most rural homes). Smile whenever possible: it smoothes the way with strangers quickly and easily.

Waving and Counting

The thumb represents the number 1, the pinkie represents the number 5, with everything in between ordered from the thumb down. It is very insulting to beckon someone with the forefinger (instead, turn your hand so that the palm is facing down and motion inward with all four fingers at once); in fact, directions are most often indicated with the chin or the head or by puckering the lips and motioning with the head in the appropriate direction. If you need to gesture for a waiter, very subtly raise your hand or make eye contact. Waving or beckoning is done with the palm down and the fingers moving forward and backward in a kind of scratching motion. It may seem as if the person making the gesture is saying good-bye to you, when in fact you are being summoned over. If you need to point to something or someone with your hand, close your fingers, open your palm and face it upward, and pass your hand in the direction you want to indicate.

Physicality and Physical Space

Some South Africans may stand closer than most North Americans are accustomed to; resist the urge to step back. Never speak with your hands in your pockets: always keep them firmly at your side when standing. If men and women must cross their legs when they sit, it must never be ankle over knee (for women, the preferred style is to cross ankle over ankle; but the bottom of the shoes must not show to the other person). Remember, even in public, formal is always better than informal: no gum-chewing; don't slouch; men, take off your hat; and don't lean against things. Many South Africans are most comfortable when they are next to other people: in a nearly empty bus, movie theater, or restaurant. In most cases, South Africans will tend to sit next to or near the other person present, instead of far away from them, if they are of the same group or background. As is the case throughout the region, needing or wanting to be alone is suspect, and maintaining privacy by insisting on being alone is considered strange, and possibly dangerous: Why would anyone want to be alone when he or she could be in the company of friends and family?

Eye Contact

Eye contact is typically not maintained when speaking with elders or people who are obvious seniors; however, when speaking with peers, or when speaking to a junior, maintaining eye contact is very important, as it shows sincerity. Typically, one does not make eye contact while eating, and conversation is often kept to a minimum while eating. Tune up your nonverbal antennae.

Emotive Orientation

South Africans are generally very warm, sensitive, friendly, and hospitable. They may not, however, be demonstrative, at least at first, as formal rules require a slow process of getting to know each other. Once they do know each other, however, there can be much touching (at least between members of the same sex) during even the most casual conversation. Two men or two women often walk hand in hand or arm in arm down the street. One should be especially careful not to interrupt others when they are speaking: a more thoughtful approach to conversation, in which you give the other person signals that he or she is being listened to, rather than chime in quickly with your own thoughts, is much preferred throughout the entire region.

Protocol in Public

Walking Styles and Waiting in Lines

On the street, in stores, and in most public facilities, people *do* pay attention to maintaining orderly lines (in contrast to much of the rest of Africa). Nevertheless, there can be some jostling, if only due to the volume of passengers on public transportation. This is not to get into a bus ahead of someone else; it is merely to get in! This is not meant to be disrespectful; if it is bothersome, just say so politely, and you will be treated well. If you ask a South African for directions, he or she will generally make every effort to show you the way (even if he or she is not that certain!).

Behavior in Public Places: Airports, Terminals, and the Market

Pride will always demand that South Africans provide you with assistance; even if they do not have an answer, they will give you one. Be careful with whom you strike up conversations, however, especially in the cities (men typically should only speak to men, and women must only speak to women).

Establish a personal relationship with everyone you must interact with, from shopkeeper to government official, and you can expect much assistance as a newcomer. Often this is one of the purposes for bargaining in the market: when you do bargain (and you can at market stalls, but not urban shops), consider that your money is, in most cases, going to the upkeep of entire families who live at subsistence levels. When bargaining, keep in mind also that it is generally considered good luck to be the first or last shopper in a store or at a stall, so you might get a better price if you can manage to be the first to arrive when they open or the last when they close. Stores in the cities are open in the evenings and on weekends, as well as during the day, as market stores and stalls usually determine their own hours; government offices in South Africa, however, often open early (around 7 or 8 A.M.) and close early (around 3 or 4 P.M.). Muslim stores may close during the Muslim Sabbath (Friday) and in preparation for it (Thursday nights), and on all Muslim holidays. A personal verbal thank-you to store owners, waiters, chefs, and hotel managers for their services is important, as it will help establish the relationship you need for continuing good service. In rural areas, marketing doubles as a social event, so plan to socialize as well as shop. Smoking is popular and, in some places, endemic, and you need not look for "no-smoking" areas, as such formal rules can rarely be enforced (be sure not to smoke during the day during Ramadan in the presence of other Muslims, when Muslims abstain; this is true for eating and drinking during the day during Ramadan, as well, when in the presence of observant Muslims). When and if you do smoke, it is critical that you offer a cigarette first to everyone else at the table before you light up, and then offer to light their cigarettes for them.

Unless they are in the company of other women, or close male relatives, women generally do not go out in public alone, especially at night; Western women traveling alone in South Africa will generally not have a problem, but should be prepared for the fact that this behavior is not typical in the region: some people won't know what to do or how to act toward them, some other women will want to assist them, and certain men, no doubt, will try to take advantage of them. The bigger issue in South Africa in the evening (and daytime, for that matter) is not gender discrimination, but general safety: violent crime is a major concern when walking on the streets, driving, and touring. Do not go out alone, avoid driving alone, and take all suggested precautions.

Bus / Metro / Taxi / Car

South Africa has a fine public transportation system of buses, rails, cars, and planes. The major roads, both in and between the cities, are generally well-maintained. Again, the problem here is more one of crime than of disrepair or lack of infrastructure or facilities. Do not attempt to drive alone and do not drive at night. Driving in South Africa is on the left (from the British tradition).

The best way to catch a cab in Johannesburg or Pretoria (and cabs are generally plentiful) is at designated taxi stands (hotels are good places, but often charge more for the same ride: a hotel surcharge is added to the meter fare, in some cases). When a taxi has been hailed—and you do this in South Africa by holding out your arm—negotiate the price before you get in. Whenever possible, have the address you need to get to written down on a piece of paper (or use the business card of the person you are going to see, if you can) before you hail the cab.

Tipping

Tipping practices are similar to those in the West, although when out in the bush and rural areas, favors are expected from individuals to individuals who are providing a service or favor. Typically, it is a way of taking care of people; when abused, it is a form of graft that in some countries in the region, South Africa included, can be a rampant form of corruption. It is traditional to always give a little something to someone who has helped you out. The offer may be refused at first in some cases, but if you insist, it will be graciously accepted and appreciated. Tips in restaurants run about 10 percent, and are typically not included in the bill (but double-check to be sure); a tip is not necessary if you have negotiated the fare for the taxi ahead of time and already figured in the tip. For everything else, a few coins are all that is needed, but you should always have a lot of spare change handy to see you through the day. The South African currency is the rand.

Punctuality

Punctuality is valued, but not required. Consider timeliness a target. People are generally more time-conscious in the cities. You should be relatively on time, but you may be kept waiting for quite a while: patience and good humor are required. Never get upset over time. If you are late, you need not have an elaborate explanation. It will be understood.

Dress

Most South Africans in the urban areas wear conservative Western dress, although some prefer to spice up the Western wardrobe with traditionally vibrant South African colors, designs, and fabrics. South African traditional dress is dependent upon the ethnic group. Women generally wear dresses that cover most of their body, some with accompanying head wraps. South African attire has a reputation, in general, for being very colorful and highly patterned. It is not appropriate for non-South Africans to dress in traditional South African clothes; Westerners should dress in conservative business clothes (as will many South African businessmen). There are generally four moderate seasons in South Africa (reversed from the order found in Europe and North America), so be prepared to dress accordingly. Never wear (and this is the case throughout most of Africa) anything that could be interpreted as a military uniform. Urban youth and Westernized people wear casual Western clothes (often secondhand from

Europe or the United States). Clothes should not be tight-fitting or revealing in any way, for men or women, and sleeveless blouses for women and shorts are not appropriate. Western women in Muslim areas should not wear pantsuits, as they reveal too much of the shape of the legs. Westerners should avoid wearing any expensive clothes or jewelry: it makes you a potential mark for thieves.

Personal Hygiene

In South Africa, cleanliness is associated with purity, and many rural South Africans try to bathe at least twice a day. Traditionally among many ethnic groups one must wash hands before and after eating every meal. Many ethnic groups may be identified by their unique hair arrangements and scarifications. Do not blow your nose in public: it is considered very rude. Spitting does occur on the street, but is also is generally regarded as rude.

Dining and Drinking

Mealtimes and Typical Foods

The typical diet is a combination of local ethnic group cuisine, Western foods, and Asian foods: much is available in South Africa. All groups enjoy barbecues, for example. Local food is rich in rice, yams, and cassava (a root vegetable), plus breads, fresh vegetables, and fruits. Meats are enjoyed when available, and fish along the coast and rivers. Each ethnic group has its own specialties and preferences, and remember, Muslims will not eat pork or drink alcohol (although it is available). A typical dish is *mealie meal* (the South African version of the ubiquitous African porridge), served in any number of different ways.

A note on hosting and dining with observant Muslims: If you are serving a meal at home, be sure you do not use alcohol or pork in any of the dishes, and if you do, so labeling the dish and serving it separately will still make your Muslim guest uncomfortable: simply don't do it. You, as a guest in the more rural regions, may be rewarded with the opportunity to either dine first, or be offered the more favored food, such as the meat: please consider that this may mean that others in the family do not eat this. Also, if you are dining with or hosting Indians, there is a very good chance they are Hindu, and therefore, will most likely be vegetarian. If you are offered something you cannot eat or drink, acknowledge the honor, and suggest that while you will always hold the honor in your heart, you in turn will bestow it on someone who can also appreciate it in his or her belly: then pass the honored dish on to a South African colleague. Alternately, you may say thank you but that you have just eaten or drunk.

Breakfast is served from about 6 to 9 A.M., lunch from 12 to 2 P.M., and dinner from 8 to 10 P.M.; the main meal of the day for most all groups is dinner. Urban South Africans will dine the Western way; rural South Africans will often dine in the more conservative African way, with a wooden spoon, a communal bowl, or no utensils (using the right hand). In such cases, traditionally, children, women, and men dine separately, and men are offered the best parts first, women next, and children typically last.

It is very important to remove your shoes before entering most South African homes (look to see if other sandals are lined up at the entrance as your cue), and when seated to always make sure that your toes and feet are not pointing to the food or to others at the meal. In such settings, typically, conversation while eating is minimal, and most South Africans avoid eye contact when dining.

Regional Differences

Remember, Islam prohibits the use of pork, and most meats of any kind for Muslims need to be prepared *halal* (meat slaughtered according to Islamic prescriptions). Do not eat in front of your Muslim colleagues, or invite them to join you for a meal, during the day during Ramadan, as Muslims typically fast (and refrain from drinking and smoking) during the day, and feast with family and friends at night. Ramadan lasts for a lunar month: this is simply not a good time to do business or go out entertaining in the Muslim world.

Typical Drinks and Toasting

Tea, coffee, beer, water, and soft drinks are all available in most places. Some of the world's best wines are now coming from South Africa. When you come to a South African home, even for just a brief visit, you will most likely be offered tea, sometimes served English style—with milk and sugar—if available. Many South Africans really do take the time to have afternoon tea. When offered, always accept the cup of tea and/or coffee, even if you only put it to your lips or just take a few sips. Your cup will always be refilled if it is less than half full. Typically, beer and other alcoholic drinks may also be served: fruit juices and lemonades, along with tea, may accompany meals.

If you are the honored guest, you are not expected to make a statement or toast, but if you offer a small compliment, it will be appreciated (and then dismissed as unnecessary); you can do this at the end of the meal, just before everyone departs. An appropriate comment would be to wish for the health of the host and all those present; always be humble.

Avoid drinking tap water anywhere in the region (this means you should brush your teeth with bottled water and not take ice in any of your drinks; drink only bottled water, or brewed tea or coffee or soft drinks, and avoid getting water from the morning shower into your mouth; never eat fresh fruits or vegetables that cannot be peeled first, and ideally cooked later before eating). This is a serious matter: there are some very nasty—and sometimes deadly—bugs going around in developing countries. In addition, avoid all dairy products except in the finest hotels, as the required refrigeration may be questionable. Do not swim in freshwater lakes, ponds, or rivers due to the possibility of serious parasitic infection.

Table Manners and the Use of Utensils

Modern urban South Africa has been significantly Westernized, as many of the Western modes of dining are understood and accepted (many South Africans, for example, dine with spoon and knife, held, as they are in Europe, in both hands, and in the same hands throughout the meal). However, understanding the traditional South African modes of dining behavior will be quite helpful as they are apparent and respected in most places. They vary group to group, but the following basic suggestions should be considered: Before meals, you must wash your hands, and wash them again when the meal is over. Traditionally, one eats with one's right hand from their plate. Never use your left hand unless you are clearly eating something that requires two hands; occasionally you may be offered a spoon or fork, which also must be held in the right hand, unless you also have a knife, in which case the knife is held in the right and the spoon or fork in the left. Keep your left hand off any bowls or serving items. If there is one communal bowl offered, eat only from that part of the communal plates or bowls that is directly in front of you. You may be seated at a table, on the floor, or on low stools. Do not smoke in the same area where the food is being served, and wait to smoke until after the meal is finished (women typically do not smoke). Typically, people stay around for a bit after the meal for some conversation.

Seating Plans

The most honored position is next to the host. Most social entertaining is done in people's homes (although in the cities there is business dining in restaurants). The home, the market, or a local café is where local people typically meet, socialize, and get things done, including business (although business is not easily done in the market), outside of the major urban centers. Your spouse might be invited with you to a meal at home, especially if the spouse of the host will be there, which will probably be the case. The invitation will then typically be phrased, "My spouse invites your spouse," and women and men may (especially in Muslim areas) eat separately. By the way, invitations, business or social, will most always be verbal, not written.

At Home, in a Restaurant, or at Work

The honored guest is served first, then the oldest male, then the rest of the men, then children, and finally women. Do not begin to eat or drink anything until the oldest man at the table has been served and has begun. At the end of the meal, it is appropriate to thank the host or hostess for a wonderful meal.

In informal restaurants, you may be required to share a table. If so, do not force conversation: act as if you are seated at a private table. Women should be sensitive to the fact that they may be seated only with other women. Waitstaff may be summoned by raising your hand or by making eye contact; waving or calling their names is very impolite. Since business and socializing in this part of the world are usually one and the same, business is often discussed over meals, once individuals know each other well enough to talk terms. Take your cue from your South African associates: if they bring up business, then it's okay to discuss it, but wait to take your lead from their conversation.

Once inside the home, do not wander around. If you move from one area to another in a South African home or restaurant, be sure to always allow more senior members of your party to enter the room ahead of you.

Being a Good Guest or Host

Usually the one who does the inviting pays the bill. If invited to a home or if you are hosted in any way, thanks and compliments may be denied; nevertheless, it is important to state humble thanks, and to accept thanks graciously.

Transportation

It's important to make sure that guests have a way to return from where they came, if they are visiting; equally, you want to be sure not to put your host out by not having made such arrangements ahead of time for yourself, if and when you visit. If cars or taxis are arranged, when seeing your guests off, you must remain at the entrance of the house or restaurant, or at the site where you deposited your guests into the car, until the car is out of sight: it is very important not to leave until your guests can no longer see you, should they look back. Guests are seated in cars (and taxis) by rank, with the honored guest being placed in the back directly behind the front passenger seat; the next honored position is in the back behind the driver, and the least honored position is up front with the driver. If there are no cars involved, hosts typically walk with their guests some distance beyond the house before saying good-bye.

When to Arrive / Chores to Do

If invited to dinner at a private home, do offer to help with the chores and to help out in any way you can. Do not leave the meal area unless invited to do so. When in the home, be careful not to admire something too effusively: South Africans may feel obligated to give it to you, and doing so might represent a great sacrifice. Your compliments will most likely be dismissed, although they will be appreciated.

Gift Giving

In general, gift giving is common for social occasions, and in business situations between trusted business colleagues. It is done not only as a gesture of thanks, but as a way of helping to ensure good business relations in the future (be careful not to go overboard here, as a gift that looks like an obvious bribe may land you in quite a bit of trouble . . . with the authorities in your home country, more than likely). In business settings, this usually takes the form of a personal gift that symbolically says the correct thing about the nature of the relationship. When going to the region on business, bringing a gift for the key decision maker is enough. Your gift does not have to be elaborate or expensive, but it should, whenever possible, be personalized (engraved or representative of the personalities of the receiver or giver or of an aspect of the relationship). You present your gift when you arrive in the country; before you leave to return home, you will receive a farewell gift usually at this last meeting. When South Africans visit your country, they will also bring you a gift, and before they leave, you should give them farewell gifts.

The most appropriate gift for a personal visit to a home, or as a thank-you for dinner, would be some special food for dessert, and something for the children, such as a toy, children's picture books, or school supplies (paper and writing utensils and calculators with a supply of batteries are very valued). In traditional homes, a man typically only gives a gift to a man, a woman to a woman; remember, any gift given by a man to a woman must come with the caveat that it is from his wife/sister/mother, or else it is far too personal. Gifts to avoid giving Muslims include alcohol (and this includes perfumes or colognes made with alcohol), pork, art or photographs that depict natural scenes or people (this runs counter to Islamic beliefs that man must not attempt to reproduce in an image what God has made), or cutlery (which symbolizes the severing of a relationship). A fine gift for a Muslim would be a silver compass, so that he will always know which direction to face when he says his daily prayers (Muslims must face Mecca no matter where in the world they are when they say their prayers). Avoid leather goods as gifts for Hindus (the cow is a sacred incarnation in the Hindu religion).

For both giving and receiving gifts, two hands may be used always, and gifts may or may not be opened by the receiver in front of the giver (this depends upon the nature of the gift, more often than not: foodstuffs meant for dessert, for example, will be opened for all to enjoy).

Gifts should be wrapped, as gift-wrapping shows extra effort and thoughtfulness.

Special Holidays and Celebrations

Major Holidays

Christian, Hindu, and Muslim holidays are celebrated by the devout, and local and seasonal celebrations are held throughout the year.

National South African holidays are:

January 1	New Year's Day
March/April	Easter
March 21	Human Rights Day
April 27	Freedom Day
May 1	Labor Day
June 16	Youth Day
August 9	National Women's Day
September 24	Inheritance Day
December 16	Reconciliation Day
December 25	Christmas
December 26	Goodwill Day

Business Culture

As most business practices among the Western-educated and white Africans, as well as many black Africans who are familiar with Western business practices, are very similar to European and North American practices, we are commenting below only on those aspects of South African business culture that may be different from traditional Western business culture, and that are practiced, in most cases, by various ethnic groups within the country. It is important not to assume that the Western business way, while well-known in South Africa, is the only way: you will most definitely need to fine-tune your business tactics and strategies to the various groups you will be working with, as everything from language to styles of work can be different.

Daily Office Protocols

The South African office may be a modern office in an urban building or a traditional stall near the market, but no matter where it is, there may be many people coming and going. This is not so much a statement about your unimportance as much as it is a statement about the importance of your host: that he is needed by many, and that in the polychronic culture, things are handled in order of their importance, and not according to the clock. Be patient. In many traditional and older South African organizations, hierarchy is strictly observed. Because faithful Muslims pray five times a day, you will need to adjust your schedules to accommodate their needs if working with Muslims. Usually, prayers are given upon awakening, and at noontime, midday, dusk, and before retiring; this means that twice during the workday, there will be time out for prayers. The prayer break usually takes a short ten or fifteen minutes or so, and any quiet area will do. If you accidentally interrupt a Muslim during his prayers, just walk quietly away: there's no need for complicated explanations or apologies. Most organizations have prayer rooms set off to the side, with carpets. In addition, devout Muslims will not work on Friday (the Muslim Sabbath), and in fact begin to end work early on Thursday before sundown. The official workweek is Monday through Friday, 9 A.M. to 4 P.M. (remember, the Muslim Sabbath is on Friday, beginning Thursday evening at sunset; the Muslim workweek therefore often includes Saturday and Sunday), and sometimes a half day Saturday morning.

Management Styles

Titles are important, and the highest ones (e.g., vice president) are usually reserved for very senior, executive-level positions, and should not be used as casually as they are in the United States. Any criticism of South African workers must be done very carefully, even privately. Traditionally, among workers, deference is shown by subordinates to their seniors; paternalistic concern is often shown by seniors to their subordinates. Superiors are not typically sensitive to inquiring about their subordinates' opinions, and once a decision is made, the superiors are followed, often unquestioningly. If you are doing business with the correct person, things will probably move quickly; it is essential to have a good and trustworthy South African contact who can make the necessary contacts for you (you can locate these people through consular and/or trade association contacts prior to your trip). Let this person take the time he needs to do this for you, for if you pressure him into making contacts sooner, he may connect you to someone who is not as useful as the one he was originally waiting for: this will not serve you. Again, be patient. Never use time as a means of pressure.

Boss-Subordinate Relations

The decision-making system usually works from the top on down, with key decisions often coming from individuals in high positions of power. Superiors are expected to provide clear and fully informed sets of instructions: that is their responsibility, and it is the responsibility of subordinates to carry out those instructions. Consequently, "management-by-objective" and other egalitarian and individually empowered management styles often may not work in this environment: without clear instruction from above, subordinates may do nothing or may make decisions independently. They also lose respect for the manager for not making the decisions he should be making. This is not a reflection of their work ethic, as South Africans can be very tireless workers, but a reflection of their expectations of the responsibilities of superiors to subordinates.

Conducting a Meeting or Presentation

There will be much hosting by your South African contacts with tea, coffee, and soft drinks. When serving any refreshments in the office, be sure they are served in porcelain, glass, or silver tea sets: the use of paper or Styrofoam shows disrespect and is very bad form. There may be more people at the meeting than you were expecting: this is typically because there are many more people who need to be consulted about the decision regarding you and your business; in most cases, you will be introduced to everyone. If you are not introduced to them, do not ask to be: acknowledge them with a smile and a nod, and proceed with your meeting. If you are meeting with a decision maker, the discussions will probably be direct, forthright, and businesslike. If you do not know the decision-making authority of the person you are with, assume that you will need to meet with many people, and perhaps repeat much of the same discussions each time with different people. There may be many interruptions throughout the meeting; stay calm and flexible. Business is generally personal throughout the region: decision makers have got to know your face. Patience and third-party connections are key.

Negotiation Styles

At first, expect no immediate decisions from your South African colleagues at the table, and be willing to provide copious information, to the degree that you can, in response to their questions and in anticipation of their needs. Presentations should be well-prepared and simply propounded. Details are best left to questions and backup material, which should be available and left behind and may be in English; such materials need to be simple, to the point, and interesting to look at. Unless you already have a well-established relationship, agendas need to be very broad and very flexible: everything unexpected will occur, and everything you did not plan to discuss will be brought up. Should you come with other team members, make sure that your roles are well-coordinated. Never disagree with each other in front of South Africans or appear uncertain, unsure, not authorized to make a decision, or out of control in any way.

Most South Africans love to bargain and see this process as a way of getting to know you: it does not imply insincerity to offer one price and then change your mind later (as it often does with Pacific Rim cultures). In fact, avoiding this process will generate suspicion, whether in the office or in the market. Final terms should be fair to all, although if you suspect something is too good to be true, or feel you are being manipulated, you are probably right in both cases. Remember to confirm what might sound like agreement with multiple inquiries: communication patterns often include reassurance, when in fact, your local associates may not be completely in agreement with you. Contracts and contract law are legitimate in South Africa, but it may take more time and effort than you are willing to expend to enforce them; nevertheless, put everything in writing that you can and insist on the same from your South African associates. If possible, the deal should be sealed with a celebratory meal. Keep communications open, especially when at a distance, and stay in touch often with your South African associates: share more information than you normally would if you can, not less; and be prepared to make many trips, as needed.

Written Correspondence

Your business letters should be informal and warm, and reflect the personal relationship you have established. Nevertheless, they must include a recognition of any titles and rank. Given names usually are written in uppercase; dates are given using the day/month/year format (with periods in between, not slashes)—in South African business correspondence, it is appropriate to use Western dates and business writing styles. When writing names, an honorific plus the title is as common as an honorific plus the last name. You should write your e-mails, letters, and faxes in an informal, friendly, and warm manner: use a brief and warm personal introduction, and segue smoothly into business. Keep the business issues and language clear and simple, however, and bulletpoint and outline all important matters. Use the Western format (name, position, company, street address, city, state/province, country, postal code) for addresses.

Note: Refer to the preceding section on South Africa for information about general South African cultural behaviors; the material that follows describes country-specific variations on general South African customs.

LESOTHO and SWAZILAND

These two countries, while being independent from each other (and their neighbors), share a few interesting commonalities: they are both small, landlocked, sovereign states almost completely surrounded by the Republic of South Africa; they emerged, in a sense, out of the struggles of their own indigenous peoples to preserve their unique ways in the face of domination by both Europeans *and* other Africans; they are both today monarchies (Swaziland is an absolute monarchy—there is no representational government—Lesotho is a constitutional monarchy with a parliament); and both are relative success stories. The people of Swaziland are often referred to as the middle class of Africa, since the country has one of the highest standards of living on the continent; Lesotho, although not nearly as economically prosperous, has one the highest literacy rates on the continent.

Lesotho is the homeland for many of the Sotho (pronounced "Sootoo," hence Lesotho is pronounced "Lesootoo") people, specifically the Basotho, one of the two major ethnic groups (along with the Nguni) in southern Africa. When the Zulus and other Ngunis were consolidating their power in this region of southern Africa, the great Sotho leader Moshoeshoe (pronounced "Moeshwayshway") gathered the Basotho under his banner and maintained their independence from the Nguni (the territory of the Sotho was considerably larger then than the territory of Lesotho is today; over the years, Moshoeshoe had to forsake, through negotiation, treachery, and battle, much of the Sotho territory). When the Boers came, the Basotho began a new battle to retain their independence, and turned to Britain, who were also enemies of the Boers, for help. Britain successfully protected the Basotho from the Boers, and then annexed the territory for themselves, calling it Basutoland. When Britain formed the colony of South Africa out of the Cape colonies, Basutoland refused to be part of it, and chose to remain with Britain, and eventually received its independence. Consequently, there are strong British traditions in Lesotho: the people are cordial and courteous, fiercely independent, and perhaps more individualistic than most other Africans in their approach to life (nevertheless, this is relative, and a Masotho—one individual of the Basotho people—is still primarily concerned about family and his or her reputation and obligations to others) and retain many British traditions, such as tea in the afternoon. Knowledge of European manners and ways is common, at least in the small capital, Maseru. Most Basotho speak some English, nearly all speak Sesotho, the Basotho language (which, unsurprisingly, is written with Latin letters), and most are Christian (infused with local animist beliefs). When greeting a Masotho, use an honorific plus the first name; once people know each other, just first names are typically used. Basotho have an unmistakable traditional dress, including a conical hat, the *mokorotlo,* which has a very decorative knob at the top (most men and women will wear some kind of hat at most all times); additionally, most Basotho, even when wearing Western clothes, will often also wear a woolen blanket across their shoulders or around their waist (it is a protection against cool evenings, and a handy carryall).

Swazis are an ethnic group that migrated into the region from Central Africa, and similarly struggled to maintain their identity against Zulu and other African groups and the encroaching Europeans. Like the Basotho, under the shrewd leadership of their king, Mswati II, they played the Boers and English off against each other, and finally allied with Britain. By cleverly buying back land from white settlers, the king was able to return land to the Swati (their real name, but because of the different pronunciation of letters in the Swati language, the mispronunciation has stuck) and thus maintain a strong sense of independence, which ultimately was officially granted by Britain in the 1960s. The economy is Swaziland's strong point: the history that was established by the king of providing people with ownership of their land fostered a strong tradition of entrepreneurship, which has been encouraged by the government; today, Swaziland is a center for much international investment in the area. Most Swazis speak English, all speak SiSwati, the local language (which is a tonal language, and one of the south African "click" languages), and most are Christian.

Unsurprisingly, the heritage of absolute monarchy has also fostered a respect for formalities and rigid gender roles (women do not typically have authority at work or in public: the roles are quite traditional), and even greetings can be quite formal: always use honorifics before the family name, and the honorific, *nkhosi* (originally used only to address Swazi royalty), is perfectly appropriate before the name when greeting anyone who needs a little extra respect (elders and superiors). Swazi have a few unique gestures, as well: use the closed fist when motioning to someone or giving a direction (also, there are no words for left or right in Siswati, so Swazis will refer to left as the direction of the hand with which you do not eat, and right as the direction of the hand with which you eat). To express frustration, Swazis will sometimes use one of their click sounds by itself. Traditional Swazi dress is quite memorable: there is the *lihiya,* the long wraparound cloth worn by both men and women; men additionally wear the *lijobo* (an animal skin at the waist) and carry a traditional club, the *knobkerrie.* It is also not uncommon for Swazi men to wear dreadlocks.

BOTSWANA

The Tswana people of northern Southern Africa, like the Basotho and the Swazi, were also caught in the vise of fighting to maintain their independence from other African groups (particularly the Zulus), and the vying Boers and British (in fact, the European presence only fueled inter-African hostilities, as the different indigenous groups fought to maintain the security of their lands); one major difference, however, was simply the size of the Tswana lands, which are far larger than either Swazi or Basotho. The Tswana were able to establish a homeland north of what is now South Africa, and south of what was then Southern Rhodesia. Seeking protection from the Boers, the Tswana turned to the British, and the British made them a protectorate: Bechuanaland, although the topography of Botswana offered much natural protection itself (over 80 percent of the country is the great Kalahari desert). As did their neighbors, the Batswana (the term used to describe the Tswana as a people) sought and eventually received independence from Britain. Today, about half the population is Batswana, while the other half is a mix of many other tribes, though predominant among them are the Kalanga people; consequently, people speak their own local language, although English is spoken by many, and the predominant national language is the language of the Batswana, Setswana. Equally, about half the population is Christian; the other half practice local animist religions. As is the case in Lesotho and to a lesser degree in Swaziland, there is a stronger tradition of individualism among Batswana than one typically finds in other parts of sub-Saharan Africa, as individual success and self-determination are parts of the Tswana heritage.

When greeting in Botswana, the handshake is very, very soft: the tips of the fingers merely glide over the palm of the other person. Additionally, as a gesture of thanks, Batswana sometimes put their hands together in a prayer position at chest level; alternately, indicating disagreement or negativity is done sometimes by extending the right arm, holding the palm open and out, and rotating the wrist from side to side. An important Setswana word, *pula,* is used as a farewell wish; it is the name of the local currency, but it is also the Setswana word, appropriately enough for a desert country so dependent upon its annual floods, for rain.

NAMIBIA

Although now an independent country, Namibia has had a particularly long and relatively recent struggle toward independence, and consequently is only now in the process of establishing a national identity and an identifiable Namibian culture. Many of the indigenous peoples of southern Africa (the Khoi and San, although the latter term is increasingly associated with the European misnomer "Bushmen," and is therefore to be avoided) live in Namibia, along with many other ethnic groups, although the country, due to its terrain, is sparsely populated. With colonialization came the Germans, and when Germany lost World War I, the colonial administration of German West Africa (what was to become Namibia) was transferred to Britain. In addition to the Khoisan (who are still a minority in Namibia), the largest ethnic group are the Owambo, a Bantu group; then there are White Namibians (Afrikaaners and descendants of Germans, Portuguese, British, and other Europeans, comprising about 10 percent of the population, although most of the wealth, in the form of land ownership, is concentrated within this group), Coloureds (descendants of both Africans and whites), and a unique group referred to as Rehoboth Basters, descendants of Europeans and Khoisan. English is the government's official language, but local languages, German, Afrikaans, and other languages are spoken by the various groups. Most Namibians practice a form of Christianity, infused with local customs. There is a unique native dress of some Namibian women, which looks like old-fashioned long and multilayered Victorian dresses, and in fact they are descended from the Victorian fashions that the Germans brought with them when they first arrived.

Index

Abu Dhabi, 38
accessories. *See* dress
Alawite sect, 41
alcohol. *See also* dining and drinking
   Israel, 47
   Oman, 37
   Qatar, 37
   Senegal, 125
   United Arab Emirates, 38
Algeria, 89–91
   background, 89–90
   communication styles, 90
   dining and drinking, 90
   dress, 90
   holidays and celebrations, 91
Arabic language, 16–18. *See also* Islam
Arab Levantine cultures, 40–41
automobiles. *See* transportation

Bahrain, 38
bathing. *See* personal hygiene
Bedouin people, 41
Benin, 165–67
   background, 165–66
   dining and drinking, 167
   greetings and introductions, 166–67
   holidays and celebrations, 167
bill paying. *See also* guests and hosts
   Egypt, 73
   Kenya, 214
   Saudi Arabia, 31
   Senegal, 127

Botswana, 260
Buddhism, 13, 55
Burkina Faso, 167–68
burping, Kenya, 213
Burundi, 221–24
   background, 221–23
   greetings and introductions, 223
buses. *See* transportation
business cards
   Egypt, 62
   Kenya, 205–6
   Nigeria, 148–49
   Oman, 37
   Saudi Arabia, 20
   South Africa, 245–46
business culture
   Congo, 196–98
   Egypt, 75–78
   Israel, 49
   Kenya, 216–19
   Kuwait, 37
   Morocco, 89
   Oman, 37
   Saudi Arabia, 33–36
   Senegal, 129–32
   South Africa, 255–58
   United Arab Emirates, 38
   Yemen, 38

Cameroon, 171–74
   background, 171–72
   communication styles, 173

Cameroon *(continued)*
  dining and drinking, 173
  greetings and introductions, 172–73
  holidays and celebrations, 174
cars. *See* transportation
celebrations. *See* holidays and celebrations
Central Africa, 169–98. *See also* specific
    countries
Central African Republic (CAR), 174–76
  background, 174
  greetings and introductions, 175
  holidays and celebrations, 176
Chad, 81–85
  background, 81–82
  communication styles, 83
  dining and drinking, 84
  dress, 83–84
  gift giving, 84
  greetings and introductions, 82–83
  holidays and celebrations, 85
children
  Kenya, 215
  Saudi Arabia, 32
Christianity
  Gambia, 132
  Lebanon, 40
  Nigeria, 143
  Sudan, 79
  Syria, 41
cigarette smoking. *See* smoking
class structure. *See* specific countries:
    cultural overview
colors. *See* dress
communication styles
  Algeria, 90
  Cameroon, 173
  Central African Republic, 175
  Chad, 83
  Congo, 186–89
  Egypt, 63–65
  Eritrea, 103
  Ethiopia, 101
  Gabon, 177

  Guinea-Bissau, 135
  Israel, 46
  Kenya, 206–9
  Morocco, 88
  Niger, 98
  Nigeria, 149–51
  Saudi Arabia, 21–23
  Senegal, 119–21
  Somalia, 105–6
  South Africa, 246–48
  Sudan, 80
  Tunisia, 91
compliments
  Chad, 84
  Egypt, 73
  Kenya, 215
  Saudi Arabia, 32
  Senegal, 127–28
Congo, 178–98
  background, 178–81
  business culture, 196–98
  communication styles, 186–89
  cultural overview, 181–84
  dining and drinking, 191–94
  dress, 190–91
  gift giving, 194–95
  greetings and introductions, 184–86
  guests and hosts, 194
  holidays and celebrations, 195–96
  public behavior, 189–90
Coptic Christians, Egypt, 54, 55
correspondence. *See* business culture
Côte d'Ivoire, 139–40
counting. *See* waving and counting
culture, defined, 3–4. *See also* specific
    countries: cultural overview

demographics. *See* religion and
    demographics
dining and drinking. *See also* mealtimes
    and typical foods; restaurants; table
    manners and use of utensils
  Algeria, 90

Bahrain, 38
Benin, 167
Cameroon, 173
Central African Republic, 175
Chad, 84
Congo, 191–94
Côte d'Ivoire, 140
Egypt, 68–73
Eritrea, 103
Ethiopia, 101
Gabon, 177
Gambia, 133
Ghana, 163–64
Israel, 47
Jordan, 41
Kenya, 212–14
Madagascar, 236
Malawi, 232
Mali, 94
Mauritania, 96
Morocco, 88–89
Mozambique, 234
Niger, 98
Nigeria, 154–57
Qatar, 37
Saudi Arabia, 26–31
Senegal, 124–27
Somalia, 106
South Africa, 251–53
Sudan, 80–81
Tanzania, 220–21
Togo, 165
Tunisia, 92
Yemen, 39
Zambia and Zimbabwe, 231
Djibouti, 106
dress
    Algeria, 90
    Chad, 83–84
    Congo, 190–91
    Eritrea, 103
    Gambia, 133
    Ghana, 163

Israel, 46–47
Kenya, 211
Kuwait, 37
Madagascar, 236
Mali, 94
Mauritania, 96
Morocco, 88
Mozambique, 234
Namibia, 261
Nigeria, 154
Oman, 37
Saudi Arabia, 25–26
Senegal, 124
Sierra Leone and Liberia, 139
Somalia, 106
South Africa, 250–51
Sudan, 80
Swaziland, 260
Tunisia, 92
Yemen, 38–39
drinks and toasts
    Congo, 192–93
    Egypt, 69–70
    Israel, 47
    Kenya, 213
    Nigeria, 155–56
    Saudi Arabia, 28
    Senegal, 125–26
    South Africa, 252
Druze religion, Syria, 41
Dubai, 38

Eastern Africa, 199–224. *See also* specific
    countries
education. *See* schools and education
Egypt, 53–78
    background, 53–56
    business culture, 75–78
    communication styles, 63–65
    cultural overview, 56–58
    dining and drinking, 68–73
    dress, 67–68
    gift giving, 73–74

Egypt *(continued)*
  greeting and introductions, 59–63
  guests and hosts, 72–73
  holidays and celebrations, 75
  public behavior, 65–67
emotional display
  Congo, 188–89
  Egypt, 65
  Israel, 45
  Kenya, 208–9
  Nigeria, 151
  Saudi Arabia, 23
  Senegal, 121
  South Africa, 248
  Sudan, 80
Equatorial Africa, 169–70. *See also* specific
    countries
Eritrea, 102–4
  background, 102–3
  communication styles, 103
  dress, 103
  holidays and celebrations, 104
Ethiopia, 99–102
  background, 99–100
  communication styles, 101
  greetings and introductions, 100–101
  holidays and celebrations, 102
eye contact
  Congo, 188
  Egypt, 65
  Kenya, 208
  Nigeria, 151, 155
  Saudi Arabia, 23
  Senegal, 121
  South Africa, 248, 252

facial expressions. *See* physical gestures
    and facial expressions
food markets. *See* stores and food
    markets
food prohibitions. *See* dining and drinking
foods. *See* dining and drinking; mealtimes
    and typical foods

Gabon, 176–78
  background, 176
  communication styles, 177
  dining and drinking, 177
  holidays and celebrations, 178
Gambia, 132–34
  background, 132–33
  dining and drinking, 133
  dress, 133
  greetings and introductions, 133
gender
  Bahrain, 38
  Egypt, 62, 66, 67
  Israel, 45, 46
  Kuwait, 37
  Lebanon, 40
  Oman, 37
  Saudi Arabia, 14, 19
  Swaziland, 259
  Syria, 41
  Yemen, 38
gestures. *See* physical gestures and facial
    expressions
Ghana, 162–64
  background, 162–63
  dining and drinking, 163–64
  dress, 163
  greetings and introductions, 163
  holidays and celebrations, 164
gift giving
  Chad, 84
  Congo, 194–95
  Egypt, 73–74
  Israel, 47–48
  Kenya, 215–16
  Nigeria, 158–59
  Saudi Arabia, 32–33
  Senegal, 128–29
  South Africa, 254–55
government. *See* politics and government
greetings and introductions
  Benin, 166–67
  Botswana, 260

Cameroon, 172–73
Central African Republic, 175
Chad, 82–83
Congo, 184–86
Egypt, 59–63
Ethiopia, 100–101
Gambia, 133
Ghana, 163
Guinea, 136
Guinea-Bissau, 135
Israel, 44–45
Kenya, 203–6
Madagascar, 236
Malawi, 232
Mali, 93
Mauritania, 95–96
Morocco, 87
Mozambique, 233–34
Niger, 97
Nigeria, 147–49
Saudi Arabia, 16–21
Senegal, 116–19
Sierra Leone and Liberia, 138–39
Somalia, 105
South Africa, 244–46
Sudan, 80
Swaziland, 259
Tanzania, 220
Togo, 165
Tunisia, 91
Yemen, 38
Zambia and Zimbabwe, 230–31
guests and hosts. *See also* bill paying
  Bahrain, 38
  Chad, 84
  Congo, 194
  Egypt, 72–73
  Jordan, 41
  Kenya, 214–15
  Nigeria, 157–58
  Saudi Arabia, 31–32
  Senegal, 127–28
  South Africa, 253–54

  Yemen, 38
Guinea, 136–37
Guinea-Bissau, 134–35
Gulf Arab cultures, 11–39. *See also* specific
  countries

handshaking. *See* greetings and
  introductions
health concerns
  Congo, 192–93
  HIV/AIDS, East Africa, 223
  Senegal, 126
  See also tap water precautions
Hebrew language, 44–45
Hinduism, 13, 55
HIV/AIDS, 223. *See also* health concerns
Hofstede, Geert, 3
holidays and celebrations
  Algeria, 91
  Bahrain, 38
  Benin, 167
  Burkina Faso, 168
  Cameroon, 174
  Central African Republic, 176
  Chad, 85
  Congo, 195–96
  Egypt, 66, 75
  Eritrea, 104
  Ethiopia, 102
  Gabon, 178
  Gambia, 134
  Ghana, 164
  Guinea, 137
  Guinea-Bissau, 135
  Israel, 46, 47, 48–49
  Jordan, 41
  Kenya, 216
  Madagascar, 237
  Mali, 94
  Mauritania, 96
  Morocco, 89
  Mozambique, 234–35
  Niger, 98

holidays and celebrations *(continued)*
  Nigeria, 159
  Qatar, 37
  Rwanda, 224
  Saudi Arabia, 33
  Senegal, 129
  South Africa, 255
  Sudan, 81
  Tanzania, 221
  Togo, 165
  Tunisia, 92
  Uganda, 224
  Yemen, 39
  Zambia and Zimbabwe, 231–32
honorifics
  Benin, 166
  Cameroon, 172
  Chad, 83
  Congo, 184–85
  Egypt, 60–61
  Ethiopia, 101
  Gambia, 133
  Israel, 45
  Kenya, 204
  Madagascar, 236
  Malawi, 232
  Mozambique, 234
  Nigeria, 147
  Saudi Arabia, 18–19
  Senegal, 117
  South Africa, 244
  Yemen, 38
Horn of Africa, 99–110
hosts. *See* guests and hosts

interpersonal relations
  Congo, 181–82
  Egypt, 56–57
  Kenya, 201–2
  Nigeria, 144–45
  Saudi Arabia, 14–15
  Senegal, 114–15
  South Africa, 241–42

introductions. *See* greetings and
    introductions
Islam
  Bahrain, 38
  Egypt, 54, 55–56
  Gambia, 132
  Jordan, 41
  Kuwait, 37
  Lebanon, 40
  Nigeria, 143–44
  Qatar, 37
  Saudi Arabia, 11–14, 16
  Senegal, 113–14
  Sudan, 78
  Yemen, 38, 39
Israel, 42–49
  background, 42–43
  business culture, 49
  communication styles, 46
  cultural overview, 43–44
  dining and drinking, 47
  dress, 46–47
  gift giving, 47–48
  greetings and introductions, 44–45
  holidays and celebrations, 48–49
  Lebanon, 40
  public behavior, 46
Ivory Coast, 139–40

jewelry. *See* dress
Jordan, 41
Judaism
  Israel, 42–44
  Orthodox, 45, 46, 47
  Syria, 41

Kenya, 199–219
  background, 199–201
  communication styles, 206–9
  cultural overview, 201–3
  dining and drinking, 212–14
  dress, 211
  gift giving, 215–16

greetings and introductions, 203–6
guests and hosts, 214–15
holidays and celebrations, 216
public behavior, 209–11
khat. See qat
Kosher laws, 47
Kuwait, 36–37

language and basic vocabulary
   Arabic, 16–17
   Benin, 166–67
   Botswana, 260
   Burundi, 223
   Cameroon, 172
   Central African Republic, 175
   Chad, 82
   Congo, 184
   Egypt, 59–60
   Ethiopia, 100–101
   Gambia, 133
   Ghana, 163
   Guinea, 136
   Guinea-Bissau, 135
   Israel, 44–45
   Kenya, 203–4
   Madagascar, 236
   Malawi, 232
   Mali, 93–94
   Mauritania, 95–96
   Morocco, 87
   Mozambique, 233–34
   Namibia, 261
   Niger, 97
   Nigeria, 147
   Rwanda, 223
   Senegal, 116–17
   Sierra Leone and Liberia, 138–39
   Somalia, 105
   South Africa, 244
   Sudan, 80
   Swaziland, 259
   Tanzania, 220
   Togo, 165

   Uganda, 223
   Zambia and Zimbabwe, 230
Lebanon, 40
Lesotho, 258–60
Liberia. *See* Sierra Leone and Liberia

Madagascar, 235–37
   background, 232, 235–36
   dining and drinking, 236
   dress, 236
   greetings and introductions, 236
   holidays and celebrations, 237
Maghreb and Sahel, 86–98
makeup. *See* dress
Malawi, 232
Mali, 92–94
   background, 92–93
   dining and drinking, 94
   dress, 94
   greetings and introductions, 93–94
   holidays and celebrations, 94
management styles. *See* business culture
markets. *See* stores and food markets
Mauritania, 94–96
   background, 94–95
   dining and drinking, 96
   dress, 96
   greetings and introductions, 95–96
   holidays and celebrations, 96
mealtimes and typical foods
   Algeria, 90
   Chad, 84
   Congo, 191–92
   Côte d'Ivoire, 140
   Egypt, 68–69
   Ethiopia, 101
   Kenya, 212
   Morocco, 88–89
   Nigeria, 154–55
   Saudi Arabia, 26–27
   Senegal, 124–25
   South Africa, 251–52
   Sudan, 80–81

mealtimes and typical foods *(continued)*
Tunisia, 92
See also dining and drinking; restaurants
meetings and presentations. *See* business
culture
metros. *See* transportation
Middle East, 9–49
cultural groups in, 10
diversity in, 9
See also specific countries
Morocco, 86–89
background, 86–87
business culture, 89
communication styles, 88
dining and drinking, 88–89
dress, 88
greetings and introductions, 87
holidays and celebrations, 89
religion and demographics, 87
Mozambique, 232–35
background, 232–33
dining and drinking, 234
dress, 234
greetings and introductions, 233–34
holidays and celebrations, 234–35
Muslims. *See* Islam

names and naming. *See* honorifics
Namibia, 261
negotiation styles. *See* business culture
Niger, 97–98
background, 97
communication styles, 98
dining and drinking, 98
greetings and introductions, 97
holidays and celebrations, 98
Nigeria, 141–62
background, 141–44
business culture, 159–62
communication styles, 149–51
cultural overview, 144–47
dining and drinking, 154–57
dress, 154

gift giving, 158–59
greetings and introductions, 147–49
holidays and celebrations, 159
public behavior, 152–54
nonverbal communication
Congo, 187–88
Egypt, 63–64
Israel, 46
Saudi Arabia, 16, 20, 21–23
See also physical gestures and facial
expressions
norms, culture, 3–4
North Africa, 51–106. *See also* specific
countries
nose blowing
Congo,191
Kenya, 211
South Africa, 251

office protocols. *See* business culture
Oman, 37
Orthodox Judaism, 45, 46, 47

personal hygiene
Congo, 191
Egypt, 68
Kenya, 211
Morocco, 88
Nigeria, 154
Saudi Arabia, 26
Senegal, 124
Somalia, 106
South Africa, 251
photography
Egypt, 62–63
Saudi Arabia, 20–21
physical gestures and facial expressions
Benin, 166
Cameroon, 173
Central African Republic, 175
Congo, 187–88
Egypt, 62, 64
Ethiopia, 101

Gabon, 177
Guinea-Bissau, 135
Israel, 45
Kenya, 207
Malawi, 232
Niger, 98
Nigeria, 150
Saudi Arabia, 20, 22
Senegal, 120
Somalia, 105–6
South Africa, 247
Sudan, 80
Swaziland, 259–60
See also nonverbal communication
physicality and physical space
Algeria, 90
Cameroon, 172–73
Chad, 83
Congo, 185–86, 188
Egypt, 62–63, 64–65
Ethiopia, 101
Gambia, 133
Ghana, 163
Guinea-Bissau, 135
Israel, 46
Kenya, 205–6, 208
Mali, 93
Mauritania, 96
Morocco, 87
Nigeria, 148–49, 151
Saudi Arabia, 19–21, 22–23
Senegal, 118–19, 121
South Africa, 245–46, 248
Togo, 165
Zambia and Zimbabwe, 230–31
Pillars of Faith. *See* Islam
politics and government
Congo, 180
Egypt, 54
Gambia, 132
Israel, 43
Jordan, 41
Kenya, 200

Kuwait, 36
Lebanon, 40
Nigeria, 142
Oman, 37
Qatar, 37
Saudi Arabia, 12
Senegal, 112
Sierra Leone and Liberia, 137–38
South Africa, 239–40
Sudan, 79
Syria, 40, 41
pornography, Egypt, 66
presentations. *See* business culture
public behavior
Congo, 189–90
Egypt, 65–67
Israel, 46
Kenya, 209–11
Lebanon, 40
Nigeria, 152–54
Saudi Arabia, 23–25
South Africa, 248–50
punctuality
Congo, 190
Egypt, 67
Kenya, 211
Kuwait, 37
Nigeria, 154
Saudi Arabia, 25, 32
Senegal, 123
South Africa, 250
See also time perspective

qat, 38, 106
Qatar, 37

relationships. *See* interpersonal
    relations
religion and demographics
Benin, 166
Burkina Faso, 168
Burundi, 223
Cameroon, 172

religion and demographics *(continued)*
  Central African Republic, 174
  Chad, 82
  Congo, 181
  Côte d'Ivoire, 140
  Egypt, 55–56
  Eritrea, 103
  Ethiopia, 100
  Gabon, 176
  Gambia, 132–33
  Ghana, 162–63
  Guinea, 136
  Guinea-Bissau, 134–35
  Kenya, 200–201
  Lebanon, 40
  Mali, 93
  Mauritania, 95
  Morocco, 87
  Mozambique, 233
  Namibia, 261
  Niger, 97
  Nigeria, 143–44
  Rwanda, 223
  Saudi Arabia, 12–14
  Senegal, 113–14
  Sierra Leone and Liberia, 138
  Somalia, 105
  South Africa, 240–41
  Sudan, 79
  Syria, 40–41
  Tanzania, 220
  Togo, 164
  Uganda, 223
  Zambia and Zimbabwe, 229–30
  See also specific religions
restaurants
  Chad, 84
  Congo, 193–94
  Egypt, 72–73
  Kenya, 214
  Nigeria, 157
  Saudi Arabia, 30–31
  Senegal, 127
  South Africa, 253
  Yemen, 39
  See also dining and drinking; mealtimes
    and typical foods
Rwanda, 179–80, 221–24
  background, 221–23
  greetings and introductions, 223
  holidays and celebrations, 224

Sahel and Maghreb, 86–98
Saudi Arabia, 11–36
  background, 11–14
  business culture, 33–36
  communication styles, 21–23
  cultural overview, 14–16
  dining and drinking, 26–31
  dress, 25–26
  gift giving, 32–33
  greetings and introductions, 16–21
  guests and hosts, 31–32
  holidays and celebrations, 33
  public behavior, 23–25
schools and education
  Congo, 180
  Egypt, 54–55
  Kenya, 200
  Nigeria, 142–43
  Saudi Arabia, 12
  Senegal, 112
  South Africa, 240
seating arrangements. *See* dining
    and drinking; greetings and
    introductions
Senegal, 111–32
  background, 111–14
  business culture, 129–32
  communication styles, 119–21
  cultural overview, 114–16
  dining and drinking, 124–27
  dress, 124
  gift giving, 128–29
  greetings and introductions, 116–19
  holidays and celebrations, 129

public behavior, 121–23

Shari'a laws, 13–14, 114, 144. *See also* Islam

Shiite Muslims. *See* Islam

shoe removal
Chad, 84
South Africa, 251–52

Sierra Leone and Liberia, 137–39

silence
Congo, 187
Egypt, 63
Kenya, 207
Saudi Arabia, 21
Senegal, 119–20
South Africa, 247

smoking
Egypt, 66
Kenya, 213
Nigeria, 156

Somalia, 104–6
background, 104–5
communication styles, 105–6
dining and drinking, 106
dress, 106
greetings and introductions, 105

South Africa, 238–58
background, 238–41
business culture, 255–58
communication styles, 246–48
cultural overview, 241–43
dining and drinking, 251–53
dress, 250–51
gift giving, 254–55
greetings and introductions, 244–46
guests and hosts, 253–54
holidays and celebrations, 255
public behavior, 248–50

Southern Africa, 225–61. *See also* specific countries

spitting
Congo, 191
Kenya, 211
South Africa, 251

stores and food markets
Kenya, 209–10
Nigeria, 152–53
Saudi Arabia, 23–24
Senegal, 122
South Africa, 249

styles. *See* dress

Sudan, 78–81
background, 78–79
communication styles, 80
dining and drinking, 80–81
dress, 80
greetings and introductions, 80

Sunni Muslims. *See* Islam

Swaziland, 258–60

Syria, 40–41

table manners and use of utensils
Congo, 193
Egypt, 70–71
Israel, 47
Kenya, 213–14
Nigeria, 156
Saudi Arabia, 28–29
Senegal, 126
South Africa, 252–53
See also dining and drinking

Tanzania, 219–21
background, 219–20
greetings and introductions, 220
holidays and celebrations, 221

tap water precautions
Congo, 192
Egypt, 70
Senegal, 126
See also health concerns

taxis. *See* transportation

telephone, Egypt, 66

terrorism, 8

thank-you notes. *See* gift giving

time perspective
Congo, 182–83
Egypt, 57–58

time perspective *(continued)*
  Israel, 44
  Kenya, 202–3
  Nigeria, 145–46
  Saudi Arabia, 15–16
  Senegal, 115–16
  South Africa, 242–43
  See also punctuality
tipping
  Congo, 190
  Egypt, 66–67
  Kenya, 210–11
  Nigeria, 153
  Saudi Arabia, 25
  Senegal, 123
  South Africa, 250
toasts. *See* drinks and toasts
Togo, 164–65
transportation
  Congo, 190
  Egypt, 66, 73
  Kenya, 210, 214–15
  Nigeria, 153, 157
  Saudi Arabia, 24, 31
  Senegal, 123
  South Africa, 249–50, 254
Tunisia, 91–92
  background, 91
  communication styles, 91
  dining and drinking, 92
  dress, 92
  holidays and celebrations, 92

Uganda, 180, 221–24
  background, 221–23
  greetings and introductions,
    223

  holidays and celebrations, 224
United Arab Emirates, 38

videotape. *See* photography
vocabulary. *See* language and basic
  vocabulary

Wahhabism, 12, 37. *See also* Islam
walking styles and waiting in line
  Egypt, 65
  Kenya, 209
  Saudi Arabia, 23
  Senegal, 121–22
  South Africa, 248–49
water precautions. *See* health concerns;
  tap water precautions
waving and counting
  Congo, 188
  Egypt, 64
  Kenya, 208
  Nigeria, 150–51
  Saudi Arabia, 22
  Senegal, 120
  South Africa, 247
West Africa, 107–68. *See also* specific
  countries
women. *See* gender
written correspondence. *See* business
  culture

Yemen, 38–39

Zambia and Zimbabwe, 229–32
  background, 229–30
  dining and drinking, 231
  greetings and introductions, 230–31
  holidays and celebrations, 231–32